New Essays on Semantic Externalism and Self-Knowledge

New Essays on Semantic Externalism and Self-Knowledge

edited by Susana Nuccetelli

A Bradford Book
The MIT Press
Cambridge, Massachusetts
London, England

This book was set in New Baskerville on 3B2 by Asco Typesetters, Hong Kong, and was printed and bound in the United States of America.

Library of Congress Cataloging-in-Publication Data

New essays on semantic externalism and self-knowledge / edited by Susana Nuccetelli.
    p.   cm.
"A Bradford book."
Includes bibliographical references and index.
ISBN 0-262-14083-7 (alk. paper)
  1. Externalism (Philosophy of mind). 2. Self-knowledge, Theory of.
I. Nuccetelli, Susana.
BD418.3 N49   2003
121'.4—dc21   2002032416

10 9 8 7 6 5 4 3 2 1

Contents

Acknowledgments

A number of people have been especially helpful to me in assembling this collection. First, I wish to thank my dissertation adviser, Stephen Schiffer, from whom I learned a great deal while writing on externalism and self-knowledge. My views on this and other matters of epistemology, philosophy of language, and philosophy of mind have also benefitted from discussions with Brian Loar, Stephen Stich, Ernest Sosa, Anthony Brueckner, Jonathan Adler, and Gary Ostertag. Matthias Steup, Bernard Baumrin, and Steven Cahn have all encouraged me to pursue this project, and I am grateful for their support. Gary Seay deserves special mention for having helped me during the whole process of putting this volume together, making comments that always led to improvements.

New Essays on Semantic Externalism and Self-Knowledge

Introduction
Susana Nuccetelli

1 The Supervenience of Content

Semantic externalism or anti-individualism is often cast as the rejection of semantic internalism or individualism, a view favored by philosophers at least since Descartes (hereafter, 'externalism' and 'internalism'). The latter takes mental properties with content to supervene upon the intrinsic properties of individuals, while the former denies that thesis, holding instead that, necessarily, two individuals could be identical in all their intrinsic properties (nonintentionally described) and have mental properties with different content. Yet it is sometimes thought that externalism, though plausible, might be incompatible with well-accepted intuitions about self-knowledge and knowledge of the empirical world. For if content varied in the ways suggested by externalists, then to know that one is having a mental property with a certain content, one might first have to know what conditions obtained in one's physical and/or social environment, that is, skepticism about privileged self-knowledge seems a consequence of their doctrine. Moreover, the attempt to hold externalism concurrently with privileged self-knowledge might face a reductio, since it would then appear that substantial propositions about one's environment could be known by simple deduction from non-empirical premises. After all, not only does it appear that one has privileged access to self-ascriptive beliefs about one's propositional-attitude contents, but knowledge of externalist entailments from those contents to the environment also seems available a priori in some sense.

More needs to be said, however, about externalism if we are to determine whether the attempt to hold it, together with some plausible epistemic intuitions, supports any of these objections. What, then, are its main claims and arguments?

2   *Externalism versus Internalism*

Externalists and internalists can first be seen as endorsing opposite theses about propositional attitudes with certain contents, such as the belief that water is wet, the fear that one has arthritis in one's thigh, or the hope that one could sit on a comfortable sofa. Roughly, when propositional attitudes are taken, as they usually are, to be mental or intentional properties of individuals (or, alternatively, predicates that they instantiate),[1] then externalism and internalism amount to opposite theses about those properties, holding, respectively,

Ext   Not all mental properties are local properties of individuals.

Int   Mental properties are local properties of individuals.

What properties may count as local could be understood *à la* Putnam:[2]

InP$_1$ A property is local, internal, or intrinsic if and only if it *does not* presuppose the existence of anything other than the contingent object that has it.

Furthermore, local properties preserve across individuals who are exact internal replicas. For example, the property of having kidneys is internal in this sense, since if an individual has it, then any internal replica of that individual would also have it. This provides an equivalent way of understanding properties of this sort, namely,

InP$_2$ A property is local, internal, or intrinsic if and only if it preserves across internal replicas.

Given internalism, *all* mental properties of individuals are local in this sense, but then surely mental properties *with content* must be local in the same way too. What shall we make of this internalist claim? To externalists such as Tyler Burge, it amounts to holding that "an individual's intentional states and events (types and tokens) could not be different from what they are, given the individual's physical, chemical, neural, or functional histories, where these histories are specified nonintentionally and in a way that is independent of physical or social conditions outside the individual's body" (1986a: 4). Externalists are committed to denying this, since on their view propositional attitudes with certain contents (e.g., the belief that water is wet, the fear that one has arthritis in one's thigh, and the hope that one could sit on a comfortable sofa) must be cashed out as nonlocal properties of individuals, where

ExP₁ A property is nonlocal, external, or extrinsic if and only if it *does* presuppose the existence of something other than the contingent object that has it.[3]

When a property is external, any object may have it only in virtue of its relationships to other objects. The property of being west of Central Park is external in this way, since whether one has it depends on how one is geographically situated with respect to Central Park. Given externalism, having either the belief that water is wet or other propositional attitudes with certain contents would be in some sense analogous to being west of Central Park, simply because the content *type* of some such attitudes would supervene on the relations of those who entertain them with their physical and/or social environments. If this is right, then the content of some (perhaps, many) propositional attitudes is determined in part by the relations of individuals who have those attitudes with things "outside" them, which are in this way external or extrinsic to them.

But since external properties are standardly defined by contrast with internal ones, and the latter can be construed in various alternative ways, let us consider another way of casting the former, one that focuses on whether or not the relevant properties are preserved across individuals who are internal replicas. By contrast with internal properties, now we must say,

ExP₂ A property is nonlocal, external, or extrinsic if and only if it may not preserve across internal replicas.

Compare being west of Central Park. When I am at the Museum of Natural History, I have that property, while my replica, who at that time is at the Metropolitan Museum, lacks it. If externalists are right, then having a propositional attitude with a certain content (e.g., the belief that water is wet) is similar to being west of Central Park in that in both cases, there could be instances in which the referred property fails to preserve across internal duplicates. If so, then the property involved is by definition an external one.

Note, however, that a mental property could be literally "inside" the person, yet supervene on factors external to that person. In the context of this debate, the 'inside/outside' distinction is, of course, a metaphor. As famously argued by Donald Davidson (1987), although a sunburn supervenes on what caused it, it is nonetheless a condition "in" one's skin. Given externalism, having the belief that water is wet or the fear that one has arthritis in one's thigh would be external to the individual who entertains any of these in the same sense that having a sunburn is: although they too are "inside" the individual who entertains them, they nonetheless supervene on external factors in his physical and/or social environment.

We can now state the crucial issue in this debate more perspicuously. Internalism consists in a supervenience thesis, which has a number of roughly equivalent construals. First, it can be seen as holding,

I_1 Necessarily, *no* two individuals x (in any possible world) and y (in any possible world) could have the same internal properties but differ in their mental properties with content (in their respective worlds).

Alternatively,

I_2 Indiscernibility with respect to internal properties entails indiscernibility with respect to mental properties with content.

Or, as the common supervenience slogan has it,

I_3 No difference in mental properties with content without a difference in internal properties.

Given the local supervenience of mental properties with content, any two individuals could not differ in those properties without some difference in their internal properties.[4] Imagine a scenario in which one individual has some mental property B while the other lacks it: the internalist would infer that the internal properties of these individuals are different. Now imagine two individuals, one of whom instantiates mental property B while the other instantiates a different mental property C: the internalist would likewise infer here that these individuals differ in their internal properties. Such conclusions are, of course, in conflict with the intuitions elicited by standard externalist thought experiments devised to show precisely that any two individuals could be exact internal duplicates yet have mental properties with different content. Externalists, then, reject the above internalist theses, claiming instead that

***Ext*$_1$**   Necessarily, any two internally identical individuals x (in any possible world) and y (in any possible world) could differ in their mental properties with content (in their respective worlds).

Alternatively,

***Ext*₂**   Indiscernibility with respect to internal properties does not entail indiscernibility with respect to mental properties with content.

Needless to say, the debate about whether mental properties with content supervene locally raises complex issues. Some of these arise from 'supervenience' itself, since this notion may be understood in several ways.[5] But, even if we adopt some adequate construal of 'supervenience', there will still be questions in need of clarification concerning the externalist and internalist modal claims.[6] And there is, of course, the large issue of alternative ways of casting externalism itself—to which we now turn.

3   Other Externalist Claims

It is not uncommon to find externalism and internalism cast in terms of opposite claims about the individuation of propositional-attitude content kinds (types). To Burge, for example, the whole debate is in fact about "how kinds are correctly individuated, how their natures are fixed" (1986a: 3). If, as externalists maintain, the content of certain propositional-attitude tokens is in part individuated by environmental factors, then those factors in part determine the content *type* instantiated by those tokens. When the debate is framed in this way, 'individuation' is, of course, a term of art that can be taken to express the following relation:

Ind   For any token y, x individuates y if and only if x determines y's type.

But the debate may also concern whether or not mental properties supervene entirely on factors within the *physical* individual—these being, for example, some behavioral dispositions or, perhaps, brain states. (Naturally, any additional claim of this sort would seem unavailable to the internalist who is also a *dualist*, but in the present context we may ignore dualistic internalism.) On this recast, internalism is the thesis that all mental properties preserve across individuals who are physical, internal replicas, and *a fortiori*, that

***Int*₂.**   Mental properties with content preserve across physical, internal replicas.

Needless to say, externalists cannot accept this version of internalism either, since their own supervenience thesis commits them to holding,

Ext₂. Some mental properties with content may not preserve across physical, internal replicas.

Standard externalist thought experiments, often run to support claims such as Ext₂., suggest that externalists take their disagreement with internalists to boil down to whether propositional-attitude contents could vary with relevant changes in the physical environment (Putnam 1975), the physical and social environments (Burge 1979), or the causal histories of individuals (Davidson 1987). In each of these cases their intuition is that, given relevant external changes, an individual could have a propositional attitude with a certain content—say believing that water is wet—while a physical internal replica may lack it. But if externalist thought experiments are sound, then the following theses also appear plausible:

Ext₃ Mental properties with certain contents depend in part on physical and/or social environmental factors.

Ext₄ Any correct psychological account of an individual's having (or lacking) mental properties with certain contents must consider some factors in that individual's physical and/or social environment.

That is, the internalist/externalist disagreement about supervenience theses is likely to carry over to a disagreement about dependency and explanatory claims. Although all that is needed to set out externalism and internalism is simply opposing supervenience theses about mental properties with content, the debate often turns into Ext₃ and Ext₄, which raise the further questions of dependency claims involving mental properties with content and the role of external properties in psychological explanation. Let us have a quick look at the latter. Externalists and internalists take opposite sides on whether or not this kind of explanation must consider only factors "inside" the individual who has those properties. Internalists hold "that an individual's being in any given intentional state (or being the subject of such an event) can be *explicated* by reference to states and events of the individual that are specifiable without using intentional vocabulary and without presupposing anything about the individual subject's social or physical environments" (Burge 1986a: 4). Externalists, on the other hand, often insist that such an account must *also* consider those factors "outside" the individual which in part determine his being in a state of having mental properties with certain contents. That is, externalists whose view of psychological explanation is along the lines of Ext$_4$ are committed to rejecting the following internalist position:

Int$_4$ Any correct psychological account of an individual's having mental properties with content must consider only the individual's internal properties.

But how are further claims of this sort related to the acceptance or rejection of local supervenience for mental properties with content? How, for example, is the externalists' explanatory claim Ext$_4$ related to their rejection of local supervenience in Ext$_1$ and Ext$_2$? A sound argument for any of the latter is likely to count as a reason for the former. The support thus provided would not be conclusive, however, since Ext$_4$ fails to be entailed by either Ext$_1$ or Ext$_2$. Clearly, there is no inconsistency in holding, for example, both the external supervenience of content *and* the view that the only properties relevant to psychological explanation are those that supervene locally.[7] At the same time, this suggests that the issues involved in trying to answer the above questions are complex, falling altogether beyond what can be examined by this introduction.[8] Whether or not the externalists' further claims are supported, there is in any case no doubt that if just their supervenience thesis is supported, that alone would suffice to undermine internalism. It is, therefore, the plausibility of that thesis that requires a closer look.

4 Externalist Thought Experiments

The externalist supervenience claim can be shown to rest on thought experiments and independent arguments. Among the former, Twin Earth and arthritis cases are often advanced to support physical externalism (Putnam 1975) and social externalism (Burge 1979), respectively. In both cases, however, the conclusion is that propositional-attitude content may vary "even as an individual's physical (functional, phenomenological) history, specified nonintentionally and individualistically, remains constant" (Burge 1986a: 6). And both thought experiments require the assumption that *that*-clauses are good guides to propositional-attitude content. A Twin Earth thought experiment runs, roughly, as follows:[9] first, imagine Oscar, a chemically ignorant inhabitant of the actual world w_1, who has had regular causal contact with H_2O and sincerely utters, 'Water is wet'—thereby reporting what can be correctly described as a belief that water is wet. Call the mental property of being a thought with that content 'B'. In w_1, then, Oscar has B. In a counterfactual situation w_2, however, an equally ignorant identical twin (who shares all Oscar's internal properties, including surface stimulations, internal chemistry, etc., nonintentionally described) similarly utters, 'Water is wet'. Here the externalist contends that since, by hypothesis, there is no H_2O in w_2 but some qualitatively identical substance (e.g., XYZ), the belief reported by twin Oscar would not have the content that water is wet. In w_2, then, Oscar lacks property B. If that intuition is found compelling, it follows that individuals who are exact replicas from the skin inwards may nonetheless have propositional attitudes with different contents. But this of course amounts to Ext_1, the thesis that mental properties with content do not supervene on the internal properties of individuals.

The 'arthritis' case (Burge 1979) has a similar structure, though it aims at showing the supervenience of propositional-attitude content on social factors in the thinker's environment. Imagine Bert, living in the actual world w_1 and having a certain propositional attitude involving the term/concept 'arthritis', which he erroneously applies (through either misconception or incomplete understanding) to a disease of both bones and joints. But now suppose a counterfactual situation w_2, where Bert's physical, behavioral, linguistic, and phenomenal events and experience (nonintentionally described) are exactly the same as in w_1, but where his propositional attitude involves a certain term, 'arthritis', that he applies correctly, as standardly used in his linguistic community: in w_2, 'arthritis' means disease of both bones and joints. The externalist contends that in w_1, when Bert sincerely tells his doctor 'I have arthritis in my thigh', although he says something false, he is nonetheless reporting what can be correctly described as the belief that he has arthritis in his thigh. Call the mental property of being a thought with that content 'C'. In w_1, then, Bert has property C. On the other hand, in w_2, when Bert sincerely tells his doctor 'I have arthritis in my thigh', although he says something true, he is *not* thereby reporting what can be correctly described as the belief that he has arthritis in his thigh. Since in w_2 Bert's speech community uses 'arthritis' to talk about a disease of both bones and joints, even though Bert's internal properties have remained constant, his propositional attitude has a different content, perhaps that he has t-arthritis in his thigh. In w_2, then, Bert lacks property C. "The upshot of these reflections," writes Burge (1979: 540), "is that the patient's mental contents differ while his entire physical and nonintentional mental histories, considered in isolation from their social context, remain the same.... The differences seem to stem from differences 'outside' the patient considered as an isolated physical organism, causal mechanism, or seat of consciousness."

Note that arthritis-type cases extend the reach of externalist claims, for now the social externalist could hold that *many* of an individual's propositional attitudes (involving artifact terms, color adjectives, social-role terms, etc.) fail to supervene locally.[10] This seems precisely what Burge's (1979, 1986b) thought experiments involving notions such as 'contract', 'brisket', 'mortgage', and 'sofa' suggest. Given Burgean externalism, there would in fact be very few concepts that may *not* qualify for either a Twin Earth thought experiment or an arthritis-type case.[11]

5   *Other Arguments for Externalism*

Assuming that words and thoughts have analogous semantic properties, certain arguments devised to show the inevitable failure of internalism about the former, would, if sound, also undermine internalism about the latter. For, clearly, if linguistic meaning and reference do not supervene on local properties of individuals, then neither does propositional-attitude content. Among those who deny the local supervenience of semantic properties are the new theorists of reference, whose reasons against a certain version of Fregean semantics may be taken to support externalism about meaning and reference. If so, then similar reasons would support externalism about intentional content. The argument runs as follows:

(1)   The new theory of reference is plausible.

(2)   If (1), then meaning and reference do not supervene locally.

(3)   If meaning and reference do not supervene locally, then neither does propositional-attitude content.

(4)   Therefore, propositional-attitude content does not supervene locally.

Premise (1) is supported by some compelling reasons undermining Fregeanism, an internalist account of public-language semantic properties, such as meaning and reference.[12] If the new theory of reference can be considered the only alternative to Fregeanism, then, given those reasons, (1) comes out true. In addition, (2) spells out an entailment of that theory, and (3) follows from the analogy of meaning and content. Reports of linguistic meaning and reports of propositional-attitude content seem, after all, parallel in their syntax and in their semantics.[13]

Note that although all premises appear well supported, the above valid argument still falls short of providing conclusive grounds for (4), the externalist supervenience claim, simply because the strength of that *conditional argument* turns on the plausibility of the new theory of reference. Yet, when taken to consist in a causal account of reference together with an account of meaning that incorporates modes of presentation (see Evans 1982), the new theory of reference appears plausible. Besides, when broadly construed, it need not be committed to the stronger, and therefore more controversial, theses of *direct-reference* semantics.

On the other hand, it is not difficult to see how externalism would follow trivially from direct-reference semantics (that is, from neo-Milleanism) *and* some common assumptions about propositional-attitude content. Direct-reference semanticists have it that not only do some singular terms such as demonstratives and other indexicals, proper names, and certain definite descriptions refer without the mediation of Fregean senses, but also that this is the only semantic contribution such terms make to the propositions in which they occur. On this view, speakers of a public language must have (or have had) contact with the relevant items of reference if their tokens of sentences containing putative singular terms of that sort are to express any proposition at all. Propositions containing genuine singular terms are in this way object-dependent: they wouldn't exist if their objects didn't exist. Suppose that *that*-clauses are the right vehicles for identifying propositional-attitude content, and that if two propositional-attitude tokens have different truth values, they cannot be of the same type. Externalism would then follow from a semantic theory that countenances object-dependent propositions. Clearly, if there are any such propositions, then neither meaning nor content supervenes upon the local properties of individuals.[14]

6   Two Incompatibility Problems

Since externalism *and* the thesis that self-knowledge is in some ways privileged are independently plausible, suppose that we wish to hold both. Incompatibilists argue that we cannot, for there are epistemic problems with any attempt to hold these two doctrines together. But incompatibilists are of different persuasions: some hold that any such attempt faces a reductio, while others maintain that, given externalism, one could *not* know one's own propositional-attitude contents without investigating the environment—that is, that externalism is incompatible with our ordinary sense that each of us has a special, first-person access to such contents.[15] Arguments for either of these conclusions, if sound, would, of course, generate at least a puzzle for the attempt to hold such independently plausible doctrines. Burge (1988b, 1996), Davidson (1987, 1991), and other externalists have offered several replies, but incompatibilists seem to remain unpersuaded.[16]

What early incompatibilists (McKinsey 1991a, 1994b; Brown 1995; Boghossian 1997) had in mind with their attempted reductio was to show that externalists could *not* retain common intuitions about self-knowledge, and that this was obvious, since their rejection of local supervenience, together with those intuitions, might open the way to simple deductions of this sort:

(1) I am thinking that water is wet.

(2) If I am thinking that water is wet, then some empirical condition obtains.

(3) Therefore, some empirical condition obtains.

Suppose that the empirical condition in question is a certain substantial matter of fact, such as that water exists. Now incompatibilists urge that, given externalism and privileged self-knowledge, a thinker could come to know the above premises a priori in the sense that neither would require any specific investigation of the environment. For he could learn externalism just by running standard Twin Earth thought experiments. And since whether or not he has a thought with a certain content may also be available to him a priori in that sense, the thinker could deduce, and thus know entirely a priori, certain substantial propositions about his environment, e.g., that water exists. But that conclusion clearly conflicts with common intuitions about knowledge of the empirical world. In short, externalists who wish to hold privileged self-knowledge appear committed to this inference:

(1) I can know a priori that I am thinking that water is wet.

(2) I can know a priori that if I am thinking that water is wet, then water exists.

(3) Therefore, I can know a priori that water exists.

Although it may be objected that an argument of this sort, originally proposed by Michael McKinsey, trades on an equivocation about the epistemic status of (1) and (2), when these premises are charitably construed, 'a priori' must be taken to apply to knowledge (or justification) that does not depend on empirical piecemeal checking of the environment, equally satisfied by (1) and (2). And since the inferential principle fueling the argument seems as independently well supported as externalism and privileged self-knowledge, it appears that the attempt to hold such doctrines would, after all, have the intolerable consequence that substantial empirical propositions could then be known entirely a priori. Not only does the McKinsey argument seems sound, but the plausibility of its premises appears as compelling as the absurdity of its conclusion. Something has gone wrong here.

There is, however, logical space for some replies. To begin with, is it really plausible that, on semantic-externalist assumptions, a thinker could know a priori that his propositional-attitude contents entail some empirical propositions? According to incompatibilists, someone could come to know externalism entirely on the basis of standard Twin Earth thought experiments and philosophical arguments, all of which amount to a priori means to knowledge. And knowing externalism in this way, he could figure out, just by thinking, that his having propositional attitudes with some contents entailed certain propositions about his environment. Yet substantial claims about the dependence of content on environmental factors may not be available a priori, if, as I would argue, the externalist conclusion from Twin Earth cases is properly construed. On my view, presented in chapter 8 of this volume, any tenable doctrine holding that concepts of some sort are individuated in terms of their referents must rest on certain semantic intuitions which are compatible only with empirical knowledge of propositions containing those concepts.

But suppose one grants that the premises of the McKinsey argument are a priori. Still more is needed to get the incompatibilist reductio off the ground. For there remains the larger issue of whether the epistemic status of premises about one's own propositional-attitude contents and their externalist entailments can transmit to the conclusion of the argument. If the principle fueling the inference merely sanctions that a priori knowledge is closed under known entailment, then since that is comparatively weaker than other closure principles, it seems therefore intuitively more acceptable. But in this volume, Martin Davies and Crispin Wright independently propose new examples to show how transmission of epistemic warrant could fail in cases involving plausible closure of just that sort. On their view, closure is one thing, transmission of epistemic warrant another. Standardly construed, the principle of closure under known entailment holds that if one knows (justifiably believes) that a proposition p obtains, and knows (justifiably believes) that p implies some other proposition q, then one also knows (justifiably believes) that q. But in a valid argument, a certain warrant may be said to transmit from premises to conclusion just in case that warrant can count as a reason for belief in the argument's conclusion. It is now possible to deny the above argument's absurd claim (3) and at the same time accept premises (1) and (2), together with the view that deductive closure of apriority obtains in that argument. All these would appear consistent if the a priori warrant for (1) and (2) failed to transmit to (3). But in a valid argument with a priori known premises, what, if anything, could block transmission of that warrant?

As a growing literature on question begging suggests, epistemic warrants may fail to transmit in more than one way.[17] In this volume, Davies and Wright offer some seemingly compatible generalizations (the "First Limitation Principle" and an "information-dependence template") to account for warrant-transmission failures of a certain type. Disagreement, however, arises in their diagnoses of what might have gone wrong with transmission in the McKinsey argument. To account for that, Davies revisits a "Second Limitation Principle" he earlier identified as being at work in that inference. The principle, which applies to valid arguments, now sanctions that in any such argument, the *acceptance* of warrant for its premises and the *acceptance* of warrant for the availability to one's thought of one of the propositions expressed by a premise cannot be rationally combined with *doubt* about the truth of its conclusion. If, as Davies maintains, these three attitudes are elicited by McKinsey's argument, then, given the Second Limitation Principle (here revised to accommodate counterexamples to a previous version), there is no transfer of warrant from premises to conclusion. As far as Davies is concerned, externalism and self-knowledge are therefore in the clear. Wright, however, rejects a diagnosis along these lines. To him, any adequate generalization on cases of transmission failure must accommodate the relative nature of warrant, since warrant of a certain kind (e.g., an a priori entitlement) may not transmit from a valid argument's premises to its conclusion, while warrant of a different sort (e.g., an empirical one) might do so in that very argument. Davies's Second Limitation Principle, where applicable, appears to block transmission of warrant of *any* sort.

Wright's compatibilist reasons are spelled out in chapter 2 of this volume, where he offers a new diagnosis of what might have gone wrong with the argument needed to generate the paradox of externalism and self-knowledge. He now holds that the warrant a thinker has to the premises of McKinsey's argument does transmit to the conclusion. A priori entitlements to such premises stem from a presumption of the integrity of concepts used to make certain self-knowledge claims and a presumption of the satisfaction of certain external conditions necessary for that integrity (assuming the conceptual necessity of externalism). Still more is needed to generate the paradox of externalism and self-knowledge. Noninferential warrants to self-knowledge claims are conferred subject to a background entitlement such as that all is in order with our concepts. When the conclusion of a valid argument spells out a known constitutively necessary condition for an entitlement one has to one's (noninferentially warranted) premises, that entitlement would, on this view, fail to transmit to the conclusion. Given externalism, scenarios such as Dry Earth and Twin Earth provide some such conditions for premises containing certain concepts. Crucial to the paradox generated by McKinsey's argument is a further conclusion ruling out content illusion, which amounts to ruling out that the thinker belongs to a speech community that has never encountered either water or any other watery substance. A priori knowledge of this condition, now the conclusion of Wright's "extended" McKinsey argument, would indeed be intolerable. Yet warrant of that sort cannot be transferred from premises to conclusion, simply because that added conclusion spells out a known constitutively necessary condition for the integrity of 'water', one of concepts contained in the premises. If this diagnosis is correct, warrant would after all transmit from premises to conclusion in the original McKinsey argument, while failing to transmit in the extended McKinsey argument, whose conclusion states what, given externalism, is a known necessary condition for freedom from content illusion. McKinsey's original conclusion, on the other hand, merely identifies the watery stuff in the thinker's environment as water, and this, even if a priori, is not enough to raise the paradox of externalism and self-knowledge. But freedom from content illusion, now added to the McKinsey argument, would be—provided that the premises of that extended argument could confer their a priori warrant to such a conclusion. But, according to Wright, this they cannot do.

Whether either this diagnosis or Davies's Second Limitation Principle has succeeded in blocking the incompatibilist reductio is, of course, a matter of dispute. Also in this volume are three other important contributions to this controversy: the reactions of Brian McLaughlin, Jessica Brown, and Michael McKinsey himself, each of whom offers an assessment of the epistemic principles that may be at work in that argument. Are Davies and Wright correct, after all, in claiming that whether deductive closure holds doesn't really matter? Have they succeeded in establishing that it is instead transmission of warrant that fails? McLaughlin remains unpersuaded by Davies's and Wright's reasons to this effect. But he also questions the plausibility of recent attempts to invoke McKinsey's argument against skepticism about the external world (Warfield 1998, Sawyer 1998). Compatibilists of this sort take externalism and privileged self-knowledge to provide a refutation of external-world skepticism by opening an a priori route to knowledge of substantial empirical propositions. Far from dismissing the plausibility of any such antiskeptical strategy outright, McLaughlin, in chapter 3 of this volume, instead argues more tentatively that the success of a proposal along those lines would be contingent upon how externalism and privileged self-knowledge are construed. Under some construals, McLaughlin contends, the warrant for believing the premises of the (valid) McKinsey argument would rest in part on an entitlement to presuppose the truth of the conclusion. In these cases warrant would fail to transmit. Yet, under other construals, warrant might transmit from premises to conclusion, and the antiskeptical strategy could then get off the ground.

If McKinsey is right, however, whether or not warrant transmits in his original argument would simply be irrelevant to the strength of its incompatibilist outcome. In his contribution to this volume, McKinsey offers a number of reasons to believe that, not a principle of *transmission of warrant*, but merely a principle of *deductive closure* of apriority is all that matters for the incompatibilist conclusion of his early argument. On his view, even if there is transmission failure in that argument, the problem for holding externalism and privileged self-knowledge will remain, since, given the appropriate closure principle, a thinker would still be in a position to deduce substantial empirical propositions from claims about his thought contents and their externalist entailments. Whether the a priori warrant for such premises is construed as being empirically indefeasible or empirically defeasible, in either case the principle of closure would be at work in that argument, and that would be enough for the incompatibilist conclusion (compare Wright, this volume). Yet the transmission-failure maneuver of compatibilists, such as Davies and Wright, may encounter responses of quite another sort. Brown, who sticks to her incompatibilists guns, finds no good reason to question the transmission of epistemic warrant in the argument she regards as a reductio of the attempt to hold both externalism and self-knowledge. In her contribution to this volume, she looks closely at Wright's compatibilist diagnoses of a transmission failure in the McKinsey argument (2000a, this volume), noting that they rely on an epistemic *internalist* notion of warrant. Why, Brown asks, frame the incompatibilist argument in those terms? Semantic externalists are, after all, more likely to construe 'warrant' in *epistemic externalist* terms. She also regards Wright's strategy as committed to a questionable assumption concerning the possibility of a priori warrant against content illusion.

In chapter 12 of this volume, Sanford Goldberg concedes that there may be a sound argument for the incompatibility of externalism and self-knowledge. Yet he suggests that, given a certain distinction within what he sees as "a catch-all category" of self-knowledge, externalism could nonetheless be retained. Also in the compatibilist camp, Gary Ebbs reacts against attempts to raise epistemic problems for externalism. According to Ebbs, once externalism, privileged self-knowledge, and the attempts to raise epistemic conflicts for these doctrines are all properly construed, it becomes clear that the last cannot succeed. More tentatively, in chapter 13 below, Richard Fumerton looks closely at various understandings of externalism and privileged self-knowledge (in his words, "introspection"), only to find that, under some construals, the latter might indeed be incompatible with any interesting versions of externalism.

Note, however, that even if the paradox of externalism and privileged self-knowledge is dissolved in some of the ways suggested above, there would still be the lingering fear that externalism might generate skepticism about self-knowledge. Such an skeptical conclusion is often drawn from externalist Twin Earth scenarios involving subjects switching unawares between superficially identical, yet chemically different, worlds. Given those scenarios—the skeptical argument runs—externalists seem committed to reasoning as follows:

(1)   If I could not know (without an investigation of the environment) that I am not living on Twin Earth, then I could not know (without an investigation of the environment) that I am now thinking that water (rather than twin water) is wet.

(2)   I could not know (without an investigation of the environment) that I am not living on Twin Earth.

(3)   Therefore, I could not know (without an investigation of the environment) that I am now thinking that water (rather than twin water) is wet.

Now (3) clearly clashes with common intuitions about self-knowledge, as we ordinarily take ourselves to know our own thought contents without piecemeal investigation of the environment. Some contributors to this volume ask whether a skeptical problem of this sort arises for externalists. Kevin Falvey explores whether, given externalism, skepticism about self-knowledge may arise when an individual's self-ascription of certain propositional-attitude contents involves memory. Falvey compares our direct and authoritative knowledge of beliefs about our own propositional attitudes with cases where these are not present tense, but past tense instead. He argues that the entitlement to rely on preservative memory depends in fact on presuppositions knowable only a posteriori. To Fred Dretske, in chapter 6 of this volume, the tension between externalism (a metaphysical doctrine about the individuation of intentional content) and a widely held view of self-knowledge (an epistemological doctrine about how one knows one's own mind) resembles other situations in which metaphysics and epistemology have come into conflict. It is not uncommon in the history of philosophy that, at a certain point, a seemingly plausible metaphysical doctrine begins to be regarded as undermining some equally plausible epistemological theory, or vice versa. The controversy we are exploring here, if Dretske is right, would be yet another instance of such a conflict. On Dretske's views, any adequate response to the tension between externalism and self-knowledge must *not* abandon the metaphysical doctrine, which he regards as plausible. He proposes instead a reexamination of what he sees as a suspect epistemology.

Yet suppose externalism is somehow shown to accommodate plausible intuitions about self-knowledge: could that metaphysical doctrine then be of any use to epistemology? Matthias Steup looks closely at some recent appeals to semantic externalism to answer the challenge of skepticism about the external world. He notes that if semantic externalism were true, then since that metaphysical doctrine introduces the possibility of content illusion, there would be a change in the epistemic rules that apply to introspective knowledge. But then, Steup contends, given semantic externalism, an appeal to introspective premises against skepticism is no more admissible than the antiskeptical appeal to perceptual premises in a Moorean "proof" of the external world. He suggests that epistemic evidentialism remains an option for those who wish to avoid skepticism about the external world.

It is important to bear in mind, however, that the parties to this debate often assume without argument a certain notion of self-knowledge. Clearly, to count as a reductio of externalism, either McKinsey-style arguments or skeptical arguments from Twin Earth cases would require cashing out self-knowledge as knowledge attainable without investigation of the environment. Incompatibilists often take this as obvious and direct their efforts to supporting other premises. But a growing literature suggests that there is room for dispute here too, as can be seen from Joseph Owens's discussion, included in this volume, of introspective knowledge in relation to the externalism/internalism debate. On his views, Davidson's doubts about the compatibility of externalism with first-person authority rest on a misunderstanding of the nature of self-knowledge, since they presuppose that, in order to have a special epistemic status, such knowledge must enable the thinker to determine sameness and difference in his thought contents without piecemeal checking of the environment. But to Owens, that condition on privileged self-knowledge is too strong, leading directly to a conflict with externalism. Ordinary practice, he suggests, points to a more modest conception of self-knowledge, which can be shown compatible with some versions of externalism. Thus construed, self-knowledge, though unavailable to the Davidsonian externalist, would still be compatible with Burgean externalism. At the same time, such self-knowledge would be robust enough to have special epistemic status when compared with other kinds of knowledge.

Yet any knowledge that lacks such metaphysical and epistemic immunities as infallibility, incorrigibility, and transparency appears to fall short of privileged self-knowledge. As is well known, at least since Descartes, self-ascriptions of propositional-attitude contents and types have been thought immune from various forms of error and/or epistemic failure. Those interested in claiming some such immunities for self-knowledge have often run transcendental arguments, persuaded that certain properties of our social and intellectual practices may be of help in making their case. Since we do seem to be moral agents responsible for what we do and also critical thinkers able to reason according to certain norms, these facts might provide transcendental arguments for some such immunities.[18] In chapter 9 of this volume, Anthony Brueckner discusses whether a robust notion of self-knowledge could be supported by a strategy along such lines. He looks closely at recent attempts by Akeel Bilgrami and Richard Moran to implement it, only to find that neither has succeeded in supporting the special status of self-knowledge with a transcendental argument. For Brueckner, given externalist Twin Earth thought experiments, it is difficult to see how those arguments could be of any help in retaining a full-blooded notion of self-knowledge.

The essays in this volume make clear that the debate about the compatibility of externalism and privileged self-knowledge has triggered interesting developments in the literature on a priori knowledge, the transmission of epistemic warrant, question-begging reasoning, the semantics of natural-kind terms, and other issues crucial to epistemology and philosophy of mind and language. At the same time, these essays show that there are not just more than one objection to the attempt to hold both externalism and privileged self-knowledge, but also more than one reply that could be mounted to block it. We thus seem left with the problem of deciding which, if any, arguments in this debate may ultimately prove sound. Needless to say, were the conflict to be found among those overdetermined issues of philosophy, apparently competing resolutions would not be rival after all. In any case, here, as well as in any rational debate, our ultimate preference should be guided by a principle of doxastic conservatism, which recommends that, *when possible*, we favor the strategy that best accommodates each of the most accepted intuitions at stake.

Notes

1. Here 'property' is used in a broad sense, according to which any meaningful predicate expresses a property, and 'content' refers to propositional-attitude content unless otherwise indicated. When, occasionally, externalists and internalists are seen as holding theses about intentional states and events without further specifications, it must be assumed that these are intentional-state and event *types*.

2. This definition of 'internal property' is, of course, inspired by Hilary Putnam's discussion (1975: 220) of internalism—or, as he calls it, "methodological solipsism."

3. Another way to understand external properties is as properties "rooted" outside the objects that have them—where property P is rooted outside the objects that have it just in case, necessarily, any object x has P only if some contingent object wholly distinct from x exists. For a view along these lines, see Kim 1982.

4. If we assume that the internalist is also a physicalist, the internal properties (in the supervenience base) would, of course, be physical properties. See this introduction, section 3.

5. Jaegwon Kim's 'Strong Supervenience IV', construed as "*A* strongly supervenes on *B* just in case cross-world indiscernibility in *B* entails cross-world indiscernibility in *A*," seems to capture what the parties in this debate wish to claim (Kim 1987: 81).

6. It will be relevant to establish not only what kind of necessity is involved but also the strength of the intended modal claims. Martin Davies (1993) has pointed out that internalist theses of local supervenience could be of different strengths, depending on how the notion of supervenience is cashed out. A weak thesis would take the local supervenience of content to hold for a single individual, or for internal duplicates in the actual world, or in two possible worlds one of which is the actual world, while a stronger thesis would take it to hold for any internal duplicates in any possible world, none of which need be the actual world. Note that although the latter appears to better capture what externalists wish to reject, the denial of any version of internalism yields a variety of externalism.

7. See, for instance, Loar 1988, Fodor 1987, and Stich 1978.

8. For more on externalist supervenience, constitutive, and explanatory claims, see, e.g., Burge 1986a, Peacocke 1993, and Davies 1993.

9. As is well known, Putnam (1975: 219) first offered the Twin Earth case to argue against two assumptions of individualistic philosophical psychology that, on his view, cannot be held concurrently, namely, that to know the meaning of certain terms is to be in some psychological state, and that the meaning of those terms determines their extension. His resolution of the conflict was, of course, to reject the first assumption.

10. The social externalist does not seem committed to holding that *all* concepts are externally determined or individuated in terms of their referents. Clearly, such a view would be untenable, for it could not accommodate the common intuition that some of our words and thoughts contain terms with no referent at all, or with no referents in our immediate environment, as in the case of logical and mathematical terms, and perhaps some theoretical terms of science. These are, however, very complex issues concerning the scope of externalist claims, which I cannot address here (see my contribution to this volume).

11. In what follows, I shall be referring principally to physical externalism (and thus to Twin Earth examples), adverting to the other variety only when the problem at issue demands it.

12. See, for example, Kripke 1972 and Putnam 1975.

13. Compare, e.g., the logical form of *sincerely saying that p* and *believing that p*. For more on the analogy of meaning and content, see Stich 1991 and Devitt 1989.

14. The direct-reference theorist's account of belief reports seems to corroborate his commitment to object-dependent propositions, and thus to externalism about semantic properties. On a common assumption, Pierre's assertion 'London is pretty', if sincere, reports what Pierre believes. Here the direct-reference theorist might represent the belief as a dyadic relation, with 'Pierre' and the *that*-clause as its relata. But then he appears committed to count the *that*-clause as a referential singular term, one that picks out an object-dependent proposition, i.e., a proposition that wouldn't exist if London, one of its constituents, didn't exist.

15. One could consistently deny that there is a reductio facing the attempt to hold externalism and privileged self-knowledge, *and* maintain that skepticism about the latter follows from the former. But one could also consistently deny that skepticism about self-knowledge follows from externalism *and* maintain that there is a reductio facing the attempt to hold these doctrines concurrently. This suggests that the incompatibilist arguments discussed below are independent.

16. Among those who take the incompatibility problem to amount to a reductio of externalism are Boghossian (1997) and Brown (1995, this volume). For discussions of the skeptical problem, see, for instance, Brueckner 1990, 1997b, this volume; Falvey and Owens 1994; and Goldberg 1997.

17. See, for instance, Davies 2000a, this volume, and Wright 2000a, this volume.

18. Another strategy available to those sympathetic to transcendental arguments stems from the (Moorean) paradox generated by ascriptions of this form:

(1)   *p*, but I do not believe that *p*.

(2)   *p*, but I believe that not-*p*.

In (1), the thinker holds a proposition to be true, yet ascribes to herself a non-belief concerning that proposition, i.e., he is agnostic about the truth of that proposition. In (2), the thinker holds a proposition to be true, yet ascribes to herself a disbelief concerning that proposition, i.e., he believes that proposition is false. Here proponents of a transcendental argument may take the paradox generated by (1) and (2) to express a conceptual constraint on higher-order self-ascriptions of belief. The predicament of a higher-order-belief self-ascriber who violates this constraint seems in some respects similar to that of a thinker who sincerely asserts logically impossible propositions. But if individuals cannot ascribe to themselves higher-order beliefs about propositions whose truth they either doubt or blatantly deny, beliefs of that sort would be infallible. Compare Brueckner, this volume.

1

The Problem of Armchair Knowledge[1]
Martin Davies

1 McKinsey's Reductio Argument: Externalism and Self-Knowledge

In "Anti-individualism and Privileged Access" (1991a), Michael McKinsey asks us to consider the following three propositions, where 'E' says that some particular externalist condition for thinking that water is wet is met:[2]

(1) Oscar knows a priori that he is thinking that water is wet.

(2) The proposition that Oscar is thinking that water is wet conceptually implies E.

(3) The proposition E cannot be known a priori, but only by empirical investigation.

McKinsey then argues that (1), (2), and (3) constitute an inconsistent triad: "Suppose (1) that Oscar knows a priori that he is thinking that water is wet. Then by (2), Oscar can simply *deduce E*, using premises that are knowable a priori, including the premise that he is thinking that water is wet. Since Oscar can deduce E from premises that are knowable a priori, Oscar can know E itself a priori. But this contradicts (3), the assumption that E *cannot* be known a priori. Hence (1), (2), and (3) are inconsistent." His conclusion is that "anti-individualism is inconsistent with privileged access" (1991a: 15).

In a more recent paper (2002a), McKinsey sets out very clearly the principles about privileged access and externalism on which his argument depends. First, (1) is a consequence of a doctrine of privileged access or first-person authority about the contents of our thoughts:

Privileged access to content (PAC)   It is necessarily true that if a person *x* is thinking that *p*, then *x* can in principle know a priori that he himself, or she herself, is thinking that *p*.

Second, if we take *E* to be an externalist condition in the sense that it "asserts or implies the existence of contingent objects of some sort external relative to Oscar," then (2) is a consequence of a doctrine of semantic externalism applied to the predicate "is thinking that water is wet":

Semantic externalism (SE)   Many *de dicto*-structured predicates of the form 'is thinking that *p*' express properties that are wide, in the sense that possession of such a property by an agent logically or conceptually implies the existence of contingent objects external to that agent.

If what can be deduced from premises that are knowable a priori can itself be known a priori, then (1) and (2) are jointly inconsistent with (3).[3] More generally, if no proposition that asserts or implies the existence of contingent external objects can be known a priori, then no pair of propositions like (1) and (2) can be true together. But if (PAC) and (SE) are both correct, then *some* such pairs must be true. So (PAC) and (SE) cannot both be true: anti-individualism, as rendered by (SE), is inconsistent with privileged access, formulated as (PAC). If 'is thinking that *p*' expresses a 'wide' property, then I cannot know with first-person authority that it is true of me. Here, then, is the reductio: "If you could know a priori that you are in a given mental state, and your being in that mental state conceptually or logically implies the existence of external objects, then you could know a priori that the external world exists. Since you obviously *can't* know a priori that the external world exists, you also can't know a priori that you are in the mental state in question" (McKinsey 1991a: 16).

McKinsey's reductio argument about externalism and self-knowledge can be adapted to provide the first instance of the epistemological problem with which I am concerned in the present paper.[4] For my own expository purposes, it is useful to separate Oscar's palpably valid argument for *E* from the epistemological commentary that generates the puzzle. To make the problem vivid, we can, in Oscar's argument, substitute a specific claim about the environment for the placeholder '*E*'. To avoid detailed consideration of different notions of a priori knowledge, we can, in the epistemological commentary, make use of the intuitive notion of knowledge that is available from the armchair.

1.1   Externalism and a first instance of the problem of armchair knowledge
Consider the argument (WATER):

WATER(1)   I am thinking that water is wet.

WATER(2)   If I am thinking that water is wet, then I am (or have been) embedded in an environment that contains samples of water.

WATER(3)   Therefore, I am (or have been) embedded in an environment that contains samples of water.

It is plausible that my first-personal knowledge that I am thinking and what I am thinking does not depend for its status as knowledge on my conducting any detailed empirical investigation either of the information processing going on inside my head or of the physical and social environment in which I am situated. I am able to know from the armchair that I am a thinking being and that I think many particular things. So I can have armchair knowledge of the first premise WATER(1). But if philosophical arguments yield knowledge, then there is more that I can know from the armchair. If externalism is correct, then I can know, not only that I have thoughts with certain particular contents, but also that having those thoughts imposes requirements on my environment. In particular, we suppose that externalist philosophical theory motivates the *externalist dependence thesis*:

WaterDep   Necessarily (*x*) (if *x* is thinking that water is wet, then *x* is, or has been, embedded in an environment that contains samples of water)

So, philosophical theorizing yields armchair knowledge of the conditional premise WATER(2).[5]

Both the premises WATER(1) and WATER(2) can be known from the armchair, and it does not require any empirical investigation to see that the conclusion WATER(3) follows. But it is overwhelmingly plausible that some empirical investigation is required if I am to settle the question of whether or not I am embedded in an environment that contains samples of water. I cannot, without empirical investigation, come to know that the answer to this question is that my environment does indeed contain samples of water. So while WATER(1) and WATER(2) can be known from the armchair, WATER(3) seems to fall outside the scope of armchair knowledge. Externalist philosophical theory, when taken together with a plausible claim about self-knowledge, gives rise to an instance of what I call *the problem of armchair knowledge*.

2   Wright on Moore: Limitations on the Transmission of Evidential Support

In his British Academy Lecture "Facts and Certainty," Crispin Wright reflects on the intuitive inadequacy of Moore's (1959) antiskeptical argument (MOORE), which we can represent as follows:

MOORE(1)   Here is one hand, and here is another.

MOORE(2)   If here is one hand and here is another, then an external world exists.

MOORE(3)   Therefore, an external world exists.

Moore's experience provides good but defeasible evidence for MOORE(1). But the question is whether this evidential support is transmitted to MOORE(3) across the modus ponens inference in which the elementary piece of conceptual analysis, MOORE(2), figures as the conditional premise.

2.1   A pattern for nontransmission
Wright (1985: 435–436) asks us to consider three examples in which the question of transmission of evidential support can arise:

(A)   The transmission of support from, *Five hours ago Jones swallowed twenty deadly nightshade berries*, to *Jones has absorbed into his system a fatal quantity of belladonna*, and thence to, *Jones will shortly die.*

(B)   The transmission of support from, *Jones has just written an 'x' on that piece of paper*, to *Jones has just voted*, and thence to, *An election is taking place.*

(C)   The transmission of support from, *Jones has kicked the ball between the two white posts*, to *Jones has scored a goal*, and thence to, *A game of football is taking place.*

In examples (B) and (C), but not in (A), Wright says, "the evidential support afforded by the first line for the second is itself conditional on the a priori reasonableness of accepting the third line.... Knowledge of the first does not begin to provide support for the second unless it is *antecedently* reasonable to accept the third" (1985: 436). Moore's mistake, then, is to suppose that the structure of evidential support in (MOORE) is like that in example (A), when it is really like that in (B) and (C): "Once the hypothesis is seriously entertained that it is as likely as not, for all I know, that there is no material world as ordinarily conceived, my experience will lose all tendency to corroborate the particular propositions about the material world which I normally take to be certain" (1985: 437).

If (MOORE) provides an example of nontransmission of evidential support across a palpably valid modus ponens inference, then it seems that other cases discussed by Wittgenstein in *On Certainty* (1969) provide examples as well. Consider *On Certainty*, secs. 208–211:

208. I have a telephone conversation with New York. My friend tells me that his young trees have buds of such and such a kind. I am now convinced that his tree is.... Am I also convinced that the earth exists?

209. The existence of the earth is rather part of the whole picture which forms the starting-point of belief for me.

210. Does my telephone call to New York strengthen my conviction that the earth exists? Much seems to be fixed, and it is removed from the traffic. It is so to speak shunted onto an unused siding.

211. Now it gives our way of looking at things, and our researches, their form. Perhaps it was once disputed. But perhaps, for unthinkable ages, it has belonged to the *scaffolding* of our thoughts.

The argument that we need to consider here is (TREE):

TREE(1)   My friend in New York has a ... tree in his garden.

TREE(2)   If my friend in New York has a ... tree in his garden, then the earth exists.

TREE(3)   Therefore, the earth exists.

Wittgenstein's remarks seem to suggest that the evidential support for TREE(1) that is provided by my telephone conversation with my friend in New York is not transmitted to TREE(3).

2.2   *Epistemic achievement and entitlement*

Towards the end of "Facts and Certainty" (1985: 470–471), Wright considers the possibility that there are propositions (including some of Wittgenstein's 'hinge' propositions) that lie outside the domain of *cognitive achievement.* Evidential support or epistemic warrant would not be transmitted to such propositions just because, lying outside the domain of cognitive or epistemic achievement, they are also "outside the domain of what may be known, reasonably believed, or doubted." But although these propositions would not be known in the sense that involves epistemic achievement, they would still be known in a more inclusive sense. Thus, *On Certainty*, secs. 357–359:

357. One might say: "'I know' expresses *comfortable* certainty, not the certainty that is still struggling."

358. Now I would like to regard this certainty, not as something akin to hastiness or superficiality, but as a form of life.

359. But that means I want to conceive it as something that lies beyond being justified; as it were, as something animal.

Wright actually explores the idea that these propositions lie outside the domain of cognitive or epistemic achievement because they lie outside the domain of truth-evaluability or are *not fact-stating*. But it seems that the structure of Wright's proposal as involving less inclusive and more inclusive notions of knowledge might be retained even if we do not go so far as to deny the fact-stating status of the propositions to which only the more inclusive notion ("comfortable certainty") applies. We might distinguish between a stricter notion of knowledge that is an *achievement* and a more inclusive notion that embraces assumptions we are epistemically *entitled* to make.

Knowledge may be an achievement in that it requires that a question-settling justification or warrant be provided for believing the known proposition. A rational thinker engaged in an epistemic project may regard the question whether *q* is true as being open *pro tempore*, and he may seek to bring to bear considerations that settle the question. Such a thinker might achieve knowledge that *q* by, for example, gathering evidential support for *q* and against alternatives, or by following through an a priori argument in favor of *q*, or by assembling considerations in favor of some premise, *p*, from which *q* palpably follows.

A fact-stating assumption may be one that we are epistemically entitled to make in the context of a particular epistemic project in the sense that a rational thinker is entitled to rely on the assumption in the conduct of that project. The project may lead to knowledge even though it involves taking the assumption for granted. No evidential support or other question-settling warrant for the assumption needs to be provided within that project. In this rough and intuitive characterization of epistemic entitlement, the notion of making an assumption should be construed in a thin way so as to include the case where it simply does not occur to a thinker to doubt that something is the case. Being epistemically entitled to make an assumption thus includes being epistemically entitled to ignore, or not to bother about, certain possibilities.[6] So suppose that a thinker sets out to settle the question whether *q* is true and that the thinker is entitled to ignore certain possible ways in which *q* might be false. Then the thinker's project may yield knowledge that q even though the positive considerations that the thinker assembles within that project do not rule out those particular alternatives to q.

In some contexts, I may be entitled to the assumption that a football match is taking place; I may be entitled to ignore the possibility, for example, that I am watching a rehearsal on a movie set. Against the background of the assumption that it is a football match, and not a movie rehearsal, that I am watching, the perceptual evidence of Jones kicking the ball between the two white posts counts very strongly in favor of the proposition that Jones has scored a goal and against many alternative possibilities. By watching the trajectory of the ball, and perhaps by observing also the behavior of the referee and the crowd, I can come to know that Jones has scored a goal. I have an epistemically adequate question-settling justification for that belief.

From the proposition that Jones has scored a goal, it surely follows that a game of football is taking place. So if I believe that Jones has scored a goal and I appreciate the entailment, then I should also believe that a game of football is taking place. If I appreciate the entailment, then since I am justified in believing that Jones has scored a goal, I am also justified in believing that a game of football is taking place. But I cannot take the question-settling justification for the first belief that is provided by watching the trajectory of the ball and augment it by recognition of the entailment so as to provide myself with a question-settling justification for the second belief. Even if I am poised to make the inference from the premise that Jones has scored a goal to the conclusion that a game of football is taking place, the perceptual evidence of Jones kicking the ball between the two white posts is of no use to me in the project of rationally settling the question whether a game of football is indeed taking place. If I begin by regarding the question as open *pro tempore*—if, for example, I regard the possibility that I am watching a rehearsal on a movie set as a live option—then I cannot take the perceptual evidence as counting in favor of the premise. For the perceptual evidence supports the premise only against the background of the assumption that it is a football match, and not a movie rehearsal, that I am watching.

In summary, because I am entitled to the background assumption, I do have an epistemically adequate question-settling justification for believing the premise. That is my epistemic achievement. But even given my appreciation of the entailment, I cannot redeploy that justification for believing the premise as a question-settling justification for believing the conclusion.[7] This, I think, is the lesson of Wright's example (C), and much the same could be said of his example (B) about voting. And I agree with Wright that the structure of evidential support in Moore's argument is relevantly similar to the structure in examples (B) and (C), even though the nature of my entitlement to the background assumption that there is an external world is surely different from the nature of my entitlement to the background assumption that I am watching a football match. These notions of entitlement and background assumptions did not, however, figure explicitly in my first attempt (1998) to use Wright's ideas about nontransmission of epistemic warrant as a way of avoiding McKinsey's reductio.

2.3 Early versions of the limitation principles

Confronted by McKinsey's reductio argument, and with Wright's discussion of Moore in mind, I proposed a principle that would limit the transmission of epistemic warrant from the premises to the conclusions of even palpably valid inferences:[8]

First Limitation Principle (early version)   Epistemic warrant cannot be transmitted from the premises of a valid argument to its conclusion if, for one of the premises, the truth of the conclusion is a precondition of our warrant for that premise counting as a warrant.

This principle appears to have the consequence that epistemic warrant cannot be transmitted from the premises to the conclusion of Moore's argument. It also seems to account for the nontransmission of evidential support in Wright's examples (B) and (C) and in Wittgenstein's example (TREE). But, in this initial formulation, the principle is problematic in a number of respects. It makes use of the unexplained notion of a precondition. If this notion is interpreted simply as a necessary condition, then the principle is certainly open to counterexamples.

Yet more pressing than these worries about the principle is the fact that it is not at all clear how it applies to the example (WATER), which is motivated by McKinsey's reductio argument. The First Limitation Principle is modeled on Wright's account of cases in which *evidential* support is not transmitted. But our knowledge of WATER(1) and WATER(2) is not based on evidence; it is armchair knowledge. What seems to be needed to block the unwanted transmission of armchair warrant from WATER(1) and WATER(2) to WATER(3) is not the First Limitation Principle, but something like this:[9]

Second Limitation Principle (early version)   Epistemic warrant cannot be transmitted from the premises of a valid argument to its conclusion if, for one of the premises, the truth of the conclusion is a precondition of the knower even being able to believe that premise.

According to externalist philosophical theory, my being embedded in an environment that contains water is a necessary condition for my believing or even thinking that water is wet. It is also a necessary condition for my thinking any other thought in which the concept of water is deployed, in particular, for my thinking that I am thinking that water is wet. So the truth of WATER(3) is a necessary condition of my even being able to think WATER(1), and this triggers the Second Limitation Principle.[10] The early version of the Second Limitation Principle has the desired result, but in other respects it is far from satisfactory. The worry is not, primarily, that the principle is open to counterexamples, but rather that no independent motivation for the principle has been provided.[11] In short, the early version of the Second Limitation Principle appears to be completely ad hoc. One of my aims in what follows is to provide a proper motivation for limitation principles that account for the nontransmission of epistemic warrant in Wright's examples, especially (MOORE), and in McKinsey's example (WATER).

3   Aunty's Argument: A Second Instance of the Problem of Armchair Knowledge

In "Aunty's Own Argument for the Language of Thought" (1992),[12] I put forward an argument for the language-of-thought (LOT) hypothesis. The argument is relatively nonempirical in character and it proceeds in two main steps. The first step makes use of neo-Fregean resources. Thinking involves the deployment of concepts, and having concepts involves commitments to certain patterns of inference. In particular, conceptualized thought involves performing certain inferences *in virtue of their form*, and this is then glossed in terms of tacit knowledge of the corresponding inferential rule. The second step makes use of a quite general connection between tacit knowledge of rules and syntactically structured representations.[13]

3.1   Eliminativism and an intuition of nonnegotiability
Aunty's argument supports a conditional: *if* we are thinking beings, *then* the LOT hypothesis is true of us; that is, we are LOT beings. Although

the argument is relatively nonempirical in character, the question of whether we really are LOT beings is a substantive empirical one, and answering it requires detailed empirical investigation.[14] It seems reasonable to allow that it is epistemically possible (whether or not it is likely) that we may turn out not to be LOT beings. But then Aunty's argument would support an eliminativist *modus tollens*. From the premise that we are not LOT beings, we would be able to conclude that we are not thinking beings.[15]

Imagine, for a moment, that empirical evidence decisively supported the thesis that we are not LOT beings. It seems that, in those circumstances, we would face a stark choice between two alternatives. On the one hand, we could perform the *modus tollens* inference and cease to regard each other and ourselves as thinking beings. On the other hand, we could conclude that there is something wrong with Aunty's argument. But the first alternative seems rationally to require that we abandon our familiar descriptions of ourselves and others as believing and wanting things, as hoping and fearing things, as engaging in reasoning and planning, and there are powerful intuitions proclaiming that this option is not genuinely available to us. Our everyday engagement in folk-psychological practice seems to be philosophically nonnegotiable. So we are driven to the second alternative. If we found ourselves to be in a disobliging world, then we would be bound to reject Aunty's argument. We would have to conclude that the philosophical theories that support the argument are in some way flawed.

It may well seem to you that, if this is how things would be in a disobliging world, then we should already conclude now that Aunty's argument is the product of flawed philosophical theories. But in my view, we can respect the intuition of nonnegotiability even while embracing the philosophical theories that support Aunty's argument. We can accept that those philosophical theories provide the best way to elaborate and make precise our current conception of a thinking being, and that Aunty's argument correctly draws out a necessary condition for falling under that conception. But we can also allow that part of our current conception is that we ourselves are thinking beings: being one of us is a sufficient condition for falling under the conception. Suppose that these claims about a necessary condition and a sufficient condition for falling under our current conception of a thinking being are both correct. It follows that if we are not LOT beings, then our current conception dictates both that we are and are not thinking beings. In a disobliging world, our current conception of a thinking being would be of no use to us, since it would dictate contradictory answers to the question of whether we are thinking beings.

If we turn out not to be LOT beings, then we must negotiate our way to a revised conception of what it is to be a thinking being.[16] This conceptual negotiation would proceed under two constraints. The revised conception should be one under which we fall, so it should not involve a commitment to the truth of the LOT hypothesis.[17] And the revised conception should rationally sustain as much as possible of our folk-psychological practice.[18] By acknowledging this pair of constraints on the process of revision, we honor the intuition of nonnegotiability concerning our engagement in folk-psychological practice.

In response to the worry about eliminativism, what is being proposed is that the concept of a thinking being has at least two components. There is an exemplar component that specifies sufficient conditions: we, at least, are thinking beings. And there is a more theoretical component that, according to Aunty's argument, imposes a necessary condition: thinking beings are LOT beings. There is no logical guarantee that the items that meet the sufficient conditions also meet the necessary conditions, and in a disobliging world the two components lead to contradictory verdicts on particular cases. The worry about eliminativism does not, in the end, constitute an objection to Aunty's argument. The importance of the worry is, rather, that it prompts us to uncover a particular structure in our conception of a thinking being. The real problem for Aunty's argument is that it gives rise to a second instance of the problem of armchair knowledge.

3.2 Aunty's argument and armchair knowledge

Suppose that the LOT hypothesis is, in fact, true and that the concept of a thinking being is in good order. It seems that, by relying on my grasp of the exemplar component of the concept of a thinking being, I can know that I am a thinking being. In fact, it seems that I have more than one way of knowing this. Since at least some thinking is conscious, first-person awareness of my own conscious mental states also assures me that I am a thinking being. Either way, provided that the LOT hypothesis is in fact true, this knowledge seems to be available to me ahead of any empirical investigation of the information-processing mechanisms inside my head.

By relying on my grasp of the theoretical component of the concept of a thinking being, engaging in some inferences to the best philosophical explanation, and following through Aunty's argument, I can, if the argument is a good one, come to know that a thinking being must be an LOT being. I know that if I am a thinking being, then I am an LOT being.

Without conducting any detailed empirical investigation, I can have two pieces of knowledge that provide the premises for a simple modus ponens inference:

LOT(1)   I am a thinking being.

LOT(2)   If I am a thinking being, then I am an LOT being.

LOT(3)   Therefore, I am an LOT being.

But it is highly plausible that settling the question of whether the LOT hypothesis is true will be the result of experiments, computational modeling, and, more generally, detailed comparison of the successes and failures of competing research programs. So Aunty's argument gives rise to a second instance of the problem of armchair knowledge. For, if the argument is a good one, then both LOT(1) and LOT(2) can be known from the armchair, yet knowledge of LOT(3) requires an investigative methodology rather than an armchair methodology.

The early and unsatisfactory version of the Second Limitation Principle mentioned towards the end of the previous section does at least have the advantage of providing a way out of this instance of the problem of armchair knowledge. If the argument that supports LOT(2) is correct, then the truth of the conclusion, LOT(3), is a necessary condition for my being a thinking being, for my being able to think anything at all, and so for my being able to think or believe the premise LOT(1). As I go on to offer more adequately motivated limitation principles, my aim is that they should account for the nontransmission of epistemic warrant in (LOT), as well as in (MOORE) and (WATER).

4 Interim Report: In the Armchair, Down and Out

In my view, being a thinking person depends on being embodied and embedded in the right way. I call the claim about embodiment, that thought requires a particular kind of internal cognitive machinery, an *architecturalist* claim. The claim about being embedded, that there are requirements that our environment must meet if we are to have thoughts with certain contents, is an *externalist* claim. Both claims are supported by philosophical arguments of a relatively a priori kind, arguments advanced from the armchair.

My concern in this paper is with the epistemological problem that these arguments pose. For both architecturalist and externalist arguments generate instances of the problem of armchair knowledge. When the arguments are combined with a claim about self-knowledge, they seem to yield deeply implausible consequences about what it is possible to know from the armchair. Given the plausibility of the claim of knowledge of our own thoughts, the problem of armchair knowledge is naturally regarded as casting doubt on the arguments that generate it. The moral that many will draw is that armchair philosophical theorizing cannot take us from everyday folk-psychological claims about our thoughts and their contents either *down*, to substantive claims about the cognitive machinery that underpins our thinking, or *out*, to substantive claims about the world that our thoughts concern. But I shall be taking a different approach.

In my view, philosophical theorizing, conducted in the armchair, can indeed support both conditional claims that link the personal level of folk psychology with the subpersonal level of information-processing mechanisms and conditional claims that link mind and world. In the armchair, we can proceed both down and out, to know what thought requires. But I also want to maintain the plausible claim of first-person knowledge of our thoughts and their contents.

In the armchair, I can know what thought requires. In the armchair, I can know about my thoughts and their contents. But I cannot, purely by armchair reflection, settle the question of whether the conditions that thought requires are conditions that actually obtain. In general, from the facts that I can have armchair knowledge of a conditional (if A, then B), and that I can have armchair knowledge of the antecedent of the conditional (A), it does not follow that I can gain armchair knowledge of the consequent of the conditional (B). In my view, then, the solution to the problem of armchair knowledge lies in limitations on our ability to achieve knowledge by inference from things that we already know. Sometimes the epistemic warrant or justification that we have for believing the premises of an argument is not transmitted to the conclusion of the argument, even though the argument is palpably valid. Sometimes even given my appreciation of the validity of the argument, I cannot redeploy the justification for believing the premises as a question-settling justification for believing the conclusion (in the terminology of section 2.2). Placing limitations on the transmission of epistemic warrant from premises to conclusion in palpably valid arguments may strike you as an extreme measure. Knowledge by inference is surely a vital component in our epistemic practices. So it may seem much more promising to reject the externalist and architecturalist arguments that generate instances of the problem of armchair knowledge. In my view, Wright's treatment of Moore's antiskeptical argument furnishes considerations that count against a blanket rejection of the idea of limiting the transmission of epistemic warrant. But there may still be a concern about the apparently ad hoc step from the First Limitation Principle, which emerged fairly naturally from what Wright said, to the Second Limitation Principle, which is needed to deal with (WATER) and (LOT).

In the remainder of this paper, I shall try to motivate my approach in two ways.[19] First, I shall show that instances of the problem of armchair knowledge, or closely related problems about transmission of epistemic warrant, are relatively widespread. It would not be right to suppose that the problem is generated only by a couple of idiosyncratic and easily rejected philosophical arguments. Second, I shall show that the proposed limitations on transmission of warrant are far from being ad hoc. Failure of transmission of epistemic warrant is the analogue, within the thought of a single subject, of the dialectical phenomenon of begging the question.[20]

5   *Problems about Transmission of Epistemic Warrant: Six Examples*

So far we have considered two examples of the problem of armchair knowledge and one closely related problem about transmission of epistemic warrant in a putative antiskeptical argument:

Example 1 (WATER): environmental requirements for thought

Example 2 (MOORE): Moore's antiskeptical argument

Example 3 (LOT): subpersonal-level requirements for thought

In this section, I shall add three further examples.

Example 4: indexical thoughts
The instance of the problem of armchair knowledge that results from externalist philosophical theorizing about thoughts involving natural-kind concepts (example 1) clearly belongs in a larger category. There are, for example, other varieties of externalism, including the externalism about so-called "object-dependent thoughts" that is familiar from the work of Gareth Evans (1982) and John McDowell (1984, 1986). More generally, these externalist examples belong with other substan-

tive requirements for thought that issue from philosophical theories about thought content, such as teleological theories of content.[21] It is not difficult to see how an instance of the problem of armchair knowledge could be generated from the claim that to be a thinker, a being must have such and such a kind of selectional history and must not have come into existence just a few minutes ago. On this issue I borrow material from Evans (1982) to provide an externalist example that involves the indexical concept 'here'. First, according to Evans, being able to think about a particular place is not a trivial matter: "We are prepared to suppose that there is a determinate thought here—that the subject has a definite place in mind—because we know that subjects do have a capacity to select one position in egocentric space, and to maintain a stable dispositional connection with it.... If the subject ... does know which place his thought concerns ..., this will be manifestable only in manifestations of that stable dispositional connection" (1982: 161).

What this suggests is that someone who is unable, for a while, either to maintain a stable dispositional connection with a position or to keep track of his movement through space is likewise unable, for that while, to have (determinate) indexical thoughts about places.

Second, Evans presents a vivid example of a thinker who fails to keep track of his movement through space: "A person might lie in bed in hospital thinking repeatedly 'How hot it was here yesterday'—supposing himself to be stationary in the dark. But his bed might be very well oiled, and be pulled by strings, so that every time he has what he takes to be the same thought, he is in fact thinking of a different place, and having a different thought" (1982: 201).

As Evans describes the case, this thinker has several instantaneous thoughts about different places. But we can adapt the example by imagining that the person thinks, slowly, carefully, not wanting to knock anything over in the dark, 'There's a bottle of whiskey just here'. In general, it is plausible that a thinker who essays a 'here'-thought, but who is moving through space even as he thinks, fails to think any determinate thought at all. If the thought that he essays as he moves several yards is, 'There's a bottle of whiskey just here', then there is no place such that the correctness of the putative thought would turn on whether there is a bottle of whiskey at that place. The subject has no determinate place in mind.

Suppose now that I am stationary in bed, in the dark, thinking 'There's a bottle of whiskey just here'—a thought that is true if there is indeed a bottle of whiskey located at a particular position just next to the bed. Suppose also that it is correct, as a matter of philosophical theory, that someone who neither maintains a stable dispositional connection with a position nor keeps track of his movement through space is unable to have indexical thoughts about places. And now consider the following argument:

BED(1)   I am thinking that there's a bottle of whiskey just here.

BED(2)   If I am thinking that there's a bottle of whiskey just here, then I am stationary.

BED(3)   Therefore, I am stationary.

By the assumption of first-person authority, I can know BED(1) from the armchair. If I follow through the philosophical theorizing indicated in the previous paragraph, then I can also have armchair knowledge of BED(2). But it is highly implausible that I can settle the question of whether I am stationary, rather than being moved silently along a darkened hospital corridor, just by giving thought. The conclusion, BED(3), seems to fall outside the scope of armchair knowledge.

Example 5: color concepts

In "Naming the Colors" (1997: 326), David Lewis begins from the thought that our folk theory of colors contains principles linking colors and color experiences, such as, when a red thing is before someone's eyes, it typically causes in him an experience of redness. If our concepts of colors and of color experiences are concepts of properties of objects and of inner states that are implicitly defined by our folk theory, then conceptual analysis is liable to lead us to such "definitions" as these (Lewis 1997: 327):

D1   *Red* is the surface property of things which typically causes experience of red in people who have such things before their eyes.

D2   *Experience of red* is the inner state of people which is the typical effect of having red things before the eyes.

The problem with D1 and D2 is that what they say, while true, does not distinguish the pair ⟨red, experience of red⟩ from other similar pairs, such as ⟨green, experience of green⟩. A further chapter must be added to the folk theory of color to individuate specific colors, and Lewis suggests that this further chapter can come in different versions, each specifying relatively parochial examples that serve well enough the needs of some subcommunity of the population. Thus, among followers of Australian Rules football, it will suffice to say "that red is the color of the diagonal stripe on an Essendon Football Club jumper."[22]

With this much by way of background, we can consider the following modus ponens inference:

RED(1)   This [pointing at the diagonal stripe on an Essendon jumper] is red.

RED(2)   If this is red, then there is a type of color experience and a type of inner state that is typically caused in people who have this before their eyes.

RED(3)   Therefore, there is a type of color experience and a type of inner state that is typically caused in people who have this before their eyes.

By relying on my mastery of the exemplar component of the concept of red (the parochial exemplar component that applies to my group), I can know that this Essendon stripe is red. Indeed, I have more than one way of knowing this, since I can often know what color something is just by looking at it. Having seen many Essendon jumpers, I can recognize this item as being the color of the Essendon diagonal stripe. Either way, knowledge of RED(1) is available to me ahead of any investigation of other people's color experiences or inner states. By relying on my grasp of the theoretical component of the concept of red (including the principles D1 and D2), I can know that if something is red, then there is a type of color experience and a type of inner state that is typically caused in people who have that thing before their eyes. So I can know RED(2). But it is implausible that, without rising from the armchair save perhaps to look at an Essendon football jumper, I can know the conclusion RED(3).

At the beginning of "Naming the Colors," Lewis says, "It is a Moorean fact that there are colors rightly so-called."[23] This remark suggests that certain claims about colors and color experiences have the status of presuppositions or unquestioned background assumptions in our everyday use of color concepts to classify the things that we see. It also suggests that these claims, like Moore's conclusion, cannot have epistemic warrant transmitted to them from premises that acquire their warrant in our everyday epistemic projects. That is just what I shall be claiming.

Example 6: meaning and tacit knowledge

The third new example to be introduced in this section concerns the meaning of sentences that are never used. Ordinary speakers of English are credited with speaking a language in which sentences that no one ever gets around to using nevertheless have determinate meanings. But what facts about ordinary speakers and their language use could make it correct for us to describe them in this way? This is the problem of *meaning without use*.

A number of philosophers of language, including Brian Loar (1981) and Stephen Schiffer (1993),[24] have argued persuasively that this problem cannot be solved without appeal to the structure of the mechanisms of language processing in speakers' heads. I myself would specifically argue that our assignments of meaning without use are correct only if speakers have subpersonal-level tacit knowledge of a compositional semantic theory for their language.[25]

Suppose, for a moment, that Loar, Schiffer, and I are right about this. Then the modus ponens inference to be considered is as follows:

MEANING(1)   Sentence *s* means that *p* in my language and would do so whether or not I ever used it.

MEANING(2)   If sentence *s* means that *p* in my language and would do so whether or not I ever used it, then I have tacit knowledge of a compositional semantic theory for my language.

MEANING(3)   Therefore, I have tacit knowledge of a compositional semantic theory for my language.

Suppose that *s* is a hitherto unused and unconsidered sentence built from words and constructions that occur in other sentences that I have used. When I hear or consider sentence *s* for the first time, I am able to assign it a meaning, say the meaning that *p*. I may know that this is what *s* means. I may know that this is what *s* does and did and would mean, whether or not I used it. Furthermore, I may know this without engaging in any empirical investigation of my language-processing system. So I have armchair knowledge of the first premise. Then, if the development of the arguments advanced by Loar and Schiffer is correct, I also have armchair knowledge of the conditional premise. But the conclusion, which follows so obviously from these premises, concerns the structure of the language-processing system, and surely I cannot gain knowledge about this cognitive structure without a substantial program of empirical research. Armchair methodologies suffice for knowledge of the premises, but knowledge of the conclusion requires an investigative methodology.

6   Limitation Principles and Begging the Question

In the previous section I tried to show that instances of the problem of armchair knowledge, or closely related problems about transmission of epistemic warrant, are relatively widespread. My aim in this section is to motivate limitation principles on transmission of epistemic warrant by making use of the idea that failure of transmission of epistemic warrant is the analogue, within the thought of a single subject, of the dialectical phenomenon of begging the question.

6.1   Moore's antiskeptical argument and a revised limitation principle

It is often said that Moore's argument begs the question against the sceptic, but what we need is an explicit account of what makes an argument question-begging, and for this I rely on Frank Jackson (1987). He says that an argument begs the question when "anyone—or anyone sane—who doubted the conclusion would have background beliefs relative to which the evidence for the premises would be no evidence" (1987: 111).

According to Jackson's view of what is achieved by advancing an argument for a conclusion, the speaker invites the hearer to borrow evidence, or other considerations, in favor of the premises of the argument. By her choice of premises the speaker provides an indication as to what kinds of considerations these are. Typically, evidence counts in favor of a proposition only relative to particular background assumptions, and often the relevant background assumptions are shared between speaker and hearer. But when background assumptions are not shared, it is possible that the considerations that count in favor of the premises relative to the speaker's background assumptions do not count in favor of the premises relative to the hearer's background assumptions. Suppose that a speaker sets out to convince a doubting hearer of the truth of some conclusion. The speaker begs the question against the hearer if the hearer's doubt rationally requires him to adopt background assumptions relative to which the considerations that are supposed to support the speaker's premises no longer provide that support. A question-begging argument "could be of no use in convincing doubters" (Jackson 1987: 112).

Convincing a doubter and settling a question both involve ruling out various ways in which a proposition could have been false. In the case of a speaker who is trying to convince a doubting hearer, the speaker's evidence for her premises rules out various ways in which those premises could have been false, ways that are left open by the speaker's background assumptions. The hearer who doubts the conclusion of the argument may have background assumptions that leave a wider range of possibilities open, and the speaker's evidence for the premises may not rule all those possibilities out. Indeed, the speaker's evidence may leave untouched ways in which, according to the hearer, the conclusion could be false.

In a similar way, a thinker who has question-settling justifications for believing the premises of an argument is able to rule out various ways in which those premises could have been false. These are ways that are left open by background assumptions that the thinker is, in that context, epistemically entitled to make. But it does not follow, even given the thinker's appreciation of the validity of the argument, that the thinker can redeploy his justifications for believing the premises so as to provide himself with a question-settling justification for believing the conclusion. For it may be that in regarding the question of the truth of the conclusion as open *pro tempore*, the thinker regards as live options certain possibilities that he was entitled to ignore when only the premises were under consideration. So the considerations that furnished epistemically adequate question-settling justifications for believing the premises may be inadequate to settle the question of the truth of the conclusion.

All this is consistent with saying that the thinker who has justifications for believing the premises of an argument is also justified in believing the conclusion. Indeed, it is consistent with saying that the speaker is epistemically entitled to believe the conclusion. The point about non-transmission of epistemic warrant is not that the thinker should believe the premises but not believe the conclusion. It is not that the thinker's beliefs in the premises are epistemically in good order while his belief in the conclusion would be epistemically out of order. It is that the thinker cannot take the question-settling justifications for believing the premises and augment them by recognition of the validity of the argument so as to provide himself with a question-settling justification for believing the conclusion.

The reason for this nontransmission of question-settling warrant is that the thinker's operative considerations amount to epistemically adequate justifications for believing the premises only against the background of certain assumptions that the thinker is entitled to make. Simply regarding a question—here, the question of the truth of the conclusion—as open *pro tempore* does not rob the thinker of that entitlement. But it may be that a doubt about the truth of the conclusion would rationally require the thinker to adopt different background assumptions relative to which the operative considerations would no longer amount to epistemically adequate justifications for believing the premises. The proposal is that, in such a case, the thinker cannot consistently make use of the original background assumptions within the context of an epistemic project that begins with the thinker regarding the question of the truth of the conclusion as open.

The analogy between convincing a doubter and providing an epistemically adequate question-settling justification for believing thus motivates the following principle about transmission of epistemic warrant:

First Limitation Principle (revised version)   Epistemic warrant cannot be transmitted from the premises of a valid argument to its conclusion if, for one of the premises, the warrant for that premise counts as a warrant only against the background of certain assumptions and acceptance of those assumptions cannot be rationally combined with doubt about the truth of the conclusion.

To apply this principle to any particular argument, we need to identify assumptions such that, for one of the premises, it is only against the background of those assumptions that the operative considerations amount to an epistemically adequate question-settling warrant for that premise. Then we need to show that acceptance of those assumptions cannot be combined with doubt about the truth of the conclusion. Wright's diagnosis of the failure of transmission of evidential support from the premises to the conclusion of Moore's argument seems to fit this pattern.[26]

6.2   *Subpersonal requirements for thought and two generalized limitation principles*

It is not so clear, however, that this revised version of the First Limitation Principle explains the failure of transmission of warrant from LOT(1) and LOT(2) to LOT(3).[27] The epistemic warrant for LOT(1) is constituted either by grasp of the exemplar component of the concept of a thinking being or else by awareness of one's own conscious mental states. But in neither case is there an obvious candidate for the role of background assumptions without which the epistemic warrant would not count as a warrant.

There is, however, a very basic assumption that lies in the background of any epistemic project, namely, the assumption that there is the proposition for which one is attempting to provide evidence, justification, or warrant. The notion of a proposition that figures in this assumption is not to be construed in a metaphysically committed way. If a thinker is attempting to provide a warrant for believing *A*, then the basic background assumption is simply that there is such a thing to think as *A*. If there were no such thing to think as *A*, then there could be no question of anything constituting an epistemically adequate warrant for believing *A*. So we can make explicit a second principle that is arguably a consequence of the first:

Second Limitation Principle (revised version)   Epistemic warrant cannot be transmitted from the premises of a valid argument to its conclusion if, for one of the premises, acceptance of the assumption that there is such a proposition for the knower to think as that premise cannot be rationally combined with doubt about the truth of the conclusion.

One way in which the assumption that figures in this principle could turn out to be false would be that one of the purported conceptual constituents in the premise were revealed to be internally incoherent, dictating contradictory answers to the question of whether some particular item falls under the concept. To that extent, the principle holds some promise of providing a solution to the instance of the problem of armchair knowledge that is posed by Aunty's argument. For the worry about eliminativism prompted us to uncover a particular structure in our conception of a thinking being. On the other hand, it is clear that acceptance of the assumption that there is such a thing to think as that I am a thinking being—and, in particular, acceptance of the assumption that the concept of a thinking being is in good order—can be rationally combined with doubt about the truth of the LOT hypothesis. It is only the acceptance of Aunty's argument that generates rational tension between acceptance of the background assumption and doubt about the conclusion.

It is clear what kind of modification of the principle is required if it is to provide a solution to the problem of armchair knowledge that arises from Aunty's argument, and the required modification is not merely opportunistic or ad hoc. To see this, we need to return to begging the question and focus on the fact that arguments may have several premises. Suppose that a speaker advances a multipremise argument in an attempt to convince a hearer who doubts that argument's conclusion. The speaker offers various considerations for borrowing; they are considerations that count in favor of the premises relative to the speaker's background assumptions. If the hearer's doubt by itself rationally requires him to adopt background assumptions relative to which one of the speaker's premises is no longer supported by the considerations that she offers for borrowing then the speaker begs the question against the hearer. That is the kind of case that Jackson describes.

But there is a more complicated scenario in which it is no less true that the argument, as advanced by the speaker, will be of no use in convincing the doubting hearer. If the hearer is to be convinced, then he must accept the considerations that the speaker offers in support of her premises. In addition, he must not differ from the speaker in his background assumptions in such a way that the premises are no longer supported by those considerations. Suppose that the hearer's doubt about the conclusion, when put together with acceptance of the considerations that the speaker offers in support of some of the premises, rationally requires him to adopt background assumptions relative to which another one of the premises is no longer supported by the considerations offered in support of it. That is enough to ensure that the argument, as advanced by the speaker, will be of no use in convincing the hearer. So, if failure of transmission of epistemic warrant is the analogue, within the thought of a single subject, of the dialectical phenomenon of begging the question, then we should expect to have the following pair of limitation principles, of which the second is arguably a consequence of the first:[28]

First Limitation Principle (generalized version) Epistemic warrant cannot be transmitted from the premises of a valid argument to its conclusion if, for one of the premises, the warrant for that premise counts as a warrant only against the background of certain assumptions, and acceptance (i) of those assumptions and (ii) of the warrants for the other premises cannot be rationally combined with doubt about the truth of the conclusion.

Second Limitation Principle (generalized version) Epistemic warrant cannot be transmitted from the premises of a valid argument to its conclusion if, for one of the premises, acceptance (i) of the assumption that there is such a proposition for the knower to think as that premise and (ii) of the warrants for the other premises cannot be rationally combined with doubt about the truth of the conclusion.

This last principle provides a solution to the instance of the problem of armchair knowledge that is posed by Aunty's argument.

7 *Applying the Limitation Principles*

In this section I shall show how the generalized versions of the two limitation principles account for the failure of transmission of epistemic warrant from premises to conclusion in five of our six examples.

Example 2 (MOORE), *Moore's antiskeptical argument*

We have seen that the First Limitation Principle in either its early version (section 2.3) or its revised version (section 6.1) accounts for the nontransmission of epistemic warrant in Moore's argument. The same goes, of course, for the generalized version of the First Limitation Principle.

Example 3 (LOT), *subpersonal requirements for thought*

Suppose that a thinker accepts that there is such a thing to think as the premise LOT(1), that he himself is a thinking being. Suppose, in particular, that he accepts that there is no internal incoherence, no source of contradictions, in the concept of a thinking being. In that case, the thinker must accept the assumption that the items, such as himself, that meet the sufficient condition for falling under the concept also meet the necessary condition. Acceptance of that assumption does not, by itself, rationally preclude doubt about whether he himself is an LOT being. But suppose, in addition, that the thinker accepts the epistemic warrants for the premises LOT(1) and LOT(2).

The epistemic warrant for believing LOT(1) is provided either by the exemplar component of the concept of a thinking being or else by his awareness of his own conscious mental states. But it is the warrant for believing the conditional premise LOT(2) that figures crucially in the solution to the problem of armchair knowledge. That warrant is provided by a battery of philosophical theory and by Aunty's argument. Acceptance of the assumption that the items that meet the sufficient conditions for falling under the concept of a thinking being also meet the necessary conditions, *and of the warrant for* LOT(2) cannot be rationally combined with doubt about whether the thinker himself is an LOT being. So the generalized version of the Second Limitation Principle is triggered and epistemic warrant cannot be transmitted from LOT(1) and LOT(2) to the conclusion LOT(3).

Example 5 (RED), *color concepts*

The problem about transmission of epistemic warrant that is presented by Lewis's account of color concepts has a solution similar to the solution to the problem presented by Aunty's argument. For the concept of red, like the concept of a thinking being, has an exemplar-based sufficient-conditions component and a theory-based necessary-conditions component.

According to the (parochial) exemplar component of the concept of red, being the color of the Essendon stripe is sufficient for being red: Essendon stripes (at least) are red things. From the theoretical component we can derive a necessary condition for being red: if something is red, then there is a type of color experience and a type of inner state that is typically caused in people who have that thing before their eyes. But there is no logical guarantee that there is a single type of color experience and a single type of inner state that is typically produced in people by the diagonal stripe on an Essendon jumper. If there is not, then the two components of the concept yield contradictory pronouncements. If the world turns out to be disobliging in this respect, then our current color concepts will be of no use to us, and we must negotiate our way to revised, presumably relativize, color concepts.

Acceptance of the assumption that there is such a thing to think as the premise RED(1) involves accepting the assumption that the items that meet the sufficient conditions for falling under the concept of red also meet the necessary conditions. But acceptance of this *and of the warrant for* RED(2) cannot be rationally combined with doubt about the truth of RED(3). So the generalized version of the Second Limitation Principle is again triggered and epistemic warrant cannot be transmitted from RED(1) and RED(2) to the conclusion RED(3).

Example 1 (WATER), *environmental requirements for thought*

We can also confirm that the generalized version of the Second Limitation Principle provides a solution to the instance of the problem of armchair knowledge that arises from externalism and self-knowledge.[29] The warrant for the conditional premise, WATER(2), is a piece of philosophical theory that supports the following two theses:

Necessarily (if I am thinking that water is wet, then I am [or have been] embedded in an environment that contains samples of water)

Necessarily (if I am thinking that I am thinking that water is wet, then I am [or have been] embedded in an environment that contains samples of water)

The theory supports the first thesis because it supports this claim:

Necessarily (if there is such a thing for me to think as that water is wet, then I am [or have been] embedded in an environment that contains samples of water)

Equally, it supports the following claim:

Necessarily (if there is such a thing for me to think as that I am thinking that water is wet, then I am [or have been] embedded in an environment that contains samples of water)

So acceptance of (i) the assumption that there is such a thing for me to think as WATER(1) and (ii) the warrant for WATER(2) cannot be rationally combined with doubt about the truth of WATER(3). According to the generalized version of the Second Limitation Principle, then, epistemic warrant cannot be transmitted from the premises WATER(1) and WATER(2) to the conclusion WATER(3).

Example 4 (BED), *indexical thoughts*

The solution to the instance of the problem of armchair knowledge that is presented by indexical thoughts follows the contours of example 1 (WATER). The warrant for the conditional premise BED(2), "If I am thinking that there's a bottle of whiskey just here, then I am stationary," is a piece of philosophical theory that also supports the conditional "If I am thinking that I am thinking that there's a bottle of whiskey just here, then I am stationary." The theory supports these conditional theses because it also supports the claims "If there is such a thing for me to think as that there's a bottle of whiskey just here, then I am stationary" and "If there is such a thing for me to think as that there's a bottle of whiskey just here, then I am stationary." Thus, acceptance of (i) the assumption that there is such a thing for me to think as BED(1) and (ii) the warrant for BED(2) cannot be rationally combined with doubt about the truth of BED(3), and this again triggers the generalized version of the Second Limitation Principle.

8   *Limitation Principles and the Objectivity of Meaning*

In section 5, I provided six examples to substantiate the claim that problems about transmission of epistemic warrant are relatively widespread. In section 6, I argued that limitation principles on transmission of epistemic warrant can be motivated by an analogy between providing a warrant and convincing a doubter. Failure of transmission is the analogue of begging the question. In section 7, I showed how five of the six problems (three instances of the problem of armchair knowledge and two closely related problems) can be solved by appeal to the generalized versions of the First and Second Limitation Principles. It remains to say something about the final example.

Example 6 (MEANING), *meaning and tacit knowledge*

According to the philosophical theory that supports the conditional premise, MEANING(2), if sentences that are never used or even considered are to have determinate meanings, then the language user must have tacit knowledge of a compositional semantic theory. If a speaker had only phrasebook knowledge of the meanings of a finite set of sentences, then there would be no basis for crediting her with speaking a language in which sentences outside that set had determinate meanings.[30] In the absence of tacit knowledge of a compositional semantic theory, the application of the concept of meaning to an unused sentence *s* would be indeterminate. Any specific judgment about the meaning of *s* in this speaker's language would be incorrect. But it does not appear to follow from this philosophical theory about the objectivity of meaning that if MEANING(3) were false, then there would be no such thing for me to think as MEANING(1). Rather, if MEANING(3) were false because I did not have tacit knowledge of a compositional semantic theory, then MEANING(1) would be thinkable but false. So it is not very plausible that the Second Limitation Principle will be applicable to this example.

The solution to the instance of the problem of armchair knowledge that is posed by the argument about meaning and tacit knowledge must lie with the First Limitation Principle. What we need to show is that the warrant for MEANING(1) counts as a warrant only against the background of certain assumptions and that acceptance of those assumptions cannot be combined with doubt about the truth of MEANING(3)—or at least that acceptance of those assumptions *together with the warrant for* MEANING(2) cannot be combined with doubt about MEANING(3).[31] A fully satisfying account of the issues surrounding the warrant for MEANING(1) would require nothing less than an adequate epistemology of understanding. But perhaps it is sufficient for present purposes to suggest that one route to knowledge of meaning is, under appropriate conditions, to take an impression of meaning at face value.

Suppose, for a moment, that the philosophical theory about the objectivity of meaning is correct and that things are as that theory says they need to be. In particular, suppose that I have tacit knowledge of a compositional semantic theory and this tacit knowledge underwrites the meanings of sentences that belong to my language even though I never get around to using them. Meaning in my language is not constituted by my having an impression of meaning, both because unconsidered sentences have meanings and because impressions of meaning can, in principle, be misleading or illusory.[32]

Suppose that *s* is a hitherto unused and unconsidered sentence built from words and constructions that occur in other sentences that I have used. And suppose that, in virtue of my having tacit knowledge of compositional meaning rules for those words and constructions, *s* determinately means that *p* in my language. If I now hear or consider *s* for the first time (hearing it in reality or in my mind's ear, as it were), then I may hear it *as* meaning that *p* and, taking that impression of meaning at face value, I may judge that *s* does mean that *p*. My suggestion is that, under appropriate conditions, this judgment amounts to knowledge.

We do not have to be in the grip of a purely reliabilist epistemology to find it plausible that one necessary condition for this judgment to be knowledge is that the same states of tacit knowledge that contribute to the constitution of *s* as meaning that *p* should figure in the causal explanation of *s*'s being heard as meaning that *p*. If taking an impression of meaning at face value is to be a route to knowledge, then the mechanisms that generate the impression of meaning should be mechanisms that reliably track the truth about meaning. It would be too restrictive to insist that every knower should be able to conceptualize this requirement and explicitly assume that it holds. Language users with no conception of mechanisms that embody tacit knowledge of semantic rules, or even with no conception of mechanisms that generate impressions of meaning, can surely come to know what sentences mean by taking impressions of meaning at face value. On the other hand, if a language user has the conceptual sophistication to consider this requirement and actually doubts that it holds, then this seems to rule out the possibility of gaining knowledge of meaning simply by taking impressions of meaning at face value.[33]

When, as in this case, there is a logical gap between having an impression and that impression's being veridical, one is justified in taking the impression at face value only against the background of an assumption (a not-calling-into-question) that certain reliabilist conditions related to the production of that impression are met. The impression furnishes an epistemic warrant for the judgment that things are as they seem to be only against the background of that assumption. The assumption against the background of which an impression of meaning furnishes a warrant when it is simply taken at face value may not be very specific; it may speak of reliability in general rather than of mechanisms that embody tacit knowledge in particular. But, given the philosophical theory that provides the warrant for MEANING(2), a general assumption of reliability can be elaborated into the particular assumption about impressions of meaning being generated by mechanisms that embody tacit knowledge of semantic rules. So it is not possible rationally to combine acceptance of (i) the assumption of reliability against the background of which the warrant for MEANING(1) counts as a warrant and (ii) the philosophical theory that provides the warrant for MEANING(2) with doubt about the truth of MEANING(3). This is what we needed to show in order to trigger the generalized version of the First Limitation Principle.

If I were to doubt that I have tacit knowledge of a compositional semantic theory for my language, then I could not resolve that doubt by reviewing the considerations that would ordinarily count in favor of MEANING(1) and MEANING(2). For, in the presence of that doubt, and given the considerations in favor of MEANING(2), the consideration that would ordinarily count in favor of MEANING(1) would no longer justify that belief. Analogously, if *you* were to doubt that I have tacit knowledge of a compositional semantic theory for my language, then I would be begging the question against you if I tried to convince you by offering those considerations.

In ordinary circumstances, it does not occur to me to doubt that the reliabilist conditions for gaining knowledge by taking an impression of meaning at face value are met. Against the background of that assumption (that not-calling-into-question), the impression of meaning provides knowledge that *s* means that *p* by ruling out various relevant alternatives to MEANING(1), such as that *s* means that *q* or that *s* means that *r*.[34] But, even taken together with the philosophical theory that supports MEANING(2), the impression that *s* means that *p* does nothing to rule out the most obviously salient alternative to MEANING(3), namely that I do not have tacit knowledge of a compositional semantic theory and that my impressions of objective meaning are illusory. My epistemic warrants for the two premises of the modus ponens inference do not add up to an epistemic warrant for the conclusion. Warrant is not transmitted from premises to conclusion.

9   *Conclusion*

I began (sections 1–3) with the instance of the problem of armchair knowledge that arises from McKinsey's reductio argument, a closely related problem about transmission of epistemic warrant in Moore's antiskeptical argument, and a second instance of the problem of armchair knowledge that arises from Aunty's argument for the language of thought. Wright's discussion of Moore's argument provides support for the general idea of limitations on the transmission of epistemic warrant, but my early proposals for limitation principles do not provide a satisfactory resolution of the problems generated by (WATER) and (LOT). In the second half of the paper I have tried to improve on that situation.

I have shown (section 5) that instances of the problem of armchair knowledge, or closely related problems about transmission of epistemic warrant, are relatively widespread. It would not be right to suppose that they arise only from a couple of idiosyncratic philosophical arguments. I have then motivated some principled limitations on transmission of epistemic warrant (section 6) and shown how these provide solutions to three instances of the problem of armchair knowledge and two closely related problems (section 7). In the final section, I have considered one instance of the problem at greater length. There are many difficult questions concerning the epistemology of understanding. But I am reasonably confident that even this last instance of the problem of armchair knowledge can be solved in a well motivated way. Being in the armchair, down and out, still seems like an attractive philosophical position.

Notes

1. An earlier version of some of this material was presented in a symposium at the Central Division meeting of the American Philosophical Association held in Minneapolis in May 2001. The other speakers were Crispin Wright and Brian McLaughlin and the symposium was chaired by Michael McKinsey.

2. Proposition (2) is actually numbered (2b).

3. In the more recent paper (2002a), McKinsey points out that his argument for the inconsistency of the triad (1), (2), and (3) depends only on a closure principle about a priori knowability, which he calls the closure of a priority under logical implication (CA): necessarily, for any person x and any propositions p and q, if x can know a priori that p, and p logically implies q, then x can know a priori that q. See also his paper in this volume.

4. See also Brown 1995 and Boghossian 1997.

5. Henceforth, I omit the parenthetical 'or have been'.

6. Burge writes, "We are entitled to rely, other things equal, on perception, memory, deductive and inductive reasoning.... Philosophers may articulate these entitlements. But being entitled does not require being able to justify reliance on these resources, or even to conceive such a justification" (1993: 458–459).

7. I hope that the terminology 'epistemic achievement' may provide a helpful contrast with 'epistemic entitlement'. But I do not want to suggest that regarding a question as open and then closing it is the only kind of epistemic achievement. Sometimes, following through an argument does not put us in a position to provide a question-settling justification for believing the conclusion, but does serve to make plain that we are rationally committed to believing the conclusion. Further reflection on the structure of evidential support may reveal the role that the conclusion plays as a background assumption in epistemic projects, and we may be able to show that we are epistemically entitled to make that assumption. Coming to see all this would be an epistemic achievement, but not the epistemic achievement of providing a question-settling justification.

8. The actual formulation is, "Epistemic warrant cannot be transferred from A to B, even given an a priori known entailment from A to B, if the truth of B is a precondition of our warrant for A counting as a warrant" (Davies 1998: 351).

9. The actual formulation is, "Epistemic warrant cannot be transferred from A to B, even given an a priori known entailment from A to B, if the truth of B is a precondition of the knower even being able to believe the proposition A" (Davies 1998: 353).

10. I assume that the unexplained notion of a precondition is to be interpreted simply as a necessary condition.

11. This is not quite true. It was suggested that we should want to block the transmission of warrant in certain putative antiskeptical arguments even if the truth of the sceptical hypothesis would render one of the premises unthinkable rather than just robbing it of its warrant (Davies 1998: 353).

12. See also Davies 1991. The Aunty in question is Jerry Fodor's. He represents her as a conservative figure who is more likely to favor connectionism than to accept that there are good reasons to adopt the LOT hypothesis: "It turns out that dear Aunty is, of all things, a New Connectionist Groupie" (Fodor 1987: 139). As I envisage her, she has some sympathy for the views of the later Wittgenstein but is fundamentally a neo-Fregean. I claim that the neo-Fregean framework offers Aunty the resources to construct her own argument for the claim that conceptualized thought requires the truth of the LOT hypothesis.

13. A background assumption for the whole argument is that personal-level events of conscious judgment and thought are underpinned by occur-

rences of physical configurations belonging to kinds that figure in the science of information-processing psychology. These physical configurations can be assigned the contents of the thoughts that they underpin. They are "proposition-sized" bearers of causal powers. This assumption is what Fodor (1985, 1987) calls *intentional realism*, and it is close to the assumption of *propositional modularity* (Ramsey, Stich, and Garon 1990). In my view, we are committed to this assumption by some of our everyday practices of mental talk and explanation, but I shall not spell out the nature of this commitment here.

14. This is so even if intentional realism is true of us.

15. Compare what Ramsey, Stich, and Garon write: "*If* connectionist hypotheses [of a particular sort] turn out to be right, so too will eliminativism about propositional attitudes" (1990: 500).

16. The process of revision will be informed by the particular ways in which the world turns out to be disobliging.

17. On the assumption that the philosophical theories supporting Aunty's argument do provide the best way to elaborate and make precise our current conception, we need to revise that conception in order to avoid a commitment to the truth of the LOT hypothesis.

18. We would not abandon the idea that we engage in deductive inference, but we would, presumably, adjust our conception of what is involved in accepting or performing an inference in virtue of its form.

19. I shall not attempt to set my approach against the background of a general epistemology. For some of the issues that would need to be addressed, see Jessica Brown's paper in this volume.

20. I am not alone in proposing a connection with begging the question here. See the title of Wright 2000a and see McLaughlin 2000: 104–105. James Pryor (forthcoming) says, "This notion of transmission-failure is basically a new piece of terminology for talking about an old phenomenon: the phenomenon of *begging the question.*" But although this looks like a point of agreement, Pryor actually disagrees with the approach that Wright and I take because he does not regard begging the question as a dialectical phenomenon.

21. See, for example, Millikan 1989. See also McLaughlin's discussion (2000: 107–109) of teleological theories such as Dretske's (1995, chap. 5) and of Davidson's (1987) example of Swampman.

22. Lewis 1997: 335. In American English, 'jersey' is more natural than 'jumper' for the item of clothing worn by football players.

23. Lewis: "It won't do to say that colors do not exist; or that we are unable to detect them; or that they never are properties of material things; or that they go away when things are unilluminated or unobserved; or that they change with every change in the illumination, or with every change in an observer's visual capacities; or that the same surface of the same thing has different colors

for different observers. Compromise on these points, and it becomes doubtful whether the so-called colors posited in your theory are rightly so-called" (1997: 323).

24. Schiffer (1993) is responding to Lewis (1992).

25. See Davies 2000b.

26. See the discussion in Davies 1998, 2000a, and compare Wright 1985.

27. In the case of the conditional premise LOT(2), it might reasonably be said that it is only against the background of the assumption of intentional realism that the premise is supported by the neo-Fregean philosophical theory on which Aunty's argument draws. But it is surely not true that acceptance of this assumption cannot be rationally combined with doubt about the conclusion LOT(3). Many philosophers sanely believe that intentional realism is true but the language of thought hypothesis is false.

28. These generalized versions of the two principles are essentially the same as the "multipremise" versions of Davies 2000a: 412.

29. The revised version of the principle is not adequate to this task. There is no immediately obvious incompatibility between, on the one hand, acceptance of the assumption that there is such a thing for me to think as that I am thinking that water is wet and, on the other hand, doubt as to whether I am (or have been) embedded in an environment that contains samples of water. It is only in the context of a philosophical theory of externalism that there is a tension between this acceptance and this doubt.

30. See Schiffer 1993 and Davies 2000b.

31. This is not, strictly speaking, the only way in which the First Limitation Principle could be triggered. But it is the most promising way.

32. The problem of meaning without use goes along with a problem of *meaning despite use* (Davies 2000b). Some examples of sentences that are typically used to communicate something other than what they mean (such as Bennett's 'No head injury is too trivial to be ignored') may provide examples of meaning illusions.

33. Peacocke says that thinkers sometimes operate in "the mode of taking the deliverances of a given informational system ... at face value." He continues, "It is in the nature of such modes of operation that they have both an objective and a subjective dimension involving reliability" (1999: 51). What I say in this paragraph closely follows Peacocke 1999: 51–52. Also, see Davies 2000b for an argument in favor of a requirement of awareness of linguistic structure.

34. I take it that I am entitled to this assumption (this not-calling-into-question) so that what is achieved is knowledge *simpliciter* and not just knowledge relative to that assumption.

2

Some Reflections on the Acquisition of Warrant by Inference

Crispin Wright

I

A valid argument is one thing. A valid argument with warranted premises is a second. But a *cogent* argument is yet a third: it is an argument, roughly, whereby someone could/should be moved to rational conviction of the truth of its conclusion—a case where it is possible to *learn* of the truth of the conclusion by getting warrant for the premises and then reasoning to it by the steps involved in the argument in question. Thus a valid argument with warranted premises cannot be cogent if the route to warrant for its premises goes—of necessity, or under the particular constraints of a given epistemic context—via a prior warrant for its conclusion. Such arguments, as we like to say, 'beg the question'.

Say that a particular warrant, *w*, *transmits* across a valid argument just in case the argument is cogent when *w* is the warrant for its premises. I do not know if anyone had registered the distinction between transmission of warrant, so characterized, and *closure* of warrant before I drew it in the 1985 British Academy lecture to which Martin Davies refers in his contribution to this volume. Closure of warrant across (known) entailment has of course been very widely discussed.[1] It is the weaker principle. A valid argument complies with closure provided that if there is warrant for its premises, there is warrant for its conclusion too. But a valid argument is transmissive if, roughly, to have warrant for its premises and then to recognize its validity is to acquire—perhaps for the first time—a warrant to accept the conclusion. My concern here will be with two forms of counterexample to transmission. Such cases need not be counterexamples to closure. Closure will hold but transmission may fail in question-begging cases—cases where there is warrant for the premises in the first place only because the conclusion is *antecedently* warranted. (I am, myself, skeptical whether there are any genuine counterexamples to closure but that issue is not on our agenda.)

Note that transmission of warrant need not be an absolute characteristic of a given valid argument. There are at least two potential sources of relativity. First, it may be that the argument is such that one type of possible ground, w_1, for its premises is transmissible—can yield a novel reason for accepting the conclusion when taken in conjunction with recognition of the validity of the inference—while another, w_2, is not, but can only be possessed in the first place by a thinker whose information already includes warrant to accept the conclusion. Second, it may happen that, even when we focus on a specific warrant, w, the question whether that warrant transmits turns on the collateral epistemic context: that some but not all possible ways of acquiring w travel through the acquisition, or anyway prior possession, of warrant for the conclusion of the argument in question. Thus it may be that whether a given warrant transmits depends, as it were, on who wants to know—on who is to be persuaded of the conclusion and what their standards and presuppositions are.

The transmissibility of warrant is what makes for the possible advancement of knowledge, or warranted belief, by reasoning. It is only because warrants are sometimes (usually?) transmitted that deductions (other than those which discharge all their premises) are of use for anything other than the disclosure of commitments. But warrants are not always transmitted. When are they not?

II

A large and important class of nontransmissible warrants connect with the holism of empirical confirmation emphasized by Quine in the last two sections of ''Two Dogmas.'' This holism is pervasive. It involves that empirical confirmation is not a simple dyadic relationship but characteristically depends upon collateral information. At work at my desk in Philosophy Hall, I hear a thunderous rumble and sense a vibration in the building. Is that evidence of an incipient electric storm? Yes, if the sky has darkened and the atmosphere is heavy and still. Probably not, if the sky outside is clear blue and my office overlooks Amsterdam Avenue with its regular cargo of outsize trucks. I see a substantial-looking brownish bird of prey perching on a fence post. A sighting of a Golden Eagle, perhaps? Quite possibly, if I am in the north-western Scottish Highlands; but not if I am knowingly in Welsh farmland, where buzzards are now quite common. Examples such as these suggest that what is normal in empirical cases is *information dependence* of warrant. A body of evidence, *e*, is an information-dependent warrant for a particular proposition *p* if whether *e* is correctly regarded as warranting *p* depends on what one has by way of collateral information, *I*. Consider a case where one's collateral information, *I*, does indeed sustain *e*'s warranting *p* but where *e* could not rationally be regarded as warranting *p* if certain elements of *I* were missing and uncompensated for. Such a relationship is always liable to generate examples of transmission failure: it will do so just when the particular *e*, *p*, and *I* have the feature that needed elements of the relevant *I* are themselves entailed by *p* (together perhaps with other warranted premises.) In that case, any warrant supplied by *e* for *p* will not be transmissible to those elements of *I*. Warrant is transmissible in such a case only if a rational thinker could cite as her ground for accepting *I* the fact that she has warrant for *p*, supplied by *e*, together with the entailment. No rational thinker could do that if the warrant for *p* supplied by *e* originally depends on prior and independent warrant for *I*.

It is easy to generate examples of transmission failures under this general template (*the information-dependence template*). For instance, (AIRPORT):
You are waiting in an airport lounge and,

(*e*)   You hear the agent utter the words, "This is a final boarding call for Northwest's flight NW644 to Minneapolis."

So you naturally infer that,

(*P*)   The agent has just orally forewarned passengers in English of final boarding for NW644.

P entails *I*:

(*I*)   The agent understands (some of) a language (English).

But clearly the warrant bestowed on *P* by *e* does not transmit across this entailment from *P* to *I*. Rather it is only in a context of collateral information in which *I* is justifiably assumed that *e* provides a warrant for *P* in the first place.

Or consider (TWINS): Jessica and Jocelyn are identical twins whom you know well but have difficulty distinguishing.

Suppose,

(*e*) You see a girl approaching you who looks just like Jessica.

There is a defeasible inference from that to,

(*P*) That girl is Jessica.

And an entailment from there to,

(*I*) That girl is not Jocelyn.

But given your discriminatory limitations, there is no question of treating *e* as a warrant for *P* and then transmitting it across the entailment to conclude *I*. Rather you—though not perhaps someone who can distinguish the twins purely visually—will need the latter already in place as collateral information before you can reasonably take *e* as a warrant for *P*.

III

As formulated, the information-dependence template engages only the transmission of *inferential* warrants: warrants consisting in the possession of evidence, *e*, which licenses a defeasible inference to one or more of the premises of the entailment in question. But what of noninferential cases—cases where warrant for a premise is acquired not on the basis of evidence but directly, via the operation of some cognitive faculty—perception, or memory (on some construals), or logical or mathematical intuition, or perhaps a faculty of immediate self-knowledge—which we regard as directly responsive to the subject matter in question? Can such, noninferential warrants fail to transmit? If so, when and why?

Here are two famous examples in modern epistemology.[2] You go to the zoo, see several zebras in a pen, and opine (ZEBRA): that those animals are zebras. Well, you know what zebras look like, and these animals look just like that. Surely you are fully warranted in your belief. But if the animals are zebras, then it follows that they are not mules painstakingly and skillfully disguised as zebras. Does your warrant transmit to the latter claim? There is a strong intuition that it does not. Did you examine the animals closely enough to detect such a fraud? Almost certainly not. The grounds you have for (ZEBRA)—essentially, just the look of the beasts—have no bearing on this possibility.

Again: you look at a wall and see that it is painted red. So you have acquired a warrant for thinking (RED): that it is red. But its being red entails that it is not a white wall cleverly illuminated by concealed lighting to look as if it is red. So have you thereby acquired a warrant for thinking *that*? Again, the strong intuition is not. Your warrant was acquired just by looking at the wall—no doubt you did enough to verify that it is red if indeed it is, but what you did simply didn't reckon with the possibility of deceptive concealed illumination.

When, in the contexts described, you form your beliefs about the zebras and the color of the wall, there are external preconditions for the effectiveness of your method—casual observation—whose satisfaction you will very likely have done nothing special to ensure. Made-up mules and tricky lighting involve the frustration of those preconditions. Can the warrants you acquire licitly be transmitted to the claim that those preconditions *are* met,—or at least that they are not frustrated in those specific respects? It should seem obvious that they cannot. While you have—no doubt quite justifiably—taken it for granted that the conditions were generally suitable for the acquisition of reliable information by casual-perceptual means, it would be absurd to pretend that you had *gained a reason for thinking so*—at least in the specific respects that you didn't have to reckon with disguised mules or deceptive lighting—just by dint of the fact that those specific possibilities are logically excluded by the beliefs which, courtesy of your background assumption, you have now confirmed.

Dretske, of course, originally presented these cases as failures of *closure*. I have just presented them as failures of transmission. But once the distinction is on the table—as it was not in Dretske's discussion—I think it is clear that the latter is the correct diagnosis. If they were cases of failure of closure, then it should be possible clear-headedly to claim a perceptual warrant for (ZEBRA) while simultaneously disclaiming all warrant for the proposition that the animals in question are not disguised mules. That would be to concede that it could be—for all one was entitled to suppose—that conditions are unsuitable for basing beliefs such as (ZEBRA) on casual perception, because it could be that the zookeeper has been cutting corners and disguising his animals, etc. *Mutatis mutandis* for (RED) and the red wall. So one ends up making a claim of the form: I have a particular kind of warrant for believing *P* but, for all I am entitled to suppose, it may be that conditions are unsuitable for getting a warrant for *P* of that kind. And that cannot be a clear-headed claim. If I assent to it, what can I possibly imagine entitles me to claim the warrant for *P* in the first place?

However, if this diagnosis is right, then we do have to reckon with a range of examples of transmission failure in which information dependence of warrant and the *e, P, I* structure is not—or at least not obviously—involved. At least at a first pass, the impression that there is a transmission failure in, e.g., the zebra case seems intuitive even when one takes it that perception is a direct engagement with the local environment and the warrants conferred by it are, in the basic case, not inferential but direct.

What form of diagnostic template do these examples suggest? Here is a suggestion I have made in other work.[3] Suppose I take myself to have a noninferential warrant for a proposition *A*. And let the question be whether this warrant transmits to a certain consequence, *B*, of *A*. However, suppose *A* stands opposed to some proposition *C* whose truth would undermine my warrant for *A* and which could be true in certain circumstances *subjectively indistinguishable* from those in which I actually find myself. And suppose *C* does not entail *B*, but would be true if *B* were false.

The set-up is thus (THE DISJUNCTIVE TEMPLATE):

(i)   that *A* entails *B*;

(ii)   that my warrant for *A* consists in my being in a cognitive state— perceiving, remembering, mathematically intuiting, or whatever— which is subjectively indistinguishable from a state in which the relevant *C* would be true;

(iii)   that *C* is incompatible with the reliable operation of the cognitive capacities involved in generating the warrant for *A*;[4]

and

(iv)   that *C* would be true if *B* were false.

Suppose I know all this. The key question is what, in the circumstances, can justify me in accepting *A*? Should I not just reserve judgment and stay with the more tentative disjunction, either (I have warrant for) *A* or *C*? For it is all the same which alternative is true as far as what is subjectively apparent to me is concerned. The answer has to be, it would seem, that the more tentative claim would indeed be appropriate unless I am somehow *additionally* entitled to discount alternative *C*. It may be that I have collateral information telling against *C*. Or it may be that, for one reason or another, I am not required to bother about *C*. But notice that either way, in order for me to be entitled to discount *C*, and so move past the disjunction to *A*, I have to be entitled to *discount the negation of B*, and therefore entitled to accept *B*; for by hypothesis, if not-*B* were true, so would C be.[5] So it would seem that I must have an appreciable entitlement to affirm B *already*, independent of the recognition of its entailment by A, if I am to claim to be warranted in accepting A in the first place. The inference from A to B is thus not at the service of addressing an antecedent agnosticism about B. So my warrant does not transmit.

It is straightforward to cast the zoo and red wall examples into this template. Let A be the proposition that the animals in question are zebras; B is accordingly the entailed proposition that they are not mules painstakingly and skillfully disguised as zebras; while for a suitable C we need look no further than a generalization of the negation of B: say, that the animals in question are not zebras but just look that way. C, so selected, meets condition (iv). It also meets condition (iii): clearly, if we are having to deal with circumstances in which animals' appearances are deceptive, then conditions are unsuitable for the reliable operation of the relevant cognitive capacities—those involved in the identification of animal species by casual observation of their appearance. Or again, let A be the proposition that the wall is red, B the entailed proposition that the wall is not a white wall cleverly illuminated by concealed lighting to look as if it is red, and C the proposition that it is not a red wall but looks just like one. C meets condition (iv). It also meets condition (iii): again, if we are having to deal with circumstances in which things' apparent colors are deceptive, then conditions are unsuitable for the reliable operation of the relevant cognitive capacities—those involved in the identification of color by casual observation of an item's appearance. However—condition (ii)—the experiences of seeing zebras and seeing mere zebra look-alikes are relevantly subjectively indistinguishable; as are the experiences of seeing a red wall and seeing a mere red-looking wall. So in treating my state as being a bona fide perception of zebras or a red wall respectively, I implicitly discount the uncongenial, deceptive alternatives C. And now, whatever my warrant for doing so, it has to be there *already*; and it must provide warrant for the respective instances of B independently of any consideration of their entailment by the corresponding choices for A.

IV

Now to content externalism and the McKinsey argument. In another essay,[6] I have suggested that the disjunctive template can be applied to corroborate the idea, independently proposed by Martin Davies in the course of recent work,[7] that McKinsey's paradox—the apparent incompatibility of content externalism with our ordinary conception of self-knowledge—turns on the presumed transmission of what is in fact an untransmissible warrant. The thought, roughly, is that in the context of my acceptance a priori of a content externalism strong enough to sustain the type of proposition typified by McKinsey's second premise—which we can take as

McKinsey (ii)   If I believe that water is wet (and hence have the concept of water), I belong to a speech community that has encountered water

—the holding of the conclusion:

McKinsey (iii)   I belong to a speech community that has encountered water,

becomes something for which I presuppose a prior entitlement in taking it that I may justifiably claim to know the other premise:

McKinsey (i)   I believe that water is wet,

in the fashion involved in normal noninferential self-knowledge. Why might one think this?

A content externalism strong enough to sustain McKinsey's second premise a priori requires not just that the *identity* of certain concepts is externally individuated—that my concept of water, for instance, varies under counterfactual variation in the actual identity of the watery stuff with which I and my speech community interact—but that the very *existence* of my concept of water turns on the existence of an appropriate extension for it: in short, that on Paul Boghossian's Dry Earth, for example[8]—in which, incredibly, all apparent interaction with watery substance is multisensory communal hallucination—I would simply have no water concept, even though my experience was subjectively indistinguishable from what it actually is. We are, in other words, implicitly entertaining types of content-externalism about common nouns which bear a relevant analogy to the strong referentialism about certain kinds of singular terms espoused by Russell and Gareth Evans. According to strong referentialism, referentless singular terms lack sense as well: they can play no role in fixing the truth conditions of a thought. On such a view, if I hallucinate a dazzlingly colored bird and say to myself, "I wonder if *that* is a kind of Oriole," I actually fail to express any thought thereby, even though subjectively my situation is just as if I were thinking a demonstrative thought. In like cases, according to the relevant kind of externalism, a thinker who lives (always or for long enough) on Dry Earth and who says to herself, "Water is wet," suffers a similar *illusion of content*, even though in a condition subjectively indistinguishable from her *doppelgänger* on Earth who thereby thinks the routine thought that water is wet.

It is this implicit provision for the possibility of content illusion which is crucial to the misgiving about transmission in McKinsey cases. Suppose that I (an English speaker) want to describe myself in the words of McKinsey's first premise: "I believe that water is wet." If some form of content externalism is true which is strong enough to sustain the second premise, then there are external preconditions of my expressing a true belief by those words—precisely the appropriate history of interaction with watery stuff in the world—whose satisfaction I may nevertheless, without compromise of the warrant for my claim, have done nothing special to ensure (just as I did—and normally would be required to do—nothing special to ensure the appropriately nondeceptive character of the situation in which I observed Dretske's purported zebras.) Does my routine psychological warrant transmit to the claim that those preconditions *are* met?

The comparison suggests not. But how do matters pan out under the disjunctive template? Take A as the proposition that I believe that water is wet, B as the proposition that I, or my speech community, has had such and such encounters with water, and C as the proposition that my tokening of "I believe that water is wet" is content-defective owing the reference failure of the purported natural kind term, "water," in my language. Then, prima facie, each of the four conditions required by the template is met:

(i)   Proposition *A*, that I believe that water is wet, entails—on the assumption of the conceptually necessary truth of the relevant strong externalism—proposition *B*, that I, or my speech community, has had such and such encounters with water.

(ii)   My warrant for *A* consists in my being in a state which is subjectively indistinguishable from a state in which the relevant proposition *C*, that my tokening of "I believe that water is wet" is content-defective owing the reference failure of the purported natural kind term, "water," in my language, would be true.

(iii)   *C* is incompatible with my having warrant for *A* in this world; for if *C* is true, there is no such thing (in this world) as the belief that water is wet; and if I have warrant for A, then that proposition exists and is exactly what (in this world) "I believe that water is wet" expresses, so that sentence is not content-defective, contrary to C.

Finally,

(iv) C would be true if B were false—for if our encounters with water had never occurred, that would suffice, in the presence of the relevant strong externalism, to divest us of the concept water and thus to ensure that all purported expressions of it are content-defective.

The consequential analysis of the transmission failure involved in the McKinsey argument—always assuming cogent a priori motivation for its externalist premise—is thus simply that once that premise is known and in play, my routine psychological warrant for taking it that A is true—and hence for dismissing the uncongenial interpretation of my subjective state as one in which C holds—must depend on antecedent warrant to think that my tokenings of 'water' comply with appropriate externalist constraints, in particular as described by B. So in taking it that I am warranted in accepting A, I presuppose a warrant for B independent of the recognition of its entailment by A. The recognition of that entailment is thus not at the service of my learning B, and the paradox—that my (broadly construed) a priori knowledge of A and of the correctness of strong content externalism would lead to similarly but incongruously a priori knowledge of B—is dissolved.

One vital clarification is required. If the demanded antecedent reason for discounting C had to be *empirically* acquired, this line of thought would indeed involve abandoning the groundlessness (a priority) of self-knowledge in the relevant kind of case; rather, empirical evidence would be presupposed that 'water' indeed possessed the appropriate historical connections and McKinsey's own original incompatibilist conclusion would then be sustained. Even then, if the diagnosis is right, there would be a transmission failure. But my contrary suggestion is this: that even if one effect of a correct externalism is indeed to introduce, via the possibility of illusions of content, a novel form of possible *defeat* for self-knowledge claims, the epistemological impact of that possibility ought to be conceived much as that of the possibility of perceptual illusion vis-à-vis the justification of perceptual claims. I propose, that is, that we may reasonably allow an *a priori presumption* against that possibility, since to allow an *empirical* issue to arise in every case would be to abrogate the means to resolve any such issues—I have to take certain perceptions to be reliable if I am to investigate the reliability of others;

I have to take certain seeming-thoughts to be well-founded if I am to investigate the well-foundedness of others. If that is broadly the right way to look at the matter, at least as a starting stance, then the ground-lessness (a priority) of basic self-knowledge—properly conceived—is unimpugned by externalism. We have a (defeasible) entitlement to set aside the uncongenial *C* without evidence, and the effect of the Mc-Kinsey deduction is, not to make available a nonempirical warrant for its conclusion but to bring out the empirically unearned but justified presumption of its conclusion, and of the satisfaction of external conditions on content in general, on which first-person authority for the contents of ones attitudes—at last within a (sufficiently strong) externalist framework—must rest.[9]

These reflections may stand some elaboration, so let me draw out their bearing upon an objection lodged by Michael McKinsey in his contribution to the present volume. McKinsey very reasonably notes that the observation of transmission failure is not enough to draw the sting of his argument—for the paradox most basically relies not on the transmissibility of the combined warrant for its premises but on the *closure* of a priori warrant across (known) entailment. Let it be conceded that I cannot *learn* of my speech community's history of interaction with water merely by reasoning from my belief that water is wet and an appropriate form of content-externalism. Still the paradox will linger so long as we are still forced to acknowledge—by an appropriate closure principle—that it is possible to come to know from the armchair, as it were, that my speech community has interacted with water, even if this possibility cannot be realized by transmitting the warrant for the McKinsey premises across the reasoning of his argument but has to be accomplished in some other—unspecified—way.

Now, we already observed (note 9) that transmission failures actually presuppose closure—that if the warrant for a set of premises fails to transmit to a consequence of them, that will be because, broadly, an antecedent warrant for the consequence needs to be in place in order for a thinker to access the warrant in question for the premises, and hence that if (that) warrant for the premises exists, so will (some kind of) warrant for the conclusion. So closure of warrant per se is not in question in the cases that interest us. But McKinsey's point needs more than that. The crucial question is: If the premises of a valid argument are warranted a priori, of what kind of warrant for its conclusion is the availability thereby ensured? In particular, is the potentially troublesome closure principle, that closure holds for a priori warrant, sound?

McKinsey distinguishes strong—empirically indefeasible—and weak —empirically defeasible—notions of a priori warrant and argues in some detail that closure holds for both. I think it is clear that he is right. Closure holds trivially where transmission does. But what characterizes cases where transmission fails is that warrant for the conclusion is presupposed by warrant for the premises—that achieving warrant for the premises has to proceed through the achievement of warrant for the conclusion. So if the latter had to go via an empirical route, so would the former; conversely, any kind of a priori warrant for the premises would have to involve no less—so to speak—of an a priori warrant for the conclusion. So isn't that enough to reinstate the paradox, failure of transmission notwithstanding?

No, it is not. We need a further distinction. What would be paradoxical would be the idea that I could *earn* a warrant for—win through to knowledge of—the proposition that, e.g., I belong to a speech community that has encountered water purely by exercise of the broadly reflective means available to me in Davies's armchair. A transmitted warrant would be such an earned warrant, but McKinsey is quite right that closure for reflectively earned armchair warrant would suffice to set the problem up. However we don't have *that* principle—quite. What we have (according to my suggestion above) is merely an *a priori presumption* in favor of the integrity of the concepts in terms of which I essay to formulate items of my self-knowledge, which in conjunction with the known conceptual necessity of an appropriate kind of externalism becomes an a priori presumption in favor of the satisfaction of the external conditions necessary for that integrity. Such an a priori presumption—or *entitlement* (now to propose a specialized use of this term)—may be counted as a subspecies of warrant. But it is conferred not by positive evidence for the proposition in question but by the operational necessity, so to speak, of proceeding on the basis of such so far untested assumptions if one is to proceed at all. I have a similar entitlement, *ceteris paribus*, to assume the proper functioning of my perceptual apparatus on a particular occasion: To be sure, the matter could be empirically investigated but only in a context in which my own or other's perceptual apparatus was again assumed, untested, to be functioning adequately.

Notice, as the latter example brings out, that an a priori entitlement to a belief is quite consistent with the only envisageable kind of positive evidence for it being empirical. I can be a priori entitled to suppose that my senses are functioning adequately right now, though a check would need to be empirical. Likewise—the proposal is—I can be a priori entitled to suppose that the seeming-concepts configured in a thought I seem to be having are all well-founded though—for externalism—their nature may be such that checking the point would demand some social and environmental history. But this is enough to save the reflective phenomenology of self-knowledge consistently both with externalism and with closure of a priori warrant, provided warrant may cover both earnings and entitlements. Once I accept the conceptual necessity of the appropriate externalism, my warrant for the thought, 'I believe that water is wet', does indeed presuppose—is accessed via—a warrant for my speech community's historical interaction with water. But the latter warrant does not need to be earned by investigation. If it did, it would of course have to be earned empirically, and the warrant for my second-order belief would have to be acquired empirically as well. Entitlements, however, are available in the armchair. After externalism, self-knowledge of the contents of one's attitudes is indeed opened to a new kind of empirical defeat. But it can remain achievable in the armchair manner allowed for by traditional ordinary psychology whenever there is an *a priori presumption that the relevant defeaters do not obtain.*

There is of course much more to say on the topic of entitlement. It is a topic of huge importance. But I hope I have said enough to make it seem plausible that the existence of a presumption in favor of the good standing of one's concepts should be an entitlement if anything is.

V

The disjunctive template discloses that the McKinsey argument does not involve a transmissible warrant. And the impression that closure of a priori warrant is anyway enough for its incompatibilist lesson trades on overlooking the possibility of a priori entitlements for beliefs for which an earned warrant would have to be empirical. So goes the proposed dissolution of the paradox.

But there is a misgiving which needs to be confronted. It concerns the fourth condition of the disjunctive template—specifically the claim that when strong externalism is assumed, freedom by me and my speech community from all historical contact with water would suffice to induce content defectiveness into our purported water thoughts. That is certainly so when the alternative scenarios considered are of the Dry Earth type. But what justifies us—theorists—in restricting attention to those?

If Twin Earth scenarios are considered as well, then our purported water thoughts would suffer not divestment of content but *change* of content. Had our actual encounters been with twater, not water, the relevant *B* would have been false. But the relevant *C* would not have been true: my term, 'water', would not have been divested of content but would have expressed the concept, *twater*, instead. So the template, it seems, does not cleanly fit the case and the diagnosis of transmission failure is compromised.

What should we make of this? It is possible, of course, that the problem is in the detail of the template—or even that it is misconceived in some more radical way. But I suspect that the truth may be a little more interesting: namely, that there is a transmission failure in the vicinity, so to speak, of the McKinsey argument but that it is not exactly as proposed; and that when we see what it is, we will be able to confirm the spirit of the original diagnosis and dissolution of the associated paradox while granting that, strictly, the conjoined warrant for the premises in the McKinsey argument *does* transmit to the original conclusion after all. Let me explain.

Put aside the detail of the disjunctive template and reflect for a minute on the intuitive diagnostic thought which motivates this response to the McKinsey paradox. Strong externalism opens up the (doubtless merely theoretical) possibility of previously unenvisaged kinds of defeaters for claims about one's own mental states, connected with illusions of content. But the situation compromises our right to such claims in the kind of circumstances in which we normally make them only if we now need to do work—specifically, to do *empirical* work—to ensure those defeaters do not obtain in any particular case. My suggestion has been that in general we do not: that, absent reason to suppose the contrary, we may take it that we have a standing (though defeasible) entitlement to the suppositions that all is in order with our concepts, as it is with our vision and other cognitive faculties, that others' testimony is sincere, and that the appearances of objects around us are not systematically misleading. In general, all noninferential warrants are conferred subject to such background entitlements. So one important general limitation on transmission will apply wherever the conclusion of an inference spells out a known constitutively necessary condition for the realization of an entitlement which conditions the acquisition of a particular kind of noninferential warrant for one of its premises. If it can be agreed that the integrity of the relevant concepts is such a background entitlement for claims of all kinds, including claims concerning one's own mental states, then it follows one cannot transmit warrants for such claims across entailments to conclusions that specify what we know to be constitutively necessary conditions for the integrity of concepts involved in those very claims.

If this basic idea is granted, it is inescapable *either* that there must be a transmission failure in the McKinsey argument, somehow not quite brought into focus by the disjunctive template, *or*—contrary to our assumption throughout—that the conclusion of the argument is not, after all, a necessary condition for the freedom from content illusion tacitly assumed as a background entitlement when I take it that I know McKinsey (i). Well, the awkwardness noted a moment ago about the fourth condition of the template now emerges, in effect, as a signal that it is the second alternative which holds: lack of water encounters would indeed *not* suffice for content illusion in my claimed item of self-knowledge (though it would impinge on the *identity* of what I claim). But if the basic diagnostic thought just adumbrated is correct, there will still be a transmission failure in the inference from that claim—advanced as a routine piece of noninferential self-knowledge—to *whatever is* a constitutively necessary condition for freedom from content illusion. So the question is: What is that necessary condition, as far as strong externalism and the (apparent) involvement of the concept of water is concerned?

Precisely, that one not inhabit Dry Earth. It is if everything which we would take to have been an actual encounter with a watery substance—water or an epistemic counterpart of water—is supposed to have been illusory that strong externalism will convict my purported claim to believe that water is wet of content illusion. So consider what happens if we run the McKinsey argument on one step further, so that it becomes (THE EXTENDED McKINSEY ARGUMENT):

McKinsey (i)   I believe that water is wet.

McKinsey (ii)   If I believe that water is wet (and hence have the concept of water), I belong to a speech community that has encountered water.

McKinsey (iii)   Therefore, I belong to a speech community that has encountered water.

McKinsey (iv)   Therefore, it is not the case that I belong to a speech community that has never encountered either water or any other watery substance.

Now, both the disjunctive template and the more general diagnostic thought which motivated it will coincide in diagnosing a transmission failure in the inference from McKinsey (i) and (ii), via McKinsey (iii), to McKinsey (iv). If McKinsey (iv) were false, my psychological claim McKinsey (i) would indeed fall prey to content illusion. But it is McKinsey (iv) that constitutes the large empirical claim about the character of the world and our history of activity within it for which it would be paradoxical to claim that warrant can be earned just by ordinary reflection on one's beliefs and an a priori warranted content externalism. It is McKinsey (iv) that is "not the kind of thing that can be known in that way." To be sure, McKinsey (iii) *looks* just as adventurous, taken in isolation. But once McKinsey (iv) is taken to be an priori entitlement, necessary to make good the local instance of the general assumption of conceptual integrity presupposed in all (self-)knowledge, the transmission of a nonempirical warrant as far as McKinsey (iii) adds to McKinsey (iv) only in respects which can indeed quite properly be viewed as nonempirical. For what McKinsey (iii) adds to McKinsey (iv) is only the identification of the watery stuff of our presumed acquaintance as *water.* And that *is* plausibly a priori. It is a priori that water is the watery stuff of our actual acquaintance, if there is any watery stuff of our actual acquaintance—compare: it is a priori that we are situated here, rather than over there, if we are situated anywhere at all.

VI

If I am right in this new diagnosis, then there is strictly no transmission failure in McKinsey's original argument after all. Relative to the entitlement to assume the integrity of the concepts drawn upon by any putative item of self-knowledge, the warrant for the claim that one believes that water is wet will—in conjunction with an a priori justification for strong externalism (if any exists)—transmit across the inference to the claim that one's speech community has a history of interaction with water. What it will not transmit to is the claim that one's speech community has a history of interaction with some watery substance. Rather, in an informational setting in which one's standing entitlement to assume the integrity of one's concepts—in particular, the concept *water*—already encompasses the latter claim, the nonempirical warrant transmitted across the McKinsey inference is merely for the identification of that substance as water. And that, I have suggested, is harmless.

In his recent work on these matters Martin Davies has been developing his own characterization of two kinds of limitation on warrant transmission. One of his principles effectively converges in its verdicts on those of the information-dependence template, and so far as I can tell, may well be just an alternative formulation of it. But the other—the Second Limitation Principle—stands somewhat in contrast to the proposal incorporated in the disjunctive template. This principle has undergone various reformulations in Davies's successive essays on the topic, but it has rejected transmission in the McKinsey argument in each of its incarnations. If my present diagnosis is right, and there is actually no such failure, then there must be some error in Davies's principle. Alternatively, if Davies is right, then the disjunctive template—and the background thought which drives it—must be too weak somehow, failing to detect the transmission failure that the McKinsey argument actually involves. Which is the fact?

Well, let me conclude on a note of tentative reservation about Davies's principle. His latest formulation (this volume) runs as follows:

> Epistemic warrant cannot be transmitted from the premises of a valid argument to its conclusion if, for one of the premises, acceptance (i) of the assumption that there is such a proposition for the knower to think as that premiss, and (ii) of the warrants for the other premises, cannot be rationally combined with doubt about the truth of the conclusion.

Both in the essay from which this formulation is taken and in earlier work, Davies has shown himself very sensitive to the issue of motivation for his principle. I have to confess to feeling that there still is an issue about that. The principle requires that, if I reason from what I regard as warranted premises to a conclusion a doubt about which would be inconsistent with the availability of one of the premises to my thought, then I cannot thereby learn of the truth of that conclusion. But why not? Suppose I am troubled by some skeptical scenario—by my inability to exclude the apparent possibility that it might be true. If Davies is right, I cannot rationally come to realize that it is not true by providing warrant for the premises (i) that I grasp a proposition describing it, and (ii), that no creature in such a scenario could have access to the conceptual wherewithal to grasp that proposition, and then proceeding to reason in the obvious way from them. But intuitively there is nothing wrong with the *strategy* of such an argument—whatever one thinks of the detail of Putnam's famous implementation of it. So the Second Limitation Principle impresses as too strong.

Naturally this point will not impress anybody who is already convinced that the cogency of Putnam's Proof stands or falls with that of the McKinsey argument in any case. But there is a second, less tendentious misgiving about the strength of Davies's principle. It concerns its apparent insensitivity to something we registered at the start—the potential warrant relativity of issues having to do with transmission. Davies's Principle speaks of the rational uncombinability of three attitudes: doubt about the conclusion of an argument, acceptance of warrants for all (but one) of the premises, and acceptance of the availability of one in particular of the premises (the other one) to one's thought. But what kind of consideration is envisaged as determining that these three attitudes cannot rationally be combined? Well, what determines that in the McKinsey case is nothing, it seems, but the relevant attitudes' respective *contents*: I cannot rationally believe simultaneously that I have a belief which draws on the concept 'water', and that there is (all things considered) warrant to accept that anyone who has such a belief meets a certain historical condition while doubting—believing that it is not the case that—I meet that condition. I cannot do so simply because that is to doubt an *obvious consequence* of things I consider that I warrantedly accept. But if that is how the Second Limitation Principle is supposed to work, then it is going to block transmission in McKinsey's reasoning *whatever* the nature of the warrant accepted for its conditional premise—McKinsey (ii). And that is clearly a bridge too far. For McKinsey's argument is fine as a vehicle for warrant transmission provided the warrant for its major premise is *empirical*. Suppose, for instance, I am a dyed-in-the-wool antiexternalist who—perhaps as a result of a brain injury—lacks all recollection of (testimony of) encounters by myself or anyone in my speech community with water. Interested in what are the actual *empirical* preconditions for possession of the concept *water*, I do some interactive anthropology. An electronic interrogation of members of a variety of societies—not extending to my own—who possess the concept discloses that they all have a history of interaction with the stuff. I therefore propose on inductive grounds that this probably goes without exception, and so reason my way to the prediction that this will also prove true of my own speech community. *This*—empirical—warrant surely transmits. Thus McKinsey's argument is not a case of transmission failure *tout court* but at best illustrates the relativity we noted at the outset. Any diagnosis of transmission failure within the argument must therefore relate specifically to the setting when its second premise is warranted in the special fashion purportedly provided for by externalism, and known to be so. This the Second Limitation Principle, at least as naturally understood, would seem to fail to do.

More generally, no restriction on warrant transmission can be generally satisfactory which is sensitive merely to rational cotenability relationships among attitudes determined *purely by their contents*. It remains to enquire, therefore, whether the disjunctive template fares better on this point. Can we use it to explain why reasoning—the very same reasoning—from the premises of the extended McKinsey argument to its conclusion may transmit warrant when the second, conditional premise is conceived as an empirical contingency but not when it is conceived as a conceptual necessity, holding a priori on externalist grounds?

One immediate difference, of course, is that in the former case the conditional premise—McKinsey (ii)—becomes essential to the deduction and we can no longer take McKinsey (i) and (iii) respectively as propositions A and B for the purposes of the template since, so identified, A does not entail B. But without here venturing to consider how best to generalize the template to cope with the multipremise case—work that would have to be taken on in a properly detailed treatment—we can still appreciate what I think is the crucial contrast. To recap. In no case can I rationally claim warrants for the premises of an argument unless I am entitled to take it that all the conditions necessary for the reliability of the cognitive functions involved in the acquisition of those warrants are met. One such condition involves the integrity of the (putative) concepts involved, so the needed entitlement must be reckoned to extend at least to whatever I know to be a conceptually necessary condition of that integrity. Suppose accordingly that I am an externalist and accept that an appropriate history of interaction with watery stuff is such a conceptually necessary condition for possession of *water*. Then in claiming that McKinsey (i) is warranted, I presuppose an entitlement—hence in the general sense of the term, a warrant—to take that condition to be met. A warrant for McKinsey (iv) thus becomes part of the stage-setting presupposed by my claim to possess warrant for the McKinsey premises: My route to warrant for them goes via warrant for that proposition, which is therefore ineligible to receive warrant by transmission down the extended argument. But now suppose by contrast that I regard McKinsey (ii) as articulating at best an inductively confirmed, causally necessary condition for possession of *water*. Then there has to be a fully intelligible possibility of counterexamples—cases of thinkers who possess the concept although the appropriate history of communal interaction with the stuff is missing. So my most fundamental grounds for crediting thinkers (myself included) with grasp of the concept will be independent of such interaction—and it will be McKinsey (ii), rather than McKinsey (i), that will be in jeopardy in cases where McKinsey (iv) is false. The fourth condition of the disjunctive template (holding that conditions unsuited to the reliable operation of the cognitive faculties involved in obtaining warrant for the premises of a targeted argument would obtain if its conclusion were false—and specifically, that concepts ingredient in the content of those premises would be compromised) is therefore not satisfied; and accordingly, the template finds no problem with the transmission of warrant in the envisaged case. Rather, augmentation of the item of self-knowledge expressed by McKinsey (i) with empirical grounds for McKinsey (ii) can provide transmissible empirical support for the prediction of McKinsey (iv) in just the straightforward fashion in which, intuitively, it should.

In brief, the key difference for the bearing of the disjunctive template in the two cases turns on the question, what would follow if McKinsey (iv) proved false? If McKinsey (ii) is accepted as a conceptual necessity, there is no option but to conclude that I would lack a concept presupposed by my endorsement of McKinsey (i)—and hence that, at least in the relevant locality, a condition on the reliability of my ordinary powers of self-knowledge would be abrogated. So the fourth condition of the template kicks in. If McKinsey (ii) is accepted as an inductive generalization, on the other hand, then should McKinsey (iv) prove false, the entitlement to presuppose the good-standing of all relevant concepts would override the (merely) inductive evidence for McKinsey (ii) and it would be discarded. So, in this case the fourth condition of the template is unsatisfied and the template does not apply.[10]

Notes

1. The initiation and locus classicus of the modern discussion is, of course, Dretske (1970). But he does not make the distinction between transmission and closure, and the subsequent literature has largely followed him in this.

2. I borrow, of course, from Dretske 1970.

3. For example, in a paper read at the 2001 Rutgers Epistemology Conference. See Wright, forthcoming.

4. In earlier work (for instance, Wright 2000a), I had a precursor of this condition which involved C's incompatibility not with the reliable operation of the

cognitive capacities involved in generating the warrant for A but with A itself. This leads, as Brian McLaughlin observed (just take C as not-A) to the template's blocking transmission—no matter what B is—of any noninferential warrant for A which one could fully convincingly *seem* to have consistently with A's falsity.

5. This is of course a *closure* step.

6. See my "Cogency and Question-Begging" (2000a).

7. See Davies 1998, 2000a, and his contribution to the present volume.

8. See Boghossian 1997.

9. It should be superfluous to remark that no case of transmission failure exemplifying the disjunctive template presents a counterexample to closure. On the contrary, it is built in to the diagnosis of the transmission failure involved that they do not. The diagnosis is precisely that a *prior* warrant to accept the relevant propositions B, appreciable independently of their entailment by the relevant propositions A, is a necessary condition for possession of the relevant kinds of warrant for the latter. So there will be warrant for the conclusions of the relevant arguments whenever there is (that kind of) warrant for their premises.

10. This paper summarizes and develops my remarks at an APA Central Divisional Meetings Symposium on Externalism, Self-knowledge, and Skepticism held at Minneapolis on 6 May 2001. I am grateful for the critical comments of the other symposiasts, Martin Davies and Brian McLaughlin, and of the chairman, Michael McKinsey. The paper has been written during my tenure of a Leverhulme Research Professorship, and I gratefully acknowledge the support of the Leverhulme Trust.

3

McKinsey's Challenge, Warrant Transmission, and Skepticism

Brian P. McLaughlin

In his seminal article, "Anti-individualism and Privileged Access" (1991a/1998: 178),[1] Michael McKinsey maintains that the following three claims are inconsistent:

(1)   Oscar knows a priori that he is thinking water is wet.

(2)   The proposition that Oscar is thinking that water is wet a priori entails E.[2]

(3)   Proposition E cannot be known a priori, but only by empirical investigation.

He is correct, given the following fairly compelling principle:

Knowledge closure   If ϕ a priori entails ψ, then if one can know a priori that ϕ, one can know a priori that ψ.

More generally, given this closure principle, any triad of claims of the following form is inconsistent:

(1a) S knows a priori that she is in m (where m is a type of mental state).

(2b)   That S is in m a priori entails E.

(3)   Proposition E cannot be known a priori, but only by empirical investigation.

This result is as secure (or insecure) as knowledge closure.[3]

   Let us call a mental state type, m, *a priori external* if and only if it is a priori that being in an m-state consists, at least in part, in being in some contingent environmental circumstance. And let us call a mental state type, m, *privileged for us* (or, for short, *privileged*) if and only if when we are in an *m*-state, our cognitive faculties are functioning properly, and we have mastered the concepts required to believe we are in an *m*-state, then we can know a priori that we are in an *m*-state.[4] Given closure, a mental state type *m* can be both privileged and a priori external only if for every contingent environmental circumstance *C* a priori required for one to be in an *m*-state, one can know a priori that *C* obtains.

The claim that a mental state type can be both privileged and a priori external is a *compatibilist* claim.[5] McKinsey (1991a) is an incompatibilist: he denies (in our terminology) that a mental state type can be both privileged and a priori external.[6] Given closure, does the fact that any triad of claims of the form (1a) to (3) is inconsistent show that no mental state can be both privileged and a priori external? That depends on whether it is possible to know a priori a contingent environmental proposition. If *C* is a contingent environmental condition, then the proposition that *C* obtains is a contingent environmental proposition. If no contingent environmental condition is such that we can know a priori that it obtains, then no mental state can be both privileged and a priori external, for given closure, if some mental state were both privileged and a priori external, then some contingent environmental proposition would be knowable a priori. Thus, given closure, the answer to our question turns on whether it is possible to know a priori a contingent environmental proposition.

Where a mental state is a priori external, McKinsey says, "Since you obviously can't know a priori that the external world exists, you also can't know a priori that you are in the mental state in question. It's just that simple" (1991a/1998: 183). This constitutes his defense of incompatibilism.

Let's use 'contingent environmental proposition' in such a way that a contingent proposition counts as such only if it a priori entails that the external world exists.[7] Given our definitions above, then, it follows that a mental state *m* is a priori external only if the fact that one is in *m* a priori entails that the external world exists. It follows that if McKinsey is right that one "obviously can't know a priori that the external world exists," then, given closure, no mental state can be both privileged and a priori external: compatibilism is false.

Unfortunately, McKinsey gives us no reason to believe that we can't know a priori that the external world exists. He claims only that we "obviously can't." Moreover, his only reason for maintaining that we can't know more specific contingent environmental propositions a priori is that we can't know a priori that the external world exists. Perhaps, however, it is only an empiricist dogma that we cannot know a priori that the external world exists. Perhaps it is possible to have an a priori proof that the external world exists. Perhaps it is even possible to have a priori proofs of some specific contingent environmental propositions. Whether such things are possible is an issue that McKinsey fails to address.

While the knowledge closure principle entails that (1) to (3) are incompatible, McKinsey himself makes no explicit appeal to closure in his defense of the claim that they are incompatible. Rather, he defends the incompatibility claim by arguing as follows:

> Suppose (1) that Oscar knows a priori that he is thinking that water is wet. Then by (2), Oscar can simply *deduce E*, using premises that are knowable a priori, including the premise that he is thinking that water is wet. Since Oscar can deduce *E* from premises that are knowable a priori, Oscar can know *E* itself a priori. But this contradicts (3), the assumption that *E cannot* be known a priori. Hence (1), (2), and (3) are inconsistent.   (1991a/1998: 182; emphases his)

If what McKinsey says in this passage is correct, then (1), (2), and (3) are indeed inconsistent. Notice, however, that if what he says in this passage is correct, then if compatibilism is true, one could arrive at a priori knowledge that *E* by deducing *E* from one's a priori knowledge that one is in a certain mental state *m* and one's a priori knowledge that if one is in *m*, then *E*. Thus, if what McKinsey says in the passage is correct, he has (inadvertently) called our attention to an interesting consequence of compatibilism, namely, that if compatibilism is true, an a priori proof of the existence of the external world is possible, and perhaps a priori proofs of the existence of various "neighborhoods" in the external world are possible as well.

Some compatibilists in fact maintain that privileged self-knowledge and a priori mental externalism provide an a priori route to knowledge of contingent environmental propositions.[8] They hold that one can come to know a priori that *E* by arguing as follows:

Premise 1   I am in *m*.

Premise 2   If I'm in *m*, then *E*.

Conclusion   Therefore, *E*.

And they maintain that such arguments—let's call them *compatibilist arguments*—can be used to refute at least some kinds of skeptical hypotheses, namely those incompatible with the contingent environmental proposition E in question. Thus, consider a skeptical hypothesis H. The skeptic claims that you don't know that not-H. If, however, the relevant E entails that not-H, you could work through the argument from premise 1 and premise 2 to E, and then deduce not-H from E. By so reasoning, these compatibilists claim, you would come to know (or to support or sustain your knowledge) that not-H and, thereby, make it the case that the skeptic's claim that you don't know that not-H is false.[9]

McKinsey's defense of the incompatibility of (1) to (3) in the passage quoted above suggests the following principle:

Knowledge transmission   If one knows a priori that ϕ and one knows a priori that ϕ entails ψ, then one can know a priori that ψ by deducing ψ from ϕ and the fact that ϕ entails ψ.

If this principle were correct, then one could indeed know a priori that E by deducing it from one's a priori knowledge of premise 1 and premise 2. The transmission principle is, however, mistaken. Suppose that one knows a priori that ψ and that one knows a priori that $\neg\phi$. Suppose also that one knows a priori that ϕ or ψ simply as a result of having deduced it from ψ. In this epistemic circumstance, one cannot sustain or support one's a priori knowledge that ψ by reasoning as follows: ϕ or ψ; $\neg\phi$; therefore, ψ. In this epistemic circumstance, this bit of reasoning would not provide a basis for knowledge that ψ. The reason is that one's belief that ψ—the conclusion of the reasoning—is one's a priori warrant for believing the first premise, namely that ϕ or ψ. Thus, the reasoning is viciously circular. Viciously circular reasoning is not cogent: it is not a basis for knowledge of the conclusion, not a means to acquiring or supporting knowledge of the conclusion. Here, then, we have a counterexample to knowledge transmission.

The reason knowledge transmission fails in the sort of case in question is that the case is a counterexample to the following principle entailed by it:

Warrant transmission   If one is a priori warranted in believing that ϕ and one knows a priori that ϕ entails ψ, then one can be a priori warranted in believing that ψ by deducing ψ from ϕ and the fact that ϕ entails ψ.

Warrant transmission fails in the kind of case in question because if ψ is one's warrant for believing ϕ, then ϕ cannot be a part of one's warrant for believing ψ. To say this is not to deny that it can ever be the case that ϕ is a reason for ψ and ψ a reason for ϕ. Of course that can happen. Two propositions can be mutually probability enhancing. That it rained last night can be a reason to believe that the grass is wet, and that the grass is wet can be a reason to believe that it rained last night.[10] But suppose that after acquiring observational knowledge that the grass is wet, one comes to believe that it rained last night by inferring it as the best explanation of why the grass is wet. Then, one cannot support or sustain one's knowledge that the grass is wet by reasoning as follows: "It rained last night; if it rained last night, then the grass is wet; so the grass is wet." Such reasoning would be viciously circular since, in the epistemic context in question, one's belief that the grass is wet is an essential part of one's warrant for believing that it rained last night. Such reasoning would not be cogent.

As talk of vicious circularity would suggest, failures of warrant transmission are intimately related to cases of question begging. Question begging is, however, a dialectical phenomenon, and as such failure of warrant transmission may fail to be a necessary condition for question begging. An argument might count as question begging relative to a dialectical purpose even if it is not an instance of failure of warrant transmission. But if an argument is an instance of failure of warrant transmission, then, I believe, the argument is viciously circular in a way that renders it question begging for any dialectical purpose.[11]

While a counterexample to knowledge/warrant transmission, the kind of case that I've been discussing is not counterexample to knowledge closure. Moreover, the kind of case in question does not itself gives us any reason to doubt closure. Suppose that one knows that ϕ and knows that ϕ entails ψ. Either ψ is part of one's warrant for ψ or it isn't. Suppose ψ is part of one's warrant for ϕ. Then, since one knows ϕ, one knows ψ. Suppose that ψ is not part of one's warrant for ϕ. Then, for all that the kind of case I've presented shows, since one knows ϕ and knows that ϕ entails ψ, one can acquire (or support or sustain) one's knowledge that ψ by inferring it from ϕ and the fact that ϕ entails ψ. One cannot sustain or increase one's knowledge by deductive inference from known premises when the conclusion of the argument is part of one's warrant for one of the premises. But that, of course, fails to entail that when ψ is not part of one's warrant for believing any of a group of propositions that one knows and knows jointly entail ψ, one can acquire or sustain one's knowledge that ψ by deducing it from those propositions. It is a difficult question under what epistemic conditions a deductively valid argument can increase or sustain knowledge. Suffice it to note here that an adequate theory of epistemic warrant must allow that we can often acquire or sustain knowledge that something is the case by deducing it from things we already know; it must allow that deductive inference can serve as a way of acquiring or sustaining knowledge.

Martin Davies (1998, 2000a) and Crispin Wright (2000a) have argued that transmission of warrant would fail in any compatibilist argument, at least when the mental state in question is one of having a propositional attitude with a certain content. (Neither Davies nor Wright challenge closure, however.[12]) If they are right, then no such compatibilist argument can serve as a proof of the existence of the external world or serve as a response to a skeptic, even if compatibilism is true. I think, however, that neither Davies nor Wright has succeeded in showing that transmission of warrant would fail in any such compatibilist argument.

In an early paper, Davies (1998) defended various "limitation principles," principles that purport to state a sufficient condition for warrant failing to transmit in a deductively valid argument. In recent papers (Davies 2000a, this volume), he has come to reject some of his earlier principles. I'll look at two of the principles that he now holds and that may be thought to be relevant.

Here is the first of Davies's limitation principles that we'll consider:

First limitation principle (generalized version)   Epistemic warrant cannot be transmitted from the premises of a valid argument to its conclusion if, for one of the premises, the warrant for that premise counts as warrant only against the background of certain assumptions and acceptance of those assumptions together with the warrants for all the premises cannot be rationally combined with doubt about the truth of the conclusion. (Davies 2000a)[13]

Were this limitation principle correct, then epistemic warrant would indeed fail to transmit from the premises of a compatibilist argument to its conclusion. However, the principle is incorrect. The main problem with it is that it entails that warrant cannot be transmitted across any one-premise valid argument, when the premise is warranted. The reason is that since the premise is warranted and entails the conclusion, one cannot rationally combine doubt about the conclusion with the acceptance of the warrant for the premise. Since that premise is the only premise of the argument, it follows that one cannot rationally combine doubt about the conclusion of the argument with acceptance of the warrants for all the premises. And since one cannot do that, it follows that one cannot rationally combine acceptance of the background assumptions against which the warrant counts as warrant for the premise with the warrants for all of the premises. So, by the limitation principle, warrant cannot transmit from the premise of a one-premise valid argument to the conclusion of the argument when the premise is warranted. But warrant can transmit from the premise of a one-premise valid argument to the conclusion of the argument when the premise is warranted: there are cogent arguments with a single premise. So, the limitation principle is false. Moreover, since any deductively valid argument can be recast as a one-premise argument (by conjoining the premises) without that affecting whether warrant transmits, the limitation principle has the obviously unacceptable consequence that warrant cannot transmit across any valid argument with warranted premises.

Here is the second principle of Davies:

Second limitation principle (generalized version) Epistemic warrant cannot be transmitted from the premises of a valid argument to the conclusion if, for one of the premises, acceptance (i) of the assumption that there is such a proposition for the knower to think as that premise and (ii) of the warrants for the other premises cannot be rationally combined with doubt about the conclusion. (Davies 2000a)

This principle too seems incorrect. Consider the following argument:

(p1) John is in pain and in the building.

(p2) If John is in pain and in the building, then someone in the building is in pain.

(c) Therefore, someone in the building is in pain.

If the first premise is warranted, then I can't rationally combine doubt about the conclusion with acceptance of the warrant for the first premise and acceptance that there is such a proposition to think as the second premise. So, according to the second limitation principle, warrant fails to transmit in the argument from (p1) to (c). But it is possible for one to come to know that someone in the building is in pain by so reasoning (by putting two and two together, so to speak); such reasoning could be cogent. Thus, the second limitation principle is false. It follows that neither of Davies's limitation principles can be used to show that compatibilist arguments will invariably involve failure of warrant transmission.

Let's turn, then, to Wright, who, as we noted, also claims that compatibilist arguments will fail of warrant transmission. He tells us,

Michael McKinsey is responsible for an influential presentation of a kind of argument—actually, a paradox—which purports to elicit an inconsistency between (allegedly) plausible externalist constraints on content and what is often termed first-person privileged access—the combination of groundlessness and authoritative standard possessed by a subject's opinions about her intentional and other psychological states. The kind of argument may be represented simply in the following (MC) form:

I have mental property *M*.

If I have mental property *M*, then I meet condition *C*.

Therefore, I meet condition *C*.   (Wright 2000a: 142)

According to Wright, this is paradoxical because it is supposed to be a priori knowable that I have *M*, a priori knowable that if I have *M* then I meet *C*, yet *C* is supposed to be a contingent environmental condition such that is "quite preposterous" (Wright's phrase) to think that I can know a priori that I meet *C*.

Wright (2000a: 150) tells us that the following would be an example of the (MC) form, on the assumption that both (1) and (2) are a priori knowable:

(1)   I believe that water is wet.

(2)   Any thinker who believes that water is wet (belongs to a speech community which) has had such and such encounters with water.

(3)   Therefore, I (or my community) have had such and such encounters with water.

Following Davies, Wright claims in response to "McKinsey's paradox" that this kind of argument would involve a failure of warrant transmission. And he maintains that we can "solve the paradox" by seeing why transmission fails.[14]

Wright proceeds as follows in making his case that warrant transmission fails here. He first presents a certain argument structure; then, he claims that no argument with that structure is warrant transmitting; finally, he claims that (1) to (3) has the structure in question, and so is not warrant transmitting.

Here is how he introduces the argument structure in question: Suppose I take myself to have a non-inferential warrant—perhaps perceptual, or introspective, or intuitive, or mnemonic—for some proposition *A*. And let the question be whether this warrant transmits to a certain consequence, *B*, of *A*. However suppose *A* stands opposed to some proposition *C* which would be true in circumstances subjectively indistinguishable from those in which I actually find myself, and which does not entail *B*, but would be true if *B* were false. The set-up is thus:

(i)   that *A* entails *B*;

(ii)   that my warrant for *A* consists in my being in a state which is subjectively indistinguishable from a state in which the relevant *C* would be true;

(iii)   that *C* is incompatible with *A*; and

(iv)   that *C* would be true if *B* were false.   (Wright 2000a: 155)

Wright goes on to tell us that in such a circumstance "the inference from *A* to *B* is not at the service of a rational first conviction that *B*," and thus that warrant fails to transmit. Following Wright, let's call the argument structure in question 'the (i)–(iv) template'. His claim, then, is that warrant fails to transmit in any argument that fits the (i)–(iv) template.

According to Wright, the (MC) argument (i.e., the compatibilist argument in question), fits the (i)–(iv) template, and so fails to transmit warrant. He asks:

How does it go with the [(MC)] argument? Take *A* as the proposition that I believe that water is wet, *B* as the proposition that I, or my speech community, has had such and such encounters with water, and *C* as the proposition that the seeming-thought which I attempt to token by "I believe that water is wet" is content-defective owing to the reference failure of the purported natural kind term, "water," in my language. Then each of the four conditions delineated is met:

(4)   Proposition *A*, that I believe that water is wet, entails—on the assumption of the necessary truth of the relevant strong externalism—proposition *B*, that I, or my speech community, has had such and such encounters with water;

(5)   My warrant for *A* consists in my being in a state which is subjectively indistinguishable from a state in which the relevant proposition *C*, that the seeming-thought which I attempt to express by "I believe that water is wet" is content-defective owing to the reference failure of the purported natural kind term, "water," in my language, would be true;

(6)   *C* is incompatible with *A*; and

(7)   *C* would be true if *B* were false.

... The recognition of that entailment is thus not at the service of a rational first conviction of *B*.   (Wright 2000a: 160)

Thus, Wright claims, (MC) fails to transmit warrant.

Wright is mistaken in claiming that every argument that fits the (i)–(iv) template fails to transmit warrant. For if that were so, then no valid argument from *A* to *B* would be warrant transmitting, when premise *A* has a noninferential, nonlogically conclusive warrant. To see this, consider, once again, the (i)–(iv) template:

(i)   *A* entails *B*.

(ii)   My warrant for *A* consists in my being in a state which is subjectively indistinguishable from a state in which the relevant *C* would be true.

(iii)   *C* is incompatible with *A*.

(iv)   *C* would be true if *B* were false.

Let *C* = ¬*A*. Then (iii) and (iv) will both hold for any *B* entailed by *A*. Moreover, condition (ii) will hold if my warrant for *A* consists in my being in a state which is subjectively indistinguishable from a state in which ¬*A*. We see, then, that if any argument that fits the (i)–(iv) template fails to transmit warrant, no valid argument from *A* to *B* would be warrant transmitting when the reasoners warrant for *A* consists in his being in a state which is subjectively indistinguishable from a state in which *A* fails to hold. But surely that is false. It would, for instance, mistakenly rule any valid argument from *A* to *B* as failing to transmit warrant, if the reasoner's warrant for *A* were anything short of logically conclusive. Falling under the Wright (i)–(iv) template doesn't suffice for failure of warrant transmission.

Neither Wright nor Davies succeeds in showing that no compatibilist argument could be one in which warrant transmits. So, for all they show, compatibilist responses to external-world skepticism will be available if compatibilism is true.

Nevertheless, I think that at least certain kinds of compatibilists arguments would involve a failure of warrant transmission. To see which kinds would, we need first to distinguish two notions of apriority.[15]

We can distinguish a weak from a strong notion of apriority.[16] Let us say that a belief that *p* is weakly a priori warranted just in case it is warranted otherwise than on the basis of empirical evidence for *p*, and let us say that a belief that *p* is strongly a priori warranted just in case it is weakly a priori warranted and the belief is empirically indefeasible.

Two points of clarification are in order. First, to be weakly a priori warranted in the intended sense, a belief must be warranted otherwise than on the basis of empirical evidence in both an epistemic internalist and an epistemic externalist sense. One is warranted in believing that *p* on the basis of empirical evidence for p just in case either (internalist disjunct) one is warranted in believing that p on the basis of empirical evidential reasons for p or (externalist disjunct) warranted in believing that p, even in part, on the basis of perception or memory of perception. Thus, to be weakly a priori warranted, a belief must be warranted otherwise than on the basis of empirical evidence in both of these ways. Second, by 'empirically indefeasible', I mean indefeasible by empirical evidence in a rebutting way, rather than in an undercutting way.[17] Empirical evidence rebuts a believer's warrant for believing that p just in case it outweighs the believer's warrant, so that given the defeating evidence, the believer's warrant fails to be adequate for knowledge. In contrast, empirical evidence undercuts a believer's warrant for believing that p just in case the evidence is evidence that the believer lacks the warrant in question. If by 'empirically indefeasible' in the definition of strong apriority we meant empirically indefeasible in either the rebutting or the undercutting way, then virtually no belief would be strongly a priori warranted. The reason is that there can virtually always be empirical evidence that a believer lacks a certain warrant for a belief. Suppose that a mathematician, Oscar, is warranted in believing a certain mathematical proposition as a result of having worked soberly, carefully, with full understanding and without mistake, through a simple proof of it. Suppose further that there is empirical evidence that Oscar was drunk or that it is widely believed by mathematicians that the pattern of reasoning Oscar went through is not in fact a proof of the mathematical proposition in question. Such evidence would undercut Oscar's warrant for believing the mathematical proposition, for such evidence would be evidence that he lacks the warrant in question for his belief in the proposition. Such evidence would not, however, be rebutting evidence, and so would not defeat Oscar's warrant in the sense relevant to the definition of 'strong apriority'. While it is always possible for there to be undercutting empirical evidence for virtually any warrant for virtually any belief, it is an important philosophical question whether one can have warrant for a belief that cannot be rebutted by empirical evidence. I can't attempt to resolve that issue here. Suffice it to note that, for present purposes, it is the distinction itself that is important.

Let us call a mental state type, m, *weakly privileged* (for one) if and only if when one is in an m-state, one's cognitive faculties are functioning properly, and one has mastered the concepts required to believe that one is in an m-state, then one can be weakly a priori warranted in believing that one is in an m-state. Let us call m *strongly privileged* (for one) if and only if it is weakly privileged and one can have empirically indefeasible warrant for believing that one is in an *m*-state (i.e., warrant that cannot be rebutted by empirical evidence). We can likewise distinguish weakly a priori warranted mental externalist theses from strongly a priori warranted ones. We can, then, distinguish four versions of the compatibilist view that a mental state can be both privileged and a priori external:

(C1)   A mental state can be both weakly privileged and weakly a priori external.

(C2)   A mental state can be both weakly privileged and strongly a priori external.

(C3)   A mental state can be both strongly privileged and weakly a priori external.

(C4)   A mental state can be both strongly privileged and strongly a priori external.

Notice that even given knowledge closure, only (C4) compatibilism entails that some contingent environmental proposition is strongly a priori knowable. Given closure, (C1) to (C3) entail only that some contingent environmental proposition is weakly a priori knowable—that is, knowable otherwise than on the basis of empirical evidence.

With the distinction between weak and strong apriority in hand, we can separate the question of whether compatibilist arguments (C1) to (C3) would involve a failure of warrant transmission from the question of whether (C4) compatibilist arguments would. Let us consider these questions in turn.

I think that compatibilist arguments (C1) to (C3) would involve a failure of warrant transmission, and so would be question begging.[18] In a (C1) or (C2) or (C3) compatibilist argument, both the privileged self-knowledge premise (premise 1) and the externalist premise (premise 2) would be warranted otherwise than on the basis of empirical evidence, but at least one of these premises would be empirically defeasible. Moreover, the premises would jointly entail *E*, a contingent environmental proposition. If both the privileged self-knowledge premise and the externalist premise were merely weakly a priori, as in (C1) arguments, then not-*E* would be an empirical defeater of their conjunction. If one of these premises were strongly a priori and the other merely weakly a priori, as in (C2) and (C3) arguments, then not-*E* would be an empirical defeater of the merely weakly a priori premise. Either way, not-E would be an empirical defeater of the premises that purport to establish the conclusion of the compatibilist argument.[19] Since (by hypothesis) the premises of arguments (C1) to (C3) are at least weakly a priori (and so warranted otherwise than on the basis of empirical evidence), E will of course not be part of the warrant for any of the premises. So the arguments will not fail of warrant transmission by the conclusion of the arguments figuring as warrant for one of the premises. Nevertheless, the arguments would, I claim, fail of warrant transmission. I'll now proceed to say why.

Not-E would defeat any of the merely weakly a priori premises in arguments (C1) to (C3). Since the premises in such arguments are not warranted on the basis of empirical evidence that would rule out not-E (since they are weakly a priori warranted, and so not based on empirical evidence at all), it must be the case that the person in question is somehow epistemically entitled to ignore the possibility that not-E. What would explain that entitlement? One might offer some sort of contextualist explanation, according to which, in certain contexts, one can properly ignore certain possibilities.[20] But perhaps some noncontextualist explanation is possible as well. In any case, the point to note is that the person must be epistemically entitled to ignore the possibility that not-E. This seems to me to amount to saying that the person is epistemically entitled to presuppose that E.[21] But, then, the person is weakly a priori warranted in believing the merely weakly a priori known premises in part in virtue of the fact that the person is entitled to presuppose that E. And for that reason, warrant would fail to transmit from the premises to E.

To employ Davies's term, the relevant 'limitation principle' here would be this:

Presupposition limitation principle Warrant fails to transmit from the premises of a valid argument to the conclusion of the argument when one is warranted in believing the premises in part because one is entitled to presuppose the truth of the conclusion.

The justification for this principle is that were one to attempt to so argue for the conclusion, one would cease to be entitled to presuppose that it is true, the entitlement would be canceled, and so one would no longer be warranted in believing the premise(s) that one was warranted in believing because of that entitlement (or at least no longer warranted in the same way). This limitation principle explains why warrant would fail to transmit in arguments (C1) to (C3), and so why such arguments would fail to be cogent. Thus such arguments could not be used to prove the existence of the external world or rebut skeptical hypotheses that entail not-*E*. So, then, I'm in agreement with Davies and Wright that compatibilist arguments (C1) to (C3) will involve a failure of warrant transmission.

What, then, about (C4) compatibilist arguments? They are not shown to involve failures of warrant transmission by the above limitation principle. The reason is that since both of their premises will (by hypothesis) be strongly a priori, the premises will be warranted in a way that does not depend on the person's being entitled to presuppose *E*. Strongly a priori warrant would not depend on entitlements to empirical presuppositions.

Might, then, a (C4) compatibilist argument be used to acquire knowledge of a contingent environmental proposition? One might well think not on the grounds that no contingent environmental proposition can be known strongly a priori—that is, on the grounds that one cannot have empirically indefeasible knowledge of a contingent environmental proposition. But I don't myself find it obvious that no contingent environmental proposition can be known strongly a priori. I am aware of no compelling argument for the claim that no contingent environmental proposition can be so known. Nonetheless, if closure is true, then I think that McKinsey has at least called our attention to a formidable challenge to (C4) compatibilism. The challenge is to provide a justification of the claim that the mental state in question is both strongly privileged and strongly a priori external that is adequate to over-rule our intuition that one cannot know strongly a priori the contingent environmental proposition(s) in question.

To illustrate McKinsey's formidable challenge at work, consider the following case. Donald Davidson (1987) has asserted an externalist claim about thinking. He maintains that thinking requires a history of causal interaction with the environment and other people. He holds for this reason that a newly emergent Swampman that is an intrinsic duplicate of him would not be thinking. Suppose, then, that someone were to maintain both that one can know strongly a priori that one is thinking and that Davidson's externalist thesis is strongly a priori.[22] Given closure, the person would be committed to the claim that it is strongly a priori knowable that one has had a history of causal interaction with the environment and other people. The person would thereby incur the formidable obligation of providing a justification for the claim that thinking is both strongly privileged and strongly a priori external in the way in question that is adequate to over-rule our intuition that one cannot have empirically indefeasible knowledge that one has a history of causal interaction with the environment and other people. Were such a justification possible, it would, I believe, yield a response to the skeptical hypothesis that one doesn't know that one is not a newly emergent Swampcreature. Unfortunately, however, I see no way to discharge the obligation in the case in question.

I myself am sympathetic to the view that there are strongly privileged mental states and strongly a priori external mental states. I find it plausible, for instance, that both the mental state type *thinking* and the mental state type *pain* are strongly privileged. Indeed I find it plausible that the mental state type *thinking that water is wet* is strongly privileged. And where the notion of a primitive natural kind concept is so understood that a concept counts as such only if it denotes a natural kind, I find it plausible that the mental state type *exercising a primitive natural kind concept* is strongly a priori external. (That would not, of course, a priori entail that *thinking that water is wet* is strongly privileged, even if the concept of water is a primitive natural kind concept. For it is not strongly a priori that the concept of water is a natural kind concept since it is not strongly a priori that water is a natural kind.[23]) But I'm skeptical that there are any states that are both strongly privileged and strongly a priori external. A main source of my skepticism is that the prospect of a (C4) compatibilist answer to McKinsey's challenge seems dim.

I want to conclude by noting that, in its essential features, the McKinsey challenge arises as well for the view that a strongly privileged mental state can have an analytical functionalist analysis. On the assumption that analytical truths are strongly a priori, according to analytical functionalism, for any mental state *m*, there will be some causal role *R* such that it is strongly a priori that one is in *m* if and only if one is in a state with role *R*. Given closure, then, if *m* is strongly privileged, this analytical functionalist claim will entail that it is strongly a priori knowable that one is in a state with causal role *R*. Since it will be contingent whether one is in a state with causal role *R*, the burden is on the analytical functionalist to make a case that one can know a priori that one is a state with causal role *R* that is adequate to over-rule our intuition that one cannot know strongly a priori that one is in such a state. As is no doubt apparent, the challenge arises as well for the weaker claim that a strongly privileged mental state strongly a priori requires being in a state with role R, even if being in a state with that role does not analytically entail being in the mental state in question. Thus, for instance, the view that *thinking* is strongly privileged and that a strongly a priori requirement for *thinking* is being in a state with a certain causal role is subject to the McKinsey challenge if closure holds.[24]

In summary, compatibilist arguments (C1) to (C3) would involve failures of warrant transmission. While we have seen no reason to think that (C4) compatibilist arguments would, the prospects of such an argument that would succeed in even refuting solipsism seem to me dim.[25]

Notes

1. The page reference here is to McKinsey 1998; similarly for other page references to McKinsey 1991a/1998.

2. McKinsey uses the expression 'necessarily depends upon' rather than 'a priori entails'. But my formulation of (2) captures his intent. See McKinsey 1991a/1998: 178 ff.

3. I won't attempt to determine here whether closure is true. For a defense of closure, see DeRose 1995.

4. As I noted when I introduced these stipulative definitions (McLaughlin 2000: 94), while a mental state is either external or not *simpliciter*, no mental state is either a priori external or privileged *simpliciter*. Strictly speaking, a state type is either a priori external or privileged only under a conceptualization, i.e., under a concept. To avoid prolixity, I shall, however, suppress the required relativization to a concept.

5. Later I'll distinguish four readings of this compatibilist claim.

6. Hereafter, I'll typically drop the qualification 'type' and speak simply of mental states.

7. Two points are in order. First, as I am using 'proposition' here, the proposition that I exist here now doesn't count as a contingent environmental proposition since it doesn't a priori entail that the external world exists. Second, I leave open whether it is contingent that the external world exists.

8. Warfield (1998) and Sawyer (1998).

9. Warfield (1998) and Sawyer (1998).

10. This example of mutually probability-enhancing propositions is from Sosa, forthcoming; see also Sosa 1997.

11. A proper discussion of the relationship between failure of warrant transmission and question begging must await another occasion.

12. Wright is one of the first philosophers to distinguish closure from transmission. See Wright 1985. While he did not distinguish closure from transmission, see Dretske 1970. See also Klein 1981, 1995.

13. Let us assume that the principle is restricted to arguments such that it isn't intrinsically irrational to doubt their conclusions; otherwise, the principle would have the unfortunate consequence that warrant cannot be transmitted in any valid argument to such a conclusion.

14. If Wright's (1) to (3) is indeed of the (MC) form, then, if I understand him, (1) and (2) must both be a priori knowable, and it must be "preposterous" to believe that (3) is a priori knowable. Notice that on the assumption that what is preposterous is false, if (1) to (3) were indeed of the (MC) form, we would have a counterexample to knowledge closure. It would be a priori knowable that (1), a priori knowable that (2), but not a priori knowable that (3), even though (1) and (2) jointly a priori entail (3). Since Wright embraces closure, he presumably does not take the fact that it is "quite preposterous" that one can know (3) a priori to entail that one cannot know (3) a priori. But, then, given that he holds closure, unless he thinks it is preposterous that both (1) and (2) can be known a priori, why does he think it is preposterous that (3) can be known a priori? Having flagged this question, I'll now drop it.

15. The next three paragraphs draw heavily from McLaughlin 2000.

16. Here I am indebted to Hartry Field (1996: 359).

17. This distinction is due to John Pollock (1974: 42 ff.; 1986: 48 ff.). See also Field's discussion of primary and secondary defeaters (1996: 361–362).

18. In McLaughlin 2000, I tried to state a sufficient condition for an argument with a contingent conclusion to be question begging. Unfortunately, the condition failed to be sufficient. I try to do better here.

19. Whether the defeaters would be undercutters or rebutters will depend on the specifics of the case.

20. See, e.g., Lewis 1996.

21. I should note that one need not actually believe all of one's presuppositions; one may be in a state of nonbelief (neither belief nor disbelief) as concerns certain of one's presuppositions. Moreover, the case I'm making could be recast in a way that doesn't depend on the assumption that being epistemically entitled to ignore the possibility that not-E amounts to being epistemically entitled to presuppose that E. Nothing essentially turns on that assumption. In the limitation principle stated immediately below, I could replace 'one is entitled to presuppose the truth of the conclusion' with 'one is entitled to ignore the truth of the conclusion'.

22. Davidson has informed me that he does not take his externalist claim to be strongly a priori.

23. For further discussion, see McLaughlin and Tye 1998 and McLaughlin 2000.

24. John Hawthorne has pointed out to me that on a Humean regularity theory of causation, analytical functionalism entails that *thinking* and *pain* fail to supervene on what's in the head since the relevant causal roles will fail to supervene on what's in the head. The reason is that on a Humean regularity theory, what causal relations there are in one's head depends on what regularities there are in one's environment. Thus, if a Humean theory is right, then the claim, for instance, that *thinking* is both privileged and such that it a priori requires being in a state with causal role R is a compatibilist claim, for if *thinking* a priori requires being in a state with role R, then it is a priori external. But whether or not a Humean regularity theory of causation is correct, and so whether or not the views in question entail (C4) compatibilist theses, is an issue I leave open.

25. This material in this paper was presented as a commentary on papers by Martin Davies and Crispin Wright in a session of the Central APA held in Chicago in spring 2000 and chaired by Michael McKinsey; hence the lengthy discussion of Davies and Wright's views. I want to thank both Peter Klein and Ernest Sosa for enormously helpful discussions of the notion of failure of warrant transmission.

4

Transmission of Warrant and Closure of Apriority
Michael McKinsey

In my paper "Anti-individualism and Privileged Access" (1991a), I argued that externalism in the philosophy of mind is incompatible with the thesis that we have privileged, nonempirical access to the contents of our own thoughts.[1] Some of the most interesting responses to my argument have been those of Martin Davies (1998, 2000a, and chapter 1 above) and Crispin Wright (2000a and chapter 2 above), who describe several types of cases to show that warrant for a premise does not always transmit to a known deductive consequence of that premise, and who contend that this fact undermines my argument for incompatibilism. I will try to show here that the Davies/Wright point about transmission of warrant does not adversely affect my argument.

Before discussing the Davies/Wright point, it will be useful to begin with, first, a brief restatement of my argument and, second, a general assessment of the dialectical situation regarding the argument and its critics.

1 The Argument for Incompatibilism

In my initial argument, I was concerned with a principle of privileged access according to which we necessarily have the capacity to obtain a priori knowledge of the *contents* of our thoughts:

Privileged access to content (PAC) Necessarily, for any person x, if x is thinking that p, then x can in principle know a priori that he himself, or she herself, is thinking that p.[2]

By 'a priori knowledge', I mean knowledge that can be achieved just by thinking, without perceptual observation or empirical investigation, and without having to make any empirical assumptions (1991a: 9; see also

McKinsey 1987: 2–3). And I argued that PAC is inconsistent with the following externalist thesis:

Semantic externalism (SE)   Many *de dicto*-structured predicates of the form 'is thinking that *p*' express properties that are wide, in the sense that possession of such a property by an agent logically implies the existence of contingent objects of a certain sort that are external to that agent.[3]

My argument was a simple reductio that considered an instance of 'is thinking that *p*' containing the natural-kind term 'water'. Suppose Oscar is thinking that water is wet. Then it follows by PAC that

(1)   Oscar can know a priori that he is thinking that water is wet.

Now since SE is supposed to apply to cognitive predicates containing natural-kind terms like 'water', we also have

(2)   The proposition that Oscar is thinking that water is wet logically implies the proposition *E*.

Here *E* is some "external proposition" that asserts or implies the existence of objects external to Oscar. For instance, *E* might be the proposition that Oscar, or members of Oscar's community, have had experiences of water, or *E* might be the proposition that water exists. But the conjunction of (1) and (2) is absurd, whatever *E* might be. If (1) is true, then according to (2), Oscar can know a priori a proposition that logically implies some empirical proposition *E*. If so, then Oscar can just *deduce E* from something he knows a priori, and so he can know *E* itself a priori. But this consequence is just absurd, since by assumption, *E* is some empirical proposition that no one could possibly know a priori. Hence the principle that we invariably have privileged access to the contents of our thoughts is inconsistent with semantic externalism.

2   *Relational Cognitive Properties*

When I first gave this reductio argument for the incompatibility of semantic externalism and privileged access (1991a), I took no stand on which of these principles is true and which is false. But shortly thereafter (1994), I provided the grounds for an argument that SE is true and hence PAC is false. I also proposed a restricted principle of privileged access to replace PAC, a principle that, unlike PAC, is consistent with SE.

SE is shown true by the semantic facts about cognitive predicates that contain small-scope proper names and indexical pronouns. Consider the case of Laura, who, when George strolls by, raises her eyebrows and whistles. Witnessing this scene, I turn to a friend and say,

(3)   Laura is thinking that George is cute.

I believe it is intuitively clear that in uttering (3), I would be using the name 'George' simply to refer to George, and I would be saying that Laura is thinking that he is cute. If the name 'George' as I use it in (3) have a descriptive meaning, then perhaps the name could semantically convey something about how Laura is thinking of George.[4] But in fact, most ordinary names, including 'George', have no such descriptive meanings, and so in (3) the name can contribute only its referent to what is said by (3).[5] As a result, (3) ascribes a cognitive property to Laura that is relational with respect to George: it says that Laura has an occurrent thought about George to the effect that he is cute.[6] It is perhaps even clearer that cognitive predicates containing small-scope indexicals ascribe relational properties. Consider (4):

(4)   Laura is thinking that *he* (or *that man*) is cute.

Since 'he' (or 'that man') in (4) refers to George, (4), like (3), says that Laura is having an occurrent thought about George to the effect that he is cute. Note that both (3) and (4) ascribe relational properties, even though the occurrences of the relevant singular terms ('George', 'he', 'that man') are assumed to fall both grammatically and logically in the scope of 'is thinking that'. Thus both (3) and (4) are *structurally* (or logically) *de dicto*, but due to the semantic character of the small-scope terms, both sentences end up saying something that is *semantically* relational, or *de re*.[7] Thus many *de dicto*-structured cognitive predicates containing small-scope names and indexicals express relational properties that are logically wide, and hence semantic externalism SE is true. Such predicates also provide straightforward counterexamples to PAC. Suppose, for instance, that (3) is true. Then given PAC, it follows that Laura can know a priori that she's thinking that George is cute. But this consequence is false. Otherwise, since what Laura supposedly knows a priori is relational with respect to George, she could just deduce that George exists from something she knows a priori, and so she could also know a priori that George exists, which is obviously absurd.

There has been much resistance to my argument for incompatibilism, mainly from externalists, who insist, contrary to my argument, that an externalist thesis should *not* assert that wide cognitive properties logically or conceptually imply the existence of external objects of a certain sort. Instead, these compatibilists claim, the relevant relation between a wide cognitive property and the external facts that make it wide is much weaker than logical or conceptual implication: perhaps the relation is only that of *metaphysical* implication, or even as weak as *counterfactual* implication.[8]

This kind of objection is always made against applications of my argument to cases of cognitive predicates that contain natural-kind terms, such as (1) and (2) above. I think that whatever plausibility this objection might have derives from the general lack of consensus about, or clear understanding of, both the semantics of natural-kind terms and the semantics of cognitive predicates that contain such terms. In my opinion, the only clear accounts of the semantics of cognitive predicates containing natural-kind terms imply that such predicates express logically wide properties that are relational with respect to external objects or substances.[9] So in my view, the semantic facts about cognitive predicates containing natural-kind terms are sufficient to support a strong form of externalism that is clearly inconsistent with the form of privileged access provided by PAC.

But even if I'm wrong about this, there should still be general agreement that PAC is false. For even in the absence of any generally accepted semantic views of singular terms, natural-kind terms, and the cognitive-attitude verbs, there should still be a consensus that many simple cases of cognitive predicates containing proper names and indexical pronouns, cases like the predicates found in sentences (3) and (4), express relational, logically wide properties. And these simple cases suffice to show that the *strongest* form of semantic externalism, SE, is true, from which it follows by my reductio argument that PAC is false.

So in my opinion, those who seek to hold on to privileged access in the form of PAC by endorsing a weak form of externalism for cognitive predicates containing natural-kind terms are engaged in a pointless exercise, like performing CPR on a long-dead horse. For the simple facts about cognitive predicates containing names and indexicals show that the strongest form of semantic externalism, SE, is in fact true anyway, and hence that PAC is false, whatever the truth may be about natural-kind terms and the cognitive predicates that contain them. A correct principle of privileged access, unlike PAC, must be restricted so as to imply at most that we can have a priori knowledge of our possession of certain logically *narrow* properties.[10]

3   Transmission of Warrant

While most critics of my argument for incompatibilism object to the argument's main premise—that externalist theses should ascribe logical relations between cognitive properties and external facts—Davies (1998) and Wright (2000a) in effect accept my premises (at least for the sake of argument) but claim that my argument is invalid.[11] They contend that even when a person knows a priori both that a given proposition p is true and that a further proposition q logically follows from p, it nevertheless does not follow that the person in question is in a position to know a priori that q.

They base this contention on an important point about the transmission of warrant made by Wright (1985). He and Davies both provide several persuasive examples to show that a person's epistemic warrant for believing a given premise p will not necessarily transmit to also provide warrant for a given deductive consequence q of p, even when the person knows that p logically implies q. Consider, for instance, Wright's nice example of the soccer game (Wright 1985: 436; Wright 2000a: 141–143; Davies 2000a: 397–399). Spectator S is apparently witnessing a soccer game in progress. Seeing a player drive the ball into the net and then seeing the referee turn and point to the center circle, S has warrant for (5):

(5)   A soccer goal has just been scored.

Of course, S also knows that (5) logically implies (6):

(6)   A game of soccer is in progress.

But S's warrant for believing (5) cannot be the *basis* of S's having warrant for (6). If S had any doubt as to whether a soccer game really is in progress (perhaps a scene is being staged for a movie), this doubt could not be settled by appeal to (5). For S will have warrant for believing that a goal has just been scored only in the context of having warrant in the first place for believing that a genuine game really is in progress. In a situation like this, any argument that S might give for (6) with (5) as premise would just beg the question.

It would seem that in general all deductively valid arguments that beg the question, or that could beg the question in a given epistemic context, provide examples in which warrant can fail to transmit from a set of premises to a known deductive consequence of those premises. For my purposes here, the important fact is that the very cases to which my argument for incompatibilism most clearly applies, cases where a premise ascribing a wide cognitive property logically implies an empirical conclusion, are also cases in which the relevant inference would beg the question. For instance, we've seen that (3) ('Laura is thinking that George is cute') logically implies that George exists. But, of course, the *source* of one's warrant for believing that George exists could not be that one has correctly deduced this conclusion from the relational premise in question, since one would not be warranted in believing the relational premise in the first place unless one were *already* warranted in believing that George exists.

Thus, in the very cases to which my argument for incompatibilism most clearly applies, warrant does not transmit from the cognitive premise to the externalist consequence. But contrary to what both Davies and Wright contend, this does not show that there is anything wrong with my argument. For the argument does not assume that warrant is always transmitted from the relevant cognitive premises to the externalist conclusions. Rather, the argument assumes a certain principle to the effect that one's capacity for a priori knowledge is closed under logical implication:

Closure of apriority under logical implication (CA)   Necessarily, for any person x and any propositions p and q, if x can know a priori that p, and p logically implies q, then x can know a priori that q.[12]

When my argument for incompatibilism is applied to a particular relational cognitive premise like (3), we assume for reductio that (3) is knowable a priori (by Laura). This assumption, as it turns out, is contrary to fact. But if (3) *were* knowable a priori, then CA generates the absurd consequence that Laura could know a priori that George exists. And surely that is the correct result. For if (3) *were* knowable a priori, then it would be knowable without empirical investigation. Hence any assumption on warrant for which knowledge of (3) is based would itself have to be knowable without empirical investigation. For otherwise, knowledge of (3) would, contrary to our assumption for reductio, be based in part on empirical investigation after all, since it would be based in part on whatever empirical investigation is required to provide warrant for the relevant empirical assumption. In this particular case, knowledge of (3) clearly depends on the agent's having warrant for the assumption that George exists. Hence one could not have a priori knowledge of (3), unless one also had a priori knowledge that George exists.

Here, then, is a clear case in which warrant fails to transmit from a premise to a deductive consequence of that premise, even though my closure principle for apriority, CA, yields the right result. And in general we may conclude that failure of warrant to transmit to a given conclusion is *not* a good reason to suspect that closure of apriority fails in the same case. Failure of warrant transmission is perfectly consistent with successful closure of apriority.

This is even more obviously shown by the simple case of conjunction. Any argument from a conjunction p & q to either conjunct as conclusion would, of course, be blatantly question-begging, and so warrant fails to transmit from premise to conclusion. But just as obviously, closure of apriority *holds* in such a case: since one can't know p & q without knowing p (and knowing q), one also cannot know p & q a priori without knowing p a priori (and knowing q a priori).

So it is difficult to understand why Davies and Wright should just assume, without argument or discussion, that failure to transmit warrant implies failure of closure for apriority. This is especially puzzling, since both Davies and Wright are careful to emphasize that failure of warrant transmission does not imply that either knowledge or warrant fail to be closed under known entailment. (See Davies 1998: 349 and 2000a: 393–394, and Wright 2000a: 140–141, 157; see also Bob Hale's useful discussion of transmission versus closure in Hale 2000.) Let us briefly consider why failure of warrant transmission does not imply failure of closure of knowledge or warrant. In cases where warrant for a given premise p transmits to a known deductive consequence q of p, we can use transmission of warrant to *explain* closure of knowledge and warrant: we can say, for instance, that a person knows (or has warrant for) q *because* he or she knows (or has warrant for) p and has correctly deduced q from p, or *because* he or she knows (or has warrant for) p and knows that p implies q. When transmission of warrant fails, then of course this sort of explanation of closure cannot be given, but this doesn't imply that closure must fail. Rather, it implies only that if closure succeeds, then the explanation of why it succeeds must be *different* from any explanation that assumes transmission of warrant. In short, transmissibility of warrant is a sufficient, but not a necessary, condition for closure of knowledge and warrant. (See Wright 2000a: 140–141; Hale 2000: 173.)

We've just seen that this same relation also holds between transmission of warrant and closure of apriority. Sometimes, when warrant successfully transmits from a premise p to a deductive consequence q of p, we can use this fact to explain how a person can know q a priori, namely, by knowing p a priori and correctly deducing q from p. When warrant fails to transmit from p to q, we no longer have *this* way of explaining why q must be knowable a priori if p is. Nevertheless, some other explanation may be available: perhaps, in the given case, we can explain why a priori knowability of premise p *requires* a priori knowability of the deductive consequence q, even though one's warrant for p fails to provide warrant for q. This is the sort of explanation that I gave earlier for the case of conjunction, and for the case in which a priori knowability of (3) ('Laura is thinking that George is cute') requires a priori knowability of the deductive consequence of (3) that George exists, even though warrant for (3) does not transmit to this consequence.

In short, for the same reason that failure of warrant transmission does not refute closure of knowledge and warrant, it also does not refute closure of apriority. Hence, my reductio argument is not shown to be unsound by the Davies/Wright point that warrant fails to transmit from premise to conclusion in many of the cases to which the argument applies. For again, my argument assumes only closure of apriority, and this principle is consistent with failure of warrant transmission.

4   Strong and Weak Apriority

The sense of 'a priori' knowledge in terms of which my argument for incompatibilism was first stated is a fairly strong one, since I meant knowledge that could be obtained without perceptual observation or empirical investigation and without having to make any empirical assumptions. (Again, see McKinsey 1991a: 9; 1987: 2–3.) Davies has recently suggested that while my reductio argument goes through with a priori knowledge understood in my strict sense, the same form of argument will not work to show the incompatibility of externalism and a form of privileged access that is understood in terms of a weaker kind of a priori knowledge. In this weaker sense, a priori knowledge is simply knowledge that is not justificatorily based on empirical investigation, though it might (in ways that Davies does not specify) involve making empirical assumptions. (See Davies 2000a: 406–408 and chapter 1 above. Wright [2000a: 152] also seems to be relying on a weak sense of the a priori.)

Davies (2000a: 407) suggests that my argument works when 'a priori' is given the strict sense but fails when 'a priori' is given the weak sense, because strict but not weak a priori warrant successfully transmits from premises to the known deductive consequences of those premises. This is wrong. No matter how strong a sense of 'a priori' we choose, there can be question-begging valid arguments whose premises are knowable a priori in that sense, even though warrant does not transmit from premises to conclusion. For instance, even the strongest a priori warrant for a conjunction will fail to transmit to its conjuncts. Transmission of warrant is not the issue. The only question for my argument that is raised by the distinction between the weak and strong a priori is the question of whether or not my closure principle CA remains true under these two different interpretations of 'a priori'.

In discussing this question, I will use explications of weak and strong a priori derived from those proposed by Hartry Field (1996).[13] I find Field's proposals salutary because they replace the obscure notion of an empirical assumption that I had used with the somewhat clearer notion of empirical defeasibility. Let us say that a person x's knowledge that p is *weakly a priori* if and only if x's knowledge that p is not based, even in part, on either perceptual observation or empirical investigation. And, following Field, let us say that x's knowledge that p is *strongly a priori* if and only if x's knowledge that p is both weakly a priori and empirically indefeasible. Here I understand that x's knowledge that p is empirically indefeasible if and only if the warrant or justification on which x's knowledge that p is based could not possibly be undermined or out-weighed by any additional empirical evidence. In Field's terminology, I mean here that the person's warrant could not be defeated "in the primary way" by any empirical evidence, where a person's warrant for a belief is defeated by additional evidence in the primary way when the person's actual warrant would no longer support the belief, given the additional evidence. (In the discussion to follow, by 'defeat' I will always mean 'primary defeat'.)[14]

Is the capacity for strongly a priori knowledge closed under logical implication? Suppose that x has strongly a priori knowledge that p, and that p logically implies q. If x's empirically indefeasible warrant for p transmits to q, then obviously x can have strongly a priori knowledge that q, by deducing q from p. But suppose that x's warrant for p does *not* transmit to q. Could it then fail to be possible for x to have strongly a priori knowledge that q? If so, then knowledge that q would have to always be either empirically defeasible or obtainable only by perceptual observation or empirical investigation. But then it certainly seems that in either case, it would follow that q could be shown false by empirical evidence, and since p logically implies q, it follows that p could *also* be shown false by empirical evidence. There certainly is a tension between this consequence and our assumption that x's knowledge that p is empirically indefeasible. However, there seems to be no inconsistency here: whatever empirical evidence that there could be against q (and hence against p) might in fact be insufficient to outweigh x's empirically indefeasible warrant for p.[15]

So while the Davies/Wright point about transmission of warrant does not show that closure of apriority fails to hold generally, the point does make it difficult to *prove* that closure of apriority does hold generally, whether we take apriority in either the strong or the weak sense. This in turn has the effect of *undermining confidence* in the closure principle on which my reductio argument depends, whether the argument is understood in terms of strong apriority or in terms of weak apriority. This difficulty can be overcome by proving restricted principles of closure for both strong and weak apriority. As we shall see, these restricted principles will serve most of the purposes of my original argument.

5   Restricted Closure Principles for Strong and Weak Apriority

In stating the restricted closure principles in question, I will make crucial use of an important idea introduced by Wright (2000a: 143) and further refined by Hale (2000: 177–181), namely, the idea of a person's warrant for a given proposition being *dependent* on a given body of collateral information I. Following Hale's definition (2000: 181), let us say that a person x's warrant w to believe that p *strictly depends* on information I if and only if (i) if it were not the case that for each $q \in I$, x has a warrant w' to believe that q, then w would not warrant x in believing that p, and (ii) x's combined warrants to believe the propositions in I do not, by themselves, warrant x's believing that p.

Now suppose again that x has strongly a priori knowledge that p and that p logically implies q. As we've seen, when x's warrant for p transmits to q, x can also have strongly a priori knowledge that q. Moreover, in cases where x's warrant for p does *not* transmit to q, this will typically be because x's warrant for p strictly depends on information containing q, so that any inference from p to q would be question-begging. It is easy to see that in such a case, it follows that x can have strongly a priori knowledge that q. For first, x's warrant for q must be empirically indefeasible, since if this warrant were empirically defeasible, then x's warrant for p, which strictly depends on warrant for q, would itself be empirically defeasible, contrary to our assumption that x's knowledge that p is strongly a priori. Second, x's warrant for q must be based on neither perceptual observation nor empirical observation; otherwise, x's warrant for p, which strictly depends on warrant for q, would itself be based in part on perceptual observation or empirical investigation, again contrary to our assumption that x's knowledge that p is strongly a priori.

These considerations show conclusively that the capacities for both strongly and weakly a priori knowledge are closed under logical implication in cases where either (i) warrant transmits from premise p to conclusion q or (ii) the agent's warrant for p strictly depends on information containing q. So we can be confident in the truth of the following restricted closure principles for strong and weak apriority, which for brevity I state together:

Restricted closure of apriority under logical implication (R-CA)
Necessarily, for any person x and any propositions p and q, if (i) p logically implies q, and (ii) x can have strongly [weakly] a priori knowledge that p in circumstances in which either (iii) x's warrant for p transmits to q or (iv) x's warrant for p strictly depends on information I such that $q \in I$, then x can have strongly [weakly] a priori knowledge that q.

Certainly, in the kinds of cases to which my reductio argument most clearly applies, use of the restricted principle R-CA effectively yields the same results as the unrestricted principle CA. Whenever a given cognitive premise such as (3) ('Laura is thinking that George is cute') is relational with respect to a given object and thus logically implies the existence of that object, a person's having warrant for believing the premise will always strictly depend on the person's having warrant for believing the conclusion. Hence, in such cases, R-CA applies to show that if a person can have strongly (or weakly) a priori knowledge of the premise, then that person can have strongly (or weakly) a priori knowledge of the conclusion.

I think it is very likely that any interesting externalist semantic thesis will imply that cognitive ascriptions are logically related to external consequences in such a way that the restricted closure principle R-CA will apply to that logical relation. The typical case is one in which a cognitive predicate ascribes the having of a thought with a logically wide content, such as a singular proposition. In such cases, the very existence of the ascribed content logically presupposes the truth of some external proposition, and so any warrant one might have for believing that a given thought has such a content will strictly depend on having warrant for the presupposed external proposition, and thus R-CA will apply.

6   *Wright's Conjecture*

Falling back to the restricted closure principle R-CA means that we have to accept at least the logical possibility that some form of semantic externalism might escape my reductio argument and perhaps be consistent with privileged access in the form of PAC. The situation would look like this: on the externalist thesis in question, (i) a cognitive premise p would logically imply an empirical externalist consequence E; (ii) warrant for p would not transmit to E; and (iii) warrant for p would also not strictly depend on any information containing E. In such a situation, R-CA could not be applied to show that given strongly (or weakly) a priori knowledge that p, one could (absurdly) have strongly (or weakly) a priori knowledge that E. How seriously should we take such a possibility?

Wright (2000a) uses Fred Dretske's (1970) famous discussion of scepticism as the basis for a conjecture that externalist theses about certain cognitive premises precisely fit the logically possible model just described. In Dretske's zebra case, a man, Jones say, is visiting the zoo and sees an animal in the pen before him that looks exactly like a zebra. Jones therefore believes (7):

(7)   The animal in the pen is a zebra.

We can assume that Jones's perceptual warrant for (7) is sufficient for knowledge and that (7) is true, so that Jones in fact knows (7). But (7) logically implies (8):

(8)   The animal in the pen is not a mule cleverly disguised as a zebra.

As Wright points out (2000a: 154), Jones's warrant for (7) clearly does not transmit to (8), since his warrant for (7), which just consists of the way the beast looks, could not provide Jones with a new reason for believing (8) for the first time. Moreover, it seems that Jones's warrant for (7) also does not strictly depend on Jones's having warrant for (8). After all, Jones has done nothing special to make sure that (8) is true. Wright (2000a: 155) suggests that while Jones lacks warrant for (8), he is nevertheless *entitled* to discount the remote possibility that (8) denies, and so he is entitled, without having warrant, to assume that (8) is true.

If Wright's description of Dretske's case is correct, then (7) and (8) provide an example of propositions p and q such that p logically implies q, but warrant for p neither transmits to q nor strictly depends on information containing q. So R-CA cannot be applied to a case like this.[16] But

Wright claims that the situation regarding cognitive premises to which externalist theses apply is closely analogous to the zebra case. Consider (9):

(9)   Oscar is thinking that water is wet.

And assume some externalist thesis according to which (9) logically implies, say, (10):

(10)   Oscar has had such and such encounters with water.[17]

According to Wright, Oscar could have (weakly) a priori knowledge of (9) purely by reflection, even though (9) entails the empirical proposition (10), which Oscar could *not* know a priori in any sense. Wright's rationale for this claim rests crucially on two further claims: first, that Oscar's warrant for (9) would not transmit to (10), and second, that Oscar's warrant for (9) would also not strictly depend on warrant for (10), even though (9) logically implies (10).

While the first of these claims is surely correct, the second is much more tenuous. In the zebra case, it's plausible to say that Jones's having warrant for believing (7) does not depend on his having warrant for believing (8), simply because it's also plausible (though not obviously true) to say that Jones would in fact *not* have warrant for (8). Since Jones has done nothing special to make sure that he's *not* seeing a cleverly disguised mule, perhaps we should say that Jones has no warrant, but merely entitlement, for assuming that (8) is true. But of course we can't say anything like this about (10). If Oscar is like the rest of us, he has seen, drunk, and washed in water several times a day on every day of his life, and so he would have as much empirical warrant for (10) as it is possible for a person to have. Thus we obviously cannot argue that Oscar's having warrant for (9) does not depend on his having warrant for (10) by appeal to the (obviously false) premise that, while Oscar has warrant for (9), he has *no* warrant, only entitlement, for believing (10).

Moreover, it does not really seem *possible* for someone to be entitled to assume that a proposition like (10) is true in the absence of any empirical warrant for that proposition. Surely, if Oscar had never had perceptual experiences of water, had never even acquired any indirect evidence for the existence of water, and thus had never acquired any empirical warrant for believing that he had had encounters with water, then he would also never have acquired any sort of *entitlement* to assume that he'd had such encounters. It in fact seems precisely as implausible to suppose that one could have unwarranted entitlement to assume that one has had watery encounters as it is to suppose that one could have a priori knowledge by pure reflection that one has had such encounters.

Why then does Wright at least implicitly endorse the implausible claim that one could have unwarranted entitlement to assume such a proposition as that one has had such and such encounters with water? It seems to be due to an analogy that Wright draws between cases of self-knowledge and cases of perception. When one looks at a wall and sees that it is red, one acquires warrant for believing that the wall is red. In such a case, according to Wright, one is entitled to assume, without having any particular warrant for doing so, that the circumstances are normal, and hence suitable for acquiring knowledge by perception. In other words, Wright is suggesting, one is normally entitled without warrant to assume that one is not the victim of an illusion of the sort that would result from, say, a white wall cleverly illuminated to look red. Similarly, Wright (2000: 152–153) suggests, in cases of self-knowledge, one is normally entitled without warrant to assume that one is not the victim of an "illusion of content" of the sort that one would have in seeming to think that water is wet, having in fact never experienced water.

But how exactly is it supposed to follow from this suggestion that one generally has unwarranted entitlement to assume the externalist presuppositions of one's thoughts? Presumably, Wright's underlying reasoning must run somewhat as follows:

(11)   When it seems to Oscar that he's thinking that water is wet, Oscar is entitled without warrant to assume that he's not then having an illusion of content. (Wright's premise)

(12)   If it seems to Oscar that he's thinking that water is wet, and Oscar is not then having an illusion of content, then Oscar has had such and such encounters with water. (Externalist premise)

(13)   Therefore, if it seems to Oscar that he's thinking that water is wet, then Oscar is entitled without warrant to assume that he's had such and such encounters with water.

Now we've already seen that (13) would be pretty obviously false: while it may well seem to a person that he or she is thinking that water is wet, it's *never* true that a person has unwarranted entitlement to assume that he or she has had such and such encounters with water. I would suggest that the inference from (11) and (12) to (13) is simply invalid, because it implicitly depends on a false principle to the effect that unwarranted entitlement is closed under implication (though it is not clear which form of implication is being invoked). That *something* is certainly wrong with this inference is shown by the following analogous inference about perception:

(14)   When it seems to Oscar that he's seeing a red wall, Oscar is entitled without warrant to assume that he's not then having a perceptual illusion.

(15)   If it seems to Oscar that he's seeing a red wall and Oscar is not then having a perceptual illusion, then Oscar is seeing a red wall.

(16)   Therefore, if it seems to Oscar that he's seeing a red wall, then Oscar is entitled without warrant to assume that he's seeing a red wall.

While premises (14) and (15) are both plausible, the conclusion (16) would normally be false. For after all, its seeming to one that one is see-ing a red wall is precisely how one typically *acquires* warrant for believing that one is seeing a red wall. In such a case, of course, the antecedent of (16) would be true and its consequent false.[18]

So it is both implausible and unjustified to suggest, as Wright does, that when a person has (weakly) a priori knowledge that *p* and *p* logi-cally implies some very strong empirical proposition *E*, the person need have no warrant, only entitlement, for assuming *E*. But Wright is surely correct when he points out (2000a: 155) that the person in question would have to be entitled to assume the relevant empirical conse-quence. In the case of Oscar, for instance, if Oscar has only weak, and hence empirically defeasible, a priori knowledge that (9) is true and (9) logically implies (10), then Oscar must be entitled to assume that (10) is true, since the falsity of (10) would empirically defeat (in the primary way) Oscar's a priori warrant for (9). However, as we've just seen, Oscar is entitled to assume that (10) is true only if Oscar has warrant for (10). Hence, Oscar's having warrant for (9) would strictly depend on his having warrant for (10). Thus my restricted closure principle R-CA applies in this case to show that, given the externalist thesis that (9) logically implies (10), then since Oscar cannot have weakly a priori knowledge that (10) is true, he also cannot have privileged (weakly) a priori knowledge that (9) is true.

So again it seems that typical forms of externalism will typically be ones to which the restricted closure principle R-CA applies, yielding in-consistency with privileged access. For most forms of externalism imply that certain cognitive premises have very strong empirical consequences, like (10). In such cases, warrant for the cognitive premise will strictly depend on information containing the empirical conclusion. In Wright's terminology, such externalisms imply that warrant for the cognitive premises in question is always *information-dependent*, where some of this information is empirical and external.[19] But as I have shown, no such cognitive proposition is one of which we can have either weakly or strongly a priori knowledge, and so there can be no privileged access to the truth of such a proposition, in any sense.

From Wright's discussion, it seems that the only forms of externalism that might escape my reductio argument are those that imply at most that some cognitive premises have weak empirical consequences to the effect that various wildly improbable skeptical hypotheses are false. Perhaps in such cases an agent's (weakly) a priori warrant for the cognitive premise would depend only on the agent's being entitled, perhaps without warrant, to assume that the relevant skeptical hypotheses are false. However, no forms of semantic externalism that I know of are this weak, and it is certainly difficult to see what the motivation for such a view might be.

7   Conclusion

The Davies/Wright point about transmission of warrant cannot be used to refute my reductio argument against incompatibilism, since my argument relies only on closure of apriority, and failure of warrant transmission is consistent with successful closure of apriority. However, the fact that warrant for a premise can fail to transmit to a known deductive consequence of that premise forces us to reexamine our intuitions about closure of apriority. When transmission of warrant fails for a given premise and conclusion, how can closure of apriority succeed? The answer lies in Wright's conception of a warrant's being information-dependent: when warrant for the premise strictly depends on information containing the conclusion, not only does transmission of warrant *fail*, but closure of both strong and weak apriority *succeeds*. This allows us to have complete confidence in a restricted principle of closure for apriority (R-CA), which says that apriority is closed under logical implication precisely when warrant for the premise either transmits from premise to conclusion or strictly depends on warrant for the conclusion. As I've argued here, this restricted principle serves most of the purposes of my original argument, which relied on the unrestricted principle CA.

I mentioned earlier that adopting a restricted closure principle for apriority opens up the logical possibility that some specific form of semantic externalism might be found to which the restricted principle does not apply, so that incompatibility of this form of externalism with privileged access in the form of PAC could not be shown. But before diehard compatibilists use this fact as an excuse to rush out and search for the relevant form of externalism, let me reiterate a point that I made earlier: such a search would be a pointless exercise. For again, the semantic facts show that *de dicto*-structured cognitive predicates containing names and indexicals express properties that are relational with respect to external objects, and the undeniable closure principle R-CA shows conclusively (by reductio) that no one could possibly have either strongly or weakly a priori privileged access to their possession of such a relational cognitive property. Hence, we already know that PAC is false, and so there is simply no point in looking for forms of externalism that are consistent with it.[20]

Notes

1. The paper in which the argument appeared (McKinsey 1991a) had earlier been presented to the Pacific Division of the American Philosophical Association (Los Angeles, March 1990). From 1978 on, I've regularly presented the argument in classes and seminars at Wayne State. I also gave the argument in a question from the floor at the April 1985 Oberlin Colloquium after Tyler Burge's presentation of his 1988a paper there, and I gave it again in a question from the floor after Burge's presentation of his 1988b paper as the Nelson lecture at the University of Michigan, February 1986.

2. Essentially, this same principle was more clearly expressed, and endorsed, by McLaughlin and Tye (1998: 286): "Privileged access thesis: It is conceptually necessary that if we are able to exercise our normal capacity to have beliefs about our occurrent thoughts, then if we are able to occurrently think that *p*, we are able to know that we are thinking that *p* without our knowledge being justificatorily based on empirical investigation of our environment." I agree with the salutary qualification that to have the relevant a priori knowledge, we must be "able to exercise our normal capacity to have beliefs about our occurrent thoughts." We can take this to be covered by the qualifier 'in principle' in PAC.

3. See McKinsey 1991a: 15, principle (Ba). Here and below I mean 'logically implies' in a broad sense that includes conceptual implication. See McKinsey 1991a: 14; 1991b: 152.

4. In McKinsey 1999, I argue that some names do in fact have descriptive meanings, and that as a result, uses of such names in cognitive contexts, unlike the use of 'George' in (3), are nonrelational.

5. I believe (McKinsey 1984, 1994, 1999) that this in part on the basis of Kripke's (1972) evidence. See also McKinsey 1984, 1994, and 1999.

6. This is in fact the standard externalist view of how cognitive ascriptions containing small-scope names and indexicals should be understood. See, for example, McDowell 1977, Evans 1982, McKay 1981, Salmon 1986, and Soames 1987.

7. It used to be common to say that demonstratives like 'he' or 'that man' must have *largest scope* relative to any cognitive operator. If so, then a sentence like (4) could not be structurally *de dicto*. But Nathan Salmon (1986: 4) effectively showed that this suggestion is a nonstarter. See also McKinsey 1998: 17–18.

8. Brueckner (1992: 113, 114, 116) seems to make *both* of these claims. See also Gallois and O'Leary-Hawthorne 1996 and McLaughlin and Tye 1998. I reply to this sort of objection at length in McKinsey 1994b, 2001, 2002a.

9. In my own work on this topic, I've provided both an explanation of precisely why cognitive predicates containing natural-kind terms express logically wide mental properties and an account of what these properties are. I know of no other externalist semantics that does these things. See McKinsey 1987, 1994a: 321–324.

10. For a statement of what I consider to be the correct principle of privileged access, see McKinsey 1994a: 308–309. See also McKinsey 2001, 2002a.

11. By contrast, McLaughlin and Tye (1998) explicitly say that my argument has a valid form (which they call 'McKinsey's recipe'), but they object to the argument's main premise. See McKinsey 2001 for my reply to their objection.

12. Most interpretations of my argument do not see it as relying on CA, but rather on another very plausible closure principle, namely, CAK: Necessarily, for any person x and any propositions p and q, if x can know a priori that p and x can know a priori that if p then q, then x can know a priori that q. (See, for instance, Brown 1995, Gallois and O'Leary-Hawthorne 1996, Boghossian 1997, Davies 1998, McLaughlin and Tye 1998, and Wright 2000a.) The serious weakness of versions of my reductio that use CAK instead of CA is that application of CAK in the argument requires the additional, and in my opinion false, assumption that externalist theses like (2) in the text are themselves knowable a priori. For a defense of my use of CA rather than CAK, and an explanation of why my argument does not have to assume that externalist theses are knowable a priori, see McKinsey 2002a. See also my discussion of Boghossian 1997 in McKinsey, 2002b.

13. Brian McLaughlin (2000 and chapter 3 above) also uses Field's conceptions of the weak and strong a priori in his discussion of issues closely related to my argument.

14. Field (1996: 361–362) distinguishes primary defeat from what he calls 'secondary defeat', where additional evidence does not undermine or outweigh the person's actual warrant, but rather would show that the person does not *have* the warrant in question. For example, suppose that x correctly claims to know a priori a theorem of logic to the effect that p, by virtue of having given a simple

proof that *p*. Possible empirical evidence that *x* was on drugs when producing the proof, or that leading logicians say that the proof is faulty, would defeat *x*'s warrant in the secondary way. As Field points out, such examples seem to show that even the most obvious cases of the strongest possible a priori knowledge would be "empirically defeasible" in the secondary way, and if so, then we should *not* understand 'strongly a priori' in terms of secondary defeat. Davies (2000a: 408) uses an example of Christopher Peacocke's (1999: 244–245) to suggest that there probably is no such thing as self-knowledge that is strictly a priori in my sense. But Peacocke's example appears to be an example of secondary defeat, and if so, then the example is not really relevant to any plausible conception of strongly a priori knowledge. In this connection, see also Burge's discussion (1993: 463–464) of the role of memory in the acquisition of knowledge by deductive proof.

15. Here I am indebted to McLaughlin (2000: 106–107), who makes a similar point.

16. Note that, if Wright's description of Dretske's case is correct, it also follows that warrant is not closed under known entailment, since Jones is supposed to have *no* warrant for (8), even though Jones has warrant for (7) and knows that (7) entails (8). Moreover, given that knowledge requires warrant, it also follows that knowledge itself is not closed under known entailment. So if his description is correct, that case is a counterexample to both closure of knowledge and closure of warrant. This fact is difficult to square with Wright's explicit skepticism (2000a: 141) as to whether there are any genuine counterexamples to closure. (See also Hale 2000: 184.)

17. The sort of externalist consequence that Wright actually considers is not (10) but disjunctions of the form 'Either Oscar or Oscar's speech community has had such and such encounters with water' (Wright 2000a: 156). I use the simpler (10) merely for ease of exposition.

18. In the above discussion, I use the phrase 'is entitled without warrant' to mean just 'both is entitled and has no warrant'. Perhaps a defender of Wright's argument would suggest that the phrase should not be understood so as to imply lack of warrant, but rather should be taken to mean 'is entitled and would still be entitled even without warrant'. Since my case against Wright is unaffected by this change, the reader is free to read the phrase in either sense.

19. In his response to Wright (2000a), Alfonso Garcia Suárez (2000) defends my reductio argument by contending that externalist theses imply that warrant for the relevant cognitive premises would be information-dependent. So my reaction to Wright's conjecture is essentially the same as that of Suárez, to whom I am indebted for his useful discussion.

20. For useful conversations about these matters, I am grateful to Martin Davies, Brian McLaughlin, Bruce Russell, and Crispin Wright. I owe a special debt to the papers of Davies (1998, 2000a) and Wright (2000a). As I hope the text indicates, by thinking about these papers I have learned a great deal about my reductio argument.

5

The Reductio Argument and Transmission of Warrant

Jessica Brown

1 Introduction

In this paper I focus on the reductio argument for the incompatibility of externalism about mental content and privileged access—the view that a subject can have a priori knowledge of her thought contents. At the core of the reductio is the idea that a subject might think through the following inference:

W1   I think that water is wet.

W2   If I think that water is wet, then I or my community has had such and such encounters with water.

W3   Therefore, I or my community has had such and such encounters with water.

The alleged incompatibility arises from the claim that if externalism and privileged access were both true, then a subject could have a priori knowledge of W1 and W2 and use this to gain by inference a priori knowledge of W3. But, it is claimed, it is absurd to suppose that a subject could have a priori knowledge of W3. Surely, a subject can know that her environment contains a certain natural kind only empirically (see McKinsey 1991a, Brown 1995, and Boghossian 1997). Some have disputed the claim that it is absurd to suppose that a subject could have a priori knowledge of W3, and have argued instead that it is an advantage of compatibilism that it has this consequence (e.g., Sawyer 1998, Warfield 1998). For if a subject can have a priori knowledge of the nature of her environment, this provides a response to skeptics who claim that we can never have knowledge of the existence or nature of the external world. However, whether or not it is absurd to suppose that a subject can have a priori knowledge of her environment, it would be a significant result if the combination of externalism and privileged access enabled a subject to gain such knowledge.

Crispin Wright and Martin Davies accept that it is absurd to suppose that a subject could gain a priori knowledge of the nature of her environment by thinking through the inference W1 to W3. They defend compatibility by arguing that even if a subject has a priori knowledge of W1 and W2, she cannot thereby gain a priori knowledge of W3 (Wright 2000a; Davies 1998, 2000a). If this is right, then the reductio intended by that inference provides neither an objection to the compatibility of externalism and privileged access nor an answer to skepticism.

In effect, Davies and Wright argue that the reductio constitutes a counterexample to the transmission of knowledge, the claim that whenever a subject knows the premises of a valid argument and believes its conclusion on the basis of her recognition of its validity, her belief in the conclusion thereby constitutes knowledge.[1] Davies and Wright are careful to separate their denial of the transmission of knowledge from a denial of the closure of knowledge: the claim that whenever a subject knows the premises of a valid argument and believes in its conclusion on the basis of her recognition of its validity, her belief in the conclusion constitutes knowledge. The main difference between closure and transmission is that the closure principle makes no claim about what makes the subject's belief in the conclusion knowledge, whereas the transmission principle claims that her belief in the conclusion constitutes knowledge in virtue of the fact that it is based on a known-to-be-valid inference from known premises. As Davies and Wright recognize, the reductio does not seem to be a counterexample to the closure of knowledge. For, plausibly, if a subject has had the kind of interactions with water an externalist thinks are required for her to have the concept of water, and thus thinks through W1 and W2, then she has empirical knowledge that she or her community has had such and such encounters with water, W3.

In principle, we have a counterexample to the transmission of knowledge whenever any component of knowledge fails to transmit across a valid argument. Both Davies and Wright argue that the reductio is a counterexample to the transmission of knowledge since warrant is a necessary condition for knowledge and the reductio is a counterexample to the transmission of warrant (the claim that whenever a subject has warrant for the premises of a valid argument and believes its conclusion on the basis of her recognition of its validity, she thereby acquires warrant for its conclusion). Davies and Wright offer different reasons for supposing that warrant fails to transmit across the reductio. In this paper, I focus only on Wright's view according to which warrant fails to transmit since the reductio has a certain conditional form. (For discussion of Davies's distinct defense of a failure of transmission, see Brown, forthcoming.)

2   Conditional Warrant

Wright (2000a: 155) argues that warrant fails to transmit across the reductio because the reductio is part of a wider class of arguments that are counterexamples to the transmission of warrant. He claims that these arguments are counterexamples to transmission since they fit the following template: they are arguments of the form "A; if A then B; B" that meet these conditions: (i) A entails B; (ii) there is a proposition C incompatible with A; (iii) my warrant for A consists in my being in a state that is subjectively indistinguishable from a state in which C would be true; and (iv) C would be true if B were false. Why, though, should we accept that warrant fails to transmit across such arguments? The key to Wright's view is his claim that any argument meeting this template has the following conditional form: warrant for the premise A is conditional on having prior and independent warrant for the conclusion, B. As a result, he says, one's warrant for the premises cannot provide one with a reason to accept the conclusion. Rather, one must already have an independent warrant for the conclusion in order to have warrant for the premises. Thus, warrant for the premises fails to transmit to the conclusion.

Wright defends his view that any argument meeting his template has the relevant conditional form in the following passage. Noting that the template includes condition (iii) that one's warrant for A consists in one's being in a state which is subjectively indistinguishable from a state in which C would be true, he says,

> The key question is what, in the circumstances, can justify me in accepting A? Why not just reserve judgment and stay with the more tentative disjunction, 'A or C'—for it is all the same which disjunct is true as far as what is subjectively apparent to me is concerned. The answer has to be, it would seem: because I am somehow additionally entitled to discount the other disjunct, C.... In order for me to be entitled to discount C, and so move past the disjunction to A, I have to be entitled to discount the negation of B, and therefore entitled to accept B; for by hypothesis, if not-B were true, so would C be. So, it would seem that I must have an appreciable entitlement to affirm B already, independent of the recognition of its entailment by A, if I am to claim to be warranted in accepting

A in the first place. So, the inference from *A* to *B* is not at the service of a rational first conviction that *B*.   (Wright 2000a: 155)

Wright's line of thought seems to be as follows. It is part of the template that my warrant for *A* consists in my being in a state that is subjectively indistinguishable from a state in which the incompatible *C* would be true. This raises the question of how it is that I am entitled to *A*, and not merely to the disjunction (*A* or *C*). He argues that I have warrant for *A* only if I have prior and independent warrant to discount *C*. But, given that (iv) (if *B* were false, then *C* would be true), he says that my warrant for *A* is conditional on my having prior and independent warrant for *B*. Thus, my warrant for *A*, even in conjunction with my warrant for (if *A* then *B*) cannot provide me with warrant for *B*. Warrant fails to transmit across the argument.

However, Wright's argument seems to reflect an internalist epistemology, which many would reject. More important, many externalists about mental content would reject epistemological internalism, for instance, as part of their response to the slow switch problem (e.g., Falvey and Owens 1994, Gibbons 1996). Notice that Wright draws no distinction between possible substitutes for *C* in terms of how remote they are from the actual situation. For Wright, if there is a state subjectively indistinguishable from one's actual state and in which *C* would be true then, no matter how bizarre *C* is, it raises the question of how one is entitled to move past the disjunction (*A* or *C*) to *A*. Wright argues that one is entitled to do so only if one has prior and independent entitlement to discount *C*. However, epistemological externalists reject the idea that one's epistemic position with respect to a true proposition *A* is putatively undermined by every proposition *C*, which is incompatible with *A*, and compatible with one's being in a state subjectively indistinguishable from one's actual state, no matter how bizarre that alternative is. Rather, they argue that only some alternatives are potentially undermining—those which are "relevant" or "nearby" (Nozick 1981; Goldman 1976, 1986). In addition, epistemological externalists reject the idea that a subject's epistemological position with respect to a proposition depends exclusively on how things are subjectively. Instead, they insist that a subject may have warrant for, and knowledge of, one of two disjuncts in virtue of her external relations to that disjunct, even when the difference between the two disjuncts makes no subjective difference to her. To illustrate both points, consider the BIV argument:

BIV1   I see a table in front of me.

BIV2   If I see a table in front of me, then it's not the case that I have just become a brain in a vat (BIV).

BIV3   Therefore, it's not the case that I have just become a BIV.

Suppose that I am actually seeing a table. I would be in a subjectively indistinguishable state were I suffering an illusion since I have just become a BIV. For Wright, this raises the question of how I am entitled to move past the disjunction (either I am seeing a table, or I have just become a BIV)? He argues that I am entitled to do so only if I have prior and independent warrant for discounting the BIV possibility. However, for the epistemological externalist, this case does not raise a problem of how the subject is entitled to move past the disjunction (I'm seeing a table, or I've just become a BIV). Nor need she accept that the subject is entitled to the first disjunct only if she has prior and independent entitlement to discount the other. For, first, epistemological externalists would regard the BIV possibility as (normally) irrelevant and therefore not a threat to my warrant for BIV1. Second, they would reject the idea that my epistemic state with respect to BIV1 is wholly determined by how things seem subjectively to me. Rather, they would hold that I have warrant for, and knowledge of, the proposition that I am seeing a table if it was produced by a reliable process of perception. Thus, the concern that drives Wright to his conditional analysis need not be shared by epistemological externalists, for whom epistemic entitlement is partly a matter of the subject's relations to her environment.

We can illustrate this by reference to Goldman's reliabilist account of warrant, according to which a subject's belief that p is warranted only if produced by a reliable process, i.e., one which tends to produce true beliefs and to inhibit false ones. As we have seen, Wright is committed to holding that one has warrant for BIV1 (I am seeing a table) only if one has prior and independent warrant for BIV3 (it's not the case that I have just become a BIV). By contrast, Goldman would hold that whether I have warrant for BIV1 depends on whether that belief was produced by a reliable process, independently of whether other beliefs, such as BIV3, are produced by such processes. Further, although Goldman would argue that I have warrant for BIV1, it seems that he should reject the claim that I have prior and independent warrant for BIV3. Perception provides one with a reliable process for producing beliefs about what one is seeing and thus warrant for such beliefs. The most obvious reliable process for producing the belief that I have not just become a BIV is by inference from other beliefs, e.g., by the inference from BIV1 to BIV3. However, although this inference is reliable, it cannot provide warrant for BIV3 that is prior and independent of my having warrant for BIV1. Further, it seems that I have no evidence that I have not just become a BIV, for, by hypothesis, everything would seem the same to me had that happened. It seems, then, that I lack a reliable process for producing the belief that I have not just become a BIV that could provide a warrant for this belief that is prior to and independent of my having warrant for BIV1. Thus, Goldman should reject Wright's claim that one has warrant for BIV1 only if one has prior and independent warrant for BIV3.

The suggested epistemological externalist approach seems better able than Wright's to deal with the threat of skepticism. On Wright's view, warrant for ordinary propositions such as BIV1 (I am seeing a table) is conditional on having prior and independent entitlement against skeptical hypotheses such as the BIV hypothesis. But we may wonder whether we have any warrant against such skeptical hypotheses. For they are designed so that everything would seem the same were they to be true. But, on Wright's view, doubt about whether we have warrant against such hypotheses would undermine the claim that we have warrant for ordinary claims, such as that I am seeing a table. But if our warrant for such ordinary claims is independent of whether we have warrant against skeptical hypotheses, then no such concern arises.

Although epistemological externalists should not accept Wright's argument for the conditional analysis, they could accept his claim that there are epistemic links between the first premise and the conclusion of arguments fitting his template. It is part of the template that the subject's warrant for the premise *A* consists in a state subjectively indistinguishable from one in which the incompatible *C* would be true, and *C* would be true if the conclusion *B* were false. Given this, an epistemological externalist may agree that the subject would lack warrant for *A* if she regards not-*B* as likely as not, or if she has strong warrant for not-*B*. (Externalists who hold that a subject's epistemic position with respect to a proposition partly depends on her external relations need not deny that it also depends on more "subjective" factors.) Further, she may agree with Wright that the subject's warrant for *A* "does not reckon with" the possibility that not-*B*, or rule it out. And she can agree that such an argument would not convince someone who anyway doubted *B*. But, this does not establish the further claim that a subject has warrant for *A* only if she has prior and independent warrant for *B*. Epistemological externalists who reject Wright's conditional analysis and his view that the subject has prior and independent warrant for assuming that she has not just become a BIV may even put their view in similar terms to Wright's by saying that the subject is "not required to bother about" the skeptical possibility, or that she is "entitled to ignore" it. But by this they would mean only that her evidence warrants propositions about the external world even though she would be in a subjectively indistinguishable state were the skeptical hypothesis to be true and although she cannot rule out the skeptical hypothesis. They need not agree with Wright's claim that she has warrant for the negation of the skeptical hypothesis.

Wright's view faces a second objection too, besides the fact that it would be rejected by many epistemological externalists. I will argue that his "solution" to the reductio is no less problematic than the original problem posed by the reductio. To set up this objection, consider how Wright applies his template for the failure of transmission of warrant to the reductio. To understand Wright's application, it is helpful to note that Wright (2000a: 145) holds that the reductio can work against only those versions of externalism according to which the existence of a natural-kind concept depends on its having a nonempty extension. Suppose, for instance, that instead of being brought in a watery environment, Sally had been brought up on Dry Earth, where, although it seems to Sally and the other inhabitants that there is a watery liquid that forms lakes and rivers and to which they try to refer with the word 'water', in fact there are no lakes and rivers; rather Dry Earth inhabitants are subject to a grand delusion. According to the kind of externalism which Wright thinks is essential to the reductio, in the Dry Earth scenario, the word 'water' would fail to express any concept. Although it would seem to the subjects as if they were thinking about a substance they call 'water', they would suffer an illusion of thought.

With this background, Wright argues that the reductio argument meets the template, taking A, B, and C to be the following:

A = I believe that water is wet

B = I, or my speech community, has had such and such encounters with water

C = The seeming thought which I attempt to token by 'I believe that water is wet' is content-defective owing to the reference failure of the purported natural-kind term 'water' in my language

So interpreted, the reductio meets Wright's four conditions for the template. In particular, "Proposition *A*, that I believe that water is wet, entails—on the assumption of the necessary truth of the relevant strong externalism—proposition *B*, I, or my speech community, has had such and such encounters with water" (Wright 2000a: 145). Proposition *C* is incompatible with *A*. "My warrant for *A* consists in my being in a state which is subjectively indistinguishable from a state in which the relevant proposition *C*, that the seeming-thought which I attempt to express by 'I believe that water is wet' is content-defective owing to the reference failure of the purported natural kind term, 'water', in my language, would be true" (Wright 2000a: 145). For the kind of externalism under discussion accepts that a subject who has in fact been brought up on Earth and thinks that water is wet could be in a subjectively indistinguishable state had she instead been brought up on Dry Earth, where she suffers an illusion of seeing a watery liquid, and thus suffers an illusion of thought. Last, *C* would be true if *B* were false: if the subject were in an environment that lacked water, then she would suffer an illusion of thought.[2] Given that the reductio meets the template, Wright argues that one's warrant for the first premise of the reductio is conditional on having prior and independent warrant for the conclusion. As a result, he says (2000a: 156), warrant fails to transmit from the premises to the conclusion and so a subject cannot gain a priori warrant for the conclusion by inference from her a priori warrant for the premises.

The fact that Wright's argument that warrant fails to transmit across the reductio depends on the claim that warrant for the premise *A* is conditional on prior and independent warrant for the conclusion *B* sets up the second objection to Wright's account. Wright's claim that warrant fails to transmit across the reductio is offered as a defense of the compatibility of externalism and privileged access, the claim that a subject can have a priori knowledge of her thought contents (Wright 2000a, esp. secs. VI and VII). So the kind of warrant which the subject has for *A*, 'I believe that water is wet', is a priori. This raises the question, what kind of prior and independent warrant does the subject have for the conclusion *B*, 'I or my community have had such and such encounters with water', on which her a priori warrant for *A* depends? Wright argues that we must suppose that the relevant warrant for the conclusion is a priori also. For, he says, if the subject's warrant for the premise *A* were conditional on her having empirical evidence for the conclusion, then her warrant for *A* would not be a priori. Thus, he holds, she has an a priori warrant for the conclusion. For example, Wright says, "If one has a priori warrant for both premises of the McKinsey argument, it is courtesy of an a priori entitlement to discount the possibility of illusions of content, and hence to discount any scenario that would generate such an illusion" (2000a: 216–217). Since Wright holds that one would suffer an illusion of thought if the conclusion, *B*, were false, this quote implies that one has an a priori entitlement to discount the falsity of the conclusion, and thus an a priori entitlement for its truth. Elsewhere Wright says that my warrant for discounting *C* and thus for holding that *A* is true, depends on "antecedent reason to think that my tokenings of 'water' comply with appropriate externalist constraints, exactly as described by *B*" (2000a: 157). But, he adds that if this "antecedent reason for discounting *C* had to be empirically acquired, this line of thought would after all involve dismissal of the groundlessness of self-knowledge in the relevant kind of case; rather, evidence would be presupposed that 'water' indeed possessed the appropriate historical connections." So he seems to hold that my having a priori warrant for the first premise of the reductio, *A*, requires me to have prior and independent a priori warrant for its conclusion, *B*.

We might wonder how Wright's account of the failure of transmission of warrant is supposed to provide a solution to the reductio if it is part of this account that the subject has a priori warrant for the conclusion of the reductio. Admittedly, Wright defends an a priori warrant to the conclusion of the reductio on grounds other than by inference from the premises. But surely what makes the reductio problematic in the first place is not merely the idea that the reductio subject gains a priori knowledge of the conclusion from the premises, but that she should have a priori knowledge of substantive facts about the world. For it seems absurd to suppose that someone could have knowledge of what substances are in her environment without grounding that knowledge on empirical investigation of her environment. If that is right, then Wright's supposed solution to the reductio is just as problematic as the original problem the reductio posed.

Now, Wright could avoid this objection if warrant for the first premise of the reductio were conditional not upon having prior and independent warrant for the conclusion, but rather just on the truth of the conclusion. For we should allow that a subject may have a priori warrant and knowledge of some proposition, even where her having that a priori warrant depends on certain empirical conditions. For example, suppose that a mathematician *S* derives a mathematical proposition *p* by inference from a priori known premises. She checks the inference carefully;

it seems to her to be valid, and indeed it is so. We should allow that such reasoning may result in a priori warrant and knowledge of the proposition in question. But S's having that a priori warrant may depend on certain empirical conditions obtaining, say that it is not the case that, through some brain deterioration, she has lost her mathematical ability and can no longer tell whether an inference is valid or not. So, in general, a subject may have an a priori warrant for some proposition even where her having that warrant depends on certain empirical conditions. However, this line of thought cannot be used to provide a better version of Wright's view which avoids the problematic claim, made by Wright himself, that the reductio subject has prior and independent a priori warrant for the conclusion of the reductio. As Wright himself notes (2000a: 214), it is central to his defense of the failure of the transmission of warrant that the subject's warrant for the premise of the reductio is conditional on her having prior and independent warrant for the conclusion, rather than merely on the conclusion's being true. If warrant for the premise of the reductio is conditional on having prior and independent warrant for the conclusion, one first needs warrant for the conclusion in order to have warrant for the premise. Given this, warrant for the premise fails to constitute a reason to accept the conclusion. However, this argument for the failure of transmission would not apply if having warrant for the first premise were conditional merely on the conclusion's truth. For then one would neither need to believe the conclusion nor have warrant for it in order to have warrant for the premise.

I have argued that Wright's solution to the reductio is no less problematic than the original problem it poses. For it is part of Wright's solution that the subject has an a priori warrant for the conclusion prior to and independent of her warrant for the premises. How, though, does Wright suppose that the subject has prior and independent a priori warrant for the conclusion of the reductio? Wright explicitly defends the idea that one has a priori entitlement against the possibility of illusions of thought analogous to one's a priori entitlement to discount the possibility of perceptual illusions: "I have to take certain perceptions to be reliable if I am to investigate the reliability of others; I have to take certain seeming-thoughts to be well-founded if I am to investigate the well-foundedness of others."[3] Further, as we have seen, Wright argues that the reductio meets the template for the failure of transmission in part because if the conclusion of the reductio were false, then the subject would suffer an illusion of thought. It may be that Wright assumes that an a priori entitlement against the possibility of illusions of thought generates an a priori entitlement against the possibility of conditions sufficient for such illusions, such as the falsity of the conclusion of the reductio.[4] But should we accept that if a subject has an a priori entitlement to discount the possibility of suffering an illusion of thought, then she has an a priori entitlement to discount any scenario sufficient to generate such an illusion? I think we can see that this suggestion is unacceptable by considering the analogous suggestion about perceptual illusion: if a subject has an a priori entitlement to discount the possibility of suffering a perceptual illusion, then she has an a priori entitlement to discount any scenario sufficient to generate such an illusion.

Suppose that Dosey attends a lecture on perceptual illusions. Seeming to see a file, she forms the (true) belief that she sees a file. Of course, if she were suffering a perceptual illusion, then she would be in a state subjectively indistinguishable from the one she is in. Nonetheless, as we have seen, Wright holds that Dosey is a priori entitled to discount the possibility of a perceptual illusion. Suppose that the lecturer reports the latest scientific discovery that lacking neural activity N is sufficient for a subject to suffer perceptual illusions. If an a priori entitlement against perceptual illusions generates an a priori entitlement against conditions sufficient for such an illusion, then Dosey should have an a priori entitlement against the possibility that she lacks N. But we can fill out the case so that this is implausible. Suppose that Dosey misses the crucial link between perception and neural activity N, since she falls asleep intermittently in the talk. She wakes up while the lecturer is describing a subject undergoing neural activity N. As a result of the lecture, Dosey forms the belief that her brain is undergoing such neural activity. She has no evidence for this, for she missed most of the lecture and, in particular, the link between vision and neural activity N. In this case, we would surely deny that her belief that she is undergoing neural activity N is one for which she has warrant or entitlement. If a subject comes to form a substantive belief about the activity in her brain on the basis of no evidence, surely she lacks warrant or entitlement for this belief. Thus, if Dosey is ignorant of the link between N and illusion, and has no other evidence about the state of her brain, she lacks a priori warrant to discount the possibility, sufficient for having a perceptual illusion, that she lacks neural state N. So, in general, having an a priori entitlement to discount illusions of perception does not generate an a priori entitlement to discount conditions sufficient for such an illusion.

Wright could attempt to defend a more restricted claim, saying that an priori entitlement to discount illusions of perception or thought generates an a priori entitlement to discount a condition sufficient for such an illusion only if the subject believes that the condition is sufficient for such an illusion. Suppose, then, that sometime after the lecture, Dosey learns of the link between illusion and activity N from another source, and uses this to make the following inference: I am seeing a file; if I am seeing a file, then my brain is undergoing activity N; so my brain is undergoing activity N. Nevertheless, it is hard for Wright to argue that she is a priori entitled to believe that she is undergoing neural activity N. For, first, Dosey has at best empirical warrant of the conditional linking N and illusion. Second, the argument from the premise that she sees a file to the conclusion that she is undergoing N fits Wright's template for the failure of the transmission of warrant, where A, B, and C are the following:

A = I am seeing a file

B = My brain is undergoing neural activity N

C = I am suffering a perceptual illusion

In particular, given the neural result linking lack of N and perceptual illusion, A entails B.[5] And A is clearly incompatible with C. My warrant for A is a state subjectively indistinguishable from one in which I would be suffering a perceptual illusion. Given the connection between lacking N and perceptual illusion, if B were false, then C would be true. Thus, on Wright's own account, Dosey cannot gain warrant for the conclusion that her brain is undergoing N on the basis of this inference. Thus her entertaining this inference cannot change her situation from one in which she lacks entitlement for the belief that her brain is undergoing N to one in which she has entitlement for that belief. So it seems that we should reject the claim that if we have an a priori entitlement against illusions of thought and perception, we also have an a priori entitlement against conditions sufficient to generate such illusions. When Dosey is ignorant of the connection between N and perceptual illusion, and has no other evidence about the state of her brain, she lacks warrant for the claim that her brain is undergoing N. If we add in the claim that Dosey knows of the connection and uses it to infer that her brain is undergoing N then, on Wright's own view, this cannot make it the case that Dosey has warrant for the claim that her brain is undergoing N.

The Dosey argument undermines one possible way for Wright to claim that the subject has a priori warrant for the conclusion of the reductio, B. On the way suggested, she has an a priori entitlement against the possibility of illusions of thought, and, it is claimed, such an entitlement generates an a priori entitlement against conditions sufficient for such an illusion, such as the negation of *B*. So she has an a priori entitlement for *B*. However, this suggestion is undermined by consideration of the implausibility of the analogous claim about perception, that an a priori entitlement against the possibility of perceptual illusions generates an a priori entitlement against the possibility of conditions sufficient for such an illusion.

3 Conclusion

We have considered one of the main responses to the reductio argument. The reductio seems to show that if externalism and privileged access were both true, then a subject could gain a priori knowledge of substantive claims about the nature of her environment by inference from a priori knowledge of her thoughts and philosophy. Some have taken this as an objection to the compatibility of externalism and privileged access; others have taken it to show that externalism combined with privileged access offers a solution to skepticism about the external world. Wright responds by arguing that warrant fails to transmit from the premises to the conclusion of the reductio and thus that even if externalism and privileged access were both true, a subject could not use her knowledge of her thoughts and of philosophy to gain by inference a priori knowledge of her environment. However, we have rejected his account of why warrant fails to transmit across the reductio. Wright's argument that warrant fails to transmit across the reductio proceeds in two steps. First, he argues that the reductio meets a certain argument template. Second, he argues that any such argument is conditional in form. But the second claim would be rejected by those endorsing epistemic externalism, the outlook adopted by many externalists about mental content. In addition, Wright's "solution" to the reductio is no less problematic than the original reductio, since it too involves the claim that a subject can have an a priori entitlement to substantive claims about the nature of the world. It is anyway unclear how the reductio subject is supposed to have such warrant. Perhaps Wright thinks that it follows from his claim that the subject has a priori warrant against the possibility that she is suffering an illusion of thought. But we have seen that it is problematic to claim that if a subject has an a priori entitlement to discount the possibility of illusions of thought and perception, she has a priori entitlement to discount conditions sufficient (or known to be sufficient) to generate such illusions. It seems, then, that we need to look for an answer to the reductio argument elsewhere.[6]

Notes

1. I have formulated transmission and closure slightly differently from Wright, who says, "Closure [of warrant], unrestricted, says that whenever there is warrant for the premises of a valid argument, there is warrant for the conclusion too. Transmission, unrestricted, says more: roughly, that to acquire a warrant for the premises of a valid argument and to recognize its validity is to acquire— perhaps for the first time—a warrant to accept the conclusion" (Wright 2000a: 141). My formulation here is designed to apply with minimal change to both warrant and knowledge. It is implausible to claim that if a subject has warrant for, or knowledge of, the premises of a valid argument, then she has warrant for, or knowledge of, the conclusion. She might not believe the conclusion of the argument or realize that the argument is valid and, even if she does, she might believe the conclusion on completely different grounds.

2. Wright (forthcoming, sec. 5) notes that it's not quite right to say that if B were false, then C would be true. Admittedly, if the subject were on Dry Earth, she would suffer an illusion of thought. But B might also be false if she were instead on Twin Earth, where instead of suffering an illusion of thought, she would have the different concept of twater. He suggests a modification of his argument to deal with this problem, which I cannot discuss here but does not undermine my arguments.

3. Coherence theorists might reject this claim and argue instead that one investigates whether a given perception is well-founded by examining overall coherence. To do this, one need not take any given seeming perception as a perception. Rather, one takes a seeming perception as a perception if it coheres with other seeming perceptions.

4. See, e.g., the above citation from Wright 2000a: 216–217.

5. Of course, the fact that I'm seeing a file does not by itself entail that my brain is undergoing N. But then neither does the first premise of the reductio by itself entail the conclusion. Nevertheless, Wright (2000a: 156) takes the reductio to fit his template, since the first premise when combined with the second entails the conclusion.

6. Many thanks to the Leverhulme Trust for a generous Philip Leverhulme Prize, which enabled me to write this paper. Thanks also to my colleagues at Bristol, and members of the departments at Glasgow and Stirling, for their comments on an earlier version of this paper.

6

Externalism and Self-Knowledge[1]
Fred Dretske

Metaphysics is always creating problems for epistemology. The fact that there is an external world, other minds, a past, a moral law, or things too small to be perceived is held to create problems for how we can know any of this to be so. If we cannot know it, then some philosophers prefer to let the epistemological tail wag the metaphysical dog. The metaphysics is wrong. There is no physical world; it is a fiction, a story that the mind spins out of elements (ideas, sense-data, or whatnot) that are epistemically more accessible. Or there is no objective moral law; only shadowy projections of subjective attitudes and feelings.

It is happening again. Externalism about the mind—the metaphysical doctrine that thought and maybe even experience are constituted by extrinsic, relational facts about a person—is held to pose problems for how we can know, in the special authoritative way that we do, what is happening in our own mind. And, once again, there is a temptation to trash the metaphysics in order to salvage the epistemology. Thought and experience cannot be relational, because if they were, people couldn't know, in the privileged way that they do, what they are thinking and experiencing. But people do know. So thought and experience are not relational.

I think the right response to this alleged conflict is not to abandon (what I regard as) a plausible metaphysics but to reexamine (what I regard as) a suspect epistemology. We do not embrace phenomenalism because skeptics find problems in how we can know there is an external world. What we do, instead, is use these problems to achieve a deeper understanding of what knowledge of the external world amounts to. We should, I submit, do the same thing with knowledge of our own minds. Opting for a more austere metaphysics to salvage a proprietary epistemology may sometimes be a good strategy (I myself prefer it in the case of the moral law), but not *always*. In some cases, we should reevaluate the epistemology. That is what I do here.

I am an externalist about mental content. I believe that the content of mental states—what it is we believe, desire, and intend (I also include the character of phenomenal states [see Dretske 1995], but I leave that more controversial claim aside for now)—is an extrinsic, relational property of a person. Beliefs are in the head, but what makes them beliefs, what gives them their intentional content, what makes them *about* something, are the relations in which these internal states stand (or stood) to external affairs. In this respect, beliefs are like money. The money is in your pocket, but what makes it money isn't in your pocket. The fact that it is money is constituted by the external conditions (in this case, economic and social) in which these objects serve as a medium of exchange.

I am not only an externalist about mental content, I am an externalist about *all* forms of representation. What makes *A* represent *B*, what makes *A* say or mean something about *B*, are not the intrinsic properties of *A* but, rather, something about the purpose or function of *A* in an larger informational enterprise. What makes an instrument on the dashboard of a car mean or say that the car is going 60 mph is the fact— and it is a relational fact—that the purpose of this instrument is to convey information about speed. Remove this purpose, this informational function, and the object becomes representationally lifeless. It no longer says anything—at least something that (like a belief or a statement) could be false. What makes splotches of ink mean something is not their shape, color, and size (i.e., intrinsic properties), but rather something about their relation to outside affairs, something (broadly speaking) about how they are used. And the same is true of the objects and events in our brains. They acquire a meaning, they become representations— thereby acquiring content and becoming mental—by acquiring (via either evolution or individual learning) an appropriate informational function.

What I have just described is metaphysical externalism about the mind. It is, in a rough and ready form, my version of externalism. Like all forms of externalism, it denies that thought supervenes on the neurobiology of the thinker. This, we are told, creates a problem. It seems to be incompatible with privileged knowledge of what is going on in one's own mind. How can one know, in the special, authoritative way that one does, that one is thinking about water if thinking about water consists of relations that exist between the thinker and other parts of the world? If, as some externalists hold, you cannot think that something is water without having stood in causal relations to water, then it seems to follow that to know, in a special authoritative way, that you think you are drinking water is to know, in that same authoritative way, that there is (or was) water. But you cannot know, at least not in *that* way (as you know that you think you are drinking water), that there *is* water. So thinking that there is water cannot consist of relations (causal, informational, functional, or what-have-you) to water. It cannot depend on there being water. Indeed, it cannot consist of any relations of the sort externalists propose, since this would imply that we could know, by introspection, by gazing inward at our own thoughts, that these external conditions obtained. So externalism is false.

There is something wrong with this argument, but the mistake is subtle and by no means obvious. It assumes that knowledge of what is in your mind is, or requires, knowledge that you have a mind. It assumes that knowledge of what you think—for instance, that there is water— is (or requires) knowledge that you think. This is false. The special authority we enjoy about our own minds is an authority about what we think—that, for instance, there is water—not about the fact that we think it. My purpose in this paper is to argue that this is indeed so, and that therefore this key assumption in epistemological arguments against externalism is false.

Let me get started in this task by talking about simple measuring instruments. People are probably tired of hearing me talk about gadgets and gauges when the topic is supposed to be the mind—presumably a more lofty topic—but I think we can learn something about self-knowledge by looking at more humble representational devices. I think we can learn something important from measuring instruments because although the representational content of an instrument is extrinsic, the instrument nonetheless carries accurate information about exactly how it is representing the world. Notice that I say it carries information about *how* it is representing the world. I do not say that it carries information *that* it is representing the world. That turns out to be an altogether different matter. If instruments knew things, they would know how they are representing the world—the content of their representational states— but they would remain completely ignorant of the fact that they are representing the world. To see how this is possible for an instrument makes it easier to see how we do it.

Think about an instrument that represents the value of some quantity Q—temperature, voltage, velocity, or whatever. When functioning normally, as it was designed to function, it carries information about the quantity Q. That is to say, it was constructed, and is connected to the source, so that, when things are working right, its registration of "5" (on a scale labeled "Value of Q") depends on the value of Q actually being 5. When it is broken or malfunctioning, the instrument might misrepresent Q. It registers "5" and thereby "says" (so to speak) that Q is 5 when Q has some other value. What gives this physical object the power to represent or say that Q is 5—even, notice, when Q is not 5—is that it has a specific information-providing function or purpose. It is, according to design, *supposed* to tell us, its users, what the value of Q is. This informational function gives it the power to say things—even things that are not so. This, of course, is a case of derived intentionality, since the purposes that give this object its representational powers are our purposes.

It is easy to modify this instrument and make it say something not only about external affairs—some object's Q value—but about itself. We can make it tell us how it is representing external affairs, what it is representing Q to be. We can give it this additional function by simply affixing an additional label to the scale. Originally it was labeled "Value of Q." We now add the label "Value that Q is represented as having." Now, when the pointer points at "5," the instrument does two things: it represents some external object as having a Q of 5 and it represents itself as representing this object as having a Q of 5. By pointing at "5," it still says that Q is 5, but again by pointing at "5," it also says that this is what it is saying. In virtue of the two interpretative schemes provided by the two labels, the instrument does two representational jobs by occupying one physical state.[2] The instrument is fallible about the first thing it says, but infallible about the second. It can be wrong about Q, but it cannot be wrong about how it represents Q. An instrument may fail to carry information about the objects it was designed to represent. If the instrument registers "5," the value of Q may or may not be 5. It all depends on how well the instrument is working. But when we interpret the pointer position according to the second label, the one that reads "Value that Q is represented as having," the device becomes infallible. It cannot, even when broken, misrepresent how it is representing Q. If instruments knew things, then this instrument might or it might not know what the value of Q is—that would depend on how well it is working—but it would certainly know (at least be able to know—having information isn't sufficient for knowing) how it is "perceiving" Q. It would know what it "thought" the value of Q was. About this topic—the content of its own thoughts about Q—it has authoritative (because infallible) and privileged (no other instrument enjoys this kind of authority about this Q-meter's representational states) information. As long as we assume that a Q-meter represents something as having a Q of 5 by pointing at the numeral "5" on a suitably calibrated scale,[3] Q-meters are infallible about what they "think" (that is, represent) about their own representational efforts.

This much, I say, is easy. It is easy to make a representational device, say, with infallible authority about how it is representing the world. It is easy because such devices necessarily carry information about how they are representing the world, and all we have to do to get them to tell us is ask them. Putting an appropriate label on their face enables them to "tell" us what they "know" about their own representational activities at the same time they are telling us what they "think" about external affairs. But although it is easy to rig an instrument that has this kind of authoritative and privileged self-knowledge about its own representational activities, it is not so easy—indeed, I think it is impossible—to make an instrument that carries the information that it is representing the world. For that an object represents Q depends not on its intrinsic nature (e.g., having a pointer that points at the numeral "5") but on its purpose, on what it was designed to do, on what it is used to do, and these are facts about the intentions and purposes of its makers and users that are not reflected in any intrinsic fact about the object—whether, for example, it has a pointer and, if it does, where that pointer is pointing. This should be evident from the fact that we could build something that was structurally (i.e., intrinsically) the same as a Q-meter with entirely different intentions. If our purposes were sufficiently different, the product, a physical twin of a Q meter, would not represent Q. Our creation might be a paperweight or a decorative *objet d'art*, but it would not be a Q-meter. Or (with apologies to Donald Davidson) we can imagine something, call it swampmeter, materializing randomly out of cosmic dust that turns out, quite coincidentally, to be physically indistinguishable from a genuine Q-meter. Lacking any informational purpose, swampmeter will be devoid of representational content. Its registration of "5" will not (unlike a real Q-meter) mean that Q is 5 in what Grice called the nonnatural sense of meaning, though it might, if connected properly, mean that Q is 5 in the natural sense (it might, that is, carry this information). Objects lacking an information-carrying function do not represent Q. They do not, in the relevant sense, say anything about Q. That is why metal flag poles and paper clips, though expanding and contracting as the temperature varies and thereby carrying the same information as thermometers, do not represent temperature as thermometers do. Thermometers (when broken or badly manufactured) can misrepresent temperature, but flagpoles (even when broken or badly manufactured) cannot—unless we somehow give them the (additional) function of indicating temperature. That is why swampmeter, though physically indistinguishable from a genuine Q-meter (a device that can misrepresent Q) lacks the power to represent (and therefore misrepresent) Q. An object's behavior testifies not to the fact that it has an information-carrying function—and hence to the fact that it represents—but only to how it represents things, given that it has that function.

It seems, then, that although there is no problem in conceiving of a representational device as infallibly representing (and thus "knowing") how it represents the world (as 5 rather than 4 or 6), there are problems—and they may be insuperable—in thinking of it as knowing (i.e., having the information) that this in fact is what it is doing— *representing Q.* As far as the instrument can tell, it could be a paperweight or a result of some cosmic accident. If it is a measuring device, it can, by the intrinsic state it occupies, eliminate some alternatives (that it is representing the value of Q as 4 or as 6) without eliminating others (that it is not representing Q at all).[4] As a result, a representational device always has information about how it represents the world, but it always lacks information that this is what it is doing. If object O represents Q, it sometimes (when it is working right) carries information about Q; it always (even when it is not working right) carries information about how it is representing Q, but it never carries the information that it is representing Q.

Enough about instruments. What does all this have to do with the mind? Well, the general drift should be obvious. If, like me, you think of the mind as the representational face of the brain and if, like me, you also understand representation in terms of informational functions, the conclusion will be evident enough: although we do not have information that we are representing the world—that we are thinking and experiencing—nonetheless, if we are representing it, if we are thinking and experiencing, we always have information about just how we are doing it, about the content of these mental states. If we think, we can know—in a privileged and authoritative way—what we think. What we can't know, at least not in the same authoritative way, is that we are thinking it. If we know it, we know it in some way other than introspection. What introspection gives us is the content of our cognitive states (that there are cookies in the jar), not the fact that this is content (something we actually think).

I know this conclusion sounds paradoxical. It flies in the face of a cherished and deeply entrenched Cartesian doctrine, the doctrine that the first and most indubitable fact is that we think. If that fact isn't secure, nothing is secure. Or so I will surely be told.

I think this fact—the fact that we think—is secure enough. I'm no skeptic.[5] Nevertheless, I do not think it is the fulcrum around which all cognition pivots. It is not a fact yielded by the same faculty— introspection—that tells us what we think and experience, nor is it a fact of which we are directly aware. Introspection is not how we know that we think and feel. It is how we know what we think and feel. Introspection is no more a way of knowing that we think and feel than is perception, our primary way of knowing what else is in the world, a way of knowing that there is something else in the world. This analogy is helpful, I think, so let me expand a bit on it.

I know my keys are still in my pocket because I can feel them there. I can see that there are still a few cans left in the fridge. That is how I know there is some beer left. I can smell—that is how I know—that the toast is burning. Notice: none of these things I come to know—things I learn by feeling, seeing, and smelling—can be true unless there is an external, mind-independent, world. Keys, beer, and burning toast (in contrast to experiences of keys, beer, and burning toast) are not mental. Does this mean I can feel, see, or smell that there is an external world? Does it mean that I can see, feel, or smell that I am not hallucinating, that there really are mind-independent objects—keys, beers, toast—that exist outside my experience of and thoughts about them? Of course not. Skepticism is not refuted so easily. We cannot see that there is an external world, although the things we come to know by seeing (that there is beer in the fridge, keys in my pocket) imply that there are things (namely, beer and keys) outside my mind. If there is an external world, sense perception gives you reliable information about what is in it, but sense perception cannot provide the information that there is such a world. To know that there is an external world, you have to discover it in some way other than by sense perception—the faculty that, if there is such a world, tells you what is in it.

Although our descriptions of what we come to know by seeing, hearing, and smelling imply there is an external world, they do not describe how we know there is an external world. They either presuppose that we know it, or (my own view) they take such knowledge to be irrelevant to the perceptual knowledge such reports describe us as acquiring. Knowing there are physical objects is irrelevant to our ability to see that there is beer in the fridge for the same reason that having information (and thus knowing) that I am actually representing something is irrelevant to having information (knowing) how I am representing it. Knowing that I represent Q as 5 implies I am representing Q, but it doesn't imply that I know I am or that I am even capable of getting the information that would let me know it.

Another way of expressing this is by saying that although you can see (and hence know) that there is beer in the fridge, you cannot see what you know to be a consequence of this—that you are not a brain in a vat or that there are physical objects in the world. You certainly cannot see that you are not a brain in a vat or that there are physical objects in the world in the way you can see that there are cookies in a jar or beer in the fridge. If you know you are not a brain in a vat, *that* is not how you know it. So your way of knowing p is not a way of knowing q, even though you know you couldn't know p unless q were true.

Thirty years ago in *Seeing and Knowing* (1969), I tried (not very successfully I now think) to describe this feature of perceptual verbs by speaking of protoknowledge. Protoknowledge was my way of talking about the things that had to be true, maybe even the things you had to take for granted, for one to see (and hence know) that something was so, but facts that one need not (perhaps could not) see to be so. Seeing that there are cookies in the jar requires there to be physical objects— cookies—yes, but it certainly doesn't require one to see, or even be able to see, that there are physical objects. Seeing that a waitress is getting angry requires the waitress to have a mental life, but it doesn't require me to see, or even be able to see, that she has a mental life, that she's not a zombie. Perception is not an answer to the skeptic's problem about other minds. The skeptical objection that you cannot see there are cookies in the jar (or that the waitress is angry) because you cannot know what is required for there to be cookies in the jar (for the waitress to be angry)—namely, that there actually are physical objects (other minds)—struck me then, as it still does today, as a misrepresentation of what we are claiming to have done when we claim to have seen that something was so. When I claim to know that there are cookies in the jar because I see that there are, I am not claiming to see, even to be able to see, nor (I would argue) to know, that there are physical objects. That there are physical objects is implied by what I find out by seeing, but it is not something I find out by seeing. I'm not even sure it is something I can find out.

In *Seeing and Knowing* I compared skepticism to worries about whether Pierre could have done what he claims to have done: walked all the way to New York City. If the worry is based on the fact that Pierre cannot walk on water—hence cannot have got to New York City from Paris (Pierre's home) by walking—it is (or may be) quite irrelevant to what Pierre said he did. For Pierre, in claiming to have walked to New York City, may have been claiming only to have walked to New York City from Hackensack, N.J., not at all a difficult feat even for a Parisian. In evaluating someone's claim to have walked to *x*, we first have to know where they walked from. Until we know that, we don't know whether they are claiming to have done something easy, hard, or physically impossible. The claim to have walked all the way to New York City doesn't provide that kind of information. Nor do perceptual claims; they tell you where the claimant is supposed to have arrived, but they don't tell you where he came from in arriving there.

Whether there are valid skeptical objections to someone seeing that there are cookies in the jar depends not only on what he learned—that there are cookies in the jar—but where, so to speak, he came from in learning it. How significant the epistemic achievement is—whether it was easy, difficult, or (as the skeptic claims) impossible—depends on what possibilities (to there being cookies in the jar) the claimant fore-closed on visual grounds. Seeing that there are cookies in the jar is a way of ruling out, on visual grounds, *some* alternative possibilities, but which possibilities were eliminated is determined by context. The perceptual report—*S* saw that there were cookies in the jar—doesn't provide this crucial piece of information.

I am not—at least not now—rejecting a general principle of closure. Closure—that you know all the things you know to be implied by what you know—is controversial, but I am not now challenging it. I have done that elsewhere. That isn't the issue here. I am here rejecting a much less plausible—indeed, I think an obviously false—cousin of closure, the notion that a way of knowing *p* is a way of knowing all the things you know to be implied by *p*. There are facts we learn by seeing, hearing, smelling, and introspection that imply things we cannot learn by seeing, hearing, smelling, and introspection. Our ways of finding out, our methods of discovery, are not closed under known implication.

My earlier discussion of a *Q*-meter was merely a way of illustrating this point in the case of information. Though instruments carry information about how they represent Q, they do not—indeed, they cannot—carry information implied by the information they do carry—that they are representing Q. Carrying information (I neglected to point out in Dretske 1981) is not closed under (known) logical implication. A pressure gauge carries information about pressure—that the pressure is 5—but it does not (indeed, cannot) carry certain pieces of information that are implied by this—that, for example, it is not malfunctioning and, as a result, misrepresenting a pressure of 4 as 5. It cannot carry the information that it is not, as it were, suffering under some instrumental illusion.

This same point holds for introspection. Whatever way we have of telling what it is we think and experience is not a way of telling that we think and experience it. In the same way that if we know there is an external world, it must be in some way other than the ways we have of knowing what is going on in the world; if we know we have minds, it has to be in some way other than the way we have of telling what is going on in our minds. Perception, our most important way of telling what is happening in the external world, doesn't tell us that there is an external world, and introspection, our authoritative way of telling what is happening in our minds, doesn't tell us we have minds.

Despite being an externalist about the mind, then, I am untroubled by the (by me) undisputed fact that we enjoy privileged and authoritative access to what is going on in our minds. Certain external conditions—I happen to think they are partly historical in nature—must obtain for thought and experience to exist. I also think that we have privileged and authoritative access to what we think and experience. But my privilege and authority do not extend to the fact that I think and experience—facts that are constituted by these external relations. My first-person authority extends only to the facts that, *given that these external relations obtain*, are internally accessible to me—to content, to what I think and experience.

This leaves me with a question: how do I know I have a mind? If introspection tells me only what I think and feel, not that I think and feel, how do I discover that I think and feel, that I'm not a zombie? I am tempted to reply, I learned this the same way I found out a lot of other things—from my mother. She told me. I told her what I thought and experienced, but she told me that I thought and experienced these things. Children make judgments about a variety of things before they understand the difference between how they judge and see the world to be (e.g., that there is candy in box A) and their judging and seeing it to be that way. Three-year-olds know, and they are able to tell you, author-itatively, what they think and see (e.g., that there are cookies in the jar, that Daddy is home, etc.), before they know, before they even under-stand, that this is something they think and see. Somehow they learn they can preface expressions of what they think (Daddy is home) with the words "I think," words that (somewhat magically) shelter them from certain forms of correction or criticism.[6] Parents may not actually tell their children that they think—for the children wouldn't under-stand them if they did—but they do teach them things (language must be one of them) that, in the end, tell them they think. Children are, at the age of two or three, experts on what they think and feel. They have to learn—if not from their mothers, then from somebody else—that they think and feel these things. Nonhuman animals never learn these things. This is exactly what one would expect on an externalist theory of the mind.

Notes

1. This paper is a descendant of a reply to Brian McLaughlin that I gave in Aix on Provence in May 1999. I wish to thank the participants in that conference, especially Elisabeth Pacherie and Simon Prosser, for many helpful suggestions. I also want to acknowledge the influence of Sven Bernecker's work (1996, 2000) on my thinking about introspection.

2. We could put two identical scales on the face of the instrument, each with its own label. In one respect, this would come closer to modeling the situation I'm interested in, namely, one representational state representing the way another representational state is representing the world. My point, however, is made as well with two labels for a single scale.

3. We needn't. As Simon Prosser at the Aix conference pointed out to me, there is the possibility that we could put the wrong numbers on the face of a properly functioning instrument and thereby make it "say" that it was representing Q to be 5 (the pointer points at the numeral "5") when, in terms of actual pointer position, it was representing Q to be 4 (the pointer occupies a position that it is designed to occupy when Q has a value of 4). This is, I concede, a way of making an instrument fallible about its own representational states. But we are fallible about our own representational states in the same way. We can teach someone to describe red things with the word "blue." Then when things look red to him, he will *say* they look blue. He will thus misrepresent, verbally misrepresent, his own representational state. Since the word "blue," even when coming out of his mouth, means *blue*, he says something false about his representational state. Our question, though, is not whether we can, in this way, verbally misrepresent our own mental states, but whether our judgments (however badly expressed) are fallible.

4. I have had it suggested to me that the on/off light found on some measuring instruments has the function of indicating that the instrument is on—thus carrying the information that the instrument is in a representational mode. When the instrument registers "0" with the light off, it does not represent Q to be 0. When it registers "0" with the light on, it represents (possibly misrepresents) Q to be 0. So the light carries the information that the instrument is representing (possibly misrepresenting) Q. I agree that the light indicates—at least it has the function of indicating—when the instrument is turned on, but I don't agree that it indicates that the instrument is representing Q. Swampmeter also has a light that goes on when a switch is closed, but swampmeter *never* represents anything. The light doesn't tell us—it has no way of telling us—that it is installed in a genuine Q meter rather than, say, a swampmeter.

5. Though I confess to being uncertain in this area. See Dretske, forthcoming.

6. See Evans 1982: 205–233 and Shoemaker 1988 for (what I regard as) attractive accounts of how we might learn to self-ascribe thoughts and experiences to ourselves without being aware (in a perceptual way) of the thoughts and experiences themselves.

7

A Puzzle about Doubt

Gary Ebbs

1   What Can an Anti-individualist Know A Priori?

My central goal in this paper is to identify and dissolve a puzzle that lies behind a vexing debate about what an anti-individualist can know a priori. In this opening section, I will review common assumptions and contested points of the debate, and briefly explain my misgivings about one of the common assumptions. In later sections I will identify and dissolve the puzzle that lies behind the debate.

Anti-individualism is the view that what a person believes and thinks is not settled by his linguistic dispositions, internal physical states, or phenomenal experiences, described independently of his social and physical environment. One central question about anti-individualism is whether it is compatible with *minimal self-knowledge*—the familiar fact that (in a sense yet to be clarified) we each know without empirical investigation what thoughts our own utterances express. If what we know without empirical investigation is what we know a priori, then the question of whether anti-individualism is compatible with minimal self-knowledge is linked to the question of what an anti-individualist can know a priori.

This question has been much discussed recently in the literature about anti-individualism. Although several answers to the question have been proposed, a single debate now dominates the discussion. On one side are those who argue that an anti-individualist who assumes she has minimal self-knowledge is committed to the unacceptable conclusion that she has a priori knowledge of some truths that in fact she *cannot* know a priori.[1] On the other side are those who argue that anti-individualists are not committed to this unacceptable conclusion.[2] Philosophers on both sides of the debate assume that minimal self-knowledge is second-order, in the sense that statements that express such knowledge have the logical form 'I am thinking that *p*', where '*p*' is replaced by a declarative sentence.[3] They also assume that both reason and introspection can be sources of a priori knowledge.[4]

Much of literature about the debate has focused on an argument by Michael McKinsey (1991a: 9). The argument presupposes that a priori knowledge is "knowledge obtained independently of empirical investigation." Suppose that I utter the sentence 'Water is a liquid at room temperature', thereby expressing the thought that water is a liquid at room temperature. Suppose also that I have minimal self-knowledge, so I know without empirical investigation that I am thinking that water is a liquid at room temperature. By assumption, a priori knowledge is knowledge obtained without empirical investigation, so I know a priori that (1):

(1)   I am thinking that water is a liquid at room temperature.

If anti-individualism is correct and I accept it, McKinsey assumes, I am in a position to know by reasoning alone, hence a priori, a *conceptual* truth of the form 'If I am thinking that water is a liquid at room temperature, then *E*', where *E* is a statement that most philosophers would say I cannot know a priori.[5] I am in a position to know a priori, for instance, that (2):

(2)   If I am thinking that water is a liquid at room temperature, then either I or members of my linguistic community have seen or touched water.

And if I can know a priori that (1) and (2), then by modus ponens I can deduce, and thereby know a priori, that (3):

(3)   Either I or members of my linguistic community have seen or touched water.

But it seems that no one can know a priori that either he or members of his linguistic community have seen or touched water. Hence anti-individualism apparently implies that a person can have a priori knowledge of some statements that in fact he cannot know a priori. I will call this McKinsey's argument.

The orthodox reply to McKinsey's argument (implicit in Burge 1982a, explicit in Brueckner 1992a and McLaughlin and Tye 1998) is that despite appearances to the contrary, an anti-individualist who assumes he has minimal self-knowledge has no reason to think he can know a priori *any* statement that most philosophers would say he cannot know a priori. According to this reply, to know what one is thinking when one utters a particular sentence, one need not know or presuppose any empirical statements. Premise (2) of McKinsey's argument may be true, but even if it is true, it is not a *conceptual* truth, as McKinsey assumes, and so we cannot know it a priori.

The initial plausibility of this reply masks a deep problem with both sides of the debate. The problem can be traced back to a widely accepted but unexamined assumption about how an anti-individualist should analyze epistemic possibility. Twin Earth thought experiments suggest that for each person we can describe *subjectively equivalent worlds* in which everything that is relevant to the person's subjective assessment of her situation seems the same to her as it does in the actual world, but her social or physical environments are different from her social or physical environment in the actual world. According to the standard analysis of epistemic possibility, no one can know by reasoning or introspecting—without empirical investigation—which of her subjectively equivalent worlds she is actually in.[6]

The problem, I will argue, is that this standard analysis of epistemic possibility conflicts with the truism that *to express a thought, one must have some idea of what that thought is.* To defend and clarify the truism, I will argue that contrary to the standard analysis of epistemic possibility, if we accept anti-individualism, there are some apparently empirical statements that we cannot make sense of doubting.

2   Anti-individualism and Self-Knowledge

To see the conflict between the truism and the standard analysis of epistemic possibility, it helps to reflect first on the methodology behind Putnam's (1975) Twin Earth thought experiments, which have persuaded many to accept anti-individualism. In my view, these thought experiments are persuasive because they are based in our practice of taking fellow English speakers' words at face value.[7]

Recall the thought experiment involving Oscar, an ordinary English speaker who is competent in the use of the English word 'water' but does not accept (or reject) the sentence 'Water is H_2O'. Suppose that Oscar utters the sentence 'Water is a liquid at room temperature'.[8] Since Oscar is a competent English speaker, other English speakers take his words at face value—they take him to have said that water is a liquid at room temperature. If they think his utterance is sincere, they also take him to believe this.

Now suppose there is a planet called Twin Earth, which is just like Earth except that wherever there is water on Earth, there is twin water, a liquid with an underlying chemical structure very different from the chemical structure of water, on Twin Earth. On Twin Earth there lives a physical, phenomenological, and behavioral twin of Oscar, Twin Oscar, who is a normal speaker of Twin English, the Twin Earth counterpart of English. When Twin Oscar utters the sentence 'Water is a liquid at room temperature', his fellow Twin English speakers take his words at face value—they take him to have said (translated into English) that twin water is a liquid at room temperature. If they think his utterance is sincere, they also take him to believe this.

Together with our trust in our practice of taking other speakers' words at face value, these observations show that what a person believes and thinks is not settled solely by his linguistic dispositions, internal physical states, or phenomenal experiences, described independently of his social and physical environment. This negative thesis is what I call anti-individualism.[9]

Putnam (1975) also argued that even in 1750, *before* scientists on Earth and Twin Earth discovered the chemical properties of water and twin water, respectively, a competent English speaker who uttered the sentence 'Water is a liquid at room temperature' thereby expressed the thought that water is a liquid at room temperature, while his twin on Twin Earth expressed the thought (translated into English) that twin water is a liquid at room temperature. In my view, it is because we endorse our practice of taking each other's words at face value across time, from moment to moment, and even for centuries, that we can see that in both linguistic communities, looking backward from today, the references of the words for water and twin water did not change when the chemical properties of the liquids to which they apply were discovered.[10]

If we endorse our practice of taking each other's words at face value, we can also see that minimal competence in the use of a word requires more than simply writing or uttering sentences in which the word occurs. We wouldn't take a speaker to be using the English word 'apple' competently if she applies it only to points of light visible in the night sky. Yet a child who at first refuses to call a green apple an 'apple' might still be taken to be able to use the word 'apple' to express thoughts about apples, and to believe of the green apple that it is not an apple, provided that she has some other beliefs about apples, including some true beliefs that she expresses by using the sentence 'That's an apple'.[11] Our firmest grip on the requirements for minimal competence is our practice of taking each other's words at face value in a given context, unless we see some concrete reason in that context for not doing so.[12]

These observations about minimal competence are intimately linked with our judgments about when a speaker has minimal self-knowledge.[13] To credit a speaker of a given natural language with minimal self-knowledge is to take her to be able to use words of her own language to express thoughts, make claims, raise questions, and so on. Any situation in which we are willing to take another's words at face value is thereby also one in which we will credit her with having minimal self-knowledge.[14] Viewed in this way, minimal self-knowledge is a practical aspect of ordinary competence in the use of language, not a kind of second-order propositional knowledge, as many philosophers assume. Unlike second-order propositional knowledge of what one is thinking, minimal self-knowledge is as widespread as the everyday use of language to express thoughts, evaluate believes, raise questions, and so on.[15] In taking other speakers' words at face value, we thereby also take them to know what they are talking about in a minimal sense that goes with competence.[16]

These observations clarify the truism that *to express a thought, one must have some idea of what that thought is.* To take someone to express a thought by using a given word is also to take him to have some beliefs that he expresses by using that word. These beliefs may be false or misleading, but not just any utterances of sentences containing a word suffice for minimal competence in the use of the word, as the 'apple' example shows.[17]

3   Apriority and Epistemic Possibility

The only assumption that McKinsey explicitly makes about a priori knowledge is that it is "knowledge obtained independently of empirical investigation" (1991a: 9). Most philosophers involved in the debate sketched above simply repeat McKinsey's characterization of a priori knowledge and agree with him about which beliefs the person can know a priori. It is widely agreed, for instance, that no one can know a priori that members of her linguistic community have seen or touched water.[18]

But McKinsey's characterization of a priori knowledge does not explain this agreement. To see why, consider my belief that physicists in my linguistic community have detected quarks. I have read this in authoritative books, but have never undertaken any empirical investigation into whether it is true. By ordinary standards, I am epistemically *entitled* to believe that physicists in my linguistic community have detected quarks; if this is true, then I know it independently of empirical investigation. Similarly, an unusually sheltered person who is *told* that members of her linguistic community have seen or touched water might be epistemically *entitled* to believe this without undertaking any empirical investigation into whether the person who told her this is trustworthy or whether it is true; if it is true, then by ordinary standards she knows it independently of empirical investigation. It therefore seems that according to McKinsey's characterization of a priori knowledge, she knows a priori that members of her linguistic community have seen or touched water. But it is supposed to be obvious that no one knows a priori that members of her linguistic community have seen or touched water.

One might think that in both of these cases the knowledge gained by testimony is not independent of empirical investigation, because it can be traced back to empirical observations made by others. But minimal self-knowledge cannot be independent of empirical observation in this sense, since it requires minimal competence, which typically depends on accepting testimony from others.[19] For a large number of words, the testimony that we accept when we acquire competence in the use of those words can be traced back through chains of similar testimony to speakers who have made empirical observations that support it. In the context of anti-individualism, then, we cannot assume that a given person's minimal self-knowledge is independent of everyone *else's* empirical observations. The most we can say is that to have minimal self-knowledge is to know what thoughts one's utterances express without going through any empirical investigation of one's own.

For this reason, McKinsey's characterization of a priori knowledge does not explain why so many philosophers agree with him about which statements can be known a priori. What does explain this? The answer, I believe, is that most philosophers presuppose a tempting but misguided analysis of epistemic possibility that looks like an immediate consequence of the Twin Earth thought experiments themselves. As I noted earlier, the Twin Earth thought experiments suggest that for each individual, we can describe *subjectively equivalent worlds* in which her physical and phenomenal states, described independently of her environment, are the same, but her environments are different.[20] Most philosophers assume that no one can distinguish between any of her subjectively equivalent worlds just by reasoning or introspecting—that all of a person's subjectively equivalent worlds are epistemically possible for her.

They find this analysis of epistemic possibility appealing on its own terms, for two reasons that I will soon discuss. In addition, I believe, they find it attractive because it is like the analysis of epistemic possibility that Saul Kripke introduced in *Naming and Necessity* to solve a puzzle about his view of reference and necessity. The puzzle is that in Kripke's view, if Hesperus is identical to Phosphorus, then there is no possible world in which Hesperus is not identical with Phosphorus. Prior to our discovery that Hesperus is identical to Phosphorus, we assumed that 'Hesperus is identical with Phosphorus' may actually be false. Hesperus is in fact identical to Phosphorus, however, and so, by Kripke's theory, Hesperus is *necessarily* identical with Phosphorus: we can't express our prior assumption by saying that it could have turned out that Hesperus is not identical to Phosphorus. Kripke therefore had to provide a new analysis of our previous assumption that 'Hesperus is identical with Phosphorus' may actually be false. He stipulated that "given the evidence that someone has antecedent to his empirical investigation, he can be placed in a sense in exactly the same situation, that is a qualitatively identical epistemic situation, and call two heavenly bodies 'Hesperus' and 'Phosphorus', without their being identical" (1972/1980: 104).

Kripke suggested that since prior to our empirical investigation, we could not discriminate between these worlds on the basis of our evidence, we may actually have been in a world in which 'Hesperus is not identical to Phosphorus' is true. He explicitly connected this analysis with the traditional idea of a priori knowledge: "Two things are true: first, that we do not know a priori that Hesperus is Phosphorus, and are in no position to find out the answer except empirically. Second, that this is so because we could have evidence qualitatively indistinguishable from the evidence we have and determine the reference of the two names by the positions of two planets in the sky, without the planets being the same" (Kripke 1972/1980: 104). I suggest that this characterization of a priori knowledge is what lies behind the agreement that a person cannot know a priori, for instance, that members of her linguistic community have seen or touched water. The idea is that she can't know without empirical investigation that she is not in any one of her subjectively equivalent worlds in which no member of her linguistic community has seen or touched water.

Most philosophers writing about what an anti-individualist can know a priori take this analysis of epistemic possibility for granted, without giving any reasons why we should accept it.[21] Kripke himself does not *argue* for his analysis of epistemic possibility; he presents it as obvious and beyond question.[22] To evaluate it, however, we need a better idea of why so many philosophers accept it.

I think that there are two main reasons. The first is that they want to make sense of Descartes' radical skeptical hypotheses about the nature and existence of an "external" world, including the hypothesis that all my experiences, from the beginning to the end of my life, are parts of an elaborate dream, and the hypothesis that I am massively deceived by an evil demon. To find these hypotheses compelling is to picture a vast gulf between how things *seem* and how they *are*. In the context of anti-individualism, a tempting way of picturing this supposed gulf is by holding our subjective experiences constant and specifying different external environments compatible with all those subjective experiences. Many philosophers assume that to entertain the thought that they are in one of these worlds, it is enough for them to *picture* the subjective experiences they would have in these worlds (experiences that are by definition the same as the subjective experiences they have in the actual world) and then add a caption that describes an "external" world that is compatible with the picture. In what follows, I'll say that to combine one's subjective experiences with a caption in this way is to *picture oneself* in a specified subjectively equivalent world. Most philosophers assume that for a person to entertain the thought that she is actually in one of her subjectively equivalent worlds, she need only *picture herself* in it.[23]

A second reason why so many accept Kripke's analysis of epistemic possibility is that it provides a natural interpretation of the traditional view that a priori knowledge is based on reasoning or introspecting, independent of any evidence from the senses, and that neither reasoning nor introspecting, by themselves or in combination, can tell us which possible world we are in.

4   The Puzzle

It follows from the standard analysis of epistemic possibility just described that if I restrict myself to what I can know without empirical investigation, I must accept (4):

(4)   I may actually be in any of my subjectively equivalent worlds.

Yet I assume that without empirical investigation, I know what thoughts my utterances express. For instance, I assume without empirical investigation that I am epistemically entitled to accept (5):

(5)   My utterances of 'Water is a liquid at room temperature' express the thought that water is a liquid at room temperature.

If I am justified in accepting (4) and (5) without empirical investigation, then I am justified in concluding (6) without empirical investigation:

(6)   In all of my subjectively equivalent worlds, my utterances of 'Water is a liquid at room temperature' express the thought that water is a liquid at room temperature.

The trouble is that the normal procedure for conducting thought experiments that support anti-individualism implies the negation of (6):

(7)   In some of my subjectively equivalent worlds, my utterances of 'Water is a liquid at room temperature' do not express the thought that water is a liquid at room temperature.

Thus I seem committed to accepting the conjunction of (6) and (7)—a contradiction.

One strategy for trying to avoid this contradiction is to question whether we can know without empirical investigation all the premises that generate it.[24] With this in mind, I constructed this puzzle so that each of its claims, (4) to (7), appears to be independent of empirical investigation. The key premise, (4), apparently follows from our understanding of the phrase "subjectively equivalent world." And we can't give up (5) without abandoning the presumption that anti-individualism is compatible with minimal self-knowledge. Given (4) and (5), we cannot deny (6). It seems that the only claim that *may* require empirical justification is (7).

To construct a thought experiment that supports (7), we need to understand the possible worlds we are describing well enough to see that in those worlds our utterances of sentences would express different thoughts from the ones we take them to express. (This is just another illustration of the truism that to express a thought one must have some idea of what that thought is.) For instance, to support (7) by constructing an anti-individualistic thought experiment involving my word 'water', I must presuppose that the subjectively equivalent world that I *take* to be different from the one that I am actually in is *in fact* different from it. But if all my subjectively equivalent worlds are epistemically possible for me, I can't know without empirical investigation which of my subjectively equivalent worlds I am in. One might therefore think that I cannot support (7) without empirical investigation.

Let's say that a *substantive* statement for a given person is any statement of hers that according to the standard analysis of epistemic possibility she cannot know without empirical investigation. A substantive statement for a person is true in some of her subjectively equivalent worlds and false in some of her subjectively equivalent worlds.[25] For instance, my statements that water is a liquid at room temperature and that I am not in the subjectively equivalent world in which I was born, raised, and now live on Twin Earth are substantive, because according to the standard analysis of epistemic possibility, I cannot know these statements without empirical investigation.

Let's also say that if a person affirms a substantive statement that *p*, then she holds a *substantive belief* that *p*, and that if she *suspends* this belief, then she does not affirm or deny that *p*. Then the reasoning presented two paragraphs above presupposes that I can have minimal self-knowledge of what thoughts I express by using a given group of terms even if I suspend all the substantive beliefs I express by using those terms. On this view, I know what thoughts I express by asserting my sentence 'Water is a liquid at room temperature', for instance, even if I suspend any substantive beliefs that I could express by using the terms 'water', 'liquid', or 'temperature'.

The trouble is that for most terms I use, I can't have minimal self-knowledge of what thoughts I express by using those terms if I suspend all the substantive beliefs I express by using those terms. To have minimal self-knowledge, one must be able to use one's own words to make claims, raise questions, express thoughts, and so forth. Moreover, as I've already noted several times, it is a truism that to make claims, raise questions, and express thoughts, one must have some idea of what those claims, questions, or thoughts are. For most terms of English, including such terms as 'water', 'liquid', or 'temperature', for instance, a person who suspends all substantive beliefs that she would express by using one of those terms is incompetent in its use and does not count as expressing any thoughts by using it.

One can appreciate this aspect of the puzzle without endorsing my view that anti-individualism implies that to make claims, raise questions, and express thoughts, one must have some idea of what those claims, questions, or thoughts are. It is enough simply to *assume* that we have minimal self-knowledge, and to accept the truism. But the account of anti-individualism that I sketched earlier deepens and consolidates this aspect of the puzzle, by explaining why anti-individualism requires that we have minimal self-knowledge, and why we can't have minimal self-knowledge unless we have some idea of what thoughts our utterances express. The key point is that in a large number of ordinary cases, to take a person to have expressed a particular thought by uttering a given sentence is to take her to be minimally competent in the use of the terms that make up the sentence. This requires that she have some substantive beliefs—affirm some substantive statements—that she expresses by *using* those terms. As I argued above, a speaker is incompetent in the use of a word—whether it be a widely shared word of a public language, or a word that only a few idiosyncratic speakers share—if she refuses to affirm *any* substantive statements in which it occurs.

The puzzle, then, is this. It seems that without empirical investigation, we are each epistemically entitled to accept (4), because it follows from the standard analysis of epistemic possibility; (5), because we have minimal self-knowledge; and (7), because it follows from the Twin Earth thought experiments. But (4) and (5) together entail (6), which is the negation of (7). If we reject (7) for this reason, we must suspend all our substantive beliefs, so we can't be credited with having minimal self-knowledge, and hence we must reject (5). Yet (5), an instance of minimal self-knowledge, is in fact a consequence of anti-individualism, as I argued above.[26] We are therefore apparently committed to each of (4) through (7), including the contradictory pair (6) and (7).

5   *My Strategy for Dissolving the Puzzle*

The weakest premise of the puzzle is the one that almost everyone accepts without reflection—premise (4). I will argue that in the same sense of 'know' in which we know without empirical investigation what thoughts our utterances express, we can know without empirical investigation that (4) is false. It is a formidable task to make this seem plausible, however, given the popularity of the standard analysis of epistemic possibility, which is sustained by two almost irresistible assumptions: first, that we can make sense of radical Cartesian doubts, and second, that we can't know by reasoning or introspecting which of our subjectively equivalent worlds we are actually in. It is no answer to these deeply entrenched assumptions simply to *assert* that we can know without empirical investigation that (4) is false.[27]

To challenge the standard reasons for accepting (4), we must distinguish between two questions:

(Q1)   Given what I know without empirical investigation, is it epistemically possible for me that I am actually in any one of my subjectively equivalent worlds?

(Q2) Are there worlds $w_1, \ldots, w_n$ such that (a) $w_1, \ldots, w_n$ are among my subjectively equivalent worlds and (b) I can know by reasoning or introspecting, without relying on any of my substantive beliefs, that I am not in any of $w_1, \ldots, w_n$?

These questions are not explicitly addressed in the literature about what an anti-individualist can know a priori, but I speculate that philosophers who are attracted to (4) would reason roughly as follows:

"The answer to (Q2) is 'No,' because I can't discriminate between my subjectively equivalent worlds by introspecting, and reasoning can only be a source of knowledge about what is in some sense necessary, but all my subjectively equivalent worlds are possible. Hence I cannot know by reasoning or introspecting, without relying on any of my substantive beliefs, which of my subjectively equivalent worlds I am in. Therefore, for all I know without empirical investigation, I may actually be in any one of my subjectively equivalent worlds. Hence the answer to (Q1) is 'Yes.' "

Against this, I will argue that to solve the puzzle we must see that the answer to both (Q1) and (Q2) is "No." Since I agree with the standard assumption that the answer to (Q2) is "No," I must show why, despite this answer to (Q2), the answer to (Q1) is "No," and, as a consequence, we can know without empirical investigation that (4) is false.

The heart of my argument is that even if the answer to (Q2) is "No" and I restrict myself to what I know without empirical investigation, not all of my subjectively equivalent worlds are epistemically possible for me. I start by assuming that it is epistemically possible that p for a given person only if she can make sense of its actually being the case that p. Most philosophers assume that all of a person's subjectively equivalent worlds are epistemically possible for her *because* they assume that each person can make sense of actually being in any one of her subjectively equivalent worlds. I will argue that this is an illusion sustained by the mistaken assumption that for a person to make sense of actually being in any one of her subjectively equivalent worlds, it is enough for her to *picture herself* existing in that world.

6   Epistemic Possibility and Doubt

To get clear about what is epistemically possible, we must make a number of distinctions and clarifications. First, at any given time t, subject *A* will have a number of beliefs and a range of observational evidence; what is epistemically possible for *A* (at *t*) depends on *A*'s beliefs and observational evidence (at *t*). Second, to say that *p* is epistemically possible for *A* (at a given time *t*) is to say that *A* can make sense of its actually being the case that *p* (at *t*). Third, *A* can make sense of its actually being the case that *p* (at *t*) only if *A* can *express* the possibility that *p* (at *t*).

Fourth, human fallibility tells us nothing about what is epistemically possible for a person at a given time. To see why, suppose that Alice has just constructed what she regards as a proof of a mathematical theorem *T*; she has checked her work carefully, and shown it to a number of prominent mathematicians, who all find it compelling and correct. It does not follow that her proof is correct, or that *T* is true, and she knows this. Nevertheless, it is not epistemically possible for her that not *T*. Epistemic possibility requires more than mere fallibility; it requires that we be able to specify a way in which the supposed epistemic possibility may be actual.[28] To specify a way in which it may actually be the case that not *T*, Alice would have to be able to specify a way in which one of her axioms may actually be false, or a way in which the logic she used may actually be inconsistent. But this she cannot do, if she has what she regards as a proof of *T*.[29]

These preliminary clarifications may be summed up as follows: *p* is *epistemically possible* for *A* (at *t*) if and only if *A* can make sense of its actually being the case that *p* (at *t*), in the sense that *A* can *specify* a way in which it may actually be the case that *p* (at *t*). These clarifications don't by themselves *rule out* the standard analysis of epistemic possibility. Together with anti-individualism, however, they can help us to see why the standard analysis of epistemic possibility is incorrect.

Anti-individualism provides a framework for investigating, for a given speaker *A* and a statement *p*, whether or not *A* can specify a way in which it may actually be the case that not *p*. For instance, suppose Alice believes that she is not in the subjectively equivalent world in which she was born, raised, and now lives on Twin Earth, but she has not looked for empirical evidence that might settle this question. She wonders whether that world is epistemically possible for her—whether she can specify a way in which she may actually be in the subjectively equivalent world in which she was born, raised, and now lives on Twin Earth.

According to the standard analysis of epistemic possibility, she can easily specify a way in which she may actually be in that world. All she has to do is describe the world and *picture* herself in it. To do this, she need only say, 'Suppose I am in a world that *seems* to me exactly like this world, except that I was born, raised, and now live on Twin Earth'.

But this does *not* show that she can specify a way in which she may actually be in that world. For if Alice understands and accepts anti-individualism, she should reason as follows:

(8)   I am now using this sentence to express the thought that water is a liquid at room temperature.

(9)   If I were actually in the world in which I was born, raised, and now live on Twin Earth, I could not use sentence (8) to express the thought that water is a liquid at room temperature.

(10)   Therefore, I am not actually in the world in which I was born, raised, and now live on Twin Earth.[30]

Alice accepts (9), because she accepts anti-individualism and realizes that if she were actually in the world in which she was born, raised, and now lives on Twin Earth, her uses of 'Water is a liquid at room temperature' would express the thought (translated into English) that twin water is a liquid at room temperature. As part of her minimal competence in the use of 'Earth', 'Twin Earth', 'water', and 'twin water', she takes for granted that Twin Earth is not Earth and that the twin water is not water. Given her understanding of the thought she expresses by affirming (9), she can't reject (10) without rejecting (8).

But Alice can't make sense of rejecting (8). She takes for granted that she has some idea what thoughts she is entertaining when she accepts the above argument, including premise (8). But the epistemological principle that supposedly should lead her to reject (8)—the principle, based on the standard analysis of epistemic possibility, that she can coherently think that she may actually be in any one of her subjectively equivalent worlds—implies that she can coherently suspend all her substantive beliefs. If Alice were somehow to suspend all her substantive beliefs, she could no longer think of herself as minimally competent in the use of *any* words, including the words that compose (8). She would no longer have any idea what thought (8) expresses, and so she could no longer think of herself as rejecting the claim that (8) expresses.

If Alice can picture herself existing in the world in which she was born, raised, and now lives on Twin Earth, then she can add to her first-person subjective experiences a caption in English that states that they are experiences of the world in which she was born, raised, and now lives on Twin Earth. When Alice uses the words 'I may actually be in the world in which I was born, raised, and now live on Twin Earth', she takes for granted that she has some idea of what she is talking about. More generally, when a person pictures herself existing in a subjectively equivalent world that she can describe, she *presupposes* that she has minimal self-knowledge of what thoughts her descriptions of that world express. For this reason, a person cannot use her capacity to picture herself existing in a given subjectively equivalent world to *undermine* her assumption that she has minimal self-knowledge.

You might think that this reasoning just expresses my *preference* for the anti-individualist's "intuitions" that we have minimal self-knowledge and that the subjectively equivalent world we are in settles what thoughts our utterances express, on the one hand, and my *rejection* of the intuition that to make sense of being in any one of our subjectively equivalent worlds, all we need to do is picture ourselves in it, on the other. Perhaps the puzzle in (4) to (7) ultimately comes down to a clash of intuitions. If so, we could just as well reject the anti-individualist's intuitions and embrace the traditional intuition that to make sense of being in any one of our subjectively equivalent worlds, it is enough to picture ourselves in it.

It is very misleading, however, to say that the anti-individualist's thought experiments depend on intuitions. Recall that to accept the conclusions of Putnam's Twin Earth thought experiments is to endorse the practice among English and Twin English speakers of taking their fellow speakers' words at face value, together with our stipulations about how sentences of Twin English are to be translated into English.[31] These clear aspects of Putnam's reasoning are obscured by the claim that the Twin Earth thought experiments merely elicit our "intuitions" about what individuals believe in different circumstances. If our best grip on thoughts and beliefs is rooted in our practices of attributing beliefs and thoughts, then the conclusions of the Twin Earth thought experiments are not based on intuitions that may be weighed against other intuitions, and possibly rejected; they challenge any philosophical assumptions that conflict with them, including the assumption that we can make sense of being in any one of our subjectively equivalent worlds just by picturing ourselves in it.

I conclude that if we accept anti-individualism, we must reject (4). Taking for granted a number of substantive beliefs, we can specify subjectively equivalent worlds that we cannot make sense of actually being in; from our perspective, any attempt to specify a way in which those worlds may be actual is self-undermining. By the criterion articulated at the beginning of this section, therefore, these worlds are not epistemically possible for us.[32] Once we reject (4), we can accept (5) without committing ourselves to (6), which is the negation of (7). This dissolves the puzzle, by leaving us free to accept (5) and (7) without contradiction.

7 Do I Know That p If I Can't Make Sense of Doubting That p?

Suppose that I use the argument (8) to (10) to support (10), applied to myself. Many readers will be inclined to respond as follows:

"You have not shown that you are not in the subjectively equivalent world in which you were born, raised, and now live on Twin Earth; you have simply *presupposed* it. To establish that you are not in that world, you must be able to show that you are not in that world without relying on any of your substantive beliefs, hence without making any prior commitments about which subjectively equivalent world you are actually in. You would be able to do that only if you had some cognitive faculty that would enable you to see directly, without relying on any empirical assumptions, which subjectively equivalent world you are actually in. But there is no such cognitive faculty. Hence you do not *know* that you are not in that subjectively equivalent world."

There is something right about this objection: by reasoning or introspecting, without relying on any substantive beliefs, I cannot derive any conclusions about what world I am in. What the objection overlooks, however, is that if I *don't* presuppose enough substantive beliefs to have some idea what am talking about, I cannot take myself to be able to describe *any* of my subjectively equivalent worlds. If I presuppose enough substantive beliefs to have some idea of what I'm talking about, then some of the subjectively equivalent worlds that I can describe are worlds that I can't make sense of actually being in.

This shows, I think, that the answer to both (Q1) and (Q2) is 'No'. In my view, we should reject (4), which was supported by the 'yes' answer to question (Q1). But we should agree with most philosophers that the answer to question (Q2) is 'No', although not for the reasons they give. We can't simultaneously take ourselves to be able to *describe* some proper subset of our subjectively equivalent worlds and *suspend* all our substantive beliefs. For this reason, the answer to question (Q2) is 'No'—we can't know by reasoning or introspecting, without relying on any of our substantive beliefs, that we are not in some proper subset of subjectively equivalent worlds that we can specify. But for the same reason, many of our substantive beliefs are beliefs that we can't actually make sense of doubting. We can see without special empirical inquiry that some subjectively equivalent worlds that we can describe are worlds that we cannot coherently describe as being actual. But if we cannot coherently describe a given world as being actual, then that world is not epistemically possible for us: given substantive beliefs that we find ourselves unable coherently to doubt, no empirical investigation is required for us to know that we are not in that world. The answer to (Q1) is 'No', and we know without empirical investigation, in the sense just explained, that (4) is false. This dissolves the puzzle and leaves us free to accept (5) and (7) without contradiction.

This proposed dissolution to the puzzle depends on distinguishing between the claim that we know a given statement *a priori* and the claim that we know the statement *without empirical investigation*. Many of the statements that we know without empirical investigation are statements that we cannot know a priori, in any standard sense of that term. What we know without empirical investigation includes what we are *entitled* to believe without going through any special empirical investigation. Empirical investigation always relies on substantive beliefs, which therefore cannot all be simultaneously supported by empirical investigation. To say that a person's belief that p is independent of empirical investigation is to say that from her perspective there is (for the moment, at least) no coherent way to doubt that p. It is in this sense that a person can know without empirical investigation that she is not in the subjectively equivalent world in which she was born, raised, and now lives on Twin Earth.[33]

One might find it odd to say that a person can know this if from her perspective there's no coherent way to doubt it. One might think, instead, that to know that p one must be able to provide a reason for believing that p that does not beg the question of whether p or in any way presuppose that p. I agree that if knowledge does require such a reason, then a person's inability to make sense of actually being in one of the subjectively equivalent worlds that she can describe does not count as knowledge that she is not in that world. I suggest, however, that not all cases of knowledge require independent justification.

To justify any knowledge claim, one must take for granted some other beliefs or claims for which we are unable to give independent reasons, but which we nevertheless take ourselves and others to be *entitled* to accept. Some of these other beliefs or claims are so fundamental to our way of thinking that they deserve to be called knowledge, even if we cannot provide independent reasons for accepting them. One indication that a belief has this kind of fundamental status for a person is that she can't make sense of doubting it—from her perspective, any attempt to specify how the belief may actually be false is self-undermining. I suggest that if a person accepts a given statement and she cannot make sense of doubting it for the reasons just described, then she is epistemically entitled to believe it. Since from her perspective, any attempt to specify how the belief may actually be false is self-undermining, she cannot provide reasons for believing it that are more firm or secure than her acceptance of the statement itself. In practice we take such beliefs to amount to knowledge, partly because they set the framework for our practice of making and evaluating knowledge claims. I propose that to understand this practice, we take ourselves to *know* that we are not in some specified subjectively equivalent world if from our perspective, any attempt to specify how we may actually be in that subjectively equivalent world is self-undermining.[34]

But why not reserve the word 'know' for cases in which we can provide independent reasons for our beliefs or claims?[35] Why not accept that without empirical investigation, we *cannot* know which subjectively equivalent world we are in?

I reject this for two reasons. First, it suggests that we *can* know which of our subjectively equivalent worlds we are in if we engage in empirical investigation. But if we don't make any assumptions about which of our subjectively equivalent worlds we are actually in *prior* to engaging in any empirical investigation, then we will be unable to find out what subjectively equivalent world we are in by engaging in what we call empirical investigation. To see why, suppose that I am trying to discover whether I am in a world in which water is a liquid at room temperature. It follows from the definition of a subjectively equivalent world that my subjective experiences don't distinguish between any of my subjectively equivalent worlds. On the basis of some of my subjective experiences, which I regard as evidence about how things are in the world, I may come to accept the sentence 'Water is a liquid at room temperature'. But from this I cannot infer that I am in a world in which water is a liquid at room temperature, unless I presuppose that I am in a world in which my uses of the sentence 'Water is a liquid at room temperature' express the thought that water is a liquid at room temperature. But I know that in some of my subjectively equivalent worlds, my uses of the sentence 'Water is a liquid at room temperature' do not express the thought that water is a liquid at room temperature. Hence an "empirical investigation" that leads me to accept the sentence 'Water is a liquid at room temperature' does not support the conclusion that water is a liquid at room temperature. In fact, it does not support any conclusion that I could express by *using*, not mentioning, my word 'water'. The shows that if I don't know what thoughts my utterances express without empirical investigation, I can't *find out* what thoughts they express even if I try to engage in empirical investigation.[36]

My second reason for resisting the proposal is that it suggests that there is a deep gulf between beliefs we can't make sense of doubting, on the one hand, and truth, on the other, a gulf that we need a philosophical theory of knowledge to bridge. This suggestion is undercut by the observation that we can't specify how these beliefs may actually be false. The illusion that we *can* specify how these beliefs may actually be false is sustained by the mistaken assumption that to think that we are in a given situation it is enough to picture ourselves in it.

This is not to say that we cannot formulate any skeptical hypotheses at all. My argument does not show that I can't make sense, for instance, of actually being on Twin Earth right now, after being whisked away from Earth yesterday without my knowledge. The supposition that I am now in this situation does not conflict with my self-knowledge, because I would not turn into a speaker of Twin English if I spent just one day on Twin Earth without my knowledge. It may *appear* that there is a slippery slope from this kind of case to the conclusion that for all I know, I have been on Twin Earth for years, and so my uses of the sentence 'Water is a liquid at room temperature' express the thought that twin water is a liquid at room temperature. But the appearance is illusory, for the same reason that I can't make sense of being in the world in which I was born, raised, and now live on Twin Earth.[37] Those who find the standard analysis of epistemic possibility appealing *overgeneralize* from the fact that we can accept anti-individualism and still make sense of being on Twin Earth right now, for instance, to the puzzling and contradictory conclusion that we can accept anti-individualism and make sense of being in *any* one of our subjectively equivalent worlds. If we want to clarify what an anti-individualist can know without empirical investigation, we must resist the temptation to overgeneralize in this way.

My central point is that if we are convinced by the anti-individualists' thought experiments, then there are some beliefs that we cannot make sense of doubting—beliefs that are so basic for us that from our perspective, any attempt to specify how those beliefs may actually be false is self-undermining. I suggest that we view such beliefs as limiting cases of knowledge. Like any beliefs that we take to be knowledge, we may find reasons later to revise them. We may revise some of the background beliefs, such as our belief that water is different from twin water, that we now treat like definitions; after such revisions, we may find that we can make sense of doubting certain beliefs that we previously found it impossible to doubt. In these cases, we lose our entitlement to accept the beliefs, and we should revise or reject the beliefs unless we can provide reasons in the new context for accepting them. In retrospect, we may conclude that we did not know what we previously could not make sense of doubting. But if we can't now make sense of doubting that p, then the abstract possibility that we may later be able to make sense of doubting that p does not imply that we don't know that p, any more than our general human fallibility implies that when Alice takes herself to have a proof of a mathematical theorem, and all the trustworthy mathematicians she has consulted agree with her, she nevertheless doesn't know the theorem. Statements that we can't make sense of doubting in the sense described above are among the statements that we properly take ourselves to know without empirical investigation.[38]

Notes

1. This kind of argument is presented in McKinsey 1991a, Brown 1995, and Boghossian 1997.

2. This kind of reply is presented explicitly in Brueckner 1992a and McLaughlin and Tye 1998, and implicitly in a number of other papers about anti-individualism and self-knowledge, including Burge 1988b and Falvey and Owens 1994.

3. Following Burge 1988b and Davidson 1987, most discussions of minimal self-knowledge—including Boghossian 1997, Brueckner 1992b, McKinsey 1991a, and McLaughlin and Tye 1998—presuppose this second-order picture of self-knowledge. I will argue later that we should reject it.

4. There is disagreement about whether it is helpful to view "introspective" knowledge—the sort of a priori knowledge that we supposedly have of our own thoughts—as based in a kind of "perception" of one's own "inner" mental states. Tyler Burge (1988b) prefers to think of it as based in *understanding*, which involves actually *thinking* the thought, not merely regarding it as an object of one's knowledge. He accepts a modified Kantian conception of a priori knowledge, according to which "understanding is capable of yielding non-empirical and non-sensible cognition of thoughts in singular form" (2000: 28–29) and "warrant can be a priori if it derives from reason or from understanding, if it does not depend on sense experience for any of the force of its epistemic war-

rant" (2000: 28). For my purposes in this paper, however, the crucial point is that philosophers on both sides of the debate think that a priori knowledge is not exhausted by what we can know by reasoning alone: knowledge of contingent statements about what one thinks and experiences can also be a priori.

5. According to McKinsey (1991a: 14), our knowledge of anti-individualism is a priori knowledge of conceptual truths independent of empirical facts. In my view, anti-individualism is not a conceptual truth, and cannot be known a priori in any traditional sense of that term, as McKinsey assumes. But it *is* independent of empirical investigation, in an ordinary sense that I will clarify below. Since my primary focus is not on the epistemological status of anti-individualism, I will not take the time in this paper to explain how my view of what we know independent of empirical investigation applies to our knowledge of anti-individualism.

6. According to this analysis of epistemic possibility, our sensory evidence is confined to our subjective experiences. This raises an apparent problem: if our sensory evidence is the same in all of our subjectively equivalent worlds, regardless of how things are in the external world, then it seems we cannot know any particular facts about the external world, *whether or not* we engage in empirical investigation. But most philosophers are not radical skeptics, and it would be wrong to attribute to them a view of epistemic possibility that immediately implies radical skepticism. By this reasoning, it appears that what I call the standard analysis of epistemic possibility would be rejected by most philosophers. This challenge is serious, but not decisive, because many philosophers assume that some epistemic possibilities are so remote from the actual world that they are not relevant to our ordinary assessments of what we know, and so we need not rule them out in order to know what we ordinarily take ourselves to know. Those who embrace the standard analysis of epistemic possibility but are not radical skeptics hold some version of this "relevant alternatives" approach to evaluating knowledge claims. This is explicit in Burge 1988b: 655–656 and Burge 1999, for instance. For a sophisticated recent version of this way of avoiding skepticism, see DeRose 1995. I assume, provisionally, that the standard analysis of epistemic possibility, when combined with the "relevant alternatives" approach to evaluating knowledge claims, does not entail radical skepticism.

7. We sometimes have reason in a context for suspending this practice, but the practice embodies our default treatment of our fellow speakers' words.

8. It helps to imagine a context in which Oscar may actually say this. One possibility is that Oscar is explaining to his son that ice is (solid) water, not just that water *turns into* ice when it freezes. In this context, 'Water is a liquid at room temperature' may be the first of two sentences that Oscar utters, the second one being 'But ice is water, too—water that is at or below the freezing point'. This is compatible with our supposition that Oscar does not know that water is H_2O— Oscar may know that ice is water at or below the freezing point, even if he forgot, or never learned, that water is H_2O.

9. Putnam (1975) is standardly credited with showing that the *references* of a person's words are not are settled by his linguistic dispositions, internal physical

states, or phenomenal experiences, described independently of his social and physical environment. Burge (1979) is credited with making the corresponding case for beliefs and thoughts—the case for the stronger thesis that I am calling 'anti-individualism'. I have reconstructed Putnam's reasoning in a way that supports anti-individualism. Although I do not accept the standard interpretation of Putnam's (1975) reasoning, my goal here is not to present an historically accurate account of what Putnam actually thought but to highlight the methodology that in my view explains what is persuasive about Putnam's reasoning, whether or not he was clear about it.

10. Many philosophers assume that in the early 1970s Putnam and Kripke accepted this aspect of the Twin Earth thought experiment only because they believed they could explain it by constructing a causal theory of reference. But both Putnam and Kripke were cautious about whether reference could be given a noncircular explanation in causal terms. Moreover, no viable causal theory of reference has yet been constructed, but the force of the thought experiment remains. In my view, the idea that there is what Putnam called a "contribution of the environment" is rooted in our practice of taking each other's words at face value across time and does not depend on the existence of a substantive theory of reference that explains this practice. For more discussion of this point, see Ebbs 1997, 2000.

11. This does not imply that to use a given word, we *must* make some true demonstrative claims by using that word. Minimal competence in the use of some words can be picked up very quickly, just on the basis of what the speaker was told, even if what she was told is false.

12. This cannot be an informative criterion, because what counts as a concrete reason for suspending the practice is itself context-sensitive.

13. A speaker may use words that have the same *spelling* as words of a public language so idiosyncratically that her words have meanings different from the meanings that the identically spelled words have in the public language. Such uses would be judged incompetent as uses of the identically spelled public-language words, and yet the idiosyncratic speaker may still express thoughts by using her identically spelled words and have minimal self-knowledge of what thoughts she expresses by using them. This happens much less frequently than most individualists believe, however. And when it does happen, there are usually some words of the public language that the idiosyncratic speaker uses competently and that help other speakers to figure out what thoughts her idiosyncratic utterances express.

14. For a more thorough presentation of the points in this and the previous paragraph, see Ebbs 1996; 1997, secs. 100–123. For a parallel point about what it is to know the meanings of one's own *words*, see Putnam 1988: 32.

15. The kind of self-knowledge embodied in these everyday uses of language is not best viewed as a disposition to form justified second-order beliefs about what one is thinking, either. To credit someone with being able to form or justify such

second-order beliefs, we must presuppose that she already has the kind of minimal self-knowledge that goes with linguistic competence. This is the kernel of truth behind Brueckner's (1992b) criticisms of Burge and Davidson.

16. Those who are inclined to think that minimal self-knowledge is a cognitive achievement that requires more than being able to use one's words in discourse (as argued, for instance, in Bar-On and Long 2001 and Fricker 1998) may be conflating what I call 'minimal self-knowledge' with a deeper kind of self-knowledge that involves knowing what one believes, desires, and feels about a given topic. This latter sort of self-knowledge does not follow immediately from linguistic competence; it is a lifelong goal of most of us to achieve it, and we invariably fail in some respects.

17. Even an idiosyncratic speaker fails to know what thoughts she expresses by using her own words if she does not affirm any beliefs by using sentences that contain those words.

18. But some authors have noticed difficulties with McKinsey's characterization of 'a priori' knowledge. See Miller 1997 and Nuccetelli 1999. Neither Miller nor Nuccetelli questions the standard analysis of epistemic possibility, as I do below.

19. As J. L. Austin observed, "Reliance on the authority of others is fundamental ... for corroboration and for the correctness of our own use of words, which we learn from others" (1979: 83, n. 1).

20. One might doubt that a person's physical and phenomenal states, described independently of her environment, exhaust all that is relevant to her subjective assessment of her epistemological situation. I accept this now for the sake of argument. But I doubt that the resulting kind of "subjective equivalence" is relevant to epistemology, for reasons I will explain below.

21. The attitude is so widespread that it would be impractical to list all the works that are shaped by it. A small sample might include Boghossian 1997, Brueckner 1990, Falvey and Owens 1994, McLaughlin and Tye 1998, McKinsey 1991a, and McGinn 1976. Even Jaakko Hintikka, who disagrees with so much else in Kripke's work, writes, "It is the easiest thing in the world to imagine epistemically possible worlds in which a proper name refers to different objects" (1999: 140), thus endorsing a key feature of the standard analysis of epistemic possibility.

22. What I call Kripke's analysis of epistemic possibility is at best only an analysis of what might be called *empirical epistemic possibility*. It does not fit Kripke's example of Goldbach's conjecture that every even number greater than 2 is the sum of two primes. Kripke points out that it is epistemically possible for us that Goldbach's conjecture is true and epistemically possible for us that it is false. But if it is true, it is necessarily true (true in every possible world), and if it is false, it is necessarily false (false in every possible world). Suppose that in fact Goldbach's conjecture is true. Then we cannot analyze the epistemic possibility that it is false, for instance, in terms of the existence of subjectively equivalent worlds

in which it is false—by supposition, there are no such worlds. This shows that Kripke's analysis of epistemic possibility in terms of subjectively equivalent worlds must be restricted to *empirical* epistemic possibilities. Kripke and others apparently assume that we can know a priori whether or not a given epistemic possibility is empirical, and hence whether or not Kripke's analysis of empirical epistemic possibility applies to it.

23. Recall that those who embrace the standard analysis of epistemic possibility but are not radical skeptics hold some version of the "relevant alternatives" approach to evaluating knowledge claims. See note 6.

24. This is similar to the orthodox response to McKinsey's argument, which I discussed in the first section.

25. It may seem that there are contingent a priori statements, as Kripke (1972/ 1980) and others have argued, and so not *all* of a person's statements that are true in some of her subjectively equivalent worlds and false in some of her subjectively equivalent worlds are substantive. But anyone who accepts the reasoning in the previous paragraph of the text must conclude that if all of a person's subjectively equivalent worlds are epistemically possible for her, then even if she can know without empirical investigation that a particular contingent sentence expresses a truth, she can't know without empirical investigation *what* truth it expresses. Therefore, no one who accepts the reasoning in the previous paragraph of the text can hold that there are contingent but nonsubstantive statements. One might think that the two-dimensional approach, as presented, for instance, in Chalmers 1996 and Jackson 1998, is relevant to what a person knows a priori. There are several problems with this thought. The main problem is that anti-individualism is the thesis that the *de dicto* contents of a person's beliefs are world-involving contents that are settled partly by external factors, not the (imaginary) world-independent contents (Chalmers calls them "primary intensions") that yield different extensions at different worlds. Another problem is that there is no reason to think that our beliefs about how to apply our terms in the actual world are a priori, as Chalmers and Jackson claim. See Stalnaker 1999: 14 and essays 9–11.

26. Those who do not accept this argument can simply conjoin our ordinary assumption that we have self-knowledge with anti-individualism to get the same result.

27. Ted Warfield (1998) claims, in effect, that we can know a priori that (4) is false, but says very little about why (4) seems so gripping and how we can avoid the strong temptation to accept (4). For this reason, in my view, he does not really address the puzzle that lies behind the current debate about what an anti-individualist knows a priori.

28. Austin (1979: 98) emphasizes that human fallibility by itself is not a good guide to epistemic possibility or to what it makes sense to doubt.

29. There is a very weak sense in which a person can "make sense of doubting" *any* statement, even a statement that she can prove: she knows she is fallible and

may have made a mistake. In this weak sense, a person can "make sense of doubting" a statement that p even though she can't actually specify how it may actually be the case that not p, hence even though it is not epistemically possible for her that not p.

30. The argument (8) to (10) is similar in form to an argument I presented in Ebbs 1996; 1997, chap. 9. Anthony Brueckner (1997b) criticizes the argument, and I reply to his criticisms in Ebbs 2001. The argument (8) to (10) also is similar to (one version of) Putnam's argument (1981, chap. 1) that we are not always brains in vats. I discuss Putnam's argument in Ebbs 1992; 1997, chap. 9. See also Tymoczko 1989.

31. For similar observations about the methodology of belief attributions, see Kripke 1979. In my view, Kripke's observations about our ordinary practices of attributing beliefs do not inevitably lead, as he argues, to a puzzle about belief. Nor do I endorse his comment that "something's having intuitive content ... is very heavy evidence in favor of anything. ... I really don't know, in a way, what more conclusive evidence one can have about anything, ultimately speaking" (Kripke 1980: 42). Perhaps he and I mean different things by "intuition," but I do not find it illuminating to describe our most fundamental judgments about beliefs, for instance, as "based" on "intuition"—as though "intuition" were a quasi-perceptual faculty, such as sight or hearing.

32. If not all of our subjectively equivalent worlds are epistemically possible for us, how can we solve the puzzle about necessity that originally led Kripke to suggest that all of our subjectively equivalent worlds *are* epistemically possible for us? I don't have the space here to address this question properly; I will just give a brief hint of how I would proceed. In my view, a reasonable person may believe (without paraphrase into Kripke's model of epistemic possibility) that Hesperus is not necessarily identical to Phosphorus, for instance, even if Hesperus *is* necessarily identical to Phosphorus. I think that to accept this, one must also be convinced that Kripke's puzzle about belief (1979) is not a genuine puzzle, but a confusion fostered by questionable assumptions about what is required to make sense of a person's beliefs.

33. A related point is that our knowledge of anti-individualism itself, like all our knowledge, presupposes a background of entrenched substantive beliefs. Contrary to what many philosophers suppose, our knowledge of anti-individualism is *not* a priori in the traditional rationalists' sense.

34. I am not suggesting that we can tell what world we are in by reasoning or introspecting without relying on any of our substantive beliefs. If my argument is correct, then contrary to what is usually supposed, there is no such thing as reasoning or introspecting without relying on any of our substantive beliefs. To avoid confusion about this, we should not use the word "a priori" when we try to say what an anti-individualist can know without empirical investigation.

35. In a very different context, Ludwig Wittgenstein asserts, "One says 'I know' when one is ready to give compelling grounds. 'I know' relates to the possi-

bility of demonstrating the truth'' (1969, sec. 243). But there are also places in Wittgenstein 1969 where he seems more open to the use of 'know' that I am proposing.

36. I made the same argument in a slightly different way in Ebbs 2001, sec. 1. The argument undermines the assumption, which I accepted provisionally in note 6 of this paper, that a relevant-alternatives conception of knowledge can be used to prevent the standard analysis of epistemic possibility from implying radical skepticism. Here I can only hint at the reasons why: if we can't know what thoughts our sentences express, then even if we are somehow entitled to say that some sentences describe possibilities that are not relevant to our ordinary knowledge claims, we will not be entitled to use those sentences to say what possibilities those are. Hence our ''ordinary knowledge'' must be regarded as metalinguistic knowledge that certain of our sentences are true, in a context in which we are not entitled to use those sentences, since we do not know what thoughts we would thereby be expressing. This is no way to avoid skepticism!

37. I do not have the space here to defend this claim, which I have discussed in Ebbs 1996, esp. sec. VIII and n. 31.

38. I am grateful to Anthony Everett, David Hills, Hilary Putnam, and Charles Travis for helpful and timely comments on a previous draft.

8

Knowing That One Knows What One Is Talking About

Susana Nuccetelli

I

Twin Earth thought experiments, standardly construed, support the externalist doctrine that the content of propositional attitudes involving natural-kind terms supervenes upon properties external to those who entertain them. But this doctrine in conjunction with a common view of self-knowledge might have the intolerable consequence that substantial propositions concerning the environment could be knowable a priori. Since both doctrines, externalism and privileged self-knowledge, appear independently plausible, there is then a paradox facing the attempt to hold them concurrently. I shall argue, however, that externalist claims about the dependence of content on environmental factors presuppose certain theses about the semantics of natural-kind terms that, if sound, would make those claims eligible for empirical justification instead. In fact, that is the only interpretation of their epistemic status that could square with the standard conclusion from Twin Earth cases. Furthermore, the interpretation can be shown to solve the paradox of externalism and self-knowledge in a more doxastically conservative way— accommodating precisely each of the well-accepted intuitions about empirical knowledge, transmission of warrant by inference, and individuation of content given up by available competitors.

II

The attempt to hold both externalism and privileged self-knowledge seems to conflict with common intuitions about knowledge, sanctioning flagrant inconsistencies of this sort:

(1) Oscar can know a priori that his current propositional attitude involves a natural-kind term k.

(2)   Oscar can know a priori that, if his current propositional attitude involves a natural-kind term *k*, then there is a certain natural kind *K* in his environment.

(3)   Oscar could not know a priori that there is a certain natural kind *K* in his environment.

Now (1) and (2) are supported by independently plausible intuitions about self-knowledge and the individuation of mental content respectively. Given these premises, if a priori warrant (or knowledge) transmits through entailment, then (3)—a claim that rests on equally plausible intuitions about knowledge of the empirical world—must be rejected. To restore consistency, either (1), (2), or (3) ought to go, but which one? Hardly (1) or (2), since self-ascriptions of propositional-attitude contents appear every bit as a priori justified as the claim that those contents may often depend in part upon factors in the physical environment. When held concurrently, however, (1) and (2) may have the absurd consequence that, just by reflecting on the contents of one's own words and thoughts and their externalistic entailments, one could come to know entirely a priori substantial propositions about the physical world—and this conflicts with (3).

A resolution of this paradox appears to require the rejection of either privileged self-knowledge, externalism, or the thesis that a priori warrant transmits through entailment. Otherwise we are left with the absurdity of holding that one can know a priori substantial propositions about the environment. Yet each of these three is independently plausible. Thus, even though some such response might provide a venue for resolving the paradox (which may be overdetermined in any case), each would score poorly in doxastic conservatism. But a closer look at the semantic commitments of externalism may provide a strategy to resolve it with a good share of that epistemic virtue.

III

Twin Earth externalists (hereafter, 'externalists') are committed to certain theses about the semantics of natural-kind terms, which can in turn be shown crucial to determining the epistemic status of externalist entailments from propositional-attitude contents to environmental conditions. First, given Twin Earth cases, the meaning of genuine terms of that sort would depend in part upon their reference. But then it seems to follow that the content of propositional attitudes involving any such terms would likewise be partially determined by the reference of the term. Standard Twin Earth cases, however, also require that in any possible worlds where tokens of natural-kind terms refer at all, they necessarily pick out samples of exactly the same substances or species referred to by those terms in the world where their extension was initially grounded. Recall Twin Earthian T-Oscar, the exact replica of Earthian Oscar in all his internal properties (nonintentionally described), who often utters the sound 'water' to refer to a substance superficially identical to water in Oscar's world but having an inner composition that differs radically from H_2O. Here the externalist urges that T-Oscar neither possesses the natural-kind concept 'water', nor could have propositional attitudes whose content might be intentionally described as involving that concept.[1] Yet such a conclusion would fail to follow unless externalism were taken to rest upon the semantic theses outlined above.

In fact, Twin Earth thought experiments were first proposed as arguments to undermine a certain semantic account, traditional Fregeanism, thought to fuel the conclusion that in spite of radical differences in the reference of some natural-kind term, internal replicas such as Oscar and T-Oscar could entertain propositional attitudes involving exactly the same content. This would indeed follow when Fregeanism is construed as holding, first, that all constituents of propositions, whether singular terms or general ones, have meanings that supervene entirely upon the local properties of those who entertain them in their speech or thought; and secondly, that meanings of that sort (hereafter, 'Fregean senses') completely determine the extension of any such constituent. But then chemically ignorant, internal replicas could certainly entertain propositional attitudes involving exactly the same natural-kind term in scenarios where tokens of their term picked out substances of altogether different inner constitutions. Since traditional Fregeanism cashes out the senses of natural-kind terms as the speaker's nondemonstrative ways of thinking about certain properties, and takes senses of that sort to determine the extension of those terms (the referent property), therefore if internal replicas came to associate exactly the same senses with superficially identical substances or species, it would then be possible that those replicas should have words and thoughts involving exactly the same natural-kind terms in worlds where the inner properties of the substances or species referred to by tokens of their terms differed radically. If traditional Fregeans must countenance such scenarios (as their theory is usually construed, e.g., by Searle 1983), then it is difficult to see how they could accommodate the externalists' doctrine.[2]

For one thing, it follows from standard externalist thought experiments that, as in the case of the individual objects referred to by logically proper names, the properties picked out by tokens of certain predicates must also be the same in any possible world were those terms have an extension at all (which, as argued by Recanati 1993, does not entail holding that they are purely referential). And crucial to the externalist conclusion from Twin Earth examples is the metaphysical claim that, in possible worlds where natural-kind terms are genuine or nonvacuous, they necessarily pick out samples of natural kinds that have the same inner composition as the exemplars referred to by those terms in the world where their extension was initially grounded. Given externalism, for any natural kind to fall within the extension of a natural-kind term conventionally available in a linguistic community, there must be a referential link between the term and some substance or species, originally established by causal commerce of the community's speakers with the referent natural kind and later transmitted to others through social interaction. Furthermore, it is not their Fregean senses, but their reference instead, fixed by causal relations of speakers with natural kinds, that individuates natural-kind terms, together with the content of any proposition embedded in a psychological attitude containing terms of that sort.

Note that these semantic intuitions invite a certain view about the epistemic status of propositions in cases where they appear to involve natural-kind terms. For if such intuitions are correct, then whether the content of any proposition actually involves genuine terms of that type would depend upon whether the individual who entertains the proposition in his speech or thought has in fact entered some causal chains relevant to fixing the reference of occurring predicates into certain substances and species in the environment (either by his direct acquaintance with these, or by interaction with other members of the linguistic community whose referential use of such predicates traces back to those of speakers who have introduced them as a result of direct acquaintance). One's belief that any of these relations obtain, when justified and true, would of course be eligible to count as knowledge in some sense, but merely of the empirical sort. Imagine a world that differs from ours only in that tokens of a certain word, 'water', have always been empty there—like our 'phlogiston', no causal chain ever related that word, conventionally available in the linguistic community, with some natural kind. By hypothesis, then, native speakers of that world are part of no causal chain grounding the extension of that term in an external property. In such a scenario, whatever the contents of a native's sincere assertion containing that term might be, they could neither involve the property of being H_2O nor be intentionally characterized as expressing, for example, the belief that water is wet. But there is no need to appeal to imagination here, since memory, when applied to Western science (whose history of ontological shrinking is also one of semantic elimination) will do just as well. Recall, e.g., the notoriously bogus scientific term 'luminiferous ether', taken to pick out the property of being a certain radiation-transmitting medium filling all unoccupied space. No doubt physicists at some point entertained propositional attitudes involving this putative natural-kind term, sincerely thinking that they were referring to a medium of that sort. (Their term, however, regularly picked out nothing external at all, and was finally discarded shortly after the failed Michelson-Morley experiment of 1887.) In such cases, intentional description would of course fall short of involving a genuine natural-kind term individuated by environmental conditions.

When it comes to putative substance and species words, the possibility of extensional emptiness seems to suggest that, to amount to knowledge, intentional description requires investigation of the causal history of those words. Tokens of a declarative sentence (type) involving such words, in scenarios where they do have referential links to substances or species in the environment, would admit intentional characterization along externalist lines, but certain propositional-attitude contents may qualify only for internalist intentional description in situations where all embedded terms supervene entirely upon the local properties of individuals.

Charitably construed, externalism is compatible with this conclusion. At the same time, precisely because externalists may countenance the supervenience of some such contents upon local properties of individuals, they seem committed to hold that the problem of determining whether certain propositional-attitude contents depend entirely upon local properties of individuals, or partially upon nonlocal ones, amounts to an epistemic question that cannot be settled just by thinking. Clearly, externalist entailments from propositional-attitude contents to the environment, if they obtain, count as metaphysically necessary. But once the scope of externalism is properly understood, together with its semantic commitments, those entailments seem to presuppose propositions involving the existence of referential links between terms, on the one hand, and substances and species in the speaker's environment on the other. Belief in propositions of that kind, when justified and true, constitutes knowledge in some sense, but only of the empirical sort.[3] That knowledge of content is a posteriori, then, appears the only view compatible with the externalist's standard conclusion from Twin Earth thought experiments. At the same time, this view can solve the paradox facing externalism and privileged self-knowledge, provided externalists can support their semantic intuitions, to which I now turn.

IV

For most of the twentieth century, philosophical semantics, chiefly under the influence of Frege (1952) and some of Russell's writings (1905, 1918–1919), offered an analysis of the semantic contribution of certain terms to the propositions in which they occur that was not to be seriously challenged until near the end of that century. Within that analysis, tokens of 'Laika is a dog' would be taken to express a proposition ascribing a certain property (in this case, being a dog) to whomever fits some definite description (e.g., the first Russian experimental animal sent into space). Direct-reference theorists famously objected that the semantic contribution of a name could be construed as that of a definite description (or a cluster of them) and thus took the Frege-Russell analysis to misrepresent the form of the expressed proposition. On direct-reference semantics (Kripke 1972, Kaplan 1977), that proposition must instead be cashed out as a singular, Russellian one, which predicates a certain property of Laika, an individual object that is a constituent of the proposition.

Although externalism typically focuses upon *de dicto* ascriptions in cases where the propositions embedded in psychological attitudes contain natural-kind terms, much could be learned about the epistemic status of those ascriptions by reflecting upon the analogous case of belief involving singular propositions. For, assuming that there are such propositions, tokens of a certain sentence type could express a proposition of that kind, provided that there is at least one term capable of picking out a certain individual entity, that is, provided the expressed proposition has at least one singular term functioning as a logically proper name capable of contributing to it the referent object itself. But the actual semantic contribution of a singular term to the proposition in which it occurs crucially depends upon the causal history of that term. For to invoke its referent, a term must latch onto it as a result of some causal commerce of its users. On the causal account of reference favored by direct theorists, speakers must have had causal contact with the referent object itself, or with other speakers whose use of the term may be traced back to those who initially had such contact and originated the usage with that reference.

Thus, if a certain proposition is indeed singular, then there is a causal chain linking at least one of its occurring singular terms with some individual object. In speech or thought, the function of such logically proper names is paradigmatically (though not exclusively) performed by ordinary proper names. Yet because any of the latter may aim at picking out an individual object while failing to do so in fact (i.e., turning out vacuous), questions concerning whether tokens of declarative sentences containing putative logically proper names actually express singular propositions are a posteriori—requiring an investigation of the causal history of, for instance, occurring ordinary names. Clearly, whether the referent of any singular term exists, with those who use it in their speech or thought having had causal commerce with that entity (or with other members of the community whose referential usage of the term is traceable back to that of those who have had such commerce) amounts to an empirical matter of fact, knowable only a posteriori.

Externalists need not be directly concerned with the controversy between Fregeans and direct-reference theorists about the correct semantic account of singular terms, and they may even follow traditional Fregeanism in taking 'water', 'tiger', and other natural- and biological-kind words to be among the general terms whose logical function is that of predicates, with properties falling within their extension. Yet, as illustrated by standard Twin Earth thought experiments, externalists must part company with the traditional semanticist in her claim that the extension of any such term could be entirely determined by its Fregean sense or mode of presentation. In this matter, their views are closer in some crucial respects to those of direct-reference theorists. As often argued by the latter for the case of ordinary proper names, the externalist's thought experiments suggest that natural-kind terms also necessarily refer to the same thing in different possible worlds where they pick out anything at all—even when it is not an individual object but the essential property of some substance or species what falls under their extension instead. And of course, unlike logically proper names, natural-kind terms need not be considered purely referential, since it can be shown that they do have meanings—though these fall short of Fregean senses (Putnam 1975). But if externalism is correct, then the metaphysical status of propositions containing natural-kind terms would be similar to that of singular propositions, in that the former seem likewise to "invoke" something in the environment. In their case, it is an essential property, external to the individual who entertains the proposition.

The analogy, however, can be extended to cover some epistemic features. Just as tokens of a singular term may fail to pick out a specific object, no doubt those of some predicate intended to pick out a certain external property could regularly fail to do so. Such failures of reference would occur in scenarios where there is no causal chain linking a putative natural-kind term with anything external to the speaker, i.e., when no essential property of a substance or species turns out to fall under the extension of tokens of that term. How is this possible? Recall that in the mid-1970s, not only did externalists reject senses as wholly determining the extension of natural-kind terms, but they also embraced the direct theorist's causal account of reference, further developing it to become the full-fledged causal account we know today (Putnam 1975, Burge 1979). That was no historical accident: without Fregean senses, some causal account of reference was needed to avoid a magic theory of reference. In the externalists' view, for any putative natural-kind terms to amount to a genuine terms of that sort, there must be a causal chain linking the term conventionally available in the speaker's linguistic community with some actual substance or species in the environment. This requires that the speaker, in his direct commerce with a certain natural kind, has introduced the term to refer to that natural kind—or else that he has taken it up from others in his linguistic community whose referential use of it is traceable back to those who originated it in their causal transactions with a certain substance or species.

Yet, as argued above, given a plausible version of externalism, there is room for holding that terms intended to refer to some natural kinds may regularly fail to pick out the right sort of property. A native of our world, when he sincerely asserts 'Ether is lighter than phlogiston', expresses a proposition that picks out no property at all external to the speaker. No doubt intentional ascription in such cases is internalist, for any two replicas sharing identical properties from the skin inward (nonintentionally described) could have the thought *that ether is lighter than phlogiston* no matter how different their environments turned out to be. Since a plausible version of externalism can countenance cases of this sort, therefore, given that doctrine, to determine whether any propositional-attitude content is externally determined requires investigation of the causal history of its occurring terms, which is an empirical matter. For how could any such question be settled just by reasoning?

I submit that if semantic externalism is correct, then the justification of belief about substantial entailments from words and thoughts to the environment rests (at least in part) on empirical investigation.

Furthermore, if one's faculty of self-understanding is properly functioning, then, given semantic externalism, it may appear on a certain epistemic view that one could come to know the implications of one's thought contents a priori. But since the notion of justification fueling the paradox of concern here is that of epistemic *internalism*, the temptation to hold that view must be completely removed (see note 5). If this is correct, there is no epistemic problem facing the attempt to hold externalism together with privileged self-knowledge, simply because the above triad may now be recast as follows:

(1*)   Oscar can know a priori that his current propositional attitude involves a *putative* natural-kind term, *k*.

(2*)   Oscar can know a priori that, if his current propositional attitude involves a putative natural-kind term *k*, then *k* *may* pick out a certain natural kind.

(3)   No one can know a priori that any natural kind exists.

Clearly, there is nothing inconsistent about the attempt to hold all of these claims at once. Yet it remains to be shown that the doctrine of privileged self-knowledge is preserved by (1*), and that externalism does not sanction entailments stronger than (2*). Let us begin with the latter, which requires a closer look at the semantic commitments of that doctrine.

V

I have argued that standard Twin Earth thought experiments suggest two things: first, that the referents of natural-kind terms partly determine their meaning, and, second, that in any possible world where tokens of those terms have reference at all, they necessarily pick out samples of exactly the same substances (or species) falling within their extension in the actual world. Given these theses, traditional Fregeanism cannot provide a correct account of natural-kind terms. For on Fregean assumptions, the extension of any general term, a certain property, is entirely determined by the term's sense (or cluster of senses), cashed out as a *nondemonstrative* concept in the speaker's mind (that is, her *nondemonstrative* way of thinking about a certain property falling under the extension of the term). Yet this leads to the internalist conclusion that T-Oscar could have psychological attitudes involving the concept 'water' on Twin Earth, where there is no H_2O but only superficially identical XYZ, and where nobody has ever been in contact with speakers having such a concept. That would be the case if his nondemonstrative ways of thinking about the superficial qualities of XYZ were relevantly similar to Oscar's when he has words or thoughts involving the concept 'water', even when it is not XYZ but H_2O what falls under the extension of Oscar's term on Earth. This internalist result (which is clear in, for example, Searle 1983) follows inevitably from a semantics that takes the meaning of any predicate to supervene entirely upon local properties of the individuals who entertain them in their speech or thought.

Needless to say, on semantic intuitions of this sort, some relatively common scenarios would become altogether mysterious: namely, those where speakers seem to succeed in having words and thoughts about certain natural kinds in spite of their profound misconceptions and errors concerning the designated substances.[4] Externalists, on the other hand, have no problem in accounting for those scenarios. In fact, well known externalist thought experiments (such as Putnam's 'elm/ beech tree', 'water/t-water', and 'aluminum/molybdenum' cases) were devised precisely to elicit the intuition that an individual whose conception of some natural kind is incomplete or partially mistaken may still be able to entertain, not just *de re* attitudes, but *de dicto* ones as well involving that natural kind (Putnam 1975; Burge 1982a, 1982b). What matters for externalist attribution of content is the existence of referential links between certain terms embedded in a psychological attitude and some substances and species in the environment. Links of that sort are thought to rest, at least initially, on the causal commerce of speakers with paradigm samples of those substances and species. Once referential links have been established in that way, they may later be transmitted to others in the linguistic community through social interaction, with no further direct causal contact needed.

Yet further contact and expert knowledge could at any time produce changes in the speakers' ways of thinking about the extension of some such terms—as happened with 'fish' when it came to be understood that porpoises and whales did not fall within its extension, or 'jade', when gemologists discovered that there are in fact two distinct minerals, nephrite and jadeite, falling within that term's extension (Quine 1969 and Putnam 1975, respectively). Note that, if it is typically the causal contact of speakers with an essential property constitutive of the relevant kind that initiates a communal practice of using some natural-kind term with a certain extension, then the extension of any such term is fixed in a manner entirely independent of whether those who begin using it have an accurate conception of the property falling within its extension. Although experts in the community may be able to provide a scientific account of such properties, they are in no way required in order to secure the extension of natural-kind words. As often emphasized by causal theorists of reference (e.g., Kripke 1972, Putnam 1975), terms such as 'water' and 'gold' were used to pick out samples of substances with a certain chemical structure long before any expert was able to discern the chemical composition of those substances—just as some essential properties of whales and porpoises fell under the extension of tokens of 'whale' and 'porpoise' long before it was discovered that those species do not qualify as fish.

Since misconceptions and even ignorance about the essential properties of natural kinds and species, however widespread among speakers, seem not at all to undermine their success in using conventionally available natural-kind terms to predicate those properties, this counts as evidence against Fregeanism, a theory standardly construed as lacking a causal account of reference. Externalists, on the other hand, offer precisely such an account, together with the view that the extension of genuine natural-kind terms necessarily remains the same in any possible world where terms of that sort pick out anything at all.[5]

VI

Semantic theses of this sort suggest that the epistemic status of propositions containing genuine natural-kind terms must be altogether different from that of propositions involving only internally determined terms. For assuming such theses, how could either self-ascriptive beliefs about externally determined propositions, or belief in their externalistic entailments qualify for nonempirical justification of the type available, for example, when one believes *that triangles have three internal angles*, or *that bachelors are unmarried men*? Since the latter are prime candidates for a priori justification, if beliefs that ordinarily do not require investigation of the environment, even when they may presuppose some empirical propositions, are held to be a priori too, this must be under a different sense of that notion, as, for instance, when one thinks that one has a headache, or that Jessie Jackson supported Al Gore in the 2000 U.S. elections. For each of these presupposes empirical propositions concerning, e.g., the existence of my head,[6] and that of Jackson and Gore, respectively.

Such contrasting cases support a distinction between a strong notion of a priori justification (or knowledge) and a weak one, construed as follows:

A priori$_S$ A property of belief in propositions which, resting on no empirical assumption at all, are not open to challenge on a posteriori grounds.

A priori$_W$ A property of belief in propositions which, though prima facie justified without empirical investigation, rest on some empirical assumptions, and are thus open to challenge on a posteriori grounds.

Under normal circumstances, when I claim to know by introspection that I believe *that water is wet*, I take for granted that water exists, and that my term 'water' refers to water—that is, in the absence of contrary evidence, I assume that my putative natural-kind term is genuine. But, given the semantic commitments of externalism, since beliefs involving such terms would ultimately rest on empirical propositions (even when ordinarily and in the absence of evidence to the contrary their justification does not require investigation of the environment), they all fall short of being a priori in the strong sense, i.e., they are *not* indefeasible on a posteriori considerations.

Yet if self-ascriptive beliefs about thought contents are not available a priori in the strong sense, doesn't that undermine their privileged epistemic status? Not at all, if that status stems, not from their apriority, but from their being available to the first person with special access and authority—which conditions, as we have seen, are both consistent with their being a priori only in the weak sense. Recall that, given special access, beliefs of that sort are directly justified, i.e., based on neither evidence nor inference. And, given first-person authority, there is a presumption that they are also predominantly true, and thus highly eligible to be counted as knowledge. Compare my belief that *I am thinking that water is wet* with my believing that, say, *water exists*. Arguably, both are in some sense empirical, but while the latter is neither truth-warranted nor direct, the former has these properties and is therefore epistemically privileged (qualifying for a priori$_W$). This is why self-ascriptions of that sort are ordinarily trusted: noticing that they are in some sense epistemically special, we simply don't bother to investigate the environment before making knowledge and justification claims about them unless presented with convincing evidence to the contrary. In light of this, there is room for yet another recasting of the self-knowledge claim in the incompatibilist triad. Claim (1) may now be construed as holding that I can know a priori$_W$ that my thought involves a certain term, 'water'.

Thus construed, the claim seems plausible. But our discussion appears to suggest that claim (2) might have a similar epistemic status, since externalism is knowable by philosophical argument. Given (1) and (2), then, I might still be in a position to know a priori (though only in a weak sense) that water exists. However, since the issue of whether or not the putative natural-kind term 'water' turns out to be genuine ultimately depends on an empirical question concerning the causal history of my tokens of that term, the specific externalist entailment in this case cannot run stronger than this:

(2**)   If my thought involves the putative natural-kind term 'water', and this term is a genuine natural-kind term, then there is (or has been) water in my environment.

It doesn't really matter that I may come to know a priori$_W$ that my thought involves the term 'water', since the antecedent of the externalist entailment in (2**) is in fact a compound proposition, with a conjunct unavailable a priori *in either sense* of that notion. For, clearly, whether my tokens of 'water' express a genuine natural-kind term depends on their causal history, something I could know with neither special access nor first-person authority. It follows that, given the semantic commitments of externalists, if entailments from propositional-attitude contents to environmental conditions need not be more demanding than (2**), then (when justified and true), they would amount to knowledge in some sense, but ultimately of the a posteriori type.[7]

VII

The incompatibilist's chief goal was to show that the attempt to hold externalism and privileged self-knowledge concurrently leads to an absurd conclusion. Suppose we grant her (as I think we should) that Oscar could figure out some general entailments from thought contents to the world by knowing externalist theory (which he could come to know through standard Twin Earth thought experiments) and the contents of his current thoughts.[8] Given externalism and privileged self-knowledge, the consequent of such entailments appears to follow by simple deduction, without Oscar's conducting any investigation of the environment at all. Yet this objection cannot be made out if the semantic theory endorsed by externalists has the epistemic consequences suggested here. Since there is more than one notion of apriority at issue in this debate, externalists could insist that only beliefs presupposing no empirical proposition whatsoever can count as a priori in the more interesting sense of *nonempirical*. Even when self-ascriptive beliefs about propositional-attitude contents may be eligible for a priori justification, that would be only under a weaker construal of that notion. At the same time, belief about specific externalist entailments would qualify for neither.

Nothing absurd then can be deduced from such premises. For even after granting that one of the needed premises has the special epistemic status of being knowable without any special investigation of the environment, the conclusion required for the reductio—that externalism and privileged self-knowledge together entail that one could come to know a priori (in the sense of nonempirically) that certain natural kinds exist—does not follow. Such a conclusion would require that the property of being knowable nonempirically be transmitted under known entailment, and this clearly cannot happen, since the premises themselves fall short of having any such epistemic property. Once externalism is properly construed, it becomes plain that the attempt to hold it concurrently with privileged self-knowledge generates no paradox at all.

Notes

1. Since here I assume that meaning and propositional-attitude content are analogous, 'term' throughout this paper should be taken to apply to either words or concepts, and 'proposition', to the content of either a declarative sentence or a propositional attitude.

2. Although Burge (1979) has argued that content externalism is compatible with Fregean semantics, he probably has in mind *neo*-Fregeanism of the sort proposed by Evans (1982) and Wiggins (1993), i.e., a causal theory of reference that incorporates modes of presentation in its account of meaning. On the other hand, Putnam (1975) famously urged that traditional Fregeanism entails "methodological solipsism," which amounts to internalism about meaning and content.

3. Note, however, that if 'justification' and 'knowledge' are construed as epistemic externalist notions, then no piecemeal empirical checking is needed, and this might be erroneously taken to suggest that self-knowledge claims are a priori

in the strong sense of being nonempirical. A reliabilist, for example, may hold that self-ascriptions of propositional-attitude contents rest upon the trustworthy faculty of self-understanding—a thesis consistent with, e.g., Burge 1998 (see also Heil 1988). On that view, if such a faculty is indeed reliable, then when one ascribes to oneself certain propositional-attitude contents on the basis of self-understanding, one's ascription is justified and amounts to knowledge that does require piecemeal examination of the environment. But to determine whether self-understanding is actually a reliable faculty would itself require some empirical investigation involving, for example, checking its track record. In any case, epistemic externalism need not be assumed here, since the types of epistemic notions that matter for the paradox of externalism and self-knowledge are internalist, requiring *knowing that one knows*, or at least, reflective justification. Suppose that, as some have pointed out (Brewer 2000, Davies 1998), in "normal" circumstances many propositional-attitude contents are in fact externally determined. Still, given internalist justification, the individual who entertains those contents may *not* know that her thoughts involve contents of that sort, even when self-understanding could indeed be reliable.

4. As argued by direct-reference theorists, not only was 'water' used to pick out H_2O long before the discovery of that property (when *a fortiori* speakers could have had *no* conception of it) but 'marsupial mouse' was once mistakenly thought to pick out a species kindred to mice (rather than to kangaroos and opossums, as we classify them today). And although a bat is not a flying mouse, it appears that German speakers once assumed that it was; hence their term 'Fledermaus'. While all these terms may prove puzzling to a theory that takes Fregean senses to determine the extension of such terms, they could be easily accommodated if the grounding of their extension were considered a matter of initial causal interaction with certain sources and social cooperation.

5. At the same time, Burge (1982a) rejects the view that natural-kind terms might be similar to indexicals, as that would seem to lend plausibility to the narrow-content versus broad-content distinction that he wishes to eschew. For, given that analogy, natural-kind terms could be said to have a narrow meaning that, like a Kaplanian character, may remain constant from world to world while its broad meaning can vary from context to context with relevant changes in the physical environment. But that clearly falls short of the conclusion externalists standardly draw from their Twin Earth cases. For objections to Burge's reasoning here, see Sosa 1993.

6. This example was suggested to me by Stephen Schiffer.

7. McKinsey (1991a, 1994b) believes he has shown that taking externalist entailments to be metaphysically necessary yet knowable a posteriori would trivialize the characteristic thesis of externalism. But this is only because he construes that thesis in a way that is far too weak to capture what externalists have in mind. Thus construed, a blatantly trivial entailment such as that *Oscar's thinking that water is wet metaphysically entails that Oscar's biological parents existed* seems to satisfy that thesis. But when externalism is properly understood, it must be taken

to make more specific dependence claims about content, e.g., holding that Oscar's thought in that case necessarily depends in part upon the existence of a certain substance external to him, which is specifically related to the content of his thought. And there is no danger that this would trivialize the characteristic thesis of externalism, since even specific claims about the dependence of an individual's thought contents upon certain environmental conditions may support general supervenience claims about the individuation of propositional-attitude content types, which are what externalists ultimately wish to make. See Brueckner 1995a.

8. Given externalism, should propositions such as 'If I have contentful thoughts, then something other than me must exist', be considered a priori, or nonempirical? This complex question has little bearing on the paradox of concern here, which involves the possibility that externalism and privileged self-knowledge open a nonempirical way to know *more substantial* empirical propositions.

9

Two Transcendental Arguments Concerning Self-Knowledge

Anthony Brueckner

1 Skepticism about Self-Knowledge

In Hilary Putnam's well-known thought experiment, we consider Earthling Ava and her twin Twava, who inhabits Twin Earth, where there is no H_2O but instead a superficially indistinguishable liquid composed of XYZ molecules. This liquid is not water, given its strange chemical structure. Call the liquid *twater*. When Twava says, 'I swim in water', she does not express the mistaken belief that she swims in water (the belief that Ava expresses when she utters the sentence).[1] Instead, she expresses the correct belief that she swims in twater. We can suppose that Ava and Twava are indistinguishable in respect of their *individualistic* properties: those which concern their qualitative perceptual experience and stream of consciousness, their behavior and behavioral dispositions, and their functional states (all nonintentionally characterized).[2] Thus we see that which type of belief a thinker possesses depends upon which sort of environment she inhabits. Given the absence of water from Twava's environment, she lacks the concept of water and thus lacks thoughts, beliefs and other propositional attitudes involving that concept. Instead, she has *twin* propositional attitudes involving the distinct concept of twater.

In light of these *anti-individualist* considerations, we can construct a skeptical argument that parallels a familiar argument aimed at generating skepticism about knowledge of the external world:

(1) If I know that I am thinking that I swim in water, then I know that I am not thinking that I swim in twater.

(2) I do not know that I am not thinking that I swim in twater.

(3) So, I do not know that I am thinking that I swim in water.

Premise (1) follows from the following closure principle:

(4)   If I know that ϕ and I know that ϕ entails ψ, then I know that ψ.

Premise (2) is supported by the reflection that I can offer no evidence or reasons that justify me in rejecting the skeptical possibility that I am thinking a *twater* thought (involving the concept of twater) instead of a *water* thought (involving the concept of water). If I have not investigated my liquid environment, then I have no way of discerning a *water* thought from its twin. There are no introspectable features of my current thought that justify me in believing that it is not a *twater* thought. Thus I do not know that it is not a *twater* thought.

One problem with this defense of premise (2) is that it rests on a controversial conception of self-knowledge. In the corresponding argument for skepticism about knowledge of the external world, the skeptic defends a corresponding premise to the effect that one does not know that one is not massively in error about the external world. He defends this premise by impugning one's sensory evidence: one's experience would be exactly the same as it is if one were a victim of massive sensory deception (e.g., if one were a brain in a vat or a plaything of a Cartesian evil genius). Hence, one's sensory evidence does not justify one in rejecting the skeptic's possibility of massive error. Thus, one does not know that one is not massively mistaken. It is doubtful, however, that this line can reasonably be extended to the self-knowledge skeptic's premise (2). This is because one's putative knowledge of one's own thoughts is typically not evidentially based, unlike one's putative knowledge of the external world. Thus, it makes no sense for the self-knowledge skeptic to try to impugn one's putative self-knowledge by impugning its evidential base.[3]

This does not show that I *do* know that I am not thinking a *twater* thought. The point about evidence only undercuts the skeptic's case for the claim that I *lack* such self-knowledge. What is needed for a fully adequate reply to the skeptic about self-knowledge is an explanation of how it is that I know that I am thinking a *water* thought. Then it could be reasonably maintained that given the existence of such self-knowledge, I know by deduction that I am not thinking a *twater* thought.

2   Accounting for Self-Knowledge

I would like to consider two recent transcendental arguments concerning self-knowledge, from work by Akeel Bilgrami and Richard Moran.[4]

Both writers argue that the existence of self-knowledge possessing a distinctive epistemic status is a condition for the possibility of some very basic feature of us. For Bilgrami, the feature is our responsible agency. For Moran, it is our rational formation of action-guiding belief. If either argument succeeds, then, given the existence of the pertinent basic feature of us, this would provide an answer to the self-knowledge skeptic's argument from the anti-individualist considerations we have discussed.[5] Further, if successful, the arguments would presumably elucidate the nature of self-knowledge.

Like many recent writers on self-knowledge, Bilgrami and Moran reject several aspects of the traditional "Cartesian" conception of self-knowledge. They reject *infallibility*, the view that all of one's beliefs about one's own mental states are guaranteed to be correct. Psychoanalytic examples are standardly employed to refute infallibility, such as an unadmitted racist's mistaken belief that he believes that all men are created equal. Beliefs about past mental states are also standardly cited as open to error. Bilgrami and Moran also reject *transparency*, the converse of infallibility, according to which mental states are all easily accessible to correct belief about them. The same examples refute this thesis. The unadmitted racist believes that not all men are created equal, but he does not believe that he has that belief and can only be made to see that he does through great effort. Alain mistakenly believes that he wanted champagne on New Year's Eve of 1980. He wanted wine, but he does not now believe that that is what he wanted and cannot easily come to believe this.

Bilgrami and Moran also deny the *observational model* of self-knowledge, according to which there is a special introspective faculty akin to perception that delivers information about one's mental states. Not only do our mental states lack any quasi-perceptual modes of presentation, but further, self-knowledge, they say, does not depend upon the existence of a highly reliable causal process linking mental states with second-order beliefs about them (beliefs that one believes, desires, intends, etc.).

So self-knowledge, according to Bilgrami and Moran, does not possess a distinctive epistemic status in virtue of its possessing the "Cartesian" features just detailed. Though the two writers differ on exactly what *is* distinctive about self-knowledge, they agree that in a broad range of cases, knowledge of one's own mental states is (as discussed above) *noninferential*: it is not *evidentially based*. Beliefs about one's own mental states are typically *not* justified, or warranted, by virtue of their relation to other beliefs that serve as evidence. Further, if the observational model is indeed mistaken, then there is nothing like perceptual experience that constitutes a source of justification for beliefs about one's mental states, and neither can *reliabilist* considerations explain how the beliefs that amount to self-knowledge come to possess a justified epistemic status. As Paul Boghossian (1989) has put it, unlike ordinary knowledge of the external world (and of others' mental states), self-knowledge is typically *not based on anything at all*. That self-knowledge has this puzzling status follows from its noninferential and nonobservational character.

3   *Bilgrami*

Let us now turn to the details of Bilgrami's views on these matters. According to his positive characterization of what is distinctive about self-knowledge, it plays a "definitional and therefore constitutive role in the very idea of a mental state" (Bilgrami 1998: 207).[6] Bilgrami's initial formulation of this *constitutive thesis* is as follows: "There is a clear sense in which ... there can be no exceptions to the claim that if someone believes that he believes that p, then he believes that p, and vice-versa" (1998: 211). Though Bilgrami does not say so, the constitutive thesis, as just formulated, is the conjunction of the infallibility and transparency theses for *belief*. As we will see below, Bilgrami actually ends up arguing for a restricted version of the biconditional (B):

B S has intentional state i iff S believes that he has i.

This is what I am calling Bilgrami's transcendental argument concerning self-knowledge: he seeks to show that the truth of (a restricted version of) B, which secures the distinctive status of self-knowledge, is a condition for the possibility of our responsible agency.[7]

Bilgrami eases into his transcendental argument after a novel discussion of the phenomenon of self-deception. This discussion is the "intuitive starting point" of his transcendental argument (Bilgrami 1998: 217). Suppose that Joseph believes that he believes that his father is worthy of respect, while his behavior reveals a hostile, contemptuous attitude towards the father. In such a case, we correctly attribute to Joseph the first-order belief that his father is *not* worthy of respect, on the basis of the behavioral evidence that is explained by such an attribution. However, according to Bilgrami, *Joseph's second-order* belief is *not mistaken*. This is because Joseph has the first-order belief that renders true the second-order belief: he believes that his father *is* worthy of respect. Thus Joseph has inconsistent first-order beliefs regarding his father.[8]

There is a crucial difference between the first-order states, according to Bilgrami. The first-order belief that renders true the second-order belief—Joseph's belief that his father is worthy of respect—"potentially leads to actions ... that can be the objects of ... justifiable reactive attitudes," such as criticism, resentment, indignation, pride, and guilt (Bilgrami 1998: 219). Bilgrami, following P. F. Strawson's famous discussion, holds that such actions are free and responsible: their free and responsible character simply consists in their accessibility to justifiable reactive attitudes.[9] By contrast, Joseph's *other* first-order belief (that is father his *not* worthy of respect) does not lead to actions that are accessible to justifiable reactive attitudes: the belief does not lead to free and responsible actions.

Let us now turn to Bilgrami's discussion of the constitutive thesis. He wants to establish the following restricted version of that thesis:

CT   For all intentional states i and all subjects S, if i meets the *condition of responsible agency* (CRA), then S has i iff S believes that he has i.[10]

An intentional state i meets CRA just in case i can lead to actions that are accessible to justifiable reactive attitudes (as was Joseph's belief that his father is worthy of respect).

What I am calling Bilgrami's transcendental argument is his argument to establish CT. He argues for the L-R direction as follows. Assume that Joseph's belief that his father is worthy of respect in fact has led to actions that are accessible to justifiable reactive attitudes, such as asserting that his father is worthy of respect. Thus, the belief meets CRA. Bilgrami maintains that "self-knowledge is a necessary condition of responsible agency" (1998: 222). According to Bilgrami, this means that in performing a free and responsible action such as asserting that his father is worthy of respect, Joseph must "not merely know that he has acted ..., but [he must] also know the intentional states which cause and explain (rationalize) the action" (1998: 222–223). Thus, he must *know that he believes that his father is worthy of respect*, since this belief is an intentional state that helps cause and explain his asserting that his father is worthy of respect.

This argument is meant to generalize to all intentional states that meet CRA. The reasoning is not meant to extend to intentional states that fail to meet CRA. For example, Joseph's belief that his father is *not* worthy of respect does not meet CRA. Joseph neither knows nor believes that he has that belief.

The foregoing argument for the L-R direction of CT is problematic. The assumption that is doing all the work is (*):

(*)   For all actions *a* and agents *S*, if *S* performs *a* and *a* is accessible to justifiable reactive attitudes (i.e., if *a* is freely and responsibly performed by *S*), then *S* knows the intentional states which cause and explain *a*.

Suppose that Charlie believes that she is firing a gun loaded with blanks at an actor who will convincingly portray an assassinated general. Suppose further that this belief is nonculpably formed. In fact, Charlie is killing a real general by firing live rounds. Since she does not know what she is doing, we do not think that Charlie is freely and responsibly killing the general, and we do not unleash justifiable reactive attitudes towards her action. An agent must know that she is ϕing if she is to ϕ freely and responsibly. This much is plausible though rough. But it is not at all clear that these considerations establish (*). Maybe it is one thing to know what you are doing and yet another to know the intentional states that cause and explain your action.

To see that there is a worry here, consider Sydney Shoemaker's notion of a *self-blind* person. This is a person who possesses concepts of intentional states such as belief and desire and who possesses such states; but the self-blind person only attributes intentional states to herself on the basis of evidence regarding her behavior. A self-blind person, then, does not possess the sort of distinctive, noninferentially based self-knowledge that we do. Shoemaker (1995) argues that a rational, self-blind person is an impossibility.[11] I do not think that his argument succeeds, and this impossibility obviously cannot simply be stipulated in the present context.

Suppose that Marty is self-blind. Marty wants to kill the general, and he correctly believes that firing this gun is a way of killing the general. Being self-blind, Marty lacks a second-order belief that he wants to kill the general, and he lacks a second-order belief that he believes that firing this gun is a way of killing the general. According to Bilgrami's (*), Marty's action is not freely and responsibly done; reactive attitudes are not justifiably directed toward the action. But it is not at all clear that this is correct. As long as Marty knows what he is doing, and as long as his first-order belief-desire pair leads to the killing in a normal manner, it is not at all clear why his lack of second-order beliefs would preclude freedom, responsibility, and appropriateness of reactive attitudes towards the killing.

We ask Marty if he knows what he has just done, and he replies that he has killed the general. We ask him why he did it. Being self-blind, he replies, "I'm not sure. Let me reason this out. I suppose that I wanted to kill the general and believed that firing this now-smoking gun was a way of doing it. That would certainly explain my behavior." Once he has acted, Marty can in this inferential way develop second-order beliefs about his motives. But, we are supposing, he had no such beliefs in acting, and it is not clear why they are at any point required for free and responsible agency. At most, knowing what he is doing is such a requirement.

Bilgrami at one point says, "We may assume (familiarly) that there is no correctly describing action except in terms of the intentional states that explain (rationalize) it" (1998: 223). According to this claim, if Marty does not know the belief-desire pair that rationalizes his action, then the action cannot be correctly described by Marty (or by anyone else) as a killing of the general. Thus the self-blind Marty does not know what he is doing in the present case, since he cannot correctly describe his action as a killing of the general (according to Bilgrami's suggestion). Hence Marty does not after all satisfy the minimal requirement for free and responsible agency that we are here acknowledging.

I do not find this to be a plausible way of defending (*). It seems fairly clear that one can know what one is doing without knowing *why* one is doing it. Why am I washing my hands again? Why did I insult my father? Why am I pacing?[12]

There is another problem for the L-R direction of CT, whose defense we have been considering. Suppose that Bilgrami ultimately did somehow establish this conditional. This would show that if an intentional state *i* of *S*'s meets the condition of responsible agency, then *S* believes that he has *i*. But this does not show that *S* has *knowledge* regarding *i*. It at best shows that *S* has a true belief that he has *i*.

Bilgrami could reply that his argument for the L-R direction of CT, if successful, establishes a stronger result. That is, the argument relies upon (*) and thus would establish a result concerning *knowledge* of intentional states that rationalize free and responsible actions. However, even if we waive the foregoing objection to (*), it still would seem that at most *correct belief* regarding an action's rationalizing intentional states is required for the action to be free and responsible. Why would such a correct belief need, further, to be *justified*, or to amount to *knowledge*, in order for the action to be free and responsible?

There is a further question about what we might call the *nonconstructive* character of the foregoing stage of the transcendental argument. The plan was to establish the existence of self-knowledge (for intentional states meeting the condition of responsible agency) without explaining *how it is* that correct belief about rationalizing intentional states amounts to knowledge. What feature, exactly, of such correct beliefs enables them to reach the epistemic status of pieces of *knowledge?* Nothing in the first stage of the transcendental argument affords an answer to this question.

Let us now turn to the R-L direction of CT: under CRA, "second-order beliefs cannot fail to be true and cannot fail to amount to self-knowledge" (Bilgrami 1998: 223). Bilgrami argues as follows. Suppose that *S* does *a*, where this action is rationalized by intentional state *i*. Suppose that *S* has a second-order belief: *S* believes that he has *i*. Suppose further that we have a justifiable reactive attitude towards *a*, i.e., *a* satisfies CRA. Given our suppositions and given (*), *S* knows that he has *i*. Thus, *S*'s second-order belief "must be true" (Bilgrami 1998: 223).

There is an obvious problem with this reasoning (which Bilgrami duly notes). It is built into the assumptions of the case considered that *S*'s second-order belief is true: it is stipulated that *S* has *i* and believes that he has *i*.

Bilgrami's reply to this objection begins with his pointing out that true belief need not amount to knowledge. Thus, *self*-knowledge "requires something more than the presence of first-order intentional states [such as *i*] when second-order beliefs are made about them" (Bilgrami 1998: 224). Before unfolding the rest of Bilgrami's reply to the objection at hand, we may pause to wonder why Bilgrami thought in the first place that establishing the R-L direction of CT would establish something important regarding self-*knowledge*. Even if second-order beliefs are shown to be invariably true when we have them (under CRA), it would not follow that any of them amounts to *knowledge*.[13] The crux of Bilgrami's reply to the objection under consideration is that true beliefs about one's intentional states *that meet CRA* amount to self-knowledge. That further condition is put forward as a necessary condition for self-knowledge, beyond the truth condition and the belief condition. Thus, the R-L direction of CT "is *not* established as relevant to self-knowledge merely on the basis of the existence of the first-order intentional state, as was being protested" (Bilgrami 1998: 224).

It seems to me that Bilgrami has not adequately addressed the "protest." The problem to be addressed was *not* that a second-order belief about *i*, in the presence of *i*, need not amount to knowledge regarding *i*. Instead, the problem was that in attempting to show that second-order beliefs are invariably true (given satisfaction of CRA), we cannot stipulate, in our analysis of a case in which *S* believes that he has intentional state *i*, that *S* indeed *has i*. It seems to me that the most that Bilgrami has shown, *granting him the controversial (*), is that if *S* has a *true* second-order belief about an intentional state meeting CRA, then that belief amounts to knowledge. In order to establish the R-L direction of CT, however, Bilgrami must somehow show that second-order beliefs are bound to be true (given satisfaction of CRA). The present reasoning fails to show this.

Bilgrami gives another argument which, if successful, would establish the R-L direction of CT. He notes that his "intuitive starting point" regarding the phenomenon of self-deception is not necessary for his arguments to show CT. Still, he wants to argue that even in cases of self-deception, one's second-order beliefs are correct. Suppose that I self-attribute a first-order belief by uttering 'I believe that *p*'. Suppose that I am not prepared to act as would a normal *p*-believer. Then, according to Bilgrami (1998: 230–232), it would be a mistake to attribute to me the second-order belief standardly expressed by my avowal (a belief that I believe that *p*). So there cannot be a case in which I am correctly attributed that second-order belief and yet lack the pertinent first-order belief (in virtue of my being unprepared to act in ways characteristic of *p*-believers).

This argument is unpersuasive. If I am not prepared to act in characteristic *p*-believing ways, then the belief attributor's rational response would be to withhold attribution of a *first-order belief that p*. Whether it is *also* rational to withhold attribution of the *second-order belief* standardly expressed, according to Bilgrami, by my apparently sincere avowal (my utterance of 'I believe that *p*') is a further question. If we already knew that second-order beliefs are invariably true, then the first- and second-order attributions would be linked in the way asserted by Bilgrami. But that thesis about second-order belief is what the argument was meant to prove.

I conclude that Bilgrami's complex transcendental argument for the constitutive thesis CT is unsuccessful. He has not shown that knowledge of one's own mind is a condition for the possibility of responsible agency.

4 *Moran*

In Richard Moran's transcendental argument concerning self-knowledge, he seeks to elucidate one of the conditions for the possibility of being a rational agent possessed of a genuine system of beliefs. In particular, he wants to argue "that we can see it as a rational requirement on belief, on being a believer, that one should have access to what one believes in a way that is radically non-evidential, that does not rely on inferences from anything inner or outer" (Moran 1997: 143).[14]

Moore's Paradox has frequently been discussed in connection with self-knowledge. The following sentences can easily be true and yet seem exceedingly odd when asserted:

(1)   *p* and I do not believe that *p*.

(2)   *p* and I believe that ¬ *p*.

When true, (1) expresses the unsurprising fact of my ignorance of *p*'s truth; when true, (2) expresses the unsurprising fact of my mistaken belief concerning *p*'s truth value. In order to explain why the foregoing Moore-paradoxical sentences can easily be true and yet seem somehow pathological when I assert them, Moran appeals to an idea found in Wittgenstein and, more recently, in Gareth Evans's work: "I can report on my *belief* about *X* by considering nothing but *X* itself" (Moran 1997: 151).[15] For example, if I am asked whether I believe that a nuclear conflict is on the horizon, I typically do not answer by turning my gaze inward, by consulting the deliverances of an introspective faculty. Neither do I answer by considering my behavior or dispositions thereto. Instead, I turn my gaze outward and consider the facts of the geopolitical situation. In short, I answer the question 'Do I believe that *p*?' by answering the related question 'Is *p* true?' In Moran's phrase, the first question, about what I believe, is transparent to the second question, which is "not about me but about the world" (1997: 146).

This idea leads Moran to draw a distinction between two points of view upon one's own intentional mental states: the *theoretical/empirical* point of view and the *transcendent* point of view.[16] The theoretical/empirical point of view will typically involve evidence regarding one's own intentional states. I come to believe, for example, that I believe that my brother betrayed me as a result of psychoanalytic investigation of a pattern of my behavior that seems to reveal the existence of such a first-order belief. Yet when I consider the facts relevant to the question whether my brother betrayed me, I do not come to believe that he did. I do not, in virtue of such consideration, commit myself to the truth of the proposition that my brother betrayed me. In the course of accessing my own intentional states from the theoretical/empirical point of view, the assertion of a Moore-paradoxical sentence will not seem pathological. From this point of view upon my own intentional states, there is nothing surprising, for example, in my judging the following:

I believe that my brother betrayed me, even though he did not betray me.

There is good evidence for judging that I have that belief even though there is no good evidence for judging that he betrayed me.

By contrast, the transcendent point of view upon my own intentional states is not grounded in evidence regarding those states. My judgment that I believe that nuclear conflict is imminent is, instead, grounded in evidence regarding the geopolitical situation.[17] In order to settle the question of what I believe, I settle the pertinent question about the world. Thus, in forming a judgment about what I believe regarding future nuclear conflict, I simultaneously undertake a commitment to the truth of the proposition that nuclear conflict is imminent.

In the course of accessing my own intentional states from the transcendent point of view, the assertion of a Moore-paradoxical sentence will indeed seem pathological. From this point of view upon my own states, there is no gap between my judging that I believe that nuclear conflict is imminent and my judging that nuclear conflict is imminent. Thus my judgment,

I believe that nuclear conflict is imminent, even though nuclear conflict is not imminent.

will seem, from the transcendent point of view, exceedingly problematic.

Now we are in a position to restate the goal of Moran's transcendental argument: if one is a rational agent possessing a genuine system of beliefs—possessing a "psychological life"—then one must have "access to what one believes in a way that is radically non-evidential" (1997: 151, 143). To show this, according to Moran, we need to show that a rational, believing agent must adopt the transcendent point of view upon his own intentional states.

To show that, let us begin by trying to imagine the circumstances of a rational believer who *exclusively* adopts the theoretical/empirical point of view upon his own intentional states. Moran wishes to consider such an allegedly possible thinker, who has an *idealized, purely theoretical relation of expertise* towards himself. Let the evidential basis for such an expert include his behavior, dreams, thoughts, associations and feelings. Suppose further that the thinker's expertise is infallible. Still, this expertise does not "provide what is known within ordinary, first-person knowledge." This is so even though the thinker's expertise is characterized by Cartesian privacy (for, according to Moran, the non-behavioral part of the expert's evidential base, strangely, includes some of his mental states, such as his dreams).[18] Even vary the proposed example so that the thinker's expertise is afforded via his infallibly "reading his own mind" without inference from anything else. Still, suppose that even given all these assumptions regarding his special expertise, the thinker never takes the *transcendent*, ordinary first-person point of view upon his own states. This means that the thinker, in uttering 'I believe that p', expresses his belief that p without committing himself to the truth of p.[19] Taking even the most exquisite theoretical/empirical point of view upon his own states, a judgment, from this point of view, that one believes that p does not provide one with any reasons for acting on p's truth. From such a point of view, one's attitude towards one's own belief is on a par with one's attitude towards another's belief. This means that there is a gap between one's judging that one believes that p (from the theoretical/empirical point of view of expertise) and one's committing, in action, to the truth of p, just as there is a gap between one's judging that *another* believes that p and one's committing, in action, to the truth of p.

Putting these various considerations together, I reconstruct Moran's transcendental argument as follows:

(A)   If one is a rational agent possessing a genuine system of beliefs, then one commits oneself to acting on the truth of various propositions that one believes.

(B)   If one commits oneself to so acting, then one cannot exclusively adopt the theoretical/empirical point of view upon one's own beliefs.

(C)   So if one is a rational agent possessing a genuine system of beliefs, then one must sometimes adopt the transcendent point of view upon one's own beliefs, from which the question 'Do I believe that p?' is transparent to the question 'Is p true?'

It is worth noting that this argument is not primarily concerned with the *nonevidential* nature of self-knowledge, contrary to some of Moran's suggestions noted above. A being who exclusively reads his own mind in the manner envisioned by Moran would not satisfy the specified condition for the possibility of being a rational agent possessed of a genuine belief system. Unless the being adopted the transcendent point of view upon his own beliefs, he would not be such an agent, notwithstanding his allegedly noninferentially based judgments about his beliefs. The argument instead focuses upon the commitment to action involved in the transcendent point of view, not upon noninferentiality of judgments about one's beliefs.

Premise (A) seems plausible. It might be wondered whether a rational *believer* must commit to acting on the truth of the propositions he believes.[20] Though Bilgrami challenges this at the end of his paper, one might hold that it is possible for an utterly passive being to have a genuine belief system that is informed by rationality. But it is clearly another matter whether a rational *agent* with a genuine belief system could altogether fail to commit himself to acting on the truth of some of the propositions he believes. Even given the plausibility of (A), it should be noted that Moran's transcendental argument turns out not to concern the conditions for the possibility of being a rational believer, but rather the conditions for the possibility of being a rational agent possessed of beliefs.

Even if the argument is sound (and I will claim that premise (B) is problematic), the argument has some shortcomings. First, it does not bear on knowledge of mental states other than belief. The question whether I desire that p be the case, for example, is not transparent to the question whether p is true. Suppose that I settle the latter question in the negative. This leaves it wide open for me whether I desire that p be the case. For belief, no such gap is possible. This limitation of the argument is not a disgrace, though, since showing that we must adopt the transcendent point of view upon our *beliefs* would be a significant achievement. Second, Moran does not link avowals such as 'I believe that p' to second-order belief. Suppose, as does Moran, that such avowals express *first-order* beliefs upon which we adopt the transcendent point of view. It is not clear how this elucidates our *knowledge* of our own beliefs. It is natural to suppose that knowing that I believe that p involves at least a true belief that I believe that p. Moran's discussion tells us nothing about such second-order beliefs. Third, an elucidation of our knowledge of our own beliefs would presumably need to tell us something about the epistemic status of second-order beliefs. It is natural to suppose that knowing that I believe that p involves a *justified belief* that I believe that p. Moran's discussion tells us nothing about the epistemic status of such beliefs. It at best tells us that transcendent avowals of first-order belief are required if one is to be a rational, believing agent.

The main problem with the transcendental argument, however, is that the second premise is false. Consider again the self-blind Marty. He is committed to the truth of many of the propositions that are the objects of his first-order beliefs. He acts on his belief that a lion is near, for example, by fleeing and warning his friends. But he exclusively adopts the theoretical/empirical point of view upon his beliefs. In order to answer the question whether he believes that a lion is near, he examines his behavior or consults others' opinions about his beliefs. He never adopts the transcendent point of view upon his own beliefs. For him, the question whether he believes that p is never transparent to the question whether p is true. When he eventually says 'I believe that p' on the basis of behavioral or testimonial evidence, this assertion leaves open for him the questions whether p is true and whether to act on p's truth. Even though he is committed to the truth of many of the propositions he believes, this commitment does not find expression in his assertions about what he believes. This is in contrast to an ordinary believer like me, whose avowals of belief are typically made from the transcendent point of view and thus do express commitment to the truth of believed propositions.

In short, it seems that there can be a rational agent with a genuine belief system who is self-blind. He commits to the truth of various propositions that he believes, but he does not express his commitment to action in avowals made from the transcendent point of view. His assertions regarding his own beliefs are made exclusively from the theoretical/empirical point of view. If such a rational agent is possible, as indeed seems so, then premise (B) of Moran's transcendental argument is false.[21] This is because it is one thing to have a commitment to acting on the truth of p and another to express that commitment in avowals, in the way that we standardly do.

5   Conclusion

I conclude that the two transcendental arguments concerning self-knowledge considered here are unsuccessful.[22] Those who are worried about the self-knowledge skeptic's argument will need to look elsewhere for a satisfying answer.[23] Further, I believe that the work of Bilgrami and Moran does not in the end succeed in providing genuine elucidation of the nature of self-knowledge.

Notes

1. See Putnam 1975 and Burge 1982a.

2. Suppose for simplicity's sake that the twins lack chemical knowledge. Otherwise, they would differ in, e.g., their utterances regarding the inner structure of what they call 'water'.

3. Thanks to Kevin Falvey for a helpful discussion of this point.

4. See Bilgrami 1998 and Moran 1997. When the current paper was in press, Moran's book *Authority and Estrangement* (Princeton: Princeton University Press, 2001) appeared in print. The article just cited is the basis for chapter 3 of that book.

5. Many think that Kant's own transcendental arguments in the Transcendental Deduction and the Refutation of Idealism *start from* the premise that I have self-knowledge. See my "Transcendental Arguments I" (1983), "Transcendental Arguments II" (1984), and "The Anti-skeptical Epistemology of the Refutation of Idealism" (1991).

6. In this section I refer frequently to this article.

7. Bilgrami wishes to distinguish the connection between first-order intentional states and second-order beliefs about them that is involved in the constitutive thesis from the connection highlighted by the observational model. The latter is a contingent, causal connection, whereas the former is, according to Bilgrami, guaranteed to hold by "the very idea of a mental state." Elizabeth Fricker (1998) argues that it could be a necessary, a priori truth that first-order states reliably cause second-order beliefs.

8. This same structure holds for cases of self-deception regarding nondoxastic first-order states, according to Bilgrami.

9. See Strawson 1962. Even though Bilgrami writes as if all and only responsible actions are free actions, this has been a matter of controversy since Harry Frankfurt's influential "Alternate Possibilities and Moral Responsibility" (1969). Frankfurt maintains that one can be a responsible agent while lacking the ability to do otherwise that is traditionally associated with freedom.

10. This is my own formulation of Bilgrami's goal.

11. For a critical discussion, see my 1998 essay.

12. One well-known approach to the concept of freedom of the will *does* focus upon second-order intentional states. Harry Frankfurt focuses upon the role of *second-order desires* in the concept of freedom. However, Frankfurt does not

connect freedom with second-order *beliefs* that amount to self-knowledge. See his 1971 paper, in which Frankfurt holds that free action involves a second-order preference that the action's motivating desire be effective. John M. Fischer and Mark Ravizza develop a theory of responsibility as a form of *control* in *Responsibility and Control: A Theory of Moral Responsibility* (1998). According to their theory, the actual mechanism that guides one's responsible action must be counter-factually responsive to reasons. On this approach, in responsible action, an agent's motivational apparatus must satisfy certain conditions of which he is typically unaware. He need not *know* his motivational apparatus, and he need not know his motives either.

13. The same objection can be made to Tyler Burge's account of the role of self-verifying judgments in self-knowledge. See his 1988b paper and my 1992b paper. The objection also applies to any approach to self-knowledge that focuses upon covariation between first- and second-order content, such as Davidson's (1988) and Heil's (1988). See my 1995 paper for this criticism of covariation strategies.

14. In this section I refer frequently to this article.

15. See Evans 1982 and also Gallois 1996.

16. Moran sometimes says "transcendental" instead.

17. However, we must be careful to note that the evidence that justifies me in believing that nuclear conflict is imminent does not justify me in believing that I believe that nuclear conflict is imminent. Evidence about the geopolitical situation is not evidence about what I believe. See my 1998 paper.

18. How does the expert have access to *these* mental states?

19. Moran, unlike Bilgrami, does not hold that such an avowal expresses a *second-order* belief about what he believes.

20. If the believer is a brain in a vat, he will never succeed in acting on his commitments.

21. Moran obviously cannot simply assume that self-blindness is impossible in rational agents. This would be to assume a necessary connection between rational agency and correct second-order beliefs about one's beliefs, which Shoemaker unsuccessfully attempted to establish. See note 12.

22. My 1999 paper discusses some work of Andre Gallois and Tyler Burge on the problem of self-knowledge. See also my 2001 and forthcoming essays.

23. Thanks to John Fischer for a helpful discussion and also to the members of a graduate seminar I gave at the University of California at Santa Barbara in the spring of 1999. This paper was presented at a conference on self-knowledge at the University of Utah in spring 2002. I thank Douglas Lavin, my commentator, and Ram Neta, who read an earlier version of this paper.

10

Externalism, Davidson, and Knowledge of Comparative Content

Joseph Owens

Psychological externalism, the offspring of semantic externalism, first clearly articulated and defended by Tyler Burge (1979), challenges a variety of deeply entrenched philosophical intuitions about the mind. It challenges entrenched philosophical thinking on physical determinism, psychophysical identity, the nature of psychological explanation, and, most important, self-knowledge. Many have argued that psychological externalism is incompatible with the immediate, authoritative knowledge we take ourselves to have of our own occurrent attitudes. And they argue so much the worse for externalism: rendering impossible the knowledge we know ourselves to have, psychological externalism must be rejected. To others, the apparent conflict is merely apparent, genuine self-knowledge is perfectly compatible with, and poses no serious challenge to, psychological externalism.[1] In a series of papers, Donald Davidson has opted for yet another response. He sides neither with those who argue that externalism is incompatible with self-knowledge, nor yet with those who argue that externalism is simply compatible with such knowledge. He argues that, in addressing this issue, we must distinguish between different brands of externalism. Some brands are compatible with self-knowledge, and the arguments of those who deny this are based on a misunderstanding of self-knowledge. Other brands of externalism, however, really are incompatible with self-knowledge, and such versions must be rejected on this score.

In this paper, I examine Davidson's treatment of externalism and self-knowledge (1987, 1991, 1989, 1990). I argue that he misunderstands why many philosophers have thought that externalism is incompatible with self-knowledge. I agree with him that such theorists do indeed misunderstand the nature of self-knowledge, but, I argue, their misunderstanding is not the one Davidson charges them with. I argue that these theorists misunderstand self-knowledge insofar as they think of such knowledge as enabling one to determine that this thought is the same or different from that thought, and do so without consulting the external world. I then turn to Davidson's own arguments purporting to show that certain other brands of externalism are incompatible with self-knowledge. His arguments, I maintain, fail; they too rest on the same misunderstanding of self-knowledge.

I   Some Metaphysical Preliminaries

First, a brief categorization of some of the different kinds of externalism. Here it is enough to draw the distinctions that are relevant to Davidson's position. I use the term 'P-externalism' for the kind of externalism ultimately derived from Putnam's thought experiment—an externalism in which the twins are ensconced in physically different environments, and this environmental difference warrants the difference in content ascriptions. I use the term 'B-externalism' for the kind of externalism initially advanced by Burge, an externalism in which the different content ascriptions reflect differences in the linguistic practice, rather than differences in the physical environment. In addition, I also distinguish between (a) the externalist who accepts such arguments as showing only that the twins warrant different ascriptions, and (b) those who accept the arguments as showing (in addition) that the twins differ in their psychological states. There is a growing consensus that Putnamian and Burgean arguments do indeed establish something of great consequence. They seem to show beyond serious doubt that the *twins merit different psychological characterizations*—one twin may truly be said to believe that he has arthritis in his thigh, while this is not true of the other. But not everyone who grants this much is prepared to take the final metaphysical step, *to assign different psychological states to the twins*. Theorists (Fodor 1987, Lewis 1981, McGinn 1982, Kim 1982) balk at this step for a variety of reasons, and they employ a variety of strategies in their efforts to explain how identical twins in externalist thought experiments can satisfy different psychological characterizations, including belief characterizations, while not differing in psychological state. They argue, for example, that the different psychological characterizations are simply contingent characterizations, in the light of relevant external factors, of inner psychological or neurological states, states that are constant across twins. They attempt to distinguish between two kinds of content, wide and narrow, etc.

Let us call those who accept these arguments in their entirety 'metaphysical externalists', and let us call those who refuse to take the final step 'linguistic externalists'. Davidson is a linguistic externalist: he agrees that twins ensconced in different physical environments admit of different psychological descriptions, but he denies that their mental states are somehow external—he denies that they differ in their mental states. He argues that, given that mental states are ordinarily designated by expressions that make appeal to external factors, one can infer that the twins admit of different descriptions, but one cannot infer that this entails that the twins differ in mental states. "I think such states are 'inner'," writes Davidson, "in the sense of being identical with states of body, and so identifiable without reference to objects or events outside the body; they are at the same time 'nonindividualistic' in the sense that they can be, and usually are, identified in part by their causal relations to events and objects outside the subject whose states they are" (1987: 444). Davidson, however, not only refuses to take the last metaphysical step, he doesn't accept B-externalism at all. Here, as we shall see, his arguments are primarily epistemological; he rejects the B-argument on grounds that it is incompatible with genuine self-knowledge (see section II.B). With this sketch of the metaphysics in hand, I turn to Davidson's treatment of the linkage between externalism and self-knowledge.

II *Davidson, Externalism, and Self-Knowledge*

Externalism is primarily a linguistic/metaphysical thesis, but shortly after it first appeared on the scene, opponents and proponents began focusing on its alleged epistemological implications: opponents argued that externalism was clearly incompatible with entrenched and reliable intuitions about self-knowledge and should be rejected on this score; proponents argued that the appearance of incompatibility was just that, an appearance, and a proper understanding of the arguments and the nature of self-knowledge dispels the apparent incompatibility. Davidson (1987: 445), one of the lead actors in this ongoing debate, has opted for a far more complex response, arguing that some forms of linguistic externalism, those of the P-variety, are compatible with self-knowledge, while other forms of externalism, including all forms of B-externalism, are incompatible and so must be rejected. In section A, I discuss Davidson's treatment of the linkage between P-externalism and self-knowledge, and in section B, I turn to his treatment of B-externalism and self-knowledge.

A   *Davidson on P-externalism and self-knowledge*

For most theorists, the distinction between P-externalism and B-externalism is not of any great import when it comes to the epistemological issue of self-knowledge. If content is determined by external factors, be they physical or linguistic, then self-knowledge appears threatened. But for Davidson, the distinction is crucial: he claims that P-externalism is indeed compatible with self-knowledge, but B-externalism is not. He sees the tension between self-knowledge and P-externalism arising from standard Twin Earth scenarios, noting that externalists such as Putnam do not seem concerned by this result, and that "they have not made much of an attempt to resolve the seeming conflict between their views and the strong intuition that first person authority exists" (1987: 446). This, he contends, is a mistake, for there is an apparent conflict here, one that must be addressed by externalist theorists. That *apparent* conflict between externalism (of the kind advanced by Putnam) and self-knowledge is, he argues, the product of two errors: (a) the metaphysical error that the externalist argument commits one to full-fledged metaphysical externalism, and (b) a mistaken picture of self-knowledge as something like perception of inner mental objects, beliefs, etc. Since according to the metaphysical externalist, thoughts are not in the head, they can hardly be grasped by the mind in the way required by first-person authority. Davidson simply rejects this line of reasoning; he rejects the supposition that externalist arguments support metaphysical externalism. He reads P-style arguments as supporting only the linguistic version of P-externalism. Just as identifying a condition as a sunburn does not mean that a sunburn is not a state of the skin, so identifying psychological states by external factors does not entail that they are not states of the head. But he recognizes that while this deflationary metaphysical reasoning may turn back the specific argument of some purveyors of incompatibility, it does not get to the heart of the epistemological problem. He urges, "An apparent difficulty remains.... In so far as the contents are identified in terms of external factors, first person authority necessarily lapses" (1987: 451).

But this is more than an *apparent difficulty*, since it clearly indicates that the move to weak, linguistic externalism fails to provide for *any* reconciliation between externalism and self-knowledge: what is at issue is the question of whether we have authoritative first-person knowledge of the *contents* of our attitudes. To use a Davidsonian phrase, what is at issue is whether we have such knowledge *of the state under a description that makes essential appeal to external objects.* Once we allow that the content description is sensitive to external factors, then the mere fact that this description happens to accidentally denote an inner state does not help at all with the epistemological issue of self-knowledge.

Sensitive to this, Davidson suggests that the real source of the tension is much deeper. It is "a picture of mind which has become so ingrained in our philosophical tradition that it is almost impossible to escape its influence" (1987: 453). The picture is one of the mind as "a theater, in which the conscious self watches a passing show": beliefs are objects present to the mind, to be recognized, entertained, etc., by the self. Ultimately, this conception of the objects of thought undermines genuine self-knowledge. His solution is equally simple, namely, "get rid of the metaphor of objects before the mind" (1987: 454).

Davidson is correct in arguing that the apparent conflict between externalism and self-knowledge is primarily due to a mistaken view of self-knowledge, but, I think, the central mistake is not the one he focuses on. The mistake is not so much a mistake about the mechanisms of self-knowledge—whether or not it is something like inner perception of mental objects—but about the very nature of self-knowledge, what self-knowledge consists in; the real issue is, *what is it I need to know if, for example, I am said to know that I am thinking the thought that this is water?* There is, I think, a largely unrecognized presupposition that I can know that I am entertaining a thought such as that this is water (in the sense in which we think of ourselves as knowing what we think) only if I can rule out the possibility that I am entertaining the thought that this is twater (where water thoughts are different from twater thoughts). I will argue that this is a mistaken view that it lies behind most of the epistemological opposition to externalism, that Davidson subscribes to it, and that it subsequently plays a key role in motivating his claim that B-externalism is incompatible with self-knowledge.

It is, indeed, as Davidson argues, difficult to shake off the shackles of that deeply misguided picture of ourselves as having something akin to inner eyes that serve to reveal the inner realm of mental objects. Davidson is correct in his outright rejection of this picture, and he has for many years played a key role in exposing the problems that plague this Cartesian conception. But, contrary to Davidson's intuitions, these Cartesian intuitions about the inner eye don't seem to play a central role in the more prominent arguments that have been advanced in support of the claim that externalism is incompatible with self-knowledge. The central arguments for the incompatibility thesis seem to rest on a somewhat weaker and lest obviously objectionable premise. Consider Davidson's own argument:

The First says to herself, when facing a glass of water, 'Here's a glass of water'; the Second mutters exactly the same sounds to herself when facing a glass of twater. Each speaks the truth, since their words mean different things. And since each is sincere, it is natural to suppose they believe different things, the first believing there is a glass of water in front of her, the second believing there is a glass of twater in front of *her*. But do they know what they believe? If the meanings of their words, and thus the beliefs expressed by using these words, are partly determined by external factors about which the agents are ignorant, their beliefs or meanings are not narrow in Putnam's sense. There is therefore nothing on the basis of which either speaker can tell which state she is in, for there is no internal or external clue to the difference available. We ought, it seems, to conclude that neither speaker knows what she means or thinks.   (Davidson 1987: 445)

I see no reason to suppose that this argument rests on some perceptual model of introspection. The idea is rather the simpler one: externalist thought experiments appear to demonstrate that given an appropriate difference in the external world, there will be a difference in content, a difference in belief, without this difference being reflected in any inner detectable manner. This seems to imply that I can't tell, without consulting the external world, which of these two thoughts I am entertaining, and hence I cannot be said to know what it is I believe. I don't see any reason to suppose that this argument rests on any view of mental states as being inner objects subject to the scrutiny of an inner eye. A number of other philosophers have indeed argued at great length that externalism is incompatible with self-knowledge. The source of the supposed tension is evident in the following reductio (Brueckner 1990: 448):

(i)   I claim to know, independently of any knowledge of the external world, that I am entertaining the thought that some water is dripping.

(ii)   Suppose that I know (without consulting my environment) that externalism is true.

(iii)   Given (ii), the thought that I am now entertaining—the water thought—is a different thought than the thought that twater is dripping (the thought I would have in an XYZ world).

(iv)   Hence, assuming my claim in (i) is true, I am in a position to know, without consulting my environment, that I am not thinking the thought that some twater is dripping.

(v)   Hence, I am in a position to know, without consulting my environment, that I am not in an XYZ world, a twater world.

(vi)   But neither I nor anyone else is in a position to know that one is not in an XYZ world without consulting one's physical context.

(vii)   Hence, if externalism is true, I don't know, without consulting my environment, that I am entertaining the thought that water is dripping.

In thus arguing for the incompatibility thesis, Brueckner assumes that (vi) is true, and I see no reason to contest this; I can ascertain that I am not in an XYZ environment only by investigating the environment.[2] Also I think Brueckner is correct in thinking that externalism does call into question some elements in the traditional conception of introspection, but the elements it calls into question are not the ones usually noted. Externalism calls into question not self-knowledge itself, as Brueckner argues, but the conception of self-knowledge that figures prominently in (iv). Why think that (iv) is true? Why think that if the thought that water is dripping is different from the thought that twater is dripping, then I can know that I am thinking the thought that some water is dripping only if I know that I am not thinking the thought that some twater is dripping? The move to (iv) rests, I believe, on an attractive but mistaken view of what one must know to know that one is thinking the thought that p— one must also know what it is one does not believe. One can fashion the mistaken view in a variety of ways. Here are three rough formulations:

(C_1)   If p and p^* are different thoughts and I know that I am entertaining the thought that p, then I am in a position to know that (in entertaining this thought) I am not entertaining the thought that p^*, and I am in a position to know this without any investigation of my external world.

(C_2)   If p and p^* are different thoughts, then the kind of knowledge I have when I know that I am entertaining the thought that p is enough to know that I am not entertaining the thought that p^*.

These two formulations are, if you like, simple expressions of the minimal premise needed to underwrite the move from (iii) to (iv). The basic background intuition is perhaps better captured by (C_3):

(C_3)   A subject's ability to recognize herself as entertaining the same or different thoughts, at times t_1 and t_2, is not contingent upon her having information about her external physical environment, at t_1 and t_2, whether it is, for example, an H_2O world or an XYZ world, nor is it contingent upon her having knowledge about the public conventions governing the terms she uses, etc.

These three formulations of (C) differ in important ways and they are all in need of refinement, but they will do for our purposes here. Since my remarks will apply equally to all three, I will simply speak of (C). I will argue, in section B, that (C) is false, but first, let us be clear about its centrality in arguments of the form canvassed by Davidson and Brueckner. Clearly, some such principle is required if arguments like Brueckner's are to work at all. The theorist who rejects the kind of self-knowledge enshrined in (C) will simply reject the move to (iv). Such a theorist will opt for a weak sense of self-knowledge, one in which one can know that one believes that p and not necessarily know whether or not one believes that p^* in believing that p. Such a theorist will insist that in Brueckner's example, I can know that I am entertaining the thought that water is dripping without knowing whether I am entertaining the thought that twater is dripping in entertaining this very thought. (Note that I am using the same language to fashion my original water/object thought and to fashion my metathought about my original thought.)

   Much more needs to be said about (C), and I will return to this topic in section B, but for the moment we can, I think, agree that a thesis of this sort, rather than some perceptual model of introspection, seems to lie behind the alleged incompatibility of P-externalism and self-knowledge.[3] I turn now to B-externalism.

B   *Davidson on B-externalism and self-knowledge*

Davidson has argued that this form of externalism is truly incompatible with self-knowledge. I contend that Davidson's argument here also rests on an implicit appeal to (C). As noted at the outset, Davidson rejects B-externalism and the arguments Burge and others offer in its favor. This kind of account, he argues, is radically different than P-externalism. It is incompatible with genuine self-knowledge and must be rejected if entrenched intuitions about self-knowledge are to be retained. I will treat separately his analysis of where the B-argument supposedly goes astray (section 1), and his argument that this brand of externalism is incompatible with genuine self-knowledge (section 2). In section 3, I maintain that (C) should be rejected.

1   The alleged error in the argument for B-externalism   Davidson rejects the Burgean intuition that an individual, Bart, might truly believe that he has arthritis in his thigh; the argument fails, he suggests because Bart's conceptual misunderstanding of "arthritis" undermines this claim:

> Suppose that I, who think that 'arthritis' applies to inflammation of the joints only if caused by calcium deposits, and my friend Arthur, who knows better, both sincerely utter to Smith the words 'Carl has arthritis'. According to Burge, if other things are more or less equal . . . , then our words on this occasion mean the same thing, Arthur and I mean the same thing by our words, and we express the same belief. . . . If Smith (unspoiled by philosophy) reports to still another . . . that Arthur and I both have said, and believe, that Carl has arthritis, he may actively mislead *his* hearers. If this danger were to arise, Smith, alert to the facts, would not simply say 'Arthur and Davidson both believe Carl has arthritis'; he would add something like, 'But Davidson thinks arthritis must be caused by calcium deposits'. The need to make this addition I take to show that the simple attribution was not quite right; there was a relevant difference in the thoughts Alfred and I expressed when we said 'Carl has arthritis'. (Davidson 1987: 449)

The first thing to note is that Burge, and others who accept B-style arguments, can accept all of this save the closing comment ("I take this to show that the simple attribution was not quite right"). Indeed, they can even accept this comment, so long as "not quite right" is not read as "not true." They do not opt for some kind of linguistic legalism, nor need they interpret each utterance literally, regardless of the speaker's competence and intentions. Nor do they deny that there is an ordinary sense of "mean" in which it is quite appropriate to say that Davidson and Alfred mean different things by the term "arthritis." All they need is that it is *true* that Davidson believes that Carl has arthritis. They allow that there might be all kinds of differences between Davidson and other speakers, and that these differences might be very relevant in specific conversational contexts. Once again, *all they need is that Davidson's inadequate understanding does not entail that he cannot believe that Carl has arthritis.* (See Burge 1979: 87–103.)

Davidson indeed recognizes that Burge is likely to opt for this kind of response, and offers a further consideration:

> Burge does not have to be budged by this argument, of course, since he can insist that the report is literally correct, but could, like any report, be misleading. I think, on the other hand, that this reply would overlook the extent to which the contents of one belief necessarily depend on the contents of others. Thoughts are not independent atoms, and so there can be no simple, rigid, rule for the correct attribution of a single thought. (Davidson 1987: 449)

Once again, this does not seem to be an accurate portrayal of the externalist argument. B-externalists are not committed to some peculiar kind of intellectual atomism—that is, to interpret individual assertions without taking any account of the rest of the subject's linguistic capacities and dispositions. In arguing for the claim that Alf believes that he has arthritis in the thigh, externalists do not simply cite the fact that he is disposed to utter "I have arthritis in my thigh." No, they draw on a variety of facts about his general competence, his other beliefs, what he has heard about arthritis, what advice he offers others, etc. If we are to do justice to these other beliefs—to the fact that he seems to believe that elderly people have arthritis, that his doctor told him that he had arthritis, that he thinks he has the same disease in his thigh, etc.—we should read him as believing that he has arthritis in the thigh. We attribute the confused belief, not in isolation from his other beliefs, but rather in the light of these other beliefs.

Elsewhere Davidson suggests a very different reason for rejecting the argument for B-externalism: "There are those who are pleased to hold that the meanings of words are magically independent of the speaker's intentions; for example that they depend on how the majority, or the best-informed, or the best-born, of the community in which the speaker lives speak, or perhaps how they would speak if they took enough care" (1990: 310–311).

There is nothing to this charge of magic. In fashioning his belief that he has arthritis, Alf employs a linguistic device that he inherits from his linguistic community. He employs the word "arthritis," not merely a sound that happens to be acoustically similar to sounds produced by other speakers around him (this acoustic similarity is, of course, preserved across the twin worlds). He employs a term that has a use and a history, and the use and history of this term is part of its very identity. This is the lesson of semantic externalism—the original story told by Kripke and Putnam. The history of a proper name or kind term enters into the identity of a term, determining, in part, who or what we refer to when we use the name or term. The fact that a speaker's reference is thus determined in part by contextual, historical factors does not make for magic, and there is no magic in the arthritis-type case either. The speaker uses the term 'arthritis' to fashion his belief, not merely to express a belief that is fashioned without the aid of any linguistic devices; he uses this term in thinking the very thought that he has arthritis. Since he uses this term to fashion the belief, there is every reason to suppose that the character of the belief thus fashioned, the very content of the belief, is in part determined by the device employed, *a device whose character is determined by public conventions.* I see no magic here, only the rejection of an inner conceptual life that is individualistic—an inner life in which the identity of the expressions is determined by the subject herself.

I think it safe to conclude that Davidson has not provided us with any reason for rejecting the specific moves in the B-externalist argument. In particular, he has not provided us with any reason for rejecting the claim that Bart believes that he has arthritis in his thigh. His objections ultimately all hang on the alleged implications of B-externalism for self-knowledge, and to this I now turn.

2 The claim that B-externalism is incompatible with self-knowledge P-hyphenate, Davidson insists, is compatible with self-knowledge, but it is another story entirely in the case of B-externalism. B-externalism, even in its linguistic form, is incompatible with self-knowledge and so should be rejected outright. Before turning to Davidson's explicit remarks on this issue, let me quickly mention and put aside a number of possible explanations for this differing treatment of P-externalism and B-externalism.

First, Davidson has argued, as noted above, that the widespread perception that there is a conflict between externalism and self-knowledge is largely due to a mistaken understanding of self-knowledge as involving something like inner perception. But that is not what is at issue here. In this case the conflict is supposedly genuine; B-externalism, he claims, really is incompatible with authoritative self-knowledge. In any case, this is an unlikely explanation of what is at stake here, since Burge and many other B-externalists share Davidson's rejection of the perceptual model of introspection. Nor can the conflict between this brand of externalism and self-knowledge rise from the mere fact that on this externalist model, content is a function of external factors, factors which the subject need not be fully cognizant of. B-externalism does not differ from P-externalism on this score. Finally, even though Davidson is not sympathetic to content essentialism, to the idea that *mental states* are individuated by content—so that a difference in content brings in its wake a difference in *state*—this is not the source of the problem either. If this were the problem, then his objection to B-externalism would rest on the move from weak linguistic externalism to strong metaphysical externalism in the argument for B-externalism. Though this move, and the resulting metaphysics, is rejected by Davidson (as noted in my discussion of P-externalism), it is not the root problem here. *Davidson rejects B-externalism as incompatible with genuine self-knowledge, even when one limits oneself to the weak linguistic version of it.* He rejects the B-form of externalism which is limited to showing that identical twins may merit different psychological characterizations, different 'arthritis' beliefs, without making the further metaphysical claim that the twins thus differ in psychological states. The problem with B-externalism and, similarly, with examples such as Burge's arthritis case, is, Davidson claims (1987: 448; 1990: 310), that these theories and examples allow public conventions to determine content. This seems to make content independent of the speaker's intentions, and so it opens the way to not knowing what it is you are thinking or saying when you think the thought, 'I have arthritis'.

In cases of that sort, how exactly is the subject's mistaken or incomplete information supposed to tell against self-knowledge? The problem seems to be simply this: in examples such as the 'arthritis' thought experiment, there is clearly a sense in which the subject misunderstands or fails to fully understand the thought she entertains, and Davidson concludes that if we insist on attributing the confused belief to the subject, then this entails that the subject does not know what she is thinking. Consider a familiar case: Jones, who is generally competent in English, thinks an agreement must be written if it is to be a genuine, legally binding contract. This is not an example of one who just mouths the word 'contract'; there is, we may assume, little or no question about Jones's usage of 'contract' save on this score. Here we seem to have a clear case of conceptual misunderstanding as opposed to mere incomplete understanding. When asked to explain, to explicate in other words, what she meant when she claimed to have no contract with Smith, she tells us that there is no written document in which she obligated herself to do such and such for Smith. In this kind of case, it is true that there is a sense in which Jones does misunderstand what it is she claimed when she claimed she had no contract with Smith. There is a sense in which she does not fully understand her initial claim or belief. The B-theorist recognizes this, but she denies that this kind of misunderstanding is incompatible with knowing what you believe—in the sense in which this is independent of knowledge of the external world.

In the case of Jones and her attempts to explicate what she meant (and believed) when she asserted 'I do not have a contract with Smith' three options present themselves.

(1)   (a) We can claim that the subject did say and believe that she had no contract, and (b) *taking her explication into account as the expression of self-knowledge, as constituting her knowledge of what she said and thought, we can say that she did not know what she said or believed.*

(2)   We can take the subject's explication as (a) an expression of genuine self-knowledge, and (b) an accurate explication of the thought the subject *actually* expressed by her utterance 'I have no contract with Smith'. In this case there is no conflict with self-knowledge, but the subject cannot be truly said to believe that she has no contract with Smith—she believes rather that she has no legally binding written agreement with Smith.

This appears to be Davidson's position.

(3)   We can say (a) that the subject did express the thought that she had no contract with Smith by her expression, 'I have no contract with Smith', and (b) that she knows the content of her thought. She knows that she meant and believed that she had no contract with Smith. We then take her explication as giving us further information as to what she took that thought to amount to, entailed, etc. She thinks that her thought *that she has no contract with Smith* amounts to pretty much the same thing as, *I have no written, legally binding, agreement with Smith.* In this, she is mistaken.

Option (1) is the one Davidson thinks the B-externalist is committed to; option (2) is Davidson's own option, his understanding of the case; and option (3) is Burge's reading, a reading shared by other externalists. Why think, as Davidson does, that the externalist is committed to (1)? That is, why think that the externalist, who is indeed committed to the claim that Jones says and believes that she has no contract (thus ruling out (2)), must also deny that she knows what she believes? Why deny the externalist option (3)? Once again, (C) appears to be the culprit. So long as we cling to (C), we close the door to the following: Jones knows what she believes when she asserts 'I have no contract with Smith' (she knows that she believes that she has no contract with Smith), and she knows what she believes when she asserts 'I have no written legally binding contract with Smith' (she knows that she believes that she has no written legally binding contract with Smith), and she *mistakenly* thinks that in asserting and believing the one, she asserts and believes the other. So long as we assume (C) is true, we close the door to this move and to (3). And this, I suggest, is why Davidson reads the externalist as committed to (1), this is why he thinks B-externalism is incompatible with self-knowledge.

3   The status of (C)   Externalism is incompatible with (C), but this does not tell against externalism, simply because there are strong reasons, independent of externalism, for thinking that (C) is false. We don't, I think, need to argue the first point; if sameness and difference in belief content is determined in part by the character of the external world, and this sameness and difference in external context need not be reflected in any inner-experiential fashion, then clearly the subject might not be able to tell, independent of knowledge of his environment, whether two tokens are tokens of the same or different beliefs. But why think that (C) is false? Introspection is of little or no help with this issue—though, of course, on traditional Cartesian models it should decide the issue. But whatever our view of introspection, our practice clearly tells against (C).

First, the question as to whether one belief is the same as or different from another has at times surfaced in philosophical debate, and the ways in which we have attempted to resolve it tells us against (C). This kind of question was center stage in Benson Mates's influential discussion of synonymy and intentional contexts (1950). Fregeans had tended to assume that synonyms are interchangeable in intentional contents, and Mates challenged this assumption by examining the behavior of synonyms in multiply embedded contexts. Here is a typical Mates's story: Jones, we suppose, is rational and so believes that whoever believes that Ann is a doctor, believes that Ann is a doctor. Thinking that 'doctor' and 'physician' are synonyms, he is tempted to believe that whoever believes that Ann is a doctor believes that Ann is a physician. Thinking about all of this, he is then led to ask himself, "Is my thought that whoever believes that Ann is a doctor believes that Ann is a doctor the same as my thought that whoever believe that Ann is a doctor believes that Ann is a physician?" My interest here is not with any specific answer to this question (Mates's or otherwise), but rather with the predicament Jones finds himself in, and with the ways in which Jones might attempt to resolve his doubt. First, Jones is fully competent in English and knows what he is thinking when he entertains the thought he expresses by 'Whoever believes that Ann is a doctor believes that Ann is a doctor', and he knows what he is thinking when he entertains the thought he expresses by 'Whoever believes that Ann is a doctor believes that Ann is a physician'. He knows all of this, but he does not know whether these thoughts are the same or different. (The story gets even more complicated and paradoxical as one deepens the embedding [Owens 1989, 1990]: are the token thoughts I entertain using the sentences 'No one doubts that whoever believes that Ann is a doctor believes that Ann is a doctor', and 'No one doubts that whoever believes that Ann is a doctor believes that Ann is a physician' tokens of the same or different thoughts?) This example clearly suggests, without any appeal to externalism, that one can, in a very ordinary sense, know that one is thinking the thought that p and not know whether or not one is also thinking the thought that p^* in thinking this very thought. Moreover, introspection is of no assistance to Jones in his efforts to determine whether or not these thoughts are the same or different. I think it is clear that Jones should take into account whatever relevant theory there is—linguistic, psychological, or philosophical. He should, for example, take into account the fact that these are embedded contexts; he should investigate whether or not the terms are genuine synonyms; he should allow for the fact that some subjects might use these same terms and not be fully acquainted of the relations between them; etc. I take it that these remarks are simply common sense, but if they are at all reliable, then our ability to distinguish sameness and difference in our thoughts *is* contingent on our having knowledge of the external world, knowledge of linguistic conventions, etc., (C) apparently is false.[4]

Second, (C) is incompatible with how we ordinarily treat examples in which conceptual confusion is involved—examples such as Jones's belief that whales are fish, his belief that contracts must be written, his belief that he has arthritis in his knee and thigh, etc. Our practice allows that the ascription '*S* believes that p' may be literally true, even though *S*'s best efforts at explicating (using other words) the belief he fashions as 'p' are inaccurate and confused, and this fact, does not tell against the kind of self-knowledge we are supposed to have independent of any investigation into the character of our environment. Consider Jones once again and his belief that he has arthritis in his knee. Here Jones's best efforts at explicating, saying in other words what he means by 'I have arthritis in my knee' (what belief he expresses with this sentence) are confused and inaccurate. When asked to explicate his belief, he claims that his belief that he has arthritis in the knee is simply the belief that he has a rheumatoid disease in the knee. As noted earlier, I think it is clear that our practice allows that the ascription 'Jones believes that he has arthritis in his knee' may be literally true even when his attempts at articulation and explication reveal such elements of confusion.[5] This is not a case of begging the question against the proponent of (C); there is really no room for doubting the practice on this score. To think otherwise is to deny that anyone could be truly conceptually confused.[6] But once we admit this, we have little or no option but to reject (C). Jones entertains the thought that he has arthritis in his knee (indeed, believes it), he entertains the thought that he has a rheumatoid disease in the knee, and the thinks these are the same thought. These thoughts are in fact different thoughts, but this is not something that he can be aware of just from the entertaining of these thoughts; no scrutiny of the "thoughts themselves," no matter how critical, will reveal their difference. Our ordinary practice simply does not conform to the strictures of (C). There really is a sense in which we can fail to know what it is we believe when we believe that p (e.g., that Joan has arthritis), but this is just how it is, and such lack of knowledge is not incompatible with the kind of self-knowledge we are assumed to have.

III   *Conclusion*

In the much-quoted paragraph 66 of the *Philosophical Investigations,* Wittgenstein admonishes his interlocutor: "Don't say there must be ... but look and see.... To repeat: don't think, but look!" In this passage, Wittgenstein was, of course, concerned with the classical intuition that there *must* be something common to the various entities answering to a general term, but the injunction is worth keeping in mind whenever one engages in abstract philosophical thought, especially when one feels the attraction of "it must be such and such." The power and refreshing character of *Naming and Necessity* is in large part due to the fact that in it Kripke breaks out of the cycle and *looks afresh* at the phenomena—naming, meaning, necessity, etc. In doing so, he abandons previous conceptions of how things *must* be. In particular he abandons the idea that reference must be determined by something in the speaker's head—descriptions, images, etc. On examining the phenomena, it is clear that reference is in large part determined by external historical factors—a historical chain linking the speaker to her referent (despite errors in her associated descriptions, incomplete descriptions, etc.).

But this is also the case with Putnam and Burge: here too we have a fresh examination of the phenomena, and here too conceptions of how things *must* be are abandoned—once again, contextual factors are seen to play a crucial role in the actual practice of interpretation, meaning, and attitude characterizations; once again, the supposition that these things *must* be determined by states of the speaker's head is abandoned. And the same is true of self-knowledge. Here too *an examination of our practices leads us to abandon a conception of what such knowledge must consist in*, to abandon the intuition that self-knowledge must enable the subject to determine sameness and difference in her beliefs without any reliance on knowledge of the external world, to abandon (C). Such an abandonment does not come easy. It is, after all, an abandonment of a conception of how things must be. And such conceptions shape and constrain the rest of the philosophical story; they are the frameworks inside which we construct and evaluate our accounts. This same conception of self-knowledge has motivated much of the antagonism to psychological externalism and underwritten the charge that they are incompatible. In this essay I have examined Donald Davidson's complex response to psychological externalism, in particular his rejection of B-Externalism, and I have argued that his response too is in large part the product of that implicit conception of what self-knowledge must be. The appropriate response, I suggest, is Wittgenstein's: look at the actual practice!

Notes

1. There is already a vast literature on the linkages, or supposed linkages, between psychological externalism and knowledge, knowledge of the self, knowledge of the world, and knowledge of other minds. See especially Putnam 1981, Brueckner 1986, Davidson 1987, Burge 1988, Falvey and Owens 1994.

2. Others have taken a very different tack, arguing that one can use externalist intuitions and self-knowledge to defeat the skeptic. See, e.g., Putnam 1981.

3. Of course, intuitions about the nature of introspection, about how it is we have self-knowledge, may underwrite a theorist's subscription to (C). But that is another matter. In the examples at hand, there is no clear commitment to a perceptual model of introspection.

4. A similar lesson can be extracted from the Russell/Strawson debate on definite descriptions. Both Russell and Strawson were more than competent in their use of definite descriptions. They both understood the sentences 'The king of France is bald', and 'There is a king of France, only one, and whoever is a king of France is bald'. And each knew what it is he expressed by each sentence. Despite this agreement, they famously disagreed as to whether these sentences encode the same or different contents—as to whether they expressed the same or different contents by these sentences. Once again, appeal to introspection is of no use.

5. This, of course, forces attention back on the character of the second-order judgment—I believe that I have arthritis in my thigh. For some discussion of this issue, see Burge 1979 and Falvey and Owens 1994.

6. Some have taken the heroic route of rejecting the possibility of genuine conceptual confusion, usually offering some kind of metalinguistic reconstrual of these cases.

11

Memory and Knowledge of Content

Kevin Falvey

I

Much recent work on first-person authority has been characterized by a desire to avoid construing it as based on a faculty of inner perception, and has sought instead to ground our knowledge of our propositional mental states on constitutive relations between the contents of the second-order attitudes that embody such knowledge and the first-order attitudes they are knowledge about. Tyler Burge's (1988b) well-known discussion of the self-verifying character of "*cogito*-like" judgments of the form "I am thinking that *p*" is one example of the sort of approach I have in mind. In a similar vein, Gareth Evans (1982: 225) has drawn attention to the fact that, at least in certain central cases, a subject considers whether to self-attribute the belief that *p* by turning his attention to those matters in the world that are relevant to the truth of the proposition that *p*. Richard Moran (1997) has developed Evans's insight and embedded it in an intriguing account of first-person thought that features prominently the notion of the self as agent. Finally, to cut short rather arbitrarily what might otherwise become a very long list—Sydney Shoemaker (1988) has outlined a neofunctionalist position on self-knowledge according to which the second-order beliefs that comprise it are simply aspects of the ways in which the first-order states that are the objects of the knowledge are realized.[1] There are, of course, differences of emphasis and point of view among these authors, but I trust the affinities among them will be recognized. One such affinity is especially salient here. Most of this work places at center stage the authoritative character of one's judgments about one's *present* intentional mental states. It is therefore reasonable to ask how well this very general approach to self-knowledge accounts for our intuitions about our knowledge of our *past* thoughts, beliefs, and desires. It is with this question, or at least one aspect of it, that I will be concerned in this paper.

To assess the adequacy of a proposed account of first-person authority in handling knowledge of one's past thoughts, we need some sense of what our intuitions are in this area. So let me begin by offering some of my own. It seems to me that our knowledge of our own past mental states is often neither as direct nor as authoritative as our knowledge of our present mental states. The conceptual distance between a past self and one's present self must at least sometimes be bridged by something like interpretation of one person by another. Note in this connection the ordinariness of the locution, "I must have been thinking . . .," which indicates an inference to a conclusion about what one's thought was. In contrast, it would in most cases be extremely odd for someone to say, "I must be thinking. . . ." In addition, the fact that one is not committed to acting, now or in the future, on a belief one merely had at some time in the past insulates past-tense self-attributions, to some extent, from one's present view of the world. I think this makes it easier for one to deceive oneself about what one thought or felt in the past. If John has deceived himself into thinking that he loves Susan, he will surely encounter some cognitive dissonance the next time he sees her. But if he has merely deceived himself into thinking that he once loved her, it is at least somewhat less likely that his present or future dealings with her need reveal the truth to him. And we are accustomed to take with a grain of salt the confession of the aging diplomat who writes in his memoirs, "I had doubts about the war as early as 1965"—it is too easy to see this as an exercise in post hoc self-justification. In such cases, first-person authority is relatively easily overridden.

On the other hand, it is a familiar truth that the distance time creates between subject and object in a past-tense self-attribution provides scope for seeing matters aright. John's reluctant, "I guess I never really cared for Susan after all," may well have the ring of truth, and self-knowledge, that his previous professions of love lacked. However, while this kind of self-knowledge is in some respects the most interesting and important to us, it is achieved through adopting a critical, objective stance toward oneself, and is to that extent not knowledge *from* the first-person perspective, but rather knowledge that comes through *transcending* that perspective. Such knowledge is hardly direct, being based on a good deal of reflection, and while it may well carry authority, its authority is not first-person authority but the authority of wisdom in general. As such, we should not expect it to be covered by an account of first-person authority of the kind described above.

In short, I think that first-person authority extends primarily over one's present-tense attributions of intentional mental states. I therefore also think that the general strategy at work in the family of accounts mentioned above is on the right track. Here I want to defend this thought against a threat to it that stems from consideration of the Twin Earth thought experiments that motivate externalism about mental content. The threat I have in mind is roughly as follows. It is one thing to say that first-person authority is *primarily* a present-tense phenomenon; it is quite another to suggest that one could retain one's direct and authoritative knowledge of one's present thoughts and beliefs while being *radically* out of touch with one's past thoughts. But on the face of it, hypothetical cases in which an individual is switched from one environment to another, with consequent alteration of his conceptual repertoire, force us to countenance such a possibility. Or at least, they force the externalist who adheres to an account of first-person authority that highlights judgments about one's present mental states to confront this possibility. My question, then, is whether this package of views can survive the confrontation. I shall argue that it can. I begin in the next section by examining an argument due to Paul Boghossian which presents the threat in a particularly sharp form. After offering a way of navigating through the issues raised by Boghossian's argument, I turn in the ensuing two sections to defending my account of the issues against three alternatives, due to Michael Tye, John Gibbons, and Tyler Burge, respectively. My discussion of Burge's work in the third section leads into a more general examination of the place of knowledge of one's past thoughts in Burge's overall account of our entitlement to self-knowledge. I offer some conclusions in the fifth and final section.

II

Boghossian's argument is directed against Burge's idea that a central part of our notion of first-person authority involves the self-verifying character of first-person attributions of the form, "I am thinking that *p*." Burge's idea is that such a judgment is self-verifying in virtue of the fact that in making this second-order judgment, I must perforce think the first-order thought that *p* that it embeds. But that I am thinking this first-order thought is precisely what the second-order judgment claims. Hence, this latter judgment is made true by the very act of judging it to be true. That is to say, it is self-verifying. This fact is not supposed by Burge to constitute a complete account of our entitlement to these judgments.[2] But it is supposed to make clear that neither the capacity to make such judgments nor their status as knowledge is threatened by radical changes in one's environment, including changes that, in accordance with externalism, bring about changes in the contents of the thoughts one is judging and judging about. In his discussion of a case in which a person has been switched between Earth and Twin Earth, Burge writes, "In the former situation, the person may think, 'I am thinking that water is a liquid'. In the latter situation, the person may think, 'I am thinking that twater is a liquid'. In both cases, the person is right and as fully justified as ever. The fact that a person does not know that a switch has occurred is irrelevant to the truth and justified character of these judgments." On the other hand, Burge says, "Of course, the person may learn about the switches and ask, 'Was I thinking yesterday about water or twater?'—and not know the answer. Here knowing the answer may indeed sometimes depend on knowing background empirical conditions" (1988b: 659).

As will be discussed below, Burge has revisited this matter and made it clear that he intended these remarks to be interpreted narrowly, as suggesting merely that a person may be unable to answer a quite specific question about a past thought that he can only pose after he has learned about the switches. I want to postpone this, however, because I think Burge's remarks suggest a broader doctrine concerning the differences between one's knowledge of one's present and past thoughts that is both correct and defensible within the confines of externalism. According to this doctrine, while a person can always make a knowledgeable present-tense self-attribution by thinking the appropriate self-verifying thought, in some cases and depending upon what changes have occurred in his environment in the interim, the person may subsequently not be in a position to remember the content of a past thought. To recover its content, the subject may need to rely on empirical considerations, knowledge of which was not necessary for the original self-attribution.

Boghossian (1989) disagrees that this is a defensible position. He thinks that there is a mystery here. Having ruled out memory failure, he concludes that the subject must never have known what she was thinking. While I think that the principle Boghossian states, namely (M), is unexceptionable, it is not at all clear that we can uncontroversially stipulate that Burge's subject remembers everything that she knew at the earlier time.

(M)   If S knows that p at t_1 and if, at a later time t_2, S remembers everything he knew at t_1, then S knows that p at t_2.

Why shouldn't the switching she has undergone not affect her ability to remember what she previously thought? Boghossian mentions *forgetting*, and seems to equate *having once known and not forgotten* with *remembering*. I think this is a mistake. In fact I think it can plausibly be stipulated that the subject has not *forgotten* anything that she knew at the earlier time. Twin Earth switching should not make one forgetful or absent-minded. For this to be of use to Boghossian, it must also be true that (M').

(M') If at t_2 a person has not forgotten anything she knew at an earlier time t_1, then she remembers everything she knew at t_1.

But I think this principle is false, which I will now attempt to show.

One type of counterexample to (M') stems from the fact that new information can lead one to question a previous judgment that was in fact warranted. If the new evidence is misleading, so that the original judgment was also true, the result could be a situation in which the original judgment represented knowledge when it was made, knowledge that is lost when the subject retreats from the earlier claim on the basis of the new evidence. Here we may assume the subject has not forgotten anything—his problem is that he has more information, not less. But it also seems wrong to say that he *remembers that p*, where p was the original judgment.[3] However, this type of case might be thought too dissimilar to the switching case under dispute between Burge and Boghossian to cast much light on what is going on there. I therefore want to develop at some length a counterexample to (M') that, I will argue, involves a phenomenon that is quite similar to what takes place in the Twin Earth switching scenario. It involves switching an object in a subject's environment, and how this can undermine a subject's ability to retain the capacity to entertain the content of a previous demonstrative judgment about one of the objects.

Suppose that Sam passed by a certain antique shop on a number of occasions over a period of time. Each time he passed by the shop, there was a chair in the window, and as he passed, Sam thought, "That's a fine Queen Anne chair." Sam is a connoisseur of antique furniture, and the chair in the window was indeed a Queen Anne chair on each occasion. So he knew, each time, of the chair in the window, that it was a Queen Anne. Suppose, however, that although Sam thinks that he saw the same chair each time, in fact he saw a different chair on each occasion, though the chairs were virtually identical. Let C be any one of the chairs of which Sam knew, on the occasion of his passing it, that it was a Queen Anne chair.

Suppose that Sam now says, recalling this stretch of time, "That was a fine Queen Anne chair." Given his erroneous belief that he saw a single chair on a number of occasions, it is reasonable to ask, what chair does he have in mind? If this question is put to him, he will presumably say, "the chair I saw in such and such shop on a number of occasions a while back." But there is no such chair, so he has not succeeded in identifying *C*, or any other object, for the demonstrative judgment he is attempting to make. So far, we can credit him at best with having judged that the chair he saw on a number of occasions a while back was a fine Queen Anne chair. But this is not the tense-adjusted demonstrative judgment he made about *C* when he saw it. In fact, this judgment is either false or truth-valueless, depending on how we treat the description occurring in the specification of its content.

If Sam's error is brought to his attention, he may be able to retrieve some individuating knowledge of *C*, enabling us to say that he is now thinking, of *C*, that it was a fine Queen Anne chair. Perhaps *C* was the chair that he saw on his wedding anniversary, and he noted at that time that it would make a nice present for his wife. If he has not forgotten this, he might be able to identify *C* in this way. But we may suppose that he does not now possess *any* identifying information concerning *C*, not because he has forgotten the facts of this kind that he once knew, but because he never possessed any such information. We may suppose that there was nothing special about *C*, or about the day on which he passed it. His capacity to make the judgment he made about *C* as he passed it did not depend on his possessing any such information. On that occasion, the presence of *C*, in plain sight in front of him, was all that was necessary for him to make the judgment about it that it was a fine Queen Anne chair. But now that he cannot identify *C* by locating it in his immediate environment, it is reasonable to require that he possess some other means of identifying it as the object he has in mind. Since he has no such means, we should say that his present utterance cannot express the tense-adjusted demonstrative judgment he made when he saw *C*, so that the knowledge about *C* expressed in the judgment he made on that occasion has been lost.

Perhaps my claim that Sam must be able to identify *C* in some way in order to have a thought about it is too strong. One basis for the claim would be what Gareth Evans (1982: 74) calls Russell's Principle, which requires that "in order to have a thought about a particular object, you must *know which* object it is about which you are thinking." Evans's intention in endorsing such a principle was to construe the notion of individuating knowledge that it incorporates broadly, certainly much more broadly than Russell himself would have permitted. For example, the knowledge required was not supposed by Evans necessarily to be articulable by the thinker in the form of a judgment of the form, "I mean the so-and-so." The ability to locate the object in space was sufficient for satisfying the principle, as was the ability to recognize the object if the subject were to reencounter it. Nevertheless, Evans's notion of individuating knowledge has seemed not nearly broad enough to many. I would agree that the way he wielded Russell's Principle led Evans to impose implausibly strong requirements on certain thoughts about objects, especially in cases where the thoughts in question were expressed using proper names. Evans was insufficiently impressed by the idea that the thinker's membership in a name-using practice might carry his thought to the bearer of the name. But Evans's strictures on thoughts expressed using names are beside the point here, as we are concerned with an isolated individual and his demonstrative thoughts; no division of linguistic labor can come to Sam's aid.

It might be urged that individuating knowledge is not required even in our case, and that it is sufficient for Sam's thought to be about C for there to be some purely contextual relation between Sam and C in virtue of which he can entertain the thought in question. I might be willing to allow this if I could see how it would help. But I do not. What are the candidates for such a relational fact? Well, C was in fact an object distinct from any of the other chairs. But we may suppose that the total pattern of stimulation of Sam's sensory surfaces was qualitatively identical, on the occasion on which he saw C, to the pattern of sensory stimulation on the occasion on which he saw a distinct chair C', so that the distinctness of these two chairs never even impressed itself on his physiology, let alone on his consciousness. Might it help that he saw C at time t, and C' at a distinct time t'? No, because we may suppose that he was not oriented to time on either of these occasions. He did not need to know what time it was in order to make the original judgment he made about C.

Let us assume, then, that Sam does not now know that *that* [C] was a fine Queen Anne chair, because he cannot even entertain this thought. Next question: does Sam *remember* that that [C] was a fine Queen Anne? I think not, for reasons that have been given by Timothy Williamson (1995). This would involve abandoning the entailment from 'x remembers that p' to 'x knows that p'. And this would mean giving up on the natural and intuitive idea that remembering is a way of knowing.

As a way of registering the thought that in *some* sense Sam's memory has not let him down, we can say, following Williamson, that Sam remembers a situation *in which* C was a fine Queen Anne. But he does not remember *that* that [C] was a fine Queen Anne.[4] On the other hand, it does not seem correct to say that Sam has *forgotten* that C was a Queen Anne chair. His loss of this piece of knowledge stems from his inability to think a thought with a certain content, which does not look like forgetting in the ordinary sense. Note, however, that little turns on this issue. For even if it is legitimate to say that Sam has forgotten that C was a Queen Anne, then while the case is not a counterexample to (M'), it does represent a kind of memory failure that cannot simply be excluded "by stipulation," in connection with situations in which we are concerned with the retention of knowledge over periods of time in which changing environmental circumstances lead an individual to undetected conflations or confusions of objects or stuffs.

Whether by virtue of being a counterexample to (M'), or by representing a kind of memory failure that cannot be stipulated to be absent, the case of Sam provides a model in terms of which we can begin to understand how the subject in the Twin Earth switching case—call her Gloria—can fail to remember that she was thinking, say that the water was choppy on that day at the [Earth] beach. Consider first the first-order judgment she now expresses by saying, "The water was choppy that day." (We may suppose that the water was choppy, and she knew this at the time, though this is not essential.) I submit that this utterance cannot be interpreted straightforwardly as expressing the proposition that the water was choppy that day, because the switch has resulted in Gloria's losing the ability to think thoughts involving the concept *water*, in much the same way that Sam has lost the ability to think thoughts involving the concept *that chair* [C]. Furthermore, given the way in which the contents of her second-order judgments are tied to the contents of the first-order propositions embedded in them, it will follow that her present utterance, "I thought that the water was choppy that day," likewise cannot be interpreted as expressing the same proposition (adjusted for tense and other cognitive dynamics) that she expressed that day by saying, "I am thinking that the water is choppy [today]." Her failure to keep track over time of water has resulted in the loss not only of a piece of knowledge about water, but also in the loss of a piece of knowledge of one of her past water thoughts.

One difference between the cases of Sam and Gloria is that while Sam had to identify the object he had in mind when he first made the judgment about it, there was no question of Gloria having to identify the content of her thought on the occasion of her thinking it, in order for her to know that she was thinking it. Our thought contents are not objects to us in anything like the way in which physical objects are. But there is one important similarity between the two cases, namely, in the initial situation in both cases, the context was such that a certain enabling condition for the subject to make a knowledgeable judgment of a certain kind obtained, whereas this condition no longer obtains in the context in which the subject is called upon to state what he or she knew formerly. In the case of Sam, this enabling condition was the presence, where he could point to it, of *C*. In the case of Gloria, this condition was the fact that she was actively engaged in thinking the very thought that she was self-attributing. This is what makes it reasonable to say that she knew what she was thinking at the time, despite the fact that she could not at that time, distinguish the concept *water* from the concept *twater* or other waterlike concepts. But it seems appropriate to ask now how she can know that she was thinking that the water was choppy—or indeed, how she can even think that the water was choppy, given that she cannot distinguish between these concepts. The content of her present second-order judgment does not seem to be tied consti-tutively to the thought it is about—not, at least, in the self-verifying way—and the intervening switches make especially relevant her inability to distinguish various waterlike concepts. She is now in a position quite like Sam's present position, where it is reasonable to ask him which of a number of possible candidate objects he has in mind. Just as Sam will now have to draw on information he did not possess when he made his initial judgment, so Gloria, in order to recall what she was thinking that day, will have to engage in a little radical autointerpretation, which will of necessity draw on information she did not possess when she made her initial judgment, and which she will not possess until she learns of the switches and sorts her situation out. But it does not follow that she did not know what she was thinking at the time, any more than it follows that Sam did not know that that object [*C*] was a Queen Anne chair. The formally self-verifying character of Gloria's initial judgment was sufficient, in the context in which it was made, for it to count as knowledge. It is only now, when (a) this mechanism is no longer opera-tive and (b) she has confused water and twater as a result of the switches, that she does not know what she was thinking (and cannot even entertain the proposition she was thinking, again like Sam).[5]

Sam confused several objects in his environment, as a result of which he failed to retain a piece of *de re* knowledge about one of them. Gloria, on the other hand, confused two natural kinds, as a result of which she lost a piece of *de dicto* knowledge. But this difference should not be overemphasized. For first, the perceptual presence of C in Sam's immediate vicinity, at the time he made his original judgment about it, arguably enabled him to entertain an individual concept—a *de re* sense—that allows us to say that the judgment he made was conceptual in character (for this notion of sense, see Evans 1982, chap. 6). Second, samples of the relevant natural kinds play a crucial role in fixing the concepts Gloria thinks with, both before and after she is switched, in a way that is similar to the way in which the objects themselves serve to fix the *de re* senses that are employed in thinking about objects. Even in cases where one employs a natural-kind concept instances of which one has not directly encountered, via the linguistic division of labor, samples of the relevant kinds will generally figure prominently in the chain of communication that led to one's acquisition of the concept. Indeed, the similarity between the cases of Sam and Gloria can be highlighted by imagining an intermediate case in which, instead of Gloria being switched to Twin Earth, an evil demon changes all of the water on Earth to twater overnight. Gloria awakes the next morning not noticing anything different, and proceeds to apply her word "water" to XYZ. The longer she persists in using the word in this way, the more pressure there will be to say that she is confusing the two substances in a way that is quite like Sam's confusion of the several chairs. Of course, it is likely that someone on Earth will soon notice the change, and Gloria will learn of it, but we may avoid this by assuming that the evil demon, when he changes the water into twater, also switches all Earthlings *except* Gloria with their Twin Earth counterparts. This situation is functionally equivalent to the original situation in which Gloria alone was switched to Twin Earth, and brings out how similar her situation is to that of Sam.

When the question arose above what judgment is expressed by Sam when he asserts, "That was a fine Queen Anne chair I saw a while back," I suggested that we must say that it is the descriptive judgment that the chair he saw on a number of occasions a while back was a Queen Anne. There being no such chair, this judgment is either false or truth-valueless. We can be a bit more charitable in interpreting Gloria's post-switch utterances of "The water was choppy that day at the beach." Given her conflation of water and twater, I have argued, we cannot straightforwardly interpret her as expressing the proposition that the *water* was choppy that day at the beach. But here it is natural to say that her word 'water' now expresses a disjunctive concept—call it *zwater*—where zwater is either water or twater. This permits us to say that the proposition she expresses about that day at the beach is true, and perhaps even counts as knowledge; being water, the stuff at the beach that day was also zwater.[6] We cannot say anything like this about Sam, because the judgment he is trying to express when he says "That was a Queen Anne chair" purports to be about an individual chair, and there are no disjunctive chairs. (A pair of chairs may be regarded as an individual, but not as a disjunctive chair.) Gloria's judgment purports only to be about a kind of stuff, and there are disjunctive kinds of stuff, even if they are not natural kinds (jade is a frequently cited example). Thus, while Gloria has lost the knowledge that the water was choppy, this loss simultaneously gives rise to a new first-order truth (which may or may not be knowledge) that she can express in terms of her new concept. On the other hand, she not only fails to remember that she thought that the water was choppy, her second-order utterance, "I thought that the water was choppy" now expresses a false apparent memory of having thought that the zwater was choppy—the concept *zwater* did not figure in her original thought.[7] Despite this, however, the self-verifying mechanism still operates to ensure that the contents of her present tense self-attributions are determined by the contents of the first-order thoughts embedded in them. Her present utterance, "I am thinking that the water was choppy that day" expresses her direct knowledge that she is thinking that the zwater was choppy that day.

III

To shore up this interpretation of the Twin Earth switching cases, I want to argue in this section for its superiority over two alternative accounts, which are based on different accounts of the concept Gloria's utterances of 'water' express after the switch. I have argued that she expresses a disjunctive, jadelike concept, so that she no longer knows what she thought previously, because she cannot even entertain the same thought. This account is intermediate, in a sense, between the two alternatives now to be considered, the first of which has it that all of Gloria's postswitch utterances of 'water' express the Twin Earth concept *twater*, the extension of which is XYZ, including her judgments about her own past thoughts. Like my account, this one entails that Gloria loses the concept of water after the switch. But unlike my account, this one also entails that all of Gloria's apparent memories of her time on Earth have become false memories. When she now says, "I swam in water as a child," what she means is that she swam in twater as a child, which is false.

I find this account implausible. It is hard to believe that the entire contribution made to her conceptual repertoire by all of her time on Earth is simply annulled by the switch.[8] Michael Tye (1998) has defended this account, arguing first, that Gloria's postswitch 'water' utterances should be interpreted univocally, and second, that the only single concept they can all be regarded as expressing is the concept *twater*. I have no problem with the first premise—Gloria's postswitch utterances of 'water' all express the disjunctive concept *zwater* on my account. Tye's argument for his second premise is based largely on the claim that if she is asked after she is switched to clarify what she means by 'water', Gloria will either point to samples of twater—there being no water around—or defer to Twin Earth experts who will identify the extension of 'water' as XYZ. But as Jane Heal (1998) has pointed out, Gloria will surely also be inclined to identify the referent of her word by saying such things as, "the stuff I swam in as a child," and it is hard to see why these explications should be accorded no weight in assigning a semantic value to her utterances of 'water'. If the univocality assumption is to be endorsed, it seems that the disjunctive concept is the only appropriate one to use in interpreting her.[9]

The second alternative drops the univocality assumption, holding that Gloria's memories of her time on Earth will involve the concept *water*, while her perceptual and other present-tense judgments will involve the concept *twater*. John Gibbons (1996) has defended this account, arguing that the content of a thought is determined by features of its causal history. Moreover, according to Gibbons, a second-order belief about one's own thought—whether a past or a present thought—is not only caused by but inherits its content from the first order thought it is about. Gloria's second-order judgment that day at the Earth beach, that she was thinking that the water was choppy, was caused by and inherited its content from her first-order thought that the water was choppy. This is the mechanism that secures the title of the second-order judgment as knowledge, and accounts for first-person authority with respect to judgments about one's present thoughts on Gibbons's view. Similarly, Gloria's postswitch recollection, which she expresses by saying, "I thought that the water was choppy," inherits its content from the postswitch judgment she expresses by saying, "The water was choppy," ensuring that the same content figures in both. Finally, Gibbons maintains that the causal connection between the prior first-order judgment and the later first-order judgment brings it about that both of these involve the concept *water*, and this link also brings it about that Gloria remembers her prior thought correctly, all the relevant judgments being, in regular, warrant-preserving ways, about water. On the other hand, a postswitch utterance by Gloria such as, "I'm drinking a scotch and water," expresses a proposition involving the concept *twater*, and its content will be passed on to the second-order utterance, "I think I'm drinking a scotch and water," accounting for the authority of the latter.

Gibbons's account is not implausible, but I think it is problematic. The question I want to press here concerns the causal content-inheritance mechanism Gibbons assumes to be operative over time between the two first-order 'water' utterances, which he maintains is not disturbed even by a switch occurring in the interval between them. Gibbons attempts to motivate this part of his account by considering cases in which an individual confuses two objects, and he holds that even in such cases the subject should be interpreted as making a judgment about whichever of the objects figures in the causal history of that particular judgment. He considers someone—call him Frank—who has two distant cousins who look much alike, and who are both named 'Vinnie', so that Frank thinks there is only one cousin Vinnie. According to Gibbons, we should interpret an utterance of Frank's such as, "Vinnie danced all night at Sara's wedding," as being about whichever of the two men figured in the causal history of the thought or belief of Frank's that this utterance expresses.

Now, depending on the extent of Frank's confusion, this is the sort of case I would be inclined to handle along the lines of what I said about Sam and the chairs in the previous section. If Frank's confusion of the two men is complete or nearly so, I do not see that it is possible to interpret any of the thoughts he essays in his utterances of 'Vinnie' as thoughts about either of the two men. He is not, in such a case, a stable party to any social practice in which the name is used as a name of a particular person. Nor is he a stable member of two distinct practices in which two distinct names 'Vinnie$_1$' and 'Vinnie$_2$' are used to refer to two distinct persons. (Many of his relatives are presumably in that position.) I do not see that the word 'Vinnie' ever functions as a name for Frank. I agree that in a particular instance, such as Frank's remark about the wedding, it would be natural for someone who knows all of the relevant facts (about the wedding, the two Vinnies, and Frank's confusion of them) to say, "Frank means *that* Vinnie," if that Vinnie is the one who in fact danced at the wedding. But I think this is an instance of our tendency, in such cases, to discount known conceptual confusions on the part of a speaker in the interest of identifying the object whose antics figured in the etiology of the utterance, this being most essential for certain communicative purposes. This is a kind of second-best interpretation, which involves making distinctions the speaker does not make. There is a clear sense in which the speaker did not *mean that* Vinnie; being unaware of any distinction between that Vinnie and the other one, Frank's thought cannot literally be said to involve a concept of *that* one. There will be a number of descriptive and demonstrative thoughts in the vicinity of the thought he tried but failed to express in his utterance of "Vinnie danced all night" that may safely be attributed to him: my cousin, who is *F* and *G*, danced all night, that guy danced all night, and so on. Most of these thoughts will presumably count as knowledge. But none of them is the thought that his unconfused relatives express when they utter the words, "Vinnie danced all night."

If this judgment seems excessively harsh, note that it must be made with respect to some of Frank's particular 'Vinnie' utterances or thoughts, namely those that are causally sustained in equal measure by encounters with each of the Vinnies. Suppose that Frank says, "Vinnie is always nattily dressed," intending to express a belief that he has in fact acquired over a period of years, and which derives from encounters with both men. Neither of the two men figures more prominently than the other in the causal history of this particular utterance. Here, even Gibbons must say that this use of the name lacks a reference. The best we can do is attribute to Frank a belief involving some descriptive concept that is true of no one. Similarly, many of Gloria's postswitch utterances, such as "I always take my scotch with water," will be causally sustained, in roughly equal measure, by encounters with water and twater. Here though, we need not say that her word 'water' is empty, we may say it expresses the disjunctive concept *zwater*. Again, I take it that even Gibbons's causal historical account of content determination yields that judgment on this case. Given Gloria's intention to express a univocal concept by her word 'water', the door is open, I think, to interpret all her utterances as expressing the disjunctive concept.

IV

I mentioned earlier that Burge intended his original remarks about the switching cases to be interpreted narrowly. His point was merely that, after being switched and learning about the switches, one would not be able to identify the content of a past thought by introspectively distinguishing its content from its twin concept. He did not mean to suggest that one would generally, merely by being switched to a different environment and thereby acquiring some new or broadened concepts, lose the concepts one possessed in the old environment, nor would one fail to remember the contents of thoughts one had before the switch.[10] In fact, Burge's view is that Gloria, for example, will still retain the concept *water* even after she is switched, and will remember (assuming no memory failures of the ordinary sort) her past thoughts accurately. The content of Gloria's past-tense self-ascriptions is inherited from the prior first-order thoughts they are about, and their entitlement to knowledge does not depend on any ability to distinguish the contents of the thoughts they are about from various alternatives. Burge appeals here to a distinctive function of memory, its role in *preserving* the contents of past thoughts and judgments for the subject's use at later times. Preservative memory does not treat past thoughts as objects the contents of which must be identified in some way. It consists in causal links between past and present thoughts that fix content and confer warrant. As such, Burge maintains that judgments that rely on preservative memory fall within the scope of the entitlement to self-knowledge that flows from the role of self-attributions of propositional attitude in critical reasoning. We must look, therefore, at the nature of that entitlement, as Burge (1996) understands it.

Critical reasoning is reasoning that is *reflective* and which involves the consideration and weighing of reasons *as reasons*. Examples of such reasoning are questioning whether one's belief that Jones is the murderer is adequately supported by the evidence, or questioning whether one's intention to vote for a certain candidate for a job is appropriately based on his qualifications rather than other considerations. Thus critical reasoning can be practical, but for simplicity I will confine myself here to critical theoretical reasoning. Not all theoretical reasoning is critical: when I straightway judge that Matt is on campus upon seeing his car in the parking lot, my inference lacks the reflective, reason-weighing features that mark reasoning as critical. However, no simple distinction between reasoning and critical can be drawn in terms of the contents of the judgments that figure in the reasoning—for example, whether they are first-order or second-order. Though explicitly first-order, a piece of reasoning may be carried out with one eye, as it were, on the relevant relations of evidence and support among thought contents, in such a way as to count as critical reasoning. Critical reasoning need not be any very elaborate, quasi-philosophical examination. With the notion so understood, much of our reasoning is critical reasoning.

The aim of (theoretical) critical reasoning is the adjustment of one's beliefs in light of new information and the relevant relations of evidence and support. Thus, critical reasoning is governed by rational norms, and a critical reasoner must have at least a rudimentary grasp of these norms. Moreover, when it is properly conducted, critical reasoning sometimes increases, at least incrementally, the warrant we have for the beliefs that survive the reasoning process. Now, since critical reasoning involves reasoning about one's own beliefs, as well as the rational relations between the contents of those beliefs and other contents (for example, those that are actual or possible justifiers of the propositions believed), being subject to the relevant norms of critical reasoning is only possible for an individual who can make knowledgeable judgments about what he does and does not believe, and about how these contents are related to other contents. We could not hold one another responsible for conducting, when indicated, critical reasoning aimed at keeping one's epistemic house in order, if we could not be expected to be in a position to make knowledgeable self-attributions of propositional attitude. Therefore, the status of being a critical reasoner, a status enjoyed by all mature persons, must bring with it an entitlement to self-knowledge.

Burge argues further that the entitlement to self-knowledge that flows from critical reasoning is epistemically distinctive. In particular, it cannot be adequately understood simply in terms of a reliable mechanism in virtue of which first-order beliefs typically cause second-order beliefs about them. If such a quasi-observational mechanism were our only access to our own first-order attitudes, then the attitudes that come under review in critical reasoning would be treated as *objects* of investigation, in such a way that the point of view of the reflective, critical reviewer and the point of view of the reviewed attitudes would be no more unified than that of one person and another. This is inconsistent with the rational *immediacy* with which it follows that I must change my first-order attitude when it becomes apparent to me that it is not adequately supported. I may of course critically examine another's belief and find it lacking. I may judge that another's belief in a certain theory is unwarranted. But any requirement that I do anything to change the other's belief in such a case is contingent upon other matters (for example, is it worth getting into a dispute about this?). I am not rationally immediately responsible, in the relevant sense, for what another believes. To that extent, his beliefs are merely objects for me. But I cannot treat my own beliefs as mere objects of curiosity or investigation. When I judge that this theory that I accept is not adequately supported by the evidence, then I am rationally immediately required to relinquish my acceptance of it. Now, if the warrant for our self-attributions of propositional mental states were fundamentally a matter of brute causal relations by virtue of which first-order attitudes cause second-order ones, there would arise the possibility of brute error in the self-attribution of attitudes, arising from the occasional failure of the second-order belief-forming mechanism. Such a possibility, Burge thinks, would produce a dissociation of the points of view of the reviewer and the reviewed attitudes. This is inconsistent with the rational immediacy with which reasons are transmitted between these points of view. Hence, one's warrant for one's own self-attributions of belief cannot consist merely in the reliability of a system of brute, causal relations.

Now, this account is clearly an instance of the general strategy of attempting to articulate constitutive connections between first-order and second-beliefs and other attitudes. The particular relation Burge focuses on is that of the responsibility the point of view of the critical reviewer has vis-à-vis the point of view of the attitudes reviewed. Yet Burge thinks that the entitlement he has outlined extends to at least some judgments concerning one's past thoughts and beliefs.

However, I am not sure that Burge can maintain that very much of our knowledge of our past beliefs is implicated in our capacity for responsible critical reasoning. The fundamental link between critical reasoning and knowledge of one's thoughts and beliefs is my responsibility for what I believe, for ensuring that my beliefs are adequately warranted, and for abandoning those that I find to be unwarranted. On the face of it, I do not bear such responsibility for my past beliefs. By 'past' here I mean 'over and done with', not past-and-present or ongoing beliefs (I will turn to them in a moment). The mere judgment that I once believed that p, unlike the judgment that I now believe that p, can comfortably coexist with the judgment that p is and was unwarranted. There is nothing to be done, in any case, if I come to realize that a belief that I have already abandoned was or is unwarranted. Since I no longer believe it, I need take no steps to abandon it. I am not committed to the truth of my past beliefs, nor to ensuring that they are or were warranted. To this extent at least, it seems to me that my relation to my past beliefs is similar to my relation to the beliefs of others. And of course, we have no special epistemic entitlement to our beliefs about the beliefs of others.

Of course, memory is frequently relied on in making judgments about what one has-believed-and-continues-to-believe. The kind of memory involved here is indeed best understood as being concerned with preserving propositions and our commitments to them in reasoning. Preservative memory has been likened by Burge to what psychologists sometimes call *semantic* memory, the kind of memory that enables one to recall such garden variety facts as that Bucharest is the capital of Romania, or that the Earth is approximately 93 million miles from the sun. Semantic memory is distinguished from *episodic* or *autobiographical* memory, the kind of memory that is relied on in judging that one vacationed in Europe in 1996, or that one had eggs for breakfast. This is the kind of memory that is invoked in remembering specific events. Of course there was presumably an event in my life, sometime in grade school I suppose, of my first coming to believe that Bucharest is the capital of Romania, but I have long since forgotten it. What semantic, or preservative memory preserves is the content of what that geography teacher told me, as well as my commitment to that content. This is the only kind of memory that is relied on in my present judgment that I believe that Bucharest is the capital. This is fortunate, because were episodic memory invoked in my self-attributions of standing beliefs, this would introduce a distressingly empirical element into the justification for such self-attributions, and first-person authority would be compromised. Given that only preservative memory is relied on in such attributions, we may say that memory plays only an enabling, rather than a justificatory role, relative to my judgment that I believe that Bucharest is the capital. For this reason, we may say that memory does not provide reasons or evidence for thinking *that I think* that Bucharest is the capital. Instead, memory presents as true the content previously endorsed—Bucharest is the capital—making it available for reendorsement at later times.

Indeed, I think that in most cases it would be odd to cite one's memory as a reason for thinking that one thinks that *p*, in something like the way the following would be odd. A student comes into my office with a copy of one of my publications, points to a certain claim that occurs in it, and asks, "Do you really believe that?" I say in response, "Well, that is indeed my paper, and I don't recall having changed my mind about anything in it, so I guess I do believe that." Here I am treating the fact that I wrote this sentence as *evidence* that I have a certain belief. Such an attitude is perfectly appropriate when attributing a belief to another, but to self-ascribe a belief on such a basis would surely be irrational, precisely because I would not be taking the stance of the person who is responsible for that belief at the same time. In most, though not all cases, to cite one's memory as evidence that I now believe that *p* would similarly amount to disavowing my responsibility for that belief. It would be to represent my belief as something that memory tells me is the case, whatever I may now think about the matter. In this way my episodic memory does now tell me that it is a fact that I vacationed in Europe in 1996, whatever I may now think about the matter. Memory presents this event as something that simply happened, and which cannot now be changed. When one merely relies in the normal way on preservative memory in making a self-attribution of a standing belief, on the other hand, one's judgment is still sensitive to the relevant first-order, facts, so that critical reasoning can still lead to my changing my belief should new facts come to light. Therefore also, reliance on preservative memory does not threaten to introduce an empirical element into the warrant for our self-attributions of standing beliefs. Moreover, the capacity to self-ascribe such standing beliefs is certainly part of what is necessary for responsible critical reasoning. Hence, to the extent that Burge is right that there is a distinctive entitlement to self-attributions that flows from their role in critical reasoning, he is also right in claiming that this entitlement must extend to self-attributions that rely on memory insofar as it merely preserves contents and ongoing epistemic commitments to them.

What is not clear to me is how far this goes in establishing a special entitlement to "past mental states and events." Here, it seems, we must rely on the same kind of memory that enables me to recall events in my past generally, that is episodic memory. Of course, Burge might argue that whatever you call the kind of memory involved, a distinctive warrant for at least some of our judgments about our own past thought events is required, due to the role of such judgments in critical reasoning. Is this so?

Suppose that one is conducting a piece of mathematical reasoning in the careful, semireflective way that warrants describing it as critical reasoning. Now it does often happen that in the course of such reasoning one makes judgments such as, "Therefore *p*, and since *I proved that p entails q*, it follows that *q*." But is the past-tense formulation of the italicized clause really essential here? Unless it is, Burge cannot claim that the capacity to make warranted judgments concerning one's past thought events is necessary for critical reasoning. Couldn't one be a critical reasoner who could only retain, via preservative memory, such judgments as, "It is established that *p*?" And even if there are some pieces of reasoning that do require the reasoner to recall past thought events or states, and not merely to retain the contents of those states and one's commitment to them, so that the distinctive entitlement to such judgments extends to them, these judgments will presumably be about one's relatively recent thought events. Or at least, we should say that any entitlement critical reasoning confers on judgments that rely on memory becomes highly defeasible the more distant in the past is the thought event judged about. In particular, it is hard to see how a critical reasoning-based entitlement is of any help in situations as disruptive as Twin Earth switching. The point is not merely that after the switch Gloria is unable to distinguish between the concept *water* and the concept *twater*. She could not distinguish these concepts before the switch either, and I agree with Burge that this was irrelevant to the content or warrant for her earthbound present- or past-tense self-attributions. The problem is that she has now actually undergone a radical change in her environment as a result of which she has developed dispositions to apply what she takes to be a single concept to samples of both water and twater, to defer to two distinct sets of experts regarding the reference of her uses of 'water', and so on. In addition, we are concerned in the switching cases with periods of time considerably longer than that over which a single piece of reasoning could extend. These facts, I suggest, override whatever general entitlement Gloria may have to rely on the preservative function of memory. I do not see, in short, that the right to rely on preservative memory is entirely free of empirical presuppositions. It may be that the entitlement it typically confers depends on the broadly empirical fact that we live in a world in which objects and stuffs are generally stable, and we are not switched by evil demons from one planet to another.

V

Boghossian maintains that the inability of the subjects in cases of world switching to make knowledgeable judgments about their past thoughts casts doubt on whether they ever knew those thoughts to begin with. Were this position to be sustained, it would threaten any account of first-person authority that prominently features constitutive relations between first- and second-order attitudes. Gibbons and Burge, on the other hand, argue that the switching cases do not threaten the directness or authoritativeness of either our present-tense or (the most important of) our past-tense self-attributions. The position argued for in this paper is intermediate between these two. I alluded at the outset to considerations that tell against the idea that our knowledge of our past mental states is as direct or as authoritative as our knowledge of our present mental states. The switching cases suggest a reason for the difference. Our epistemic right to our present-tense mentalistic self-attributions is free of the kinds of empirical considerations that may be disturbed by radical environmental change, as accounts such as those of Burge and others have begun to make clear. But it appears that the authority of memory concerning one's past thought events—though not the authority of memory in its purely content-preserving role—can be undermined by such change. This is one respect in which the proper function of memory, even of one's own mind, is dependent on broadly empirical considerations. Thus it can happen that one may need to rely on empirical considerations to know what one thought at some point in the past, even though one's original knowledge of that thought had a nonempirical warrant. This type of situation is readily intelligible when placed in the context of other cases in which a person fails to remember something she once knew, not because she has forgotten anything, but because crucial enabling conditions for the original knowledge have lapsed in the interim.[11]

Notes

1. Since the list is arbitrary anyway, let me add to it my own contribution, "The Basis of First Person Authority," which owes much to all of the authors mentioned above.

2. I think Burge has sometimes been misinterpreted on this point. The fundamental source of the warrant for our self-attributions of propositional attitudes—including the attribution of self-verifying, *cogito*-like thoughts—is the role of such attributions in critical reasoning. This will be discussed in section III below.

3. That such cases as these are counterexamples to (M′) is pointed out by Kobes (1996).

4. Williamson made his point in a discussion of a case in which old knowledge is driven out by new, misleading evidence. There as well, we cannot say that the subject remembers what he previously knew, for then he would still know it. But as noted above, we may assume he hasn't forgotten anything either. He has simply changed his mind.

5. Boghossian has suggested (in conversation) that the main point he was driving at in the memory argument was that whatever knowledge one may have of

one's present thoughts by virtue of Burge's contextual self-verifying mechanism is merely formal and insubstantial—it is like the knowledge a person kidnapped, blindfolded and transported somewhere in the trunk of a car might express by saying, "I am here." There is a clear sense in which such a person does not really know *where* he is. This fact can be *brought out* by noting that even if his memory is perfect, there will be no judgment subsequently available to the victim that encodes the knowledge of where he was at the earlier time. But it might be suggested that appealing to memory in this way is merely a device for bringing out the intuitively obvious fact that the victim locked in the trunk of the car does not know where he is. I think something like this may be what leads Goldberg (1997) to claim that Boghossian's main point does not depend essentially on any principles about memory. However, I think the example involving the Queen Anne chairs shows that a judgment may express knowledge the warrant for which depends essentially on relations the knower bears to his present context, in such a way that the knowledge may subsequently be lost even though the subject has not forgotten anything, but where the original piece of knowledge is not for all that merely formal or insubstantial. Certainly the knowledge, of a particular object in one's immediate environment, that it is a Queen Anne chair, is a substantive piece of knowledge.

6. It is not correct to say that she remembers that the zwater was choppy that day, since she did not know this at the time. Partly for this reason, and the fact that the change in her concept is undetectable, we may not want to say that her present judgment represents knowledge of the condition of the water that day.

7. Though her error is mitigated by the fact that *zwater* is a broadening of the concept that did figure in her thought.

8. This account is sometimes attributed to Burge (1988b) but in fact he never endorsed it. It seems to have been assumed by Falvey and Owens (1994), though they did not consider questions about memory. I thank Tyler Burge for disabusing me of it.

9. Heal does not endorse the univocality assumption.

10. In "Memory and Self-Knowledge" (1998b), Burge acknowledges that some switched individuals might be best interpreted in terms of disjunctive or "amalgam" concepts, though he seems to think that such cases are not central to our understanding of the switching phenomenon. And even where the attribution of a disjunctive concept is appropriate, Burge does not think this automatically means that the original concept has been lost.

11. I thank Matthew Hanser for his comments on a previous draft of this paper. Thanks also to the participants in a seminar I gave on self-knowledge at UCLA in the spring of 2001, where some of the issues addressed in this paper were discussed.

12

What Do You Know When You Know Your Own Thoughts?

Sanford C. Goldberg

1 Introduction

I believe that there is at least one sound argument showing that the doctrine of semantic externalism is incompatible with a doctrine regarding authoritative self-knowledge of one's thoughts. I also believe that, despite this, the motivation for semantic externalism remains strong. This is admittedly a strange combination: most people who write on these issues assume that if there exists a sound argument for an incompatibilist conclusion, the case for semantic externalism is severely (and perhaps even fatally) weakened. The present paper aims to defend the "strange" combination by making a distinction within the catch-all category of 'knowledge of one's thoughts'. The distinction I propose differs from distinctions employed by externalists in previous work on self-knowledge (e.g., in Burge 1989a and Falvey and Owens 1994), and it can be independently motivated. Externalism is the thesis that some propositional attitudes depend for their individuation on features of the thinker's (social and/or physical) environment. The doctrine of authoritative self-knowledge of thoughts is the thesis that for all thinkers *S* and occurrent thoughts that *p*, *S* has authoritative and nonempirical knowledge of her thought that *p*. A much-discussed question in the literature is whether these two doctrines are compatible. My thesis is that the expression 'knowing one's own thought' actually masks at least one important distinction, and that once the distinction is brought to light, various considerations from the compatibilism debate acquire a very different significance.

2 Burge on Basic Self-Knowledge

In his seminal discussion on the compatibility of externalism and self-knowledge (1988b), Burge identifies the relevant class of judgments as those involved in *cogito* judgments. Examples include the judgments expressed by 'I think (with this very thought) that writing requires concentration' and 'I judge (or doubt) that water is more common than mercury'. Let me use 'FPPTJ' to designate any member of the relevant class of first-person present-tense judgments. However far this class extends (see, e.g., Boghossian 1989 and Goldberg 1999a), FPPTJs include judgments regarding one's own occurrent thinkings.

Burge writes, "It is certainly plausible" that FPPTJs "constitute knowledge, that they are not products of ordinary empirical investigation, and that they are peculiarly direct and authoritative." He continues, "Indeed, these sorts of judgments are self-verifying in an obvious way: making these judgments itself makes them true. For mnemonic purposes, I shall call such judgments *basic self-knowledge*" (1988b: 649). It is important to be clear about the role that the self-verifying nature of FPPTJs plays in rendering these judgments *knowledge*. Trivially, a judgment that is self-verifying is true. More important, a judgment that is self-verifying would also appear to enjoy a favorable epistemic status. In subsequent work Burge speaks of the subject's "entitlement" to make such judgments, where an 'entitlement' is defined as a positive epistemic status that accrues to a judgment when the subject, insofar as her making the judgment is concerned, is "operating in an appropriate way in accord with the norms of reason, even when these norms cannot be articulated by the individual who has that status" (Burge 1998a: 241). The result is that, insofar as a true judgment to which one is entitled would amount to knowledge, the subject who makes a self-verifying judgment that *p* would *ipso facto* count as knowing that *p*. There are two important lessons.

First, no one should try to establish an incompatibilist conclusion by way of arguing that, given semantic externalism, questions arise regarding the epistemic status enjoyed by FPPTJs. To make such a case, one would have to reveal as objectionable either Burge's notion of an entitlement or else his account of a thinker's entitlement to make FPPTJs. Neither option is very attractive. Burge's notion of an entitlement would appear to be as defensible as any run-of-the-mill externalist notion of epistemic justification. And if Burge's notion of an entitlement is acceptable, then I cannot see any way to challenge his account of the entitlement thinkers have for making FPPTJs. The second lesson is this. No would-be argument for incompatibilism should question the status as knowledge of what Burge calls "basic self-knowledge." Burge has effectively sealed off such an option if he is correct to hold that thinkers enjoy an entitlement to make FPPTJs, simply in virtue of the self-referential (and hence self-verifying) nature of these judgments.[1]

3 The Incompatibilist Argument in Boghossian 1989

It is interesting to note that the incompatibilist argument from Boghossian 1989, though directed at the self-knowledge at play in *cogito*-like FPPTJs, coheres with the two lessons just drawn:

(I) It makes no appeal to considerations regarding the justificatory status of the relevant (*cogito*-like) FPPTJs.

(II) It is consistent with the existence of Burgean "basic self-knowledge."

The argument to be presented here is not the argument as Boghossian himself presents it.[2] Rather, the argument to be presented here is a variation on Boghossian's version, arising in reaction to a particular difficulty faced by Boghossian's own version. The virtue of the present variation is that it presents a prima facie case for incompatibilism, without disagreeing with Burge on the existence and nature of basic self-knowledge.

Boghossian's 1989 version of his argument is a response to an objection that was anticipated in Burge 1988b. Burge had argued that FPPTJs amount to a kind of authoritative and nonempirical self-knowledge of one's thought. But suppose a person *S* undergoes a series of slow switches between Earth and Twin Earth, and that *S* was told of the switches at some *future* time, and then asked which thought she had at that earlier time. Burge's response involved (a) conceding that at that later time she "may not know" which thought she had, while (b) insisting that nonetheless she knew its content when she entertained it at that earlier time.

Boghossian responded to Burge's account of slow-switching by presenting the "Memory Argument," designed to bring out the absurdity of the claim that "although *S* will not know tomorrow what he is thinking right now, he does know right now what he is thinking right now" (1989: 22). Ludlow (1995) offered a helpful formalization of the argument:

(1) If *S* forgets nothing, then what *S* knows at t_1, *S* knows at t_2.

(2) *S* forgot nothing.

(3)   *S* does not know that p at t_2.

(4)   Therefore, *S* did not know that p at t_1.

In what follows I want to suggest how a variation on this argument can be understood so as to satisfy (I) and (II). The variation emerges when we consider an internal difficulty facing Boghossian's own version.

While most criticisms of Boghossian's argument have focused on premises (1) and (2) (see, e.g., Ludlow 1995, Gibbons 1996, and Brueckner 1997a), I think that the real difficulty lies in what Boghossian takes to support (3). On Boghossian's presentation (1989: 22), the reason why *S* fails to know at t_2 what she thought at t_1 is that "no self-verifying judgment" is available at t_2 regarding what she thought at t_1. But we can note that the same point does not hold for *S* at t_1: at t_1, *S* does have available a self-verifying judgment regarding her thought at t_1. The upshot would be that to any compatibilist-minded externalist who is willing to grant (3), either premise (1) or premise (2) must be false. The 'must' here is that of logical necessity: given Burge's points about the self-verifying nature of FPPTJs—points which support the claim that these judgments invariably amount to knowledge—(4) is false; so if (3) is true, either (1) or (2) must be false (assuming that the argument is valid).

Now this criticism would be avoided if a support for (3) were to be found elsewhere rather than in the nonavailability to *S* a self-verifying thought at t_2 regarding her thought at t_1. Consider then the following version.[3] *S* is thinking a thought which she expresses (at t_{before}) with the sentence 'I am thinking that water is wet'. *As she is thinking this thought*, she comes to find out about her world-switching history. She learns merely that at some point in the past she has been the victim of slow switching; she does not learn, and she remains ignorant of, both her present world residency and the length of time she has spent on either planet. But even after she learns of her switching, she continues to think a thought (at t_{after}) that she would express with the very same sentence form, 'I am thinking that water is wet'. Under these circumstances I submit that the following is an intuitive description of *S*'s situation:

(*)   Though *S* is thinking the same thought throughout the brief interval from t_{before} to t_{after}, she does not count as knowing this thought at t_{after}, even though at t_{after} *she is still in a position to form the relevant FPPTJ regarding the thought she is thinking at t_{after}*.

Of course, if (*) is true, then it would appear possible to use this new thought experiment to support (3), and by extension the incompatibilist conclusion of (4), without (I) making a point about the justificatory status of the relevant judgments or (II) calling into question the existence of basic self-knowledge. However, as we have just seen, this claim depends on the cogency of (*), and there are at least two objections one might have to (*).

The first one, the *concept-shift* objection, holds that it is true that S uses the same (self-ascriptive) form of words ('I am presently thinking that water is wet') throughout the interval from t_{before} and t_{after}. But S's use of 'water' shifts in meaning once she finds out about her world-switching history. This contention can be supported as follows. The self-verifying nature of FPPTJs ensures that (A):

(A)   At any time t at which S is thinking a thought, S has (or is in a position to have) authoritative and nonempirical knowledge of the thought she is thinking at t.

Now from (A) it follows both that at t_{before} S knows the thought she is thinking at t_{before}, and that at t_{after} S knows the thought she is thinking at t_{after}. Assuming (with Boghossian) that at t_{after} S fails to know the thought she had at t_{before}, we conclude that the thought she had at t_{after} differs from the thought she had at t_{before}. And we chalk this up to the shift in meaning of 'water' as used at these two times. This shift in meaning might be ascribed to the different functional role played by S's use of the word 'water' prior to and after t_{after}. For surely it is open to the externalist to hold that the individuation of attitudes involves (not just externalist considerations but also) considerations of functional role (this is suggested in Gibbons 1996: 307–310.)[4]

But there is a price that will be paid by anyone who responds to (*) using the objection from concept shifting. There are two different accounts of world-switching cases. On the 'replacement' account, the 'water'-concept that S acquires after having been switched from Earth to Twin Earth replaces the 'water'-concept she had prior to switching: once S acquires her Twin Earthian 'water'-concept, she can no longer express (and consequently can no longer think) the 'water'-thoughts she had while on Earth. Most people (regardless of auxiliary ideology) find the replacement account of switching cases to be very implausible. Consequently, there is a second account of switching, widely acknowledge to be much more plausible. On this 'supplementation' account, switching merely provides the subject with more concepts that she had prior to switching, but it does not deprive her of any preswitching concepts she had.

Now I want to claim that the concept-shift objection to (*), on which S expresses two different thoughts with the same sentence form 'I am presently thinking that water is wet' despite the brevity of the interval from t_{before} to t_{after}, implicitly depends on the (less plausible) replacement interpretation. For consider: what is to prevent S from forming and avowing the intention to be using 'water' univocally, i.e., as expressing the same concept throughout the brief interval from t_{before} to t_{after}? Of course, if she did form such an intention, then, on the assumption that this intention was realized, the thought she expressed at t_{before} = the thought she expressed at t_{after}—with the result that S's failure at t_{after} to know the thought she had at t_{before} is tantamount to S's failure at t_{after} to know the thought she had at t_{after}, that is, is tantamount to S's failure to know her thought even as she thinks it self-ascriptively. The only reaction to this would appear to be that, having come to learn of her world-switching, she is *precluded* from thinking the same thought throughout the interval. (The point would then be that, even if S were to avow the intention to be using 'water' univocally throughout the brief interval, this intention is doomed to frustration given the change in the functional role of her use of 'water'.) I conclude that, on pain of having no way to resist the conclusion that at t_{after} S fails to know her thought even as she thinks it self-ascriptively, the concept-shift objection to (*) presupposes the replacement interpretation. Since the replacement interpretation is taken by most (including compatibilist-minded authors as well) to be implausible, and since whatever minimal plausibility the replacement interpretation has should be even less when it is employed in the context of such a short interval as that between t_{before} and t_{after}, this result is a reason not to object to (*) by suggesting that S undergoes a concept shift upon being apprized of her world-switching.[5]

That brings me to a second possible objection that a compatibilist might level against (*), which I will call the objection from *knowledge-preservation*. Here it is agreed that S is thinking the same thought throughout the interval, but it is denied that her becoming apprized of her world-switching undermines her knowledge of that thought. Rather, on the grounds that S retains her ability to form the relevant self-verifying judgment regarding the thought she has been thinking all along, the knowledge in question is preserved. (See Brueckner 2000 for an argument of this sort.)

But the knowledge-preservation objection does nothing to undermine the core incompatibilist intuition behind (*). The intuition in question is this: once *S* is apprized of her world-switching, then, so long as she remains uncertain as to (i) the length of time she has spent on either planet, (ii) her world residency at the time of the original thinking, and (iii) her world residency now (at the time of 'recollection'), there is a sense of 'knowing one's thought' on which she does not count as knowing her thought. To be sure, the sense in question is not that of 'basic self-knowledge:' it is common ground that *S* has basic self-knowledge of her thought throughout this interval (and indeed that she cannot fail to have such knowledge on any occasion on which she forms an FPPTJ). But despite *S*'s possession of basic self-knowledge, there remains a sense in which she fails to know her thought.

We can make this sense vivid by supposing that (upon being apprized of her world-switching) *S* is provided with a full explication of both the concept expressed by 'water' in English as well as the concept expressed by 'water' in Twin English. For simplicity, let us say that in English 'water' expresses the concept: *the liquid that is uniquely ϕ*, whereas in Twin English 'water' expresses the concept: *the liquid that is uniquely ψ*. Even granting that she now knows these things, the point is that, whatever *S* can be said to know regarding her thought, she cannot be said to know which if either of the following two argument forms, as they occur in her language, is sound (we will imagine that she considers these arguments just as she is making the FPPTJ expressed in premise 1):

Argument 1

Premise 1   I am presently thinking that water is wet.

Premise 2a   Water is the liquid that is uniquely ϕ.

Conclusion 1   There is a type of liquid that is uniquely ϕ which is such that, on at least one occasion I have thought, of that liquid, that it is wet.

Argument 2

Premise 1   I am presently thinking that water is wet.

Premise 2b   Water is the liquid that is uniquely ψ.

Conclusion 2   There is a type of liquid that is uniquely ψ which is such that, on at least one occasion I have thought, of that liquid, that it is wet.

What *S* knows—or at least what *S* can know, given that she has been apprized of her world-switching, and that she has been informed of the difference between English and Twin English regarding the word form 'water'—is that at least one of these arguments exhibits the fallacy of equivocation. If she knew which argument exhibits this fallacy (and it may be both), then she would know which argument is not sound. But, she cannot determine, merely by reflecting on the thought self-ascribed in premise 1, which argument exhibits this fallacy. This is curious, since the premises of both arguments all appear to have an a priori character. Premise 1 can be known a priori to be true—or so I am assuming, since my version of Boghossian's argument is supposed to satisfy (I) and (II). And each instance of the second premise is such that, if true at all, it is true in virtue of the relevant 'water'-concept. In short, it would appear that S's failure to know which (if either) of these arguments is sound reflects a failure on S's part to know the thought self-ascribed in premise 1.

Now there are two things that must be said regarding the point I am presently making. First, I am *not* maintaining, as Boghossian (1992) tried to argue, that given externalism, someone such as S is not in a position to determine whether arguments which appear to be valid really are valid. I am speaking of soundness, and the difference here is important. I believe, what has been argued elsewhere (Schiffer 1992, Burge 1998a, Goldberg 1999b), that someone such as S would be in a position to determine whether the argument forms above are valid, when these argument forms are expressed by her in her own language—namely, by *stipulating* that she is using 'water' in a univocal fashion. But for precisely this reason the issue of soundness becomes problematic: for if she simply stipulates that she is using 'water' univocally, then the *truth value* of the relevant instance of premise 2 (i.e., either 2a or 2b) becomes open to doubt. (See Goldberg 1999b for a further discussion of this point.)

Second, my claim that S's ignorance is to be interpreted as amounting to a failure to know her thought requires defense, since there are at least two distinctions in the literature that appear available to compatibilist-minded externalists to resist this claim. The first distinction, from Falvey and Owens 1994, is the distinction between knowledge of one's own thought and discriminatory knowledge of one's thought, where the latter is a matter of being in a position to discriminate between one's actual thought and thought one would have had in some counterfactual situation.[6] The second distinction, from Burge 1989a, is that between knowledge of one's thought and knowledge of the proper explication of the concepts figuring in the thought. A compatibilist-minded externalist might attempt to argue that S's ignorance is either a failure of discrimination or of explication, but that in any case it is not a failure to know the thought in question.

But *S*'s ignorance cannot be assimilated in either of the proposed ways. First, her ignorance cannot be understood as a mere inability to discriminate the actual thought from a counterfactual one. *S*'s inability to determine which of the two arguments is not sound does not appear to derive from any inability to say whether she was thinking a water thought or a twater thought: for arguably she *can* say whether she was thinking a water thought or a twater thought, namely, simply by saying 'I'm thinking a water thought', intending to use 'water' as she had in the original self-ascriptive thinking. (I say that this claim is arguable: the cost of denying it appears to be a commitment to the replacement interpretation discussed above.) Rather, *S*'s inability to make this determination derives from the fact that nothing that she knows regarding her thought suffices to determine which premise (2a or 2b) captures the 'water'-concept in play. What is more, her ignorance is not to be understood as a failure of explicational ability of the sort envisaged by Burge (1989a). His distinction between knowledge of one's thought and explicational knowledge regarding the concepts figuring in the thought, reflects something that should be conceded by anyone who recognizes the possibility of cases involving a subject's *incompletely grasping* a concept figuring in her own thought:[7] the point is that a subject's incomplete grasp of a concept figuring in her thought should not be taken to imply that the subject fails to know the thought in which that concept figures. But in the case above, *S*'s ignorance cannot be explained away as a kind of incomplete grasp: for, having been informed of the difference between what is expressed in English, and what in Twin English, with a use of 'water', *S* has a *complete grasp* of both concepts. At any rate, she can fully explicate both concepts! What she lacks is the knowledge that would enable her to connect her explicational knowledge to the thought she has in mind (more on this below).

To reinforce my point, we can ask: why is it that *S* cannot determine which of 2a or 2b captures the 'water'-concept in play in the thought self-ascribed in premise 1? The answer cannot be that she needs more explicational material; for by hypothesis she has been supplied with all of the relevant conceptual explications. Rather, the natural answer is that there is a sense in which she does not 'know the thought' she is (self-ascriptively) thinking. To fail to know one's thought in this sense is to fail to be able to connect one's explicational knowledge regarding the concepts involved in the thought, to the thought itself, when this failure cannot be chalked up to a lack of explicational material regarding any of the concepts figuring in the thought. If compatibilist-minded externalists think to reject this account of what *S* fails to know, in their hope of repudiating (*) (and with it the argument from Boghossian 1989 as here construed), then they owe an alternative explanation of the ignorance in question. I have merely suggested that no distinction yet proposed—whether between knowledge of one's thought and discriminatory knowledge of one's thought (Falvey and Owens 1994), or between knowledge of one's thought and explicational knowledge regarding the concepts figuring in the thought (Burge 1989a)—will do the trick.

4   Our Incompatibilist Result and the Status of Semantic Externalism

I have just argued that a reconstructed version of Boghossian's 1989 'memory argument' succeeds in establishing an incompatibilist result, while at the same time squaring with the constraints (I) and (II) imposed by Burge's reflections on basic self-knowledge. Here I want to suggest that, despite this result, the viability of semantic externalism remains intact. The significance of my account of these matters will be twofold: it will enable us to see how one can concede the success of certain arguments for incompatibilism, without thereby calling into question the viability of semantic externalism; and it will enable us to grasp more clearly the nature of 'basic self-knowledge'.

The position I am advocating is to distinguish basic self-knowledge from the kind of self-knowledge at play in Boghossian's argument. The basis for this distinction lies in considerations already presented. In particular, in the context of the preceding arguments, a failure to distinguish them will result in a paradox. On the one hand, Burge's reflections on the nature of FPPTJs suggest that these judgments invariably amount to a kind of a priori self-knowledge of one's thoughts. On the other hand, I have argued that a variation on Boghossian's 1989 argument succeeds in establishing that, given externalism, FPPTJs do not, or do not invariably, amount to a priori knowledge of one's thoughts. Of course, one need only formulate this 'paradox' in order to see its proper dissolution: what a subject is represented as knowing, when she is described as having basic self-knowledge of her thoughts, is not what the conclusion of Boghossian 1989 (as presented here) would represent her as failing to know regarding her thoughts. Such a claim is reinforced by the fact that Boghossian's argument need not call into question any of the points Burge makes regarding basic self-knowledge.

Some terminology may help. Let us say that someone has *self-ascriptive* knowledge of her own thought that *p* just in case she can be said to know that she herself is thinking that *p*. This is the type of knowledge of one's thought that one has when one has basic self-knowledge of the thought. The argument above suggests that self-ascriptive knowledge of one's thought is a rather insubstantial kind of knowledge.[8] One who has self-ascriptive knowledge of her thought that *p* is correctly describable as knowing that she herself is thinking that *p*; but to be correctly describable as knowing that one oneself is thinking that *p* is consistent with failing to have, and failing to have an a priori route to, the kind of knowledge of the thought that is necessary for applying one's relevant conceptual-explicational knowledge to the thought itself. Of course, self-ascriptive knowledge of one's thought is not totally insubstantial: presumably there are conditions one must satisfy if one is to be correctly described as knowing that one oneself is thinking that *p*. Among other things, one must be in a position to use the verb 'to think' in the first-person, present-tense way; and in addition one must satisfy the preconditions on thinking that *p*, i.e., one must possess the relevant concepts. And this latter point requires that one be able to connect at least *some* of one's explicational knowledge to the thought itself: a subject who uttered 'Dogs are friendly', but who does not know, e.g., that dogs are animals, would be a subject about whom it would be reasonable to suppose that she did not possess the concept DOG in the first place. At the same time, on the assumption of externalism, the conditions on concept possession can be satisfied by a subject who, though possessing exhaustive conceptual-explicational knowledge of all relevant concepts, and though able to draw on this knowledge to the minimal degree required by the condition on possessing the relevant concepts, is nonetheless not able to draw on this knowledge to determine which sentence(s) are true in virtue of the concepts figuring in the thought she has in mind—at least in the kind of context envisaged above.

We might also try to capture the more substantive sense of 'knowing one's own thought' at play in Boghossian's argument. Let us say that a subject *S* has *C self-knowledge* (conceptual self-knowledge) of her thought that *p* when she has the kind of self-knowledge of her thought which is required if, e.g., she is to be in a position to determine which of the two arguments, argument 1 or 2, is sound. Whatever C-self-knowledge comes to, the take-home point is that (on the assumption of externalism) one can have basic self-knowledge of one's thought that p without having C-self-knowledge of one's thought that p.

This distinction opens up a new perspective on Boghossian's argument. One can allow that (a variation on) Boghossian's argument shows that (R1):

(R1)   Given semantic externalism, a subject S might fail to have C-self-knowledge of her thought that p.

In this sense one allow that Boghossian's argument is a successful incompatibilist argument while maintaining that Boghossian's argument does not (and indeed cannot) establish the stronger result that (R2):

(R2)   Given semantic externalism, a subject S might fail to have basic self-knowledge of her thought that p.

That neither Boghossian's argument, nor any other would-be incompatibilist argument, can establish. (R2) is itself a bridgehead against all future arguments against externalism from self-knowledge.

Still, one might ask, Given that the goal is to defend semantic externalism against arguments from self-knowledge, why should we endorse this indirect response to Boghossian's argument, which has us concede that Boghossian's argument establishes an incompatibilist result? Why not try instead to make out a direct refutation? After all, if Burge is correct in his assertion that externalism is compatible with authoritative basic self-knowledge, then we can leave it to the reader to infer that for this reason there can be no successful argument against externalism from self-knowledge, and leave it at that.

The superiority of the indirect response to an argument such as Boghossian's, I submit, is that it identifies a core intuition behind incompatibilist arguments, and it shows how the proponent of externalism can accommodate such an intuition. We might initially formulate the intuition in question, as it was formulated in Goldberg 1997, as the intuition that being in a position to *knowingly* self-ascribe a thought is consistent with not knowing the thought self-ascribed. However, to many this initial formulation is likely to seem paradoxical. It is here that we can see the utility of the technical vocabulary introduced above, which enables us to clarify the relevant intuition to the point where the following nonparadoxical formulation can be given: having self-ascriptive knowledge of one's thought that p is consistent with failing to have C-self-knowledge of one's thought that *p*. I would suggest further that a failure to identify, articulate, and respond directly to this intuition, as in the case of attempts at a direct refutation of Boghossian's argument, will leave us with the nagging feeling that, still, there is something fishy about externalism on the score of self-knowledge. However, once we identify what it is about Boghossian's argument that makes it strangely compelling, and better yet when we show that we can acknowledge the point behind Boghossian's argument without surrendering externalism itself, we are in a better position altogether.

5   An Independent Motivation for the Proposal

It is perhaps worth concluding this discussion by way of suggesting some independent motivation for the present proposal, which otherwise might appear to be an ad hoc way to preserve externalism in the face of Boghossian's (1989) argument. To do so, I submit that the kind of distinction that I am trying to make (by suggesting that 'knowledge of one's own thought' covers distinct relations one can bear to one's own thoughts) mirrors a distinction already present in the literature. For, in discussing the logic of knowledge attributions, Hintikka notes, "The criteria of *knowing that* do not completely determine ... what counts as knowing who, what, when, where, and so forth. This result is immanently in agreement with what is found in ordinary discourse" (1998: 86). What is more, he goes on to write,

In order to understand ... a *knows who* statement, one must know what the criteria of identification are that the speaker or writer is presupposing.... Moreover, the same criteria must be used throughout any coherent argument or discourse. But they do not reduce to the criteria of *knowing that* (knowing facts). Accordingly, different criteria can be adopted, and are adopted, on different occasions.... A choice between all these different criteria of identification is ... guided by general epistemological considerations plus the specific purpose of the discourse in question.   (1998: 86–87)

Interestingly, Hintikka is explicit in extending these reflections to cover "higher-order knowledge." Thus he suggests that his observation regarding different criteria for the application of different knowledge-constructions "can be extended to knowledge of higher-order entities, for instance, knowledge of functions" (1998: 87). I submit that one's knowledge of the concepts figuring in one's thoughts (and, by extension, knowledge of the thoughts themselves) is a case in point. We might connect our discussion of self-knowledge to Hintikka's discussion by borrowing a point suggested to me by Sidney Morgenbesser: one can count as knowing *that* one is thinking that *p* without knowing *what* one is thinking in (knowing that one is) thinking that *p*.[9] Such a way of putting matters provides a natural way to gloss the lesson from Boghossian's memory argument. And I would speculate that much can be made of the *knows that/knows what* distinction in the present context. To cite just one example: perhaps the very appearance of a McKinsey-style a priori route to substantive knowledge of the world (by way of externalism and authoritative self-knowledge) can be explained away as based on the illegitimate conflation of knowing that one is thinking that *p* and knowing what one is thinking in thinking that *p*. For example, it might be argued, first, that such a refutation depends on a 'knows what' ascription, and second, that in contexts where what is at issue is the possibility of a refutation of skepticism from externalism and self-knowledge, we have very demanding standards for ascriptions of 'knowing what (you are thinking)'!

6   Conclusion

In this paper I have taken on the prevailing orthodoxy which holds that if there are any successful arguments establishing an incompatibility between semantic externalism and authoritative self-knowledge of one's thoughts, then this is so much the worse for semantic externalism. I have done so in two stages. First, I defended (a revised version of) Boghossian's 1989 incompatibilist argument. But second, I argued that, since this argument squares with the main points Burge (1988b) was anxious to make, the proper reaction on the part of semantic externalists would be to accept Boghossian's argument but deflate its pretensions. Such can be done by distinguishing the self-knowledge at play in that argument from 'basic self-knowledge'. The advantage of this roundabout response to Boghossian's argument with respect to "straight" responses that aim to refute it directly is that I can embrace the intuition driving Boghossian's incompatibilist argument, while at the same time insisting that this embrace does nothing to undermine the viability of semantic externalism itself. Reflecting on Boghossian's argument in this way shows the general point that, though semantic externalism does appear to require some modification of our pretheoretic beliefs regarding a thinker's relation to her own mind, the externalist can explore this matter safe in the thought that none of the required modifications will undermine externalism.[10]

Notes

1. One might hope to rebut this latter contention by endorsing an internalist notion of justification. But it is to be hoped that, if Burge's views regarding basic self-knowledge are to be rebutted, such a rebuttal could proceed without having to take on such heavy baggage.

2. Boghossian has suggested (in conversation) that he does not endorse the version I will be presenting on his behalf.

3. This version is presented in greater length in Goldberg 1997, where it is formalized so as not to rely on any principles involving memory.

4. Throughout this argument I am moving back and forth, without argument, from claims about the semantic evaluation of words, to claims about the content of the attitudes expressed. This is concessive to the compatibilist critics of Boghossian. Any gap that is postulated to exist between them could be exploited by Boghossian, in order to argue, e.g., as follows: given that the meaning of a word is (by Burge's own lights) to be individuated by appeal to facts about the relevant linguistic community, and given that the concepts figuring in a person's thoughts are to be individuated by appeal to the thinker's own "epistemic perspective," the result is that a thinker can utter 'I am presently thinking that water is wet', where, given the meaning assigned to 'water is wet' by the relevant linguistic community, 'water is wet' fails to capture the concepts composing the content of the thinker's attitude. Arguments of this sort have actually been given in Bach 1988 and Elugardo 1992 (but see Goldberg, forthcoming, for a reply). In moving back and forth from claims about the semantic evaluation of words, to claims about the content of the attitudes expressed, I am tabling the possibility of such an argument against Burge.

5. This line of argument may not compel; some compatibilist-minded externalists may think to bite the bullet and accept the replacement interpretation. But the conclusion of this paper is that externalism can be defended against objections from self-knowledge without surrendering the supplement interpretation of world-switching cases. So even if at this point a compatibilist would be inclined to bite the bullet, by the end of this paper this temptation should dissolve.

6. Falvey and Owens formulate this distinction in terms of knowledge of content; but at this point of my dialectic it will be helpful to cast the distinction without introducing the technical term 'knowledge of content'.

7. Some will not recognize this possibility, on the grounds that any case that Burge would describe as a case of a subject's incompletely grasping a concept *C*

that figures in her own thought is better described as a case in which *C* does not figure in her thought at all (but rather a different, completely grasped concept figures in her thought). Bach (1988) endorses a view of this sort.

8. This thought is not new. Boghossian himself has made it (in conversation, among other places). What I am trying to add is that in its insubstantiality lies the secret to understanding the crux of the externalism/self-knowledge debate.

9. See also Bernecker 2000 for an alternative use of the knows that/knows what distinction, as applied to the compatibilism issue.

10. I would like to express my deepest gratitude to Sidney Morgenbesser for the many discussions (over many years) I have had with him on these topics, and I would like to thank as well Sven Bernecker, Akeel Bilgrami, Paul Boghossian, Tony Brueckner, Tyler Burge, Gary Ebbs, Kevin Falvey, Dien Ho, Peter Ludlow, Brian McLaughlin, and Michael McKinsey.

13

Introspection and Internalism
Richard Fumerton

A heated controversy has developed over the question of whether one can reconcile externalist (or anti-individualist) theories of intentional states with alleged data about the nature of our access to those states.[1] Put crudely, the externalist seems to argue that a given internal state is the belief, desire, fear, or more generally, thought that it is, only if that state bears appropriate *relations* to objects, conditions, or states that lie outside the individual. A causal theory of mental content, for example, might attempt to identify the fact that I am now thinking of the color red with the fact that some past encounter with redness is causally responsible (in the right way) for some image in my mind.[2]

At the same time, it has seemed perfectly obvious to a lot of philosophers that we have a special kind of epistemic access to our thoughts and beliefs. When I'm thinking of red, for example, I typically seem to know that that's what I'm thinking about, and know it in a way better than anyone else could know. Some have claimed that the justification I have in support of my belief that I'm thinking of red is *infallible* (precludes the possibility of error). Others have been content to claim that the justification is noninferential, and about as strong as justification gets for believing contingent propositions. Still others talk of a kind of introspective access one has to one's own thoughts, an access that either constitutes a kind of justification or precludes the necessity of seeking justification.

All of these characterizations of the special epistemic access one has to one's own thoughts (and other intentional states—desires, fears, hopes, etc.) might seem to be incompatible with views that *identify* being in a mental state with being in a state that bears certain relations (usually construed as partially causal) to other people and objects. One doesn't have the same sort of special epistemic access to the external world, the argument goes, that one has to one's intentional states, and if one's analysis of mental states burdens knowledge of these states with both knowledge of the external world and the particularly problematic knowledge of causal connections, then so much the worse for externalist analyses of intentional states.

I want to focus on the claim that we have introspective knowledge of our own intentional states and explore the implications of that claim for externalist analyses of intentionality. I believe that given the correct account of introspection and the most interesting construals of what the externalist is arguing, externalism really is incompatible with facts about the introspective access one has to one's own mental states. Rarely, however, are there knockdown arguments against well-entrenched philosophical positions, and this is no exception. The philosophical debate inevitably raises a host of controversial issues concerning the nature of both analysis and introspection. I probably won't change any minds, but I do hope to make distinctions that bring to the foreground what I take to be the pivotal issues around which the debate turns.

1   *The Argument*

Put crudely, the critic of externalism might be tempted to advance the following argument (where again I'll employ a crude causal theory as the target on the assumption that a similar argument will apply *mutatis mutandis* to other externalist views):

(1)   I know through introspection that I am currently thinking that my son is tall.

(2)   I can't know through introspection even that I have ever had a son, let alone that this son figures into the causal explanation of my present state of mind.

(3)   Therefore, any view about what is involved in thinking that my son is tall that makes my son's existence a necessary condition for having that thought is false.

The argument relies implicitly on half of Leibniz's law. If a thing x is identical with a thing y, then whatever is true of x is true of y and vice versa. It's true of my thought of my son's being tall that I know that it exists through introspection. It is not true of my son's causally interacting with some internal state that I know that it exists through introspection. There is something true of the one that isn't true of the other, so you better not try to identify my thinking that my son is tall with my being in a state that involves past interactions with my son.

This kind of argument has a troubled history. A much criticized version of it seemed to constitute the basis of Descartes' argument for dualism. I know that I exist in a way different from the way in which I know that my body exists. Therefore, I cannot be identical with my body. Critics of the argument relied on powerful analogies. Lois Lane knew that Clark Kent existed before she knew that Superman existed, but it hardly follows that the legend of Superman is unintelligible. Lots of people know that water exists, but have no idea that a substance with molecular structure H_2O exists, but it hardly follows that water isn't H_2O. How could one possibly reach a conclusion about the distinctness of self and body based on the fact that the way in which I know that I exist differs from the way in which I know that my body exists?

If Descartes' argument for dualism fails, why should the externalist about mental states have anything to fear? So I know that I'm thinking of my son in a way different from the way in which I know that I am in a state with a certain causal origin. Why should that preclude one from identifying the thought of my son's height with my being in a state having a certain causal origin? Both the dualist and the internalist have a response to this reply, but its development requires the defense of a number of controversial metaphilosophical and philosophical views.

2   The Internalism/Externalism Controversy

Let me begin by trying to define more clearly the internalism/externalism controversy about the nature of intentional states. At first the dispute seems straightforward. As the labels imply, internalists identify intentional states such as belief, imagining, desire, etc., with states that are purely *internal* to the subject who is in those states. The internalist who is a physicalist puts the thought in the head or in the brain. The dualist, of course, puts that same thought "in" the mind. Externalists (causal theorists, for example) claim that my thinking that p is constituted in part by my being in a state (quite plausibly an internal state) that is related to factors that lie outside of me.

While this characterization of the dispute is superficially clear, it is also problematic for a number of reasons. First, the discussion often employs the language of *content*. Intentional states have content, they are *directed at*, or are *about*, objects. Externalists sometimes put their thesis as a thesis about the *objects* of intentional states. *S*'s thought of *p* is a thought of *p* only in virtue of factors that lie outside of *S*. But all internalists will surely insist on a distinction between something like content understood as the *meaning* of a thought (narrow content) and content understood as the object or state of affairs in the world which the thought is of, *assuming that its object exists* (wide content). One can put the point more clearly first in the context of language. Frege and Russell are most commonly put in the internalist camp. But both Frege and Russell would insist, of course, on distinguishing the meaning of certain linguistic expressions (say ordinary names) and their referents. According to Russell, for example, 'the tallest man in the world right now' has a meaning (when embedded in a sentence) even if it fails to denote anything. Furthermore, its having meaning is independent of its denoting. Just as one can distinguish the meaning and referent of the definite description, so one can distinguish the 'meaning' and 'referent' of the thought expressed by the definite description. Suppose Rob is the tallest man in the world. Then when I am thinking that the tallest man in the world has a difficult life, there is a sense in which that is a thought about Rob. On the other hand, according to the internalist, there is another perfectly clear sense in which that thought has the content it has (the meaning it has) whether or not Rob exists, indeed, whether or not there is a tallest man.

There is, of course, a real philosophical problem about how to understand the nature of intentional states whose intentional "objects" don't exist. Convinced that we must not abandon a relational analysis of intentional states, Meinongians develop a rather rich ontology replete with objects having being but no existence.[3] Adverbial theorists construe intentional states as nonrelational properties, and understand their intentional character in terms of their *capacity* to correspond to objects.[4] When one is thinking of something that doesn't exist, there simply is no object to which the thought "corresponds." In a different world, that same thought might stand in a correspondence relation to an object or state of affairs. Our present concern is not to settle these ontological controversies. It is rather simply to note that internalists will allow that there is a sense (a *trivial* sense) in which my thought that the Eiffel Tower is in France, for example, is a thought of the Eiffel Tower only if that tower exists. There is another sense, however, in which the internalist is convinced that this very thought (with its content—with its *capacity* to refer) could have existed without an Eiffel Tower. It's only that second sense of thought in which thought is claimed to be an internal state, something to which an internalist thinks one can have introspective access.

The above discussion might become even more complicated if we introduce a distinction between *de re* and *de dicto* intentional states. So some philosophers will distinguish my thinking *of* the *F* that it is *G* (a *de re* thought) from my thinking *that* the *F* is *G* (a *de dicto* thought). Again, on *some* views, a *de re* thought includes the entity that is *F* as literally a *constituent* of the thought in a way that the *de dicto* thought does not. And if one holds such a view, one might well suppose that any remotely plausible version of internalism should be restricted to *de dicto* intentional states. The *de re/de dicto* distinction can easily be the subject of an entire paper or, indeed, a book. I note here only that one must sharply distinguish the highly controversial thesis that there is a *metaphysical* distinction to be made between two kinds of intentional states, and what should be the relatively innocuous claim that there is an ambiguity between what we can call *de re* and *de dicto ascriptions* of belief (an ambiguity that is not always or even usually marked in English by employing the terminology 'believe *of* the *F* ... /believe *that* the *F* ...'). Certainly, when I describe Henry Hudson as having believed that Hudson's Bay was a passage to the Orient, I hardly intend to describe Hudson as having had the idiotic belief that a bay was a passage. But I also need not be attributing to Hudson something other than a *de dicto* belief. I may only be attributing to Hudson a belief in *some* proposition or other whose subject concept denotes that body of water that we know as Hudson's Bay and whose predicate involves being a passage to the Orient. In general, when one says of someone *S* that he believes *of* the *F* that it is *G*, we may only intend to assert that there is one and only one thing that is *F* and that *S* believes a proposition whose subject concept denotes the *F* and whose predicate involves being *G*.[5] In any event, the internalist need not and should not deny that there are *de re ascriptions* of intentional states that carry with them existential import with respect to entities outside the subject who is in the intentional state. An internalist would (or at least should) recognize that there is often scope ambiguity involving definite descriptions (or, if Russell is right, ordinary names that should be treated as disguised definite descriptions), and that in attributing to someone an intentional state, we sometimes mean to imply the existence of the object denoted by the definite description (or ordinary name). That same internalist might insist, however, that there is only one metaphysical sort of intentional state and claim that it should always be identified with an internal state.

Another problem concerning our initial characterization of internalism involves the notion of *internal* state. Perhaps the most straightforward way of defining an internal state is to contrast it with a relational state. My internal states are states that we can identify with my exemplifying nonrelational properties—they are states that could exist in a world containing no other entity but me. The difficulty, however, is that many paradigm internalists themselves endorse a relational analysis of at least some intentional states. Consider again a philosopher like Russell. Simple thoughts, for Russell, were analyzed employing the relational concept of acquaintance. My thought of red, for example, is just my being acquainted with the universal red. My thought that red is darker than yellow similarly involves my acquaintance with universals. Is thought understood this way an internal state? Well, it depends on what you mean, of course. Certainly, Russell thought that the universal red had an existence outside of me. If you destroy me, you don't destroy the universal red.[6]

If we want to allow that one can be an internalist and identify thought with a self standing in a *de re* relation of acquaintance to something like a universal, then in what sense is *this* internalist committed to the view that thoughts are "in" the head or "in" the mind? Well, perhaps the internalist is attempting to stress an *epistemological* feature of thought. When Berkeley claimed that all ideas are *in* the mind, it's at least possible that he was claiming only that we have a kind of direct, introspective access to ideas. If in this way we saddle the externalist with the denial of introspective access to intentional states, however, we will have defined into self-contradiction those externalists who claim to be able to reconcile their externalism with familiar facts about our phenomenological access to our mental states (e.g., Burge 1988b and Davidson 1987).

I suspect that in the end we will simply need to understand internal states as including both nonrelational properties of the self and the self's standing in certain sorts of *nonnatural* relations (such as acquaintance) with certain entities. Though inelegant, that's the only way I can see how to define internalism so that paradigm internalists stay in the right camp. Externalists claim not only that intentional states involve relations but that those relations can be understood naturalistically, in terms, for example, of nomological connections. Supposing that we get clear about how to understand an internal state, we still have a problem concerning the precise nature of the externalist's thesis. Earlier I characterized the externalist as holding that we must *identify* the intentional states of a subject *S* with states of *S* that bear certain relations to objects, people, or states of affairs that exist outside of, or independently of, *S*. But externalists could understand this claim of identity in quite different ways. We can distinguish at least the following *forms* an externalist thesis might take (where *y* and *z* are objects outside of the self):

Ext1 The proposition that *S* is thinking that *p* is analytically equivalent to the proposition that *S* is in a state that bears relation *R* to objects *y* and *z*.

Ext2 It is *necessarily* the case that *S* is thinking that *p* only if *S* is in a state that bears relation *R* to objects *y* and *z*.

Ext3 *S*'s thinking that *p* is a state that has *essentially* the property of standing in relation *R* to objects *y* and *z*.

Ext4 *S* wouldn't have been thinking that *p* were *S* not in a state that bears relations *R* to objects *y* and *z*.

Ext5 *S*'s thought that *p* has the property of bearing *R* to *y* and *z*.

Ext6 *S*'s thought that *p* is identical with the state of *S* that bears *R* to *x* and *z*.

Ext7 The fact that *S* is thinking that *p* is identical with the fact that *S* is in a state that bears *R* to *y* and *z*.

Ext8 The fact that *S* is thinking that *p* is *constituted* by *S*'s being in a state that bears *R* to *y* and *z*.

We can eliminate Ext5 as a claim of philosophical interest. No doubt my beliefs, hopes, imaginings, and fears have many causes and many effects. They stand in temporal relations to infinitely many other states of affairs. There are, therefore, infinitely many truths one can assert about the relations intentional states have to other objects and states. These are commonplace truths that no internalist would reject. Ext6 might initially seem to be a more plausible candidate for a philosophical thesis, but it should quickly become apparent that without a modal operator it is no more interesting than Ext5. The color red is identical with the color that my aunt likes more than any other. Knowing is the epistemic state that Descartes was most interested in discussing. These identity claims might be true, but no philosophers in their right minds would think that these truths shed any light on the correct philosophical analyses of red or knowledge. Intentional states may be identical with states that have a certain causal origin, but no philosopher should think that this sheds any *philosophical* light on the nature of intentional states. To be sure, my examples are a bit misleading. Our externalist will no doubt purport to uncover true *generalizations* about intentional states. Surely, we might be interested as philosophers in the discovery, for example, that *all* intentional states have a certain causal origin. I don't want to get into an argument about what does or doesn't interest philosophers, but I would insist that if it is only a *contingent* feature of intentional states that they have the origin they have, we still haven't discovered anything that illuminates the *nature* of intentional states. A cornerstone of British empiricism was the doctrine that all simple ideas are produced by prior experiences of which they are copies. Someone like Hume was committed to the view that the thesis, if true, is only contingently true (knowable only through induction!). But true or not, the thesis doesn't tell us what an idea is. In precisely the same sense, no true claim about the causal origin of thought tells us what a thought is.

Ext7 is also a claim about identity, but as made by philosophers it typically carries with it additional commitments. When one identifies the fact that *p* with the fact that *q in the context of offering a philosophical analysis*, one is often making a claim about the *constituents* of a fact—one is making a claim like Ext8. But one can make *philosophically* uninteresting identity claims about facts just as one can make *philosophically* uninteresting identity claims about red and knowledge. The fact that I know that I exist is identical with the fact I used as an example in class yesterday. As long as one can pick out facts through contingent properties of those facts, one can make informative, but philosophically unilluminating, identity claims about facts. In philosophical analysis we want to uncover the constituents of facts, not merely properties that facts have. Ext8 is the form a philosophically illuminating analysis of facts must take. Ext4 seems to fare no better than Ext5 and Ext6 as a thesis that deserves the attention of philosophers. Subjunctive conditionals can be understood in a number of different ways, but without a modal operator strengthening the thesis, no internalist would be interested in denying any number of true subjunctives about intentional states. I wouldn't have been thinking that my son is tall today had I not been playing catch with him yesterday. I wouldn't have been thinking that my son is tall had I not had a son. I wouldn't have been thinking that my son is tall if my parents hadn't existed. All true; all philosophically uninteresting.[7]

The modal operator in Ext2 can be interpreted in any number of different ways. If we want Ext2 to be different from Ext1, however, we will need to understand the necessity as something different from analyticity. But if we want to avoid our thesis degenerating once again into a philosophically uninteresting *empirical* claim, we will want the necessity to be something stronger than nomological necessity. That leaves us with the philosophically problematic category of synthetic necessary truth. In fact, I think that there are fairly obvious candidates for synthetic necessary truths, but I also doubt that most contemporary externalists are all that comfortable employing this modal concept in advancing their theses. For reasons that I don't understand, some philosophers who have no truck with the synthetic and necessary seem perfectly comfortable with the concept of essential properties, and for that reason Ext3 might be a live option for the interpretation of some externalist claims. It is, however, a kind of claim that I'm not going to address in this paper. The reason is simple. I have no idea how to evaluate nontrivial claims about essential properties even when those claims are made about so called natural kinds, like gold and water. When it comes to psychological states like belief, it seems to me that the category of essential properties becomes even more mysterious. If an externalist is advancing a claim about the essential properties of intentional states, that claim will remain untouched by any of the arguments we will be considering in this paper. So in the final analysis, it seems to me that the most interesting externalist theses are Ext1 or Ext8.

3   The Argument Revisited

Is either Ext1 or Ext8 threatened by the internalist's argument from introspection? Let us briefly return to Descartes' much maligned argument for dualism. Why can't we conclude that the self isn't the body upon discovering that we know that we exist in a way different from the way in which we know that our bodies exist? Why doesn't this epistemological difference indicate that there is something that is true of the self that isn't true of the body and thus that self and body are distinct? One might try to argue that the problem lies with Leibniz's law. Although I can't argue the point here, I am convinced that if one avoids the fatal error of confusing Leibniz's law with false principles concerning the substitutivity *salva veritate* of coreferential, or even synonymous expressions, one will find no difficulties with Leibniz's law. There are no counterexamples to it.

The better response of the identity theorist to Descartes' argument is to distinguish claims about the identity of *propositions* (or of the *meaning*s of statements) from claims about the identity of what is described by those propositions or statements (this sort of response was made by J. J. C. Smart in 1962). There is no problem with Leibniz's law, but we need to be clear about *what* precisely *has* the property of being known or not known before we attempt to employ these properties in arguing identity claims. If the knowledge in question is *de dicto* knowledge, then what is known is a *proposition*. From the fact that I can know that I exist in a way in which I cannot know that my body exists, it *does* follow, by Leibniz's law, that the proposition *that I exist* is a different proposition from the proposition *that my body exists*. If knowledge is of statements-with-a-meaning, we can infer from the difference in knowledge that the statement that I exist has a different meaning from the statement that my body exists. But it doesn't follow that the two propositions (statements) have a different subject matter. Unbeknownst to me, the two propositions (statements) can turn out to be about one and the same entity. By analogy, an internalist might claim that while I can know through introspection that I am thinking that my son is tall and cannot know through introspection that I'm in a state whose causal origin involves my son—all that follows from this is that the *proposition* that I am thinking that my son is tall is different from the *proposition* that I'm in a state whose causal origin involves my son. From that it doesn't follow that the two distinct propositions have a different subject matter.

Notice, however, that our hypothetical externalist has given up on one of the two most obvious interpretations of externalism, Ext1. This externalist no longer even purports to have a thesis with the status of an analytic truth. It is *conceded* that the proposition that I am thinking that my son is tall is not analytically equivalent to a proposition describing the causal genesis of some internal state (or any other propositions implying the existence of my son). The retreat, then, is to a claim about the common subject matter of two propositions. The concept of common subject matter, however, requires close attention. It may not be all that easy simply to abandon claims about equivalence in meaning and retreat to claims about commonality of subject matter. On some correspondence theories of truth, for example, the identity conditions for propositions are isomorphic with the identity conditions for the facts that make those propositions true. On a crude picture theory, for example, if we have two different propositions, two different "pictures" of reality, then there must be two different features of reality that make the respective pictures true. On certain theories of truth, then, one can move directly from facts about the distinctness of propositions to facts about the distinctness of the facts that would make them true. The collapse of Ext1, on these views, carries with it the collapse of Ext8.

Correspondence conceptions of truth are hardly uncontroversial, however, and even if one is a correspondence theorist one need not posit a different fact as the truth maker for each distinct proposition.[8] In addition, I suspect many externalists are going to be unhappy with my implicit suggestion that facts are the most appropriate candidates for being the "subject matter" of propositions. Someone like Davidson, for example, might be much happier formulating the externalist's identity thesis by employing the category of event. The *fact* that I am thinking that my son is tall may not be constitutionally identical with the *fact* that I'm in a state with a certain causal origin. But that doesn't mean that the *event* that is my thinking of my son is something different from the *event* that is a certain internal state occurring for a certain (causal) reason. If one rejects a correspondence conception of truth, one might even deny that claims about the distinctness of facts are interestingly different from claims about the distinctness of propositions. Talk about facts is just a misleading way to talk about the truth of propositions. If reference to the fact that p is just reference to p's being true, and reference to the fact that q is just reference to q's being true, then it trivially follows from the distinctness of the propositions p and q that the facts p and q are distinct. Correspondence theorists who want facts to serve as representation-independent truth makers for propositions have a radically different view. But even some of them might want to allow that one should distinguish the identity conditions for facts from the identity conditions for events. To take a well-worn example, the fact that Oedipus killed his father might be a different fact from the fact that Oedipus killed the king of Thebes (the corresponding propositions are certainly different). But there does seem to be some intuitive sense in which only one event occurred (in space and time), an event that could be alternatively described as Oedipus killing his father or as Oedipus killing the king of Thebes.

If the externalist insists on this distinction between the identity conditions for facts and the identity conditions for events, and restricts the claim of identity to events, we would need to turn at this point to thorny issues concerning the identity conditions for events. There is a vast literature on the subject and no consensus has ever been approached. Is my playing the piano loudly last night the same or a different event from my waking up the neighbor? Is it the same or a different event from my pounding out the *Star Spangled Banner*? Is it the same or a different event from my playing my daughter's favorite tune? To be honest, I don't even have intuitions about how to answer these questions. I simply don't *understand* those who claim that we need to individuate events through their causes and effects. If events are the relata of causal connections, then it would seem we need some independent understanding of what *constitutes* the event if we are even to assess a claim about that event's causal origin or causal effects.[9]

Rather than confront the externalist who advances a thesis employing the language of events, I would simply recommend that we internalists be content to stay with a claim about facts. The identity conditions for facts are no more (nor less) complicated that the identity conditions for particulars and properties. The fact that p is constitutionally identical with the fact that q when the facts are constituted by the same particulars exemplifying the same (relational and nonrelational) properties. We should declare victory if we can get the externalist to concede that the fact that I am thinking of my son does not involve as a constituent any individual or state that lies outside of me.

In the problematic dualist claims we considered by way of analogy, there was another candidate for common subject matter of the distinct propositions. When I believe that I'm in pain and I believe that my brain is in a certain state, both beliefs may be about the same particular, in the Russellian sense we discussed earlier. Just as my belief that Rob is tall and my belief that the tallest man in America is tall may be about the same person (in the sense that both thoughts might turn out to be about one and the same individual), so my belief that I'm in pain and my belief that my brain is in a certain state may be "existential" beliefs whose "variables in thought" take the value of the same individual.[10]

In the case of the internalism/externalism controversy about intentional states, however, the focus of the controversy seems not to be the individual who is in the intentional state (the individual who exemplifies the property of representing the world a certain way), but rather the *property* of representing that the individual exemplifies. To be sure, the properties may themselves be complex and two distinct properties may have common constituents. Being in a certain internal state and being in that internal state having certain causes both, intuitively, involve being in the internal state.[11] So there is a sense in which the proposition that I am thinking of my son and the proposition that I am in an internal state whose causal genesis involves my son have *overlapping* subject matter. But overlapping subject matter and common subject matter are surely not the same thing. The internalist claims that the existence of my son and his causal connections to my internal state is no part of what *constitutes* my thinking of my son. That internal state may, of course, be included in the subject matter of propositions that describe features of the world that go beyond the internal state.

Davidson gives an example that is supposed to help reconcile externalism with the possibility of introspective knowledge of intentional states. It serves better, I think, to underscore the problems the externalist faces. Davidson (1987: 103–105) argues that just because my being sunburned implies the existence of the sun, it surely doesn't follow that being sunburned isn't a condition of my skin. In the context of the present debate, this might seem to imply that we can surely notice (be aware of) someone's sunburn without having to reach conclusions about the existence of the sun or the sun's causal role in producing the burn. And this is true despite the fact that one couldn't develop a plausible story about what sunburn *is* without talking about the way in which the sun causes the skin to change color. Presumably, the pink skin color is supposed to be analogous to the internal state that we know through introspection. The causal origin of the skin color, a necessary condition for the person's being sunburned, is supposed to be analogous to the causal origin of the internal state, a necessary condition for its being an intentional state with the content it has. For many of us the analogy is problematic because we don't think that we are *directly* aware of skin color the way we are directly aware of our mental states. But leaving that aside, does the analogy help the externalist? I think not. To see *that* someone is sunburned, to be aware of the *fact that* someone is sunburned, *does* involve knowing that the skin color has a certain causal origin. If, for example, I see someone with reddish skin that is, in fact, caused by a rash, it is simply false that I am aware of the fact that the person is sunburned. Without some *reason* to believe that the skin color is caused by exposure to the sun, I have no *reason* to conclude that the person is sunburned, and I won't *know* that the person is sunburned. Without employing the concept of causation, I can't even see the person *as* sunburned. In such a case, I might still be described as seeing a sunburn.[12] But notice that the sense in which someone can see an *F* without even believing that the thing is *F* is irrelevant to knowing *that* an *F* exists. The alleged claim about intentional states is not merely that one is aware of them in the sense in which one can be aware of a coatrack without seeing it as a coatrack. It is, rather, that one is aware of them *as* intentional states—one is aware of them in a way that can give propositional knowledge of what one is thinking.

4 Introspective Knowledge

In the preceding discussion, I have been supposing that the externalist will concede that we know through introspection what we are thinking of in a way in which we cannot know through introspection truths about the causal origin of our internal states. I have argued that such a concession is fatal to Ext1 and, when combined with certain controversial theses about truth, may prove fatal to Ext8. But need the externalist make the concession? Can the externalist argue that I have introspective knowledge of *both* the proposition that I am thinking of my son's being tall and the proposition that I am in a state whose causal origin involves my son? The answer to the question, not surprisingly, hinges on how we understand introspective knowledge.

Externalists with respect to the ontological analysis of intentional states are also likely to be epistemic externalists. How would an epistemic externalist understand introspective knowledge? Rather than discuss the question in the abstract, let's consider a specific version of externalism, and for our present purposes let's use a fairly crude form of reliabilism. When Goldman (1979) first introduced a reliabilist account of justification, he introduced a distinction between two importantly different kinds of justified belief: (1) justified beliefs whose justification derives from their being produced by conditionally reliable processes which take as input justified beliefs, and (2) justified beliefs whose justification derives from their being produced by unconditionally reliable processes which take as input stimuli other than beliefs. Conditionally reliable processes are those that produce mostly true beliefs when the input beliefs are true. Unconditionally reliable processes are those that produce mostly true beliefs when prompted by the relevant noncognitive stimuli.

This version of reliabilism is a form of both epistemic and conceptual foundationalism. All justified beliefs owe their justification ultimately to beliefs whose justification does not derive from the having of other justified beliefs. And the very *concept* of a justified belief is (through a recursive definition) parasitic on the concept of a noninferentially justified belief (defined in the base clause of the recursive definition). While the theory itself takes no stand on which beliefs are noninferentially justified and which are only inferentially justified, one presumes that beliefs about the contents of one's mind might be pretty good candidates for noninferentially justified beliefs. The mind (or brain), one might suppose, monitors itself with respect to some of its characteristics, and monitors some of those characteristics rather reliably. We simply identify introspective knowledge with those beliefs about mental states that take as their input the mental states and produce as their output *beliefs* that the mental states are occurring.

Now it is important to note that reliabilism in particular, and externalism in general, places no a priori restrictions on which beliefs turn out to be noninferentially justified (which beliefs are the results of belief-independent, unconditionally reliable processes). Beliefs about the past, the external world, the future, God (as Plantinga [2000] has reminded us) might all turn out to be "basic" on an externalist account of justification (or in Plantinga's case, warrant). As a result, there would be nothing inconsistent in an externalist's arguing that we can have noninferentially justified belief in the very propositions that constitute the externalist's analysans for propositions describing intentional states. One could reconcile one's externalism with the alleged phenomenology of our knowledge of intentional states by simply greatly expanding the class of propositions to which one has noninferential (spontaneous, immediate) knowledge. Whether an externalist would make such a move depends on how daring the externalist is when it comes to expanding foundations for knowledge. On externalist accounts, it is always an empirical question as to which belief-forming processes are or are not unconditionally reliable. It probably won't be that hard for the externalist to construe various propositions about the past, and perhaps even about the external world, as noninferentially justified.[13] When my past interactions with my son caused that image in my mind (making the image an image *of* my son), they might also have reliably caused a belief that my son is tall, thus generating a justified belief (whose content will involve my son). I suspect that most externalists, however, are going to get cold feet when it comes to allowing noninferential knowledge of propositions asserting *causal* connections, though perhaps it depends on one's account of causation.

There is a quite different approach the metaphysical externalist might take to arguing parity of justification for belief in both the analysans and analysandum of an externalist theory. Burge (1988b: 117) and others sometimes seem to assume that we have all learned from futile bouts with the skeptic that we shouldn't burden everyday knowledge with the requirement that we know all of the presuppositions for the truth of various claims we make. I've never found these sorts of arguments very convincing. As far as I can see, Dretske better have some reason to believe that the animal isn't a cleverly disguised mule, or he simply *isn't* justified in believing that he is seeing a zebra.[14] But whether or not we need justified belief in the many propositions whose truth is a necessary condition for the truth of commonplace claims we make about the world, it is surely obvious that we do not bring these largely dispositional beliefs to the fore of consciousness when forming indefinitely many beliefs (or better, expectations). After emphasizing this point, an externalist might go on to argue that beliefs based on introspection may not be as straightforward as they initially seem. To be sure, I do not *consciously* infer that I'm thinking of my son when I immediately conclude that this is the content of my present thought. But then I don't consciously infer most of what I believe about my immediate physical environment, my immediate past experience, or even most of what I expect with respect to the near future. This kind of psychological observation should be neutral with respect to the epistemic status of these "spontaneous" beliefs, but it is not unfair to suggest that many in the history of epistemology have been too quick to slide from the absence of conscious inference in what strikes us as obvious, to the conclusion that the belief in question must be noninferentially justified. In any event, there is no reason why an externalist might not attempt to cash out introspective knowledge in terms of psychologically spontaneous belief whose justification may involve a number of different conditionally and unconditionally reliable belief-forming processes.

There are, then, externalist epistemological accounts of introspection that might allow one to retain Ext1 (and with it, Ext8) by arguing that both analysandum and analysans of the externalist account of mental content can be known through introspection. I myself don't think any of the externalist accounts of knowledge or justified belief capture philosophically interesting epistemic concepts, something I have argued elsewhere (1995). As I indicated earlier, however, my primary purpose in this paper is to make clear the philosophical choices available in evaluating the argument from introspection against externalist accounts of intentional states.

But what sort of account might an *internalist* give of introspective knowledge? In a number of places (e.g., Fumerton 1995) I have defended the concept of direct acquaintance as the key conceptual building block in constructing an internalist foundationalism. Externalists are rarely all that comfortable with talk of phenomenological aware-ness, direct awareness, or direct acquaintance. And that's because on the most natural interpretation of these concepts, we are trying to get at something that is not just another intentional state with a content that may or may not correspond to reality. Direct acquaintance is a real *rela-tion* that a subject bears to features of the world. When the internalist speaks of the acquaintance you have with your pain, the internalist is calling your attention to the way in which the pain itself is before your mind. But if awareness is a relation that a subject bears to features of the world, in what sense can we speak of introspective knowledge? It's sim-ply a category mistake to think of pain, for example, as something that is true or false. How do we get from awareness of something that is neither true nor false to justified belief in a proposition? Although I can hardly defend the view here, I have argued that the key to answering this ques-tion is to recognize that one can be directly acquainted not only with properties, and, perhaps, particulars, but also with facts. Facts are the truth makers of thoughts; thoughts are the primary bearers of truth values. When one is directly acquainted with the fact that one is in pain while one is directly aware of a correspondence between the thought that one is in pain and the pain, that just *is* having noninferential justi-fication for believing that one is in pain. And if that justification pro-duces the belief that one is in pain, then one knows that one is in pain. When internalists argue from the phenomenology of introspection to a rejection of externalism about mental content, they do so because they are convinced that they are directly acquainted with facts about what they are thinking of, facts that do not contain as constituents nomo-logical relations to objects that lie outside them.

If acquaintance is a real relation that a subject bears to features of the world, then one cannot deploy the classic response to Descartes' argu-ment for dualism in defending externalism. Propositions may have the property of being believed or not believed, known or not known. But on the classical foundationalist view, it is *facts* with which we are or are not acquainted. Employing this concept of acquaintance, we can present a revised argument against externalism:

(1)   I am directly acquainted with the fact that I'm thinking of my son's being tall.

(2)   I am not directly acquainted with the fact that I'm in a state whose causal origin involves my son.

(3)   Therefore, the fact that I am thinking that my son is tall is not identical with that fact that I am in a state whose causal origin involves my son.

I suspect that Descartes was implicitly relying on something like this notion of direct acquaintance. Convinced that he was directly aware of his thoughts, but not directly aware of any physical states, he concluded that he couldn't identify his thoughts with his exemplifying physical properties. I am under no illusions with respect to the prospect of using the above argument to change an externalist's mind about the plausibility of externalist analyses of mental content. The *sui generis*, nonnatural concept of direct acquaintance upon which the argument relies is something externalists would (and should, given their views) reject. Some of us are convinced, however, that without a phenomenological direct acquaintance with features of the world, we have nothing on which to anchor our metaphysical speculations.[15]

Notes

1. Two relatively recent anthologies (Ludlow and Martin 1998; Wright, Smith, and MacDonald 1998) contain papers devoted to the subject.

2. I have yet to encounter anything resembling an even prima facie plausible account of how to distinguish the "right" sort of causal chain from "deviant" causal chains. I'll continue to use a crude causal theory as my example of an externalist account of intentional states. There are, of course, others. The kind of functionalism that identifies intentional states with second order properties (being in an intentional state is being in a state that plays a functional role) is another common version of externalism. This sort of functionalism must be distinguished from those views according to which the reference of intentional states gets "fixed" via definite descriptions that characterize functional roles.

3. One of the most elaborate of such accounts is Butchvarov 1979.

4. For the development of such an account, see Fumerton, forthcoming.

5. The precise way in which to "translate" what I've called *de re* ascriptions of belief into propositions attributing certain *de dicto* beliefs is a matter of some difficulty.

6. A similar problem arises when trying to define the internalism/externalism controversy in epistemology. Epistemic internalists are sometimes characterized as holding that being justified is being in some internal state. But again, paradigmatic internalists like Russell hold that the source of noninferential justification is the relation of acquaintance one bears to various particulars and properties. This version of foundationalism is compatible with any number of

different views concerning the *objects* of direct acquaintance. It is important to remember that in the final analysis we are trying to make technical philosophical distinctions when we try to clarify internalism/externalism controversies. There is no one correct way to understand the distinctions. Our goal is only to make philosophically interesting distinctions. One could, therefore, construe Russell (and Frege also) as a kind of externalist both with respect to mind and epistemology, and go on to sharply distinguish this kind of externalism from its more recent versions.

7. That externalists want their claims to be understood as claims about what is *necessarily* true of intentional states is evident by the way in which they conduct their arguments. It's clear that both they and their critics feel free to explore possible worlds far removed from this one in evaluating their claims.

8. It is entirely plausible (though not uncontroversial) to suppose, for example, that there are no disjunctive facts. There is only one fact that is the truth maker for both the proposition that grass is green and the distinct proposition that grass is green or the moon is made of green cheese. One might also argue there are no existential facts corresponding to existential propositions. It is only the existence of particular horses, one might suppose, that makes true the existential proposition that there are horses, and that despite the fact that the existential proposition is not logically equivalent to any disjunction of atomic propositions.

9. Here again, the philosopher putting forth this thesis might be intending only to make an assertion about essential properties of events. As I indicated earlier, I am not interested in addressing claims about essential properties in this paper.

10. So it is clear that the debate over dualism is sometimes a debate over whether there is one substance exemplifying both mental and physical properties, or two substances: one exemplifying mental properties, the other exemplifying physical properties. Property dualists and "fact" dualists leave open the question of what bears properties and focus their attention instead on what they take to be an important distinction between kinds of properties, a distinction that carries over to the facts that are constituted partially by those properties.

11. This can actually get a bit complicated. If one is offering something like a functionalist account of intentional states, then the second-order property of having a property with certain causal properties only indirectly involves the property that realizes that functional role. The thought of the second-order property involves the mental counterpart of a variable whose value may take the very internal property that the internalist takes to be the intentional state.

12. This is, presumably, the point that Davidson would emphasize.

13. I have argued (in Fumerton 1988) that it won't be that easy either, particularly in the case of belief about the external world.

14. The reference is to Dretske's highly influential discussion (1970) of whether we need to know implications of what we know. To be sure, one would need

to qualify the claim that one needs to know every presupposition of a proposition before one can know the proposition. Every necessary truth is a (trivial) necessary condition for the truth of every proposition, and it is hardly plausible to suppose that one needs to know every necessary truth before one can know anything. One of the keys to distinguishing relevant from irrelevant presuppositions may involve the development of a relevance logic.

15. I'd like to thank Ken Williford, Susana Nuccetelli, and Diane Jeske for their helpful comments on a draft of this paper.

14

Two Forms of Antiskepticism
Matthias Steup

1 McKinsey's Inconsistent Triad

According to semantic externalism (SE), my thinking that water is wet implies that I either have been in causal contact with water or have been a member of a speech community that has been in causal contact with water. So SE is the view that my thinking that water is wet implies that water exists. Michael McKinsey has argued that when SE is conjoined with the privileged access thesis—the thesis that we know the contents of our own thoughts a priori (PAC: privileged access to content)—an inconsistent triad results, for SE and PAC imply a third proposition: the thesis that we can have privileged access to, a priori knowledge of, specific facts about the external world (PAW: privileged access to the world).[1] Let us immediately settle the meaning of 'a priori'. *Strict* a priori knowledge is knowledge of necessary truths, gained through conceptual analysis. *Broad* a priori knowledge is either knowledge of necessary truths or knowledge acquired through introspection, understood as a faculty that gives us knowledge of our mental states in a way that does not involve any sense perception. Henceforth, I will follow McKinsey's usage and mean by 'a priori' broad apriority as just defined.

Now consider the following three propositions:

M1 Oscar knows a priori that if he is thinking that water is wet, then water exists.

M2 Oscar knows a priori that he is thinking that water is wet.

M3 Oscar knows a priori that water exists.

SE is the thesis that a natural-kind term like 'water' receives its meaning from causal connections to water. So when Oscar is thinking about water, water must exist. This is something Oscar can know a priori, for

SE derives its support from philosophical thought experiments and conceptual analysis.[2] Thus we get M1. PAC gives us M2. M1 and M2 imply M3, which is an example of PAW.

McKinsey considers PAW unacceptable. Since he accepts SE, his view is that M1 to M3 amount to a reductio of PAC.[3] But this is just one of altogether three responses to the puzzle. A second option would be to embrace M3, a third to reject SE. The latter option is not frequently endorsed in the literature on the subject. Thus we may think of the problem as a *dilemma* for semantic externalists. They must choose between M1 and M3, between giving up PAC and getting stuck with PAW. This is a dilemma because, as received opinion would have it, it is *plausible* to assume that our epistemic position relative to our thoughts is privileged compared to our epistemic position relative to the external world, and it is *implausible* that we can know a priori specific facts about the external world. McKinsey, in any case, thinks that PAW is out of the question, and thus concludes that PAC needs revision. So he thinks that SE and PAC are not compatible, which makes him an *incompatibilist*. In contrast, Sawyer (1988) and Warfield (1999) argue for embracing PAW. They think that SE and PAC are compatible, which makes them *compatibilists*.[4]

There is, in fact, no reluctance at all in Sawyer's and Warfield's endorsement of PAW. Following the path originally paved by Putnam (1981), they see virtue in the fact that SE, if conjoined with PAC, implies PAW. It permits us to deduce from the contents of our thoughts not only that there is an external world, but, to a large extent, what that world is like. If this were true, it would appear to be good news as far as rebutting skepticism is concerned. Oscar, for example, could then know, by knowing that he is thinking about water, that water exists. And he would only need to start thinking about things like spinach, zinc, and mice to deduce that spinach, zinc, and mice exist, which would allow him to dismiss skeptical alternatives that involve the nonexistence of spinach, zinc, and mice. Alas, such an easy dismissal of skeptical alternatives might be too good to be true. I will argue that there is reason to think it would be.

2 Semantic Antiskepticism

Suppose, then, Oscar is a semantic externalist and feels inspired to refute skepticism. He might want to argue thus:

THE SEMANTIC ANTISKEPTICAL ARGUMENT

S1 I am thinking about water.

S2 If I am thinking about water, then water exists.

S3 Water exists.

The conclusion of this argument makes a rather specific existential claim. One might wonder whether one couldn't argue for the existence of unicorns in parallel fashion. Warfield's argument avoids this problem because its conclusion asserts something else: I'm not a brain in a vat (BIV) in an otherwise empty world. It goes as follows:

WARFIELD'S ARGUMENT

W1 I think that water is wet.

W2 No brain in a vat in an otherwise empty world can think that water is wet.[5]

W3 I am not a brain in a vat in an otherwise empty world.

A first point to note is that W2 might assert less than what SE implies. Arguably, SE in fact implies the stronger premise:

W2* No brain in a vat in a world without water can think that water is wet.

From the conjunction of W1 and W2*, the conclusion follows that water exists. If SE indeed implies W2*, then Warfield's actual, weaker antiskeptical argument would not alleviate the concerns of incompatibilists, i.e., of those who find PAW unacceptable and thus reject PAC. Warfield, in any case, prefers W2 to W2* because, as he explicitly states, he does not want to appeal to the premise that 'water' in his language refers to water. I will argue that in spite of the relative modesty of W2, the argument nevertheless vulnerable to serious objections.

Warfield defends the two premises of his argument as follows: W2 is supported by Putnam/Burge-style thought experiments, and W1 is unproblematic because it's easy to know the contents of our thoughts. There is, of course, the concern that SE undermines self-knowledge. A critic might argue that it is inconsistent to use one premise that is underwritten by SE and another one that asserts self-knowledge. Warfield (1999: 83) replies that SE merely implies the possibility of a lack of self-knowledge. From this possibility, it doesn't follow that in fact he fails to know W1. I must agree with him there.

There is, however, a further problem with W1. Warfield claims that, unlike Moore's hand-waving refutation of skepticism, his argument does not beg the question against the skeptic. It doesn't because, Warfield claims, he knows his premises a priori: W1 through introspection and W2 through conceptual analysis. The kind of knowledge the skeptic calls into question is empirical knowledge. Warfield's argument does not appeal to any empirical knowledge; so it isn't question begging. This would be true enough if Warfield's knowledge of W1 would indeed be based solely on introspection. It's not obvious, however, that it really is. If it isn't, then Warfield's argument would be question-begging by his own admission. I will get back to this question in section 5.

Another worry is registered by Warfield himself. In response to Putnam's (1981) argument against the BIV hypothesis, it has been pointed out that it is ineffective if the hypothesis involves *recent* envatment. Warfield (1999: 88) argues that we don't know enough about the semantics of thought and reference to assert with confidence that a BIV's water thoughts continue to refer to water if envatment occurred only recently. I find this reply implausible. Consider Robinson Crusoe. After fifteen years or so of solitude, wouldn't his thoughts about oaks, with which he had been in causal contact back in England but which are not to be found on his island, still be thoughts about oaks? But even if Warfield were right and this is something we just don't know, his point would cut both ways. If we don't know whether or not 'water'-water reference survives recent envatment, then surely Warfield doesn't know, on the basis of his argument, that he is not a *fresh* BIV in an otherwise empty world. So even if Warfield's argument were otherwise successful, it would be of limited scope.

3   A Priori Knowledge of the External World

Let us turn our attention to the semantic antiskeptical argument. It would appear to be the sort of argument McKinsey has in mind when he argues for the incompatibility of SE and PAC on the basis of rejecting PAW. In his contribution to this volume, McKinsey suggests that SE applies not only to natural kind terms, but even more clearly to indexical pronouns and small-scope proper names. It is the latter two that convince him that SE is correct. As an example, he uses the proposition 'Laura is thinking that George is cute'. 'George' is a nondescriptive proper name. Thus, as McKinsey puts it, this proposition "ascribes to Laura a cognitive property that is relational with respect to George" (this volume, p. 99). If that's right, then Laura's thought that George is cute implies George's existence. Laura, then, could argue as follows:

LAURA'S ARGUMENT

L1 I am thinking that George is cute.

L2 If I am thinking that George is cute, then George exists.

L3 George exists.

If Laura could acquire knowledge of L3 by reasoning in this way, she could acquire a priori knowledge of George's existence. McKinsey considers this to be sufficient grounds for doubting the apriority of L1. The situation with regard to Warfield's argument is different. If it were successful, it would give Warfield a priori knowledge of the proposition that he isn't a BIV in an otherwise empty world. With regard to that conclusion, apriority is not quite as worrisome as it is when it comes to the existence of George. Still, can a person know a priori that she isn't a BIV? It seems doubtful. But would it be right to conclude that at least one of the premises of Warfield's argument must be false because his conclusion just isn't the sort of thing that's knowable a priori? Warfield thinks it wouldn't be. It should not merely be *asserted* that we cannot have a priori knowledge of the external world. What's needed here is an argument.

It seems to me that incompatibilists might as well leave it an open question whether we can have a priori knowledge of the external world. In fact, I will now present what I take to be an a priori argument for the existence of external objects that I think has *some* claim to prima facie plausibility:

THE EXISTENCE ARGUMENT

E1 I exist.

E2 Necessarily, if I exist, then at least one physical thing T exists.

E3 Therefore, at least one physical thing, T, exists.

E4 Necessarily, if at least one physical thing, T, exists, then in addition to T, many other physical things exist.

E5 Therefore, in addition to T, many other physical things exist.

The two problematic premises are E2 and E4. Are they at all plausible? Well, physicalists believe that persons are physical organisms. And surely they do not believe that persons simply happen to be physical organisms. Rather, what the standard arguments against Cartesian dualism suggest is that a person *could not* be a nonphysical thing. Moreover, surely the arguments physicalists employ against dualism are a priori in nature. So, arguably, if physicalism is correct, I can know E2 a priori. Certainly a priori knowledge of E1 is uncontroversial. E3, then, is arguably something I can know a priori.

Now consider E4. Is there a possible world in which just one physical thing T (without any parts) exists? This would be a world in which the existence of T, as well as its activities, would be an unexplainable, brute fact. T would neither have originated from anything else nor be sustained by anything else. It and its activities would be utterly mysterious. So E4 is not altogether implausible. I do not, however, wish to assert that E4 true. Rather, the point is that E4 is not obviously false. A sharp metaphysician might be able to make a good case for it. My reason, then, for presenting the existence argument is not make a case for its conclusion. Rather, the question I'm interested in is whether saying that E5 is simply not the sort of thing you can know a priori would be a good objection to the existence argument. I think it would not be. A good objection would have to engage directly with E2 or E4.[6]

So I think that a priori knowledge of the external world should not be dismissed too quickly. However, even if we could know E5 (or other general propositions like it) a priori, arguments like the semantic antiskeptical argument or Laura's argument remain nevertheless problematic because it is hard to believe that we can have a priori knowledge of *specific* facts about the external world. As far as these arguments go, I side with McKinsey: the thought that their conclusions are knowable a priori is highly implausible. This by itself is reason enough to doubt that such arguments are sound.

Warfield's argument is a different matter. Knowing a priori that one is not a BIV is perhaps less problematic than knowing a priori that George exists, or that water exists. Thus my objection to Warfield's argument is not going to be that we simply cannot have any a priori knowledge of the external world. Rather, I will argue that there is reason to think that, while it might be possible to gain a priori knowledge of some very general propositions about the external world, the premises of Warfield's argument are, in point of fact, *not* knowable a priori.

4   Semantic Antiskepticism and Transmission Failure

Consider Laura's argument again. Can Laura know L1 solely trough introspection? Her thought has the content it has only if George exists. So we might wonder whether she can know that she is thinking about George without relying on perceptual experiences that give her knowledge of George's existence. If reliance on such experiences is necessary, then arguably her knowledge of the content of her thought could not have introspection as its sole source. McKinsey, in any case, seems to suggest that this is so:

> But of course the source of one's warrant for believing that George exists could not be that one has correctly deduced this conclusion from the relational premise in question, *since one would not be warranted in believing the relational premise in the first place, unless one were already warranted in believing that George exists.* (This volume, p. 102)

In this passage, McKinsey applies to his Laura example a point that was initially made by Martin Davies (1998) and Crispin Wright (2000a): arguments from the contents of one's thoughts to the existence of their referents (or perhaps some broader, external condition) suffer from transmission failure; they do not succeed in transmitting the warrant for the premises to the conclusion.[7] Arguments that beg the question are examples of arguments that suffer from transmission failure. Laura's argument is a case in point. It begs the question, and thus suffers from transmission failure. It begs the question, McKinsey argues, because I couldn't be warranted in believing L1 unless I was warranted in believing L3 in the first place. Consequently, my warrant for the existence of George, which is perceptual, is a part of my warrant for attributing to myself the thought that George is cute.

Now consider the semantic antiskeptical argument. The charge of transmission failure would proceed in parallel fashion. I couldn't be warranted in believing that I am thinking about water unless I was warranted to begin with, on the basis of perceptual experiences, in believing in the existence of water. As a consequence, my perceptual warrant for believing in the existence of water is part of my warrant for believing that I am thinking about water. A parallel point applies to Warfield's argument. Perceptual warrant for believing that water exists is part of my warrant for attributing to myself a thought with the content that water is wet. So just like Laura's argument, both the semantic antiskeptical argument and Warfield's argument are vulnerable to the charge of transmission failure.

If an argument suffers from transmission failure, it is not a *cogent* argument: it cannot be used for *generating* warrant for, or rational acceptance of, the conclusion. But that's not the only problem that arises for Warfield's argument if the charge of transmission failure sticks. A second problem is that transmission failure would undermine Warfield's antiskeptical strategy, which relies on appealing to premises that are knowable a priori: through reasoning and introspection alone.

Suppose it is indeed a consequence of SE that part of my warrant for W1 is perceptual evidence for the existence of what my thought is about: water. If so, I cannot know W1 through introspection alone. Rather, I would know it on the basis of both introspection and perception. But then my knowledge of these premises would not be a priori, for it would in part depend on perceptual evidence. As a result, Warfield's argument would beg the question against the skeptic, assuming rebutting skepticism on the basis of empirical premises, as Warfield assumes, is indeed question begging.

5   Begging the Question against the Skeptic

It is one thing to acquire knowledge of the external world, another to defend the claim to such knowledge against the skeptic. We obtain knowledge of the external world through our perceptual experiences. Thus we can construe perceptual arguments for the existence of particular objects or substances, and from their existence deduce the existence of an external world. Consider, for example:

MOORE'S ARGUMENT
Here is a hand.
If so, then there is an external world.

There is an external world.

This argument has the virtue of succeeding in explaining how we in fact know that there in an external world. We know that there is an external world precisely because we know, on the basis of perception, that there are particular, external objects such as our hands. In this regard, Moore's argument is clearly different from the semantic antiskeptical argument. We know that water exists. But we enjoy this bit of knowledge not on the basis of the evidence identified by the semantic antiskeptical argument. Rather, we know its conclusion to begin with and independently: on the basis of innumerable perceptual encounters with water.

How does Warfield's argument compare with Moore's argument? If it is indeed correct that, if we wish to avoid begging the question against the skeptic we must not use any premise whose warrant would be (even partially) perceptual, then it would seem that Warfield's argument begs the question no less than Moore's argument does. Next, I will pursue this line of thought further, developing it from a different angle. Consider:

THE BIV ARGUMENT

I do not know that I am not a BIV.

If so, then I do not know that I have hands.

I do not know that I have hands.

Warfield's response to this argument is to deny the first premise, and to appeal to his semantic argument as a justification for denying it. However, if the possibility of being a brain in a vat threatens knowledge of the external world, doesn't that possibility, given SE, also threaten knowledge of the content of our thoughts? After all, according to SE, thoughts like 'Water is wet' imply the existence of water (or in the very least a suitable speech community). So if the BIV possibility threatens our knowledge of the existence of water (or a suitable speech community), then doesn't SE lead to the consequence that it also threatens our ability to know that we are thinking about water? Let us back up one step and consider why surprisingly many epistemologists think that it is extremely difficult to know that one isn't a BIV.[8] The reason why they think this is the BIV hypothesis:

The BIV hypothesis   I am not what I take myself to be, but am instead a mere BIV *whose memories and sense-experiences are type-identical to the ones I have now in the real world*, being a normal person who is considering the hypothesis of being a BIV. In the imagined circumstances, there is no external world around me except for what is necessary to sustain me as a BIV. More specifically, water does not exist.

The significance of the italicized passage is this: introspectively—just by inspecting the contents of our minds—it is undetectable whether one is a BIV or not. This is why many philosophers think it is extremely difficult, if not outright impossible, to have any warrant for believing that one is not a BIV. Now, the problem is that if Warfield were a BIV, it would introspectively *seem* to him that he is thinking about water. After all, it is the very essence of the BIV hypothesis that, if he were a BIV, *everything would look and feel to him exactly the same way it does now*. Thus, like Boghossian's Dry Earth example,[9] the BIV hypothesis raises the specter of *content illusion*—a sort of illusion that one need not worry about (at least not to the same degree) if one isn't a semantic externalist. For then one would hold that one can think that water is wet whether or not water (or a suitable speech community) exists.

SE, then, engenders the specter of content illusion. As a result, knowing your mind becomes as difficult as knowing the world. Before the emergence of SE, philosophers thought that knowing one's mind was unproblematic. If only one could find a deductive link between the contents of the mind and the world, then knowledge of the world would be secured. Semantic externalism undermines this strategy in a novel way: by making knowing one's mind as fallible, and thus as difficult, as knowing the world.[10] The point is nicely put by Sarah Sawyer: "The self can no longer be regarded as an entity completely separate from her environment. As a result, the apparent clear divide between the mind and the world is eroded."[11] This is bad news for semantic anti-skepticism. It would not be bad news if, unlike sense experience, introspection was infallible. If introspection were infallible, there wouldn't be such a phenomenon as content illusion. But given that SE makes water thoughts dependent on the existence of external objects, it would seem that SE leads to the consequence that, in addition to possibility of *sensory* illusion, there is the possibility of *content* illusion: the possibility that one can think one is having water thoughts when in fact one is having thoughts with a different content. If this is correct, then the endeavor of rebutting skepticism will have to follow a new set of rules. Consider:

THE OLD RULES   Find a mix of premises that are knowable through introspection and conceptual analysis. Appealing to premises whose warrant would be *perceptual* is forbidden. If your premises imply propositions about the external world, you have avoided question-begging. You win; the skeptic loses.

If SE is true, we get the new rules:

THE NEW RULES   Find a mix of premises that are knowable a priori (in the strict sense). Appealing to any premises whose warrant would be *perceptual* or *introspective* is forbidden. If your a priori premises imply any propositions about the external world, you have avoided question begging. You win, the skeptic loses.

Why is it a consequence of SE that the new rules replace the old ones? It is a consequence of SE because, if SE is true, whether your are a BIV has a significant impact on the contents of your mind. If you are not a BIV, then of course you can think about water (given that water exists). If you are a BIV (in a world without water), you cannot. It follows that, if you accept SE and wish to argue that the skeptical hypothesis is false, appealing to the contents of your mind is no different from appealing to your hand, or, for that matter, to the sticks and stones you find in your environment. If the latter begs the question against the skeptic, then so does the former.

Perhaps this consequence could be avoided by showing that introspection, notwithstanding the deductive link between the contents of (at least some of) our thoughts and the external world, is infallible. So my point is merely a conditional one: unless there are good reasons for assuming that we are infallible when it comes to introspecting that we think that water is wet, appealing to such a premise begs the question if appealing to the existence of water itself begs the question. Let us assume that introspective access to the contents of our thoughts is not infallible. If so, then SE changes the rules for rebutting skepticism: an appeal to introspective premises is no more admissible than an appeal to perceptual premises. As a consequence, the semantic antiskeptical argument and Warfield's argument are in the same boat as Moore's argument. If it begs the question, then so do the semantic argument and Warfield's argument.

Perhaps, however, the new rules as well as the old rules should be rejected. If so, neither of these arguments would be begging the question simply because each would appeal to the kind of knowledge the skeptic calls into question. In the next section, I will present an alternative strategy of rebutting skepticism. According to this strategy, there is no reason to accept that arguing against skeptical hypotheses requires of us not to appeal to the kind of knowledge these hypotheses are meant to undermine. Thus from this point of view, neither Moore-type antiskepticism nor semantic antiskepticism should be accused of begging the question against the skeptic since they rely on the sort of evidence that the skeptic calls into doubt. This point is not meant to establish that Moore's argument, the semantic argument, and Warfield's argument are cogent after all. Rather, the point is that if they are not, the explanation of that would not, from the point of view I will advocate, reduce to the simple point that their premises require perceptual warrant.

6   Evidentialist Antiskepticism

Consider the following evidentialist conception of knowledge: S knows that p if and only if p is true, S is not in a Gettier situation, and S has evidence for p that is good enough to put p beyond any reasonable doubt. Assume further that what's required for p to be beyond a reasonable doubt for S is that there not be any defeaters for p that are themselves beyond a reasonable doubt. Put differently, you know that p only if you have defeaters for all of p's defeaters. But if you have defeaters for all the defeaters for p, then you are in a position to know that all the defeaters for p are false. So according to evidentialism, you know that p only if you are in a position to know that all of p's defeaters are false. Many would say that this is an unreasonably strong requirement for knowledge. It makes knowledge of the external world impossible, for we don't know that a defeater such as 'I'm a mere BIV' is false. But let us see whether we really don't know that such a defeater is false. Let us begin with some familiar epistemological scenarios:

THE RED WALL   I'm standing before a wall that looks red to me.

SKEPTICAL ALTERNATIVE   Perhaps it is white and illuminated by a red light.

Whether I know that the wall is red depends on the circumstances. In ordinary circumstances, the objects in my environment are not illuminated by red lights. This is not just a presupposition I am making. It is something that I in fact know. Of course, I might happen to be in an area where the presence of red lights is not unlikely. In that case, the wall's looking red would not by itself be enough for me to know that it is red. But in ordinary situations, I know that the skeptical alternative is false. *How* do I know that it is false? Well, I have background evidence that defeats the skeptical alternative, and thus know it to be false. Below, I'll explain what I take that evidence to be. Next, consider Dretske's (1970) famous example:

ZEBRAS   In the zoo, I'm at an enclosure with animals that look like zebras.

SKEPTICAL ALTERNATIVE   Perhaps they are cleverly disguised mules.

It is uncontroversial that I know that the animals are zebras. What's controversial is whether I know that they are not cleverly disguised mules (without examining them). I suggest we have background evidence that defeats the skeptical alternative, and hence know it to be false. Finally, consider this example:

EXTERNAL WORLD   I appear to have a body, and there appears to be rich and complex external world.

SKEPTICAL ALTERNATIVE   Perhaps I'm just a brain in a vat.

I know that I have a body, and that there is an external world. I know this because I can know that the skeptical alternative is false. I can know it is false because it is defeated by my background knowledge.

If skeptical alternatives like these are indeed defeated by our background knowledge, then we can have knowledge of the external world, *p*, notwithstanding the strong requirement that all defeaters for *p* be defeated. But can they really be defeated? It is now time to examine whether we really have the sort of background knowledge that defeats the defeaters we considered. Let me ask three questions: Do you know that there isn't an atom bomb in your basement? Do you know right now, without looking, that there isn't a rattle snake under your chair? Finally, do you know that there isn't a million dollars hidden in your mattress? If you reply that you don't know these things, the game is over. In that case, you and I must mean different things by 'knowledge'. We would have to backtrack and sort out from scratch what we are talking about. But if you say that you do know these things, we have significant common ground from which to approach the question of whether we know that that skeptical alternatives considered above are false.

So how do you know that there isn't an atom bomb in your basement? You know it on the basis of your general knowledge of the world. There is a story to be told here: only a few countries have them, they are extremely well guarded, they are very difficult to produce, and so forth. We need not go into further details. Suffice it to say that we know the general facts pertaining to atom bombs. And these facts imply that it's beyond a reasonable doubt that there is not an atom bomb in your basement. The arguments for the other two questions are analogous. Your general knowledge of the world has a rattle-snake chapter and a million-dollar chapter. In each case, you have background knowledge that puts you in a position to know that the proposition in question is false.

Let us return to the epistemological scenarios. We have general knowledge of how things are ordinarily illuminated. When you go out on a walk during daylight, things are illuminated by daylight. When you go out on a walk at night time, things are illuminated by street lights, or perhaps the moon. A story can be told about these things, and this story is good enough for you to know, without having to engage in a special examination of your environment, that what you see is not illuminated by any red lights.

As far as Dretske's zebras go, there is a story to be told here too. Why would anybody *want* to replace the zebras with cleverly disguised mules?

What would be the *point* of it? Would it be worth the risks it involves (potential embarrassment, hefty fines, or even a criminal record)? Such reasoning, I suggest, defeats the skeptical alternative. This is not to say, of course, that there couldn't be special circumstances where things are different. We can easily describe circumstances where entertaining the thoughts in question—an atom bomb in your basement, a rattle snake under your chair, red-light illumination, mules instead of zebras—is reasonable after all. But that just means it is possible for these things to occur, which is compatible with saying that under normal circumstances you know that they do not obtain because they are defeated by your background knowledge of how the real world works.

Finally, let us consider the possibility of being a BIV. If you do know that you are not a BIV, how do you know it? I suggest that our general knowledge of the world includes a chapter on BIVs. It includes things like the following: We know that neurophysiology and medical science are not advanced enough to keep a BIV alive for an extended period of time. We know that, given current scientific advancement, scientists are nowhere near the point where they could stimulate a brain so as to generate the illusion of a normal life. If scientists could do that, surely it would have been reported in the media, and a public debate would be raging about the ethics of envatting people's brains. Certainly, it would be made illegal in short order. More items could be added to the list easily. In the end, all of this adds up to a compelling case against the existence of (live) brains in vats anywhere. So is the doubt that I might be a brain in a vat reasonable? Surely not. It is defeated by our background knowledge.

Before proceeding, I will consider two objections to the account of knowledge I proposed. One goes like this: "Yes, you do have background knowledge giving you reasons to suppose that you are not a BIV. But these reasons are too weak to give you knowledge." In reply, I would like to have it explained what it takes for a reason to be strong enough to give us knowledge. What are the criteria? Without further explanation, the objection is ad hoc. Moreover, I suspect that if my reasons for believing I'm not a BIV are too weak to give me knowledge, then my reasons for believing that there isn't an atom bomb in my basement are also to weak to give me knowledge. But the latter strikes me as highly implausible. So what I would like to know from the objector is, in case he takes himself to know that there isn't an atom bomb in his basement, why it is that he knows *that*, but does not know that he isn't a BIV.

According to the second objection, to defeat the BIV hypothesis, I would have to show that it is logically impossible for me to be a BIV. But that is something I cannot do. The reply can be stated in one word: fallibilism. To have knowledge of *p*, our warrant for *p* need not come with a logical guarantee of *p*'s truth. So from the mere fact that it is logically possible that I'm a BIV, it certainly doesn't follow that I don't know that I'm not a BIV.[12]

7 Why Evidentialist Antiskepticism Does Not Beg the Question

I have suggested defeating skeptical alternatives by appealing to our background knowledge. But my background knowledge about general illumination conditions, zebra-mule replacements in zoos, and BIVs is empirical, and what the skeptic calls into question is the entire body of my empirical knowledge. Why, then, is it that evidentialist antiskepticism avoids begging the question against the skeptic? Well, evidentialist antiskeptics hold that for a skeptical hypothesis to call into question any of my empirical knowledge, it must not be defeated by anything that is reasonable for us to believe. But the skeptical alternatives do not satisfy this requirement. They are defeated in the strong sense that their negations are beyond a reasonable doubt.

Consider again our examples. In ordinary situations, you are warranted in disbelieving the proposition 'What I see is illuminated by red light'. In fact, you know this proposition to be false. Thus it does not call into question whether the red-looking wall is really red. And when you are in a normal zoo, the proposition 'The animals in the pen are cleverly disguised mules' does not call into question your belief that the animals you see are zebras. It does not because the negation of that proposition is beyond a reasonable doubt. You know it to be false. Finally, consider the alternative 'I am a BIV'. For this alternative to call into question the entire body of your empirical knowledge, it would have to have some minimal warrant for you. But in fact it has none. Rather, in light of your background knowledge, its negation is beyond a reasonable doubt for you. You know it to be false.

The point can be summed up as follows. Evidentialist antiskepticism demands that for defeaters to succeed in defeating anything, they must not themselves be defeated. But the skeptical alternatives we considered are defeated, and thus do not call into question knowledge of propositions that are incompatible with them. So in rebutting skepticism, we may appeal to our background knowledge after all. We may do so because, since the skeptical alternatives fail to be reasonable, they do not raise any question that we could beg in the first place. Now, this kind of reasoning presupposes that we can know what our background knowledge is. And for that, we need to rely on introspection. But that is all right as long as there is no reasonable doubt that introspection leads us astray. No more is required. So if we rebut skepticism in the evidentialist way, we may rely on introspection even if we accept SE and thus have to live with the consequence of content illusion, that is, with the consequence that we don't know our mind any better than we know the world. Evidentialist antiskepticism, therefore, should be an attractive option for semantic externalists.

Notes

1. McKinsey 1991a and this volume.

2. See the thought experiments by Putnam (1975) and Burge (1979) that semantic externalists cite as the chief reasons in support of their view.

3. See McKinsey, this volume, pp. 97 ff.

4. This terminology was introduced by Boghossian (1997).

5. If one is a BIV in an otherwise empty world, one is in a world which contains nothing except for what is necessary for sustaining the BIV.

6. A different objection would be that I know E5 in fact on the basis of sense perception, not on the basis of the existence argument. So surely the existence argument doesn't have the consequence that I know a priori that the external world exists. This seems right to me. However, it also seems right to me that one *could* acquire, through the existence argument, a priori knowledge of the external world. Suppose you have always been a brain in a vat. Contrary to what you believe, you have never really perceived any external objects. Suppose further one day a tragic thing happens: the world turns black, and the vat mister lets you know that you are a mere brain in a vat. Now you wonder what truly exists. You reflect, and the existence argument occurs to you. Supposing E2 and E4 are really true, why shouldn't you, by reasoning this way, acquire a priori knowledge of the existence of external physical objects.

7. The transmission of warrant (or knowledge) under known entailment is to be distinguished from the closure of warrant (or knowledge) under known entailment, which says that whenever I am warranted in believing (or know) that p, and also am warranted in believing (or know) that p entails q, then I am warranted in believing (or in a position to know) that q. Consider Dretske's famous zebra example. Standing before the zebra enclosure in a zoo and looking at animals that appear to be zebras, I form the belief that these animals are zebras

(*A*). *A* entails that these animals are not cleverly disguised mules (CDMs) (*B*). Suppose that I recognize the entailment. Am I warranted in believing (or do I know) that these animals are not CDMs (*C*)? If we assume that I do not, then the case is a counterexample to the closure principle. However, as I will argue in section 6, I think there are good reasons for thinking that I do in fact know *C*. If we actually do know *C*, closure is preserved. But even if I am warranted in believing *C*, it does not seem I can acquire warrant for believing *C* by inferring *C* from *A* and *B*. This inference, it would seem, suffers from transmission failure: it does not transmit the warrant I have for *A* and *B* to *C*. My warrant for *C*, it would seem, must have has its origin elsewhere.

8. See DeRose 1995, Dretske 1970, Lewis 1996, Nozick 1981.

9. See Boghossian 1997.

10. The old way of rejecting the Cartesian strategy was to go along with the assumption that knowing one's mind is easy, but to reject any deductive link between the contents of one's mind and the external world.

11. Sawyer 1998: 532. Citing Sawyer in this context is a bit ironic, since she endorses semantic antiskepticism herself. But what she says in the passage I quoted strikes me as correct. What I would disagree with is her conclusion, which is not that, given SE, we lose privileged access to the mind, but rather that, given SE, we gain privileged access to the world.

12. For a doubts about fallibilism, see Lewis 1996.

References

Austin, J. L. 1946. "Other Minds." *Proceedings of the Aristotelian Society*, supp. vol. 20. Reprinted in J. L. Austin, *Philosophical Papers*, edited by J. O. Urmson and G. J. Warnock, pp. 76–116. Oxford: Oxford University Press, 1979.

Bach, K. 1988. "Burge's New Thought Experiment: Back to the Drawing Room." *Journal of Philosophy* 85: 88–97.

Bar-On, D., and D. C. Long. 2001. "Avowals and First-Person Privilege." *Philosophy and Phenomenological Research* 62: 311–335.

Beebee, H. 2001. "Transfer of Warrant, Begging the Question, and Semantic Externalism." *Philosophical Quarterly* 51: 356–374.

Bernecker, S. 1996. "Externalism and the Attitudinal Component of Self-Knowledge." *Noûs* 30: 262–275.

Bernecker, S. 2000. "Knowing the World by Knowing One's Mind." *Synthese* 123: 1–34.

Bilgrami, A. 1998. "Self-Knowledge and Resentment." In Wright, Smith, and Macdonald 1998, pp. 207–241.

Boghossian, P. 1989. "Content and Self-Knowledge." *Philosophical Topics* 17: 5–26.

Boghossian, P. 1992. "Externalism and Inference." *Philosophical Issues* 2: 11–28.

Boghossian, P. 1997. "What the Externalist Can Know A Priori." *Proceedings of the Aristotelian Society* 97: 161–175. Reprinted in Wright, Smith, and Macdonald 1998, pp. 271–284.

Boghossian, P., and C. Peacocke. 2000. *New Essays on the A Priori*. Oxford: Oxford University Press.

Brewer, B. 2000. "Externalism and A Priori Knowledge of Empirical Facts." In Boghossian and Peacocke 2000, pp. 415–432.

Brown, J. 1995. "The Incompatibility of Anti-individualism and Privileged Access." *Analysis* 55: 149–156.

Brown, J. Forthcoming. *Externalism and Self-Knowledge.* Cambridge: MIT Press.

Brueckner, A. 1983. "Transcendental Arguments I." *Noûs* 17: 551–575.

Brueckner, A. 1984. "Transcendental Arguments II." *Noûs* 18: 197–225.

Brueckner, A. 1986. "Brains in a Vat." *Journal of Philosophy* 83: 148–167.

Brueckner, A. 1990. "Scepticism about Knowledge of Content." *Mind* 99: 447–451.

Brueckner, A. 1991. "The Anti-skeptical Epistemology of the Refutation of Idealism." *Philosophical Topics* 19: 31–45.

Brueckner, A. 1992a. "What an Anti-individualist Knows A Priori." *Analysis* 52: 111–118.

Brueckner, A. 1992b. "Semantic Answers to Skepticism." *Pacific Philosophical Quarterly* 73: 200–219.

Brueckner, A. 1994. "Knowledge of Content and Knowledge of the World." *Philosophical Review* 103: 327–343.

Brueckner, A. 1995a. "The Characteristic Thesis of Anti-individualism." *Analysis* 55: 146–148.

Brueckner, A. 1995b. "Trying to Get Outside Your Own Skin." *Philosophical Topics* 23: 79–111.

Brueckner, A. 1997a. "Externalism and Memory." *Pacific Philosophical Quarterly* 78: 1–12.

Brueckner, A. 1997b. "Is Skepticism about Self-Knowledge Incoherent?" *Analysis* 57: 287–290.

Brueckner, A. 1998a. "Moore Inferences." *Philosophical Quarterly* 48: 366–369.

Brueckner, A. 1998b. "Shoemaker on Second-Order Belief." *Philosophy and Phenomenological Research* 58: 361–364.

Brueckner, A. 1999. "Two Recent Approaches to Self-Knowledge." *Philosophical Perspectives* 13: 251–271.

Brueckner, A. 2000. "Ambiguity and Knowledge of Content." *Analysis* 60: 257–260.

Brueckner, A. 2001. "Problems for a Recent Account of Introspective Knowledge." *Facta Philosophica.*

Brueckner, A. Forthcoming. "Problems for the Agency Model of Self-Knowledge." *Dialogue.*

Burge, T. 1979. "Individualism and the Mental." In *Studies in Metaphysics*, edited by P. A. French, T. E. Uehling, and H. K. Wettstein, Midwest Studies in Philosophy, no. 4, pp. 73–121. Minneapolis: University of Minnesota Press. Reprinted in *The Nature of Mind*, edited by D. Rosenthal, pp. 536–567. New York: Oxford University Press, 1991.

Burge, T. 1982a. "Other Bodies." In Woodfield 1982, pp. 97–120.

Burge, T. 1982b. "Two Thought Experiments Reviewed." *Notre Dame Journal of Formal Logic* 23: 284–293.

Burge, T. 1986a. "Individualism and Psychology." *Philosophical Review* 95: 3–45.

Burge, T. 1986b. "Intellectual Norms and Foundations of Mind." *Journal of Philosophy* 12: 697–720.

Burge, T. 1988a. "Cartesian Error and the Objectivity of Perception." In *Contents of Thought*, edited by R. Grimm and D. Merrill, pp. 62–76. Tucson: Arizona University Press.

Burge, T. 1988b. "Individualism and Self-Knowledge." *Journal of Philosophy* 11: 649–663. Reprinted in Ludlow and Martin 1998, pp. 111–128.

Burge, T. 1989a. "Wherein Is Language Social?" In *Reflections on Chomsky*, edited by A. George, pp. 175–191. Oxford: Basil Blackwell.

Burge, T. 1989b. "Individuation and Causation in Psychology." *Pacific Philosophical Quarterly* 70: 302–322.

Burge, T. 1993. "Content Preservation." *Philosophical Review* 102: 457–488.

Burge, T. 1996. "Our Entitlement to Self-Knowledge." *Proceedings of the Aristotelian Society* 96: 91–116.

Burge, T. 1998a. "Reason and the First Person." In Wright, Smith, and Macdonald 1998, pp. 243–270.

Burge, T. 1998b. "Memory and Self-Knowledge." In Ludlow and Martin 1998, pp. 351–370.

Burge, T. 1999. "Comprehension and Interpretation." In *The Philosophy of Donald Davidson*, edited by L. E. Hahn, pp. 229–250. La Salle, Ill.: Open Court.

Burge, T. 2000. "Frege on Apriority." In Boghossian and Peacocke 2000, pp. 11–42.

Butchvarov, P. 1979. *Being Qua Being.* Bloomington: Indiana University Press.

Chalmers, D. 1996. *The Conscious Mind.* New York: Oxford University Press.

Davidson, D. 1987. "Knowing One's Own Mind." *Proceedings and Addresses of the American Philosophical Association* 60: 441–458. Reprinted in Ludlow and Martin 1998, pp. 87–110.

Davidson, D. 1989. "The Myth of the Subjective." In *Relativism*, edited by M. Krausz, pp. 159–172. Notre Dame: University of Notre Dame Press.

Davidson, D. 1990. "The Structure and Content of Truth." *Journal of Philosophy* 87: 279–328.

Davidson, D. 1991. "Epistemology Externalized." *Dialectica* 45: 191–202.

Davies, M. 1991. "Concepts, Connectionism, and the Language of Thought." In *Philosophy and Connectionist Theory*, edited by W. Ramsey, S. Stich, and D. Rumelhart, pp. 229–257. Hillsdale, N.J.: Lawrence Erlbaum Associates.

Davies, M. 1992. "Aunty's Own Argument for the Language of Thought." In *Cognition, Semantics, and Philosophy: Proceedings of the First International Colloquium on Cognitive Science*, edited by J. Ezquerro and J. M. Larrazabal, pp. 235–271. Dordrecht, Netherlands: Kluwer.

Davies, M. 1993. "Aims and Claims of Externalist Arguments." *Philosophical Issues* 4: 227–249.

Davies, M. 1998. "Externalism, Architecturalism, and Epistemic Warrant." In Wright, Smith, and Macdonald 1998, pp. 321–361.

Davies, M. 2000a. "Externalism and Armchair Knowledge." In Boghossian and Peacocke 2000, pp. 384–414.

Davies, M. 2000b. "Persons and Their Underpinnings." *Philosophical Explorations* 3: 43–62.

DeRose, K. 1995. "Solving the Skeptical Problem." *Philosophical Review* 104: 1–52.

Devitt, M. 1989. "A Narrow Representational Theory of the Mind." In *Representation: Readings in the Philosophy of Mental Representation*, edited by S. Silvers, pp. 369–402. Dordrecht, Netherlands: Reidel.

Donnellan, K. 1966. "Reference and Definite Descriptions." *Philosophical Review* 75: 281–305.

Dretske, F. 1969. *Seeing and Knowing*. Chicago: University of Chicago Press.

Dretske, F. 1970. "Epistemic Operators." *Journal of Philosophy* 67: 1007–1023.

Dretske, F. 1981. *Knowledge and the Flow of Information*. Cambridge: MIT Press.

Dretske, F. 1995. *Naturalizing the Mind*. Cambridge: MIT Press.

Dretske, F. Forthcoming. "How Do You Know You Are Not a Zombie?" In *Privileged Access and First Person Authority*, edited by Brie Gertler. Ashgate Press.

Ebbs, G. 1992. "Skepticism, Objectivity, and Brains in Vats." *Pacific Philosophical Quarterly* 73: 239–266.

Ebbs, G. 1996. "Can We Take Our Words at Face Value?" *Philosophy and Phenomenological Research* 56: 499–530.

Ebbs, G. 1997. *Rule-Following and Realism*. Cambridge: Harvard University Press.

Ebbs, G. 2000. "The Very Idea of Sameness of Extension across Time." *American Philosophical Quarterly* 37: 245–268.

Ebbs, G. 2001. "Is Skepticism about Self-Knowledge Coherent?" *Philosophical Studies* 105: 43–58.

Elugardo, R. 1993. "Burge on Content." *Philosophy and Phenomenological Research* 53: 367–384.

Evans, G. 1973. "The Causal Theory of Names." *Proceedings of the Aristotelian Society*, supp. vol. 47: 187–208.

Evans, G. 1981. "Semantic Theory and Tacit Knowledge." In *Wittgenstein: To Follow a Rule*, edited by S. Holtzman and C. Leich, pp. 118–137. London: Routledge.

Evans, G. 1982. *The Varieties of Reference.* Oxford: Oxford University Press.

Falvey, K. 2000. "The Basis of First Person Authority." *Philosophical Topics* 28 (2): 69–99.

Falvey, K., and J. Owens. 1994. "Externalism, Self-Knowledge, and Skepticism." *Philosophical Review* 103: 107–137.

Field, H. 1996. "The Apriority of Logic." *Proceedings of the Aristotelian Society* 96: 359–376.

Fodor, J. 1985. "Fodor's Guide to Mental Representation." *Mind* 94: 55–97.

Fodor, J. 1987. *Psychosemantics.* Cambridge: MIT Press.

Frege, G. 1952. *Translations from the Philosophical Writings of Gottlob Frege.* Translated by P. Geach and M. Black. Oxford: Blackwell.

Frankfurt, Harry. 1969. "Alternate Possibilities and Moral Responsibility." *Journal of Philosophy* 66: 829–839.

Fricker, E. 1998. "Self-Knowledge: Special Access versus Artefact of Grammar: A Dichotomy Rejected." In Wright, Smith, and McDonald 1998, pp. 155–206.

Fumerton, R. 1988. "Externalism and Epistemological Direct Realism." *Monist*: 393–406.

Fumerton, R. 1995. *Metaepistemology and Skepticism.* Lanham, Md.: Rowman and Littlefield.

Fumerton, R. Forthcoming. *Realism and the Correspondence Theory of Truth.* Lanham, Md.: Rowman and Littlefield.

Gallois, A., and J. O'Leary-Hawthorne. 1996. "Externalism and Scepticism." *Philosophical Studies* 81: 1–26.

Gibbons, J. 1996. "Externalism and Knowledge of Content." *Philosophical Review* 105: 287–310.

Goldberg, S. 1997. "Self-Ascription, Self-Knowledge, and the Memory Argument." *Analysis* 57: 211–219.

Goldberg, S. 1999a. "The Psychology and Epistemology of Self-Knowledge." *Synthese* 118: 165–199.

Goldberg, S. 1999b. "The Relevance of Discriminatory Knowledge of Content." *Pacific Philosophical Quarterly* 80: 136–156.

Goldberg, S. Forthcoming. "Do Anti-individualistic Construals of the Attitudes Capture the Agent's Conceptions?" *Noûs.*

Goldman, A. 1976. "Discrimination and Perceptual Knowledge." *Journal of Philosophy* 73: 771–791.

Goldman, A. 1979. "What Is Justified Belief?" In *Justification and Knowledge*, edited by G. Pappas, pp. 1–23. Dordrecht, Netherlands: Reidel.

Goldman, A. 1986. *Epistemology and Cognition.* Cambridge: Harvard University Press.

Hale, B. 2000. "Transmission and Closure." *Philosophical Issues* 10: 172–190.

Heal, J. 1988. "Externalism and Memory." *Proceedings of the Aristotelian Society* 88: 183–209.

Heil, J. 1988. "Privileged Access." *Mind* 97: 238–251.

Hintikka, J. 1998. *The Principles of Mathematics Revisited.* Cambridge: Cambridge University Press.

Hintikka, J. 1999. "The Emperor's New Intuitions." *Journal of Philosophy* 96: 127–147.

Jackson, F. C. 1987. *Conditionals.* Oxford: Blackwell.

Jackson, F. C. 1998. *From Metaphysics to Ethics: A Defence of Conceptual Analysis.* Oxford: Oxford University Press.

Kaplan, D. 1977. "Demonstratives." Manuscript. In *Themes from Kaplan*, edited by J. Almog et al., pp. 481–563. Oxford: Oxford University Press, 1989.

Kim, J. 1982. "Psychophysical Supervenience." *Philosophical Studies* 41: 51–70. Reprinted in Kim 1993, pp. 175–193.

Kim, J. 1987. "'Strong' and 'Global' Supervenience Revisited." *Philosophy and Phenomenological Research* 48: 315–326. Reprinted in Kim 1993, pp. 79–91.

Kim, J. 1993. *Supervenience and Mind: Selected Philosophical Essays.* Cambridge: Cambridge University Press.

Klein, P. 1981. *Certainty: A Refutation of Skepticism.* Minneapolis: University of Minnesota Press.

Klein, P. 1995. "Skepticism and Closure: Why the Evil Genius Argument Fails." *Philosophical Topics* 23: 213–236.

Kobes, B. 1996. "Mental Content and Hot Self-Knowledge." *Philosophical Topics* 24: 71–99.

Kripke, S. 1972. "Naming and Necessity." In *Semantics of Natural Languages,* edited by D. Davidson and G. Harman, pp. 253–355. Dordrecht, Netherlands: Reidel. Reprinted as *Naming and Necessity.* Cambridge: Harvard University Press, 1980.

Kripke, S. 1979. "A Puzzle about Belief." In *Meaning and Use,* edited by A. Margalit, pp. 239–283. Dordrecht, Netherlands: Reidel.

Lewis, D. 1981. "What Puzzling Pierre Does Not Believe." *Australasian Journal of Philosophy* 59: 283–289.

Lewis, D. 1992. "Meaning without Use: Reply to Hawthorne." *Australasian Journal of Philosophy* 70: 106–110.

Lewis, D. 1996. "Elusive Knowledge." *Australasian Journal of Philosophy* 74: 549–567.

Lewis, D. 1997. "Naming the Colors." *Australasian Journal of Philosophy* 75: 323–342.

Loar, B. 1981. *Mind and Meaning.* Cambridge: Cambridge University Press.

Loar, B. 1988. "Social Content and Psychological Content." In *Contents of Thought,* edited by R. H. Grimm and D. D. Merrill, pp. 99–110. Tucson: University of Arizona Press.

Ludlow, P. 1995. "Social Externalism, Self-Knowledge, and Memory." *Analysis* 55: 157–159.

Ludlow, P., and N. Martin. 1998. *Externalism and Self-Knowledge.* Stanford: CSLI.

McDowell, J. 1977. "On the Sense and Reference of a Proper Name." *Mind* 86: 159–185.

McDowell, J. 1984. "De Re Senses." *Philosophical Quarterly* 34: 283–294.

McDowell, J. 1986. "Singular Thought and the Extent of Inner Space." In *Subject, Thought, and Context,* edited by P. Pettit and J. McDowell, pp. 137–168. Oxford: Oxford University Press.

McGinn, C. 1976. "*A Priori* and *A Posteriori* Knowledge." *Proceedings of the Aristotelian Society* 76: 195–208.

McGinn, C. 1982. "The Structure of Content." In Woodfield 1982, pp. 97–120.

McKay, T. 1981. "On Proper Names in Belief Ascriptions." *Philosophical Studies* 39: 287–303.

McKinsey, M. 1978. "Names and Intentionality." *Philosophical Review* 87: 171–200.

McKinsey, M. 1984. "Causality and the Paradox of Names." In *Causation and Causal Theories*, edited by P. A. French, T. E. Uehling, and H. K. Wettstein, Midwest Studies in Philosophy, no. 9, pp. 391–415. Minneapolis: University of Minnesota Press.

McKinsey, M. 1987. "Apriorism in the Philosophy of Language." *Philosophical Studies* 52: 1–32.

McKinsey, M. 1991a. "Anti-individualism and Privileged Access." *Analysis* 51: 9–16. Reprinted in Ludlow and Martin 1998.

McKinsey, M. 1991b. "The Internal Basis of Meaning." *Pacific Philosophical Quarterly* 72: 143–169.

McKinsey, M. 1994a. "Individuating Beliefs." *Philosophical Perspectives* 8: 303–330.

McKinsey, M. 1994b. "Accepting the Consequences of Anti-individualism." *Analysis* 54: 124–128.

McKinsey, M. 1998. "The Grammar of Belief." In *Thought, Language, and Ontology*, edited by F. Orilia and W. J. Rapaport, pp. 3–24. Dordrecht, Netherlands: Kluwer.

McKinsey, M. 1999. "The Semantics of Belief Ascriptions." *Noûs* 33: 519–557.

McKinsey, M. 2001. "The Semantic Basis of Externalism." In *Topics in Contemporary Philosophy: Meaning and Truth*, edited by J. Campbell, M. O'Rourke, and D. Shier, pp. 34–52. New York: Seven Bridges Press.

McKinsey, M. 2002a. "Forms of Externalism and Privileged Access." *Philosophical Perspectives (Language and Mind)* 16: 199–224.

McKinsey, M. 2002b. "On Knowing Our Own Minds." *Philosophical Quarterly* 52: 107–116.

McLaughlin, B. 1998. "Is Privileged Access Incompatible with Content-Externalism?" *Philosophical Review* 107: 349–380.

McLaughlin, B. 2000. "Self-Knowledge, Externalism, and Skepticism." *Proceedings of the Aristotelian Society*, supp. vol. 74: 93–117.

McLaughlin, B., and M. Tye. 1998. "Externalism, Twin Earth, and Self-Knowledge." In Wright, Smith, and Macdonald 1998, pp. 285–320.

Mill, J. S. 1952. *A System of Logic*. London: Longman.

Miller, R. 1997. "Externalist Self-Knowledge and the Scope of the A Priori." *Analysis* 57: 67–75.

Millikan, R. G. 1989. "Biosemantics." *Journal of Philosophy* 86: 281–297. Reprinted in her *White Queen Psychology and Other Essays for Alice*, pp. 83–101. Cambridge: MIT Press, 1993.

Moore, G. E. 1959. "Proof of an External World." In *Philosophical Papers*, pp. 127–150. London: Allen and Unwin.

Moran, R. 1997. "Self-Knowledge: Discovery, Resolution, and Undoing." *European Journal of Philosophy* 5: 141–163.

Moran, R. 2001. *Authority and Estrangement.* Princeton: Princeton University Press.

Nozick, R. 1981. *Philosophical Explanations.* Oxford: Oxford University Press.

Nuccetelli, S. 1999. "What Anti-individualists Cannot Know *A Priori.*" *Analysis* 59: 48–51.

Nuccetelli, S. 2001. "Is Self-Knowledge an Entitlement? And Why Should We Care?" *Southern Journal of Philosophy* 39: 143–155.

Owens, J. 1989. "Contradictory Belief and Cognitive Access." In *Contemporary Perspectives in the Philosophy of Language, II*, edited by P. A. French, T. E. Uehling, and H. K. Wettstein, Midwest Studies in Philosophy, no. 14, pp. 289–316. Minneapolis: University of Minnesota Press.

Owens, J. 1990. "Cognitive Access and Semantic Puzzles." In *Propositional Attitudes: The Role of Content in Logic, Language, and Mind*, edited by C. A. Anderson and J. Owens, pp. 147–173. Stanford: CSLI Press.

Owens, J. 1993. "Content, Causation, and Psychophysical Supervenience." *Philosophy of Science* 60: 242–261.

Owens, J. 1995. "Pierre and the Fundamental Assumption." *Mind and Language* 10: 250–273.

Peacocke, C. 1993. "Externalist Explanation." *Proceedings of the Aristotelian Society* 93: 203–230.

Peacocke, C. 1999. *Being Known.* Oxford: Oxford University Press.

Plantinga, A. 2000. *Warranted Christian Belief.* Oxford: Oxford University Press.

Pollock, J. 1974. *Knowledge and Justification.* Princeton: Princeton University Press.

Pollock, J. 1986. *Contemporary Theories of Knowledge.* Totowa, N.J.: Roman and Littlefield.

Pryor, J. Forthcoming. "Is Moore's Argument an Example of Transmission-Failure?"

Putnam, H. 1975. "The Meaning of 'Meaning'." In his *Philosophical Papers*, vol. 2: *Mind, Language, and Reality*, pp. 215–271. Cambridge: Cambridge University Press.

Putnam, H. 1981. *Reason, Truth, and History*. Cambridge: Cambridge University Press.

Putnam, H. 1988. *Representation and Reality*. Cambridge: MIT Press.

Quine, W. V. 1969. "Natural Kinds." In *Ontological Relativity and Other Essays*, pp. 114–138. New York: Columbia University Press.

Ramsey, W., S. Stich, and J. Garon. 1990. "Connectionism, Eliminativism, and the Future of Folk Psychology." *Philosophical Perspectives* 4: 499–533.

Recanati, F. 1993. *Direct Reference: From Language to Thought*. Cambridge: Blackwell.

Russell, B. 1905. "On Denoting." *Mind* 14: 479–493.

Russell, B. 1918–1919. "Lectures on the Philosophy of Logical Atomism." *Monist* 28.

Salmon, N. 1986. *Frege's Puzzle*. Cambridge: MIT Press.

Sawyer, S. 1998. "Privileged Access to the World." *Australasian Journal of Philosophy* 76: 523–533.

Schiffer, S. 1992. "Boghossian on Externalism and Inference." *Philosophical Issues* 4: 29–37.

Schiffer, S. 1993. "Actual-Language Relations." *Philosophical Perspectives* 7: 231–258.

Searle, J. 1983. *Intentionality*. Cambridge: Cambridge University Press.

Shoemaker, S. 1988. "On Knowing One's Own Mind." *Philosophical Perspectives* 2: 183–209.

Smart, J. J. C. 1962. "Sensations and Brain Processes." In *The Philosophy of Mind*, edited by V. C. Chappell, pp. 160–172. Englewood Cliffs, N.J.: Prentice-Hall.

Soames, S. 1987. "Substitutivity." In *On Being and Saying: Essays in Honor of Richard Cartwright*, edited by J. Thompson, pp. 99–132. Cambridge: MIT Press.

Soames, S. 1988. "Direct Reference, Propositional Attitudes, and Semantic Content." In *Propositions and Attitudes*, edited by N. Salmon and S. Soames, pp. 197–239. Oxford: Oxford University Press.

Sosa, E. 1991. *Knowledge in Perspective: Selected Essays in Epistemology*. Cambridge: Cambridge University Press.

Sosa, E. 1993. "Abilities, Concepts, and Externalism." In *Mental Causation*, edited by J. Heil and A. Mele, pp. 309–328. New York: Oxford University Press.

Sosa, E. 1997. "Reflective Knowledge in the Best Circles." *Journal of Philosophy* 8: 410–430.

Sosa, E. Forthcoming. "Virtual Epistemology."

Stalnaker, R. 1993. "Twin Earth Revisited." *Proceedings of the Aristotelian Society* 93: 297–311.

Stalnaker, R. 1999. *Context and Content: Essays on Intentionality in Speech and Thought.* Oxford: Oxford University Press.

Stich, S. 1978. "Autonomous Psychology and the Belief-Desire Thesis." *Monist* 61: 573–591.

Stich, S. 1991. "Narrow Content Meets Fat Syntax." In *Meaning in Mind: Fodor and His Critics,* edited by B. Loewer and G. Rey, pp. 239–254. Oxford: Blackwell.

Strawson, P. 1962. "Freedom and Resentment." *Proceedings of the British Academy.* Reprinted in *Freedom and Resentment and Other Essays,* pp. 1–25. London: Methuen, 1974.

Suárez, A. G. 2000. "On Wright's Diagnosis of McKinsey's Argument." *Philosophical Issues* 10: 140–164.

Tye, M. 1998. "Externalism and Memory." *Proceedings of the Aristotelian Society* 72: 77–94.

Tymoczko, T. 1989. "In Defense of Putnam's Brains." *Philosophical Studies* 57: 281–297.

Warfield, T. 1998. "A Priori Knowledge of the World: Knowing the World by Knowing Our Minds." *Philosophical Studies* 92: 127–147. Reprinted in *Skepticism: A Contemporary Reader,* edited by K. DeRose and T. Warfield, pp. 76–90. New York: Oxford University Press, 1999.

Wiggins, D. 1993. "Putnam's Doctrine of Natural Kind Words and Frege's Doctrine of Sense, Reference, and Extension: Can They Cohere?" In *Meaning and Reference,* edited by A. W. Moore, pp. 192–207. New York: Oxford University Press.

Williamson, T. 1995. "Is Knowing a State of Mind?" *Mind* 104: 533–565.

Wittgenstein, L. 1953. *Philosophical Investigations.* Oxford: Blackwell.

Wittgenstein, L. 1969. *On Certainty.* Oxford: Basil Blackwell.

Woodfield, A. 1982. *Thought and Object: Essays on Intentionality.* Oxford: Oxford University Press.

Wright, C. 1985. "Facts and Certainty." *Proceedings of the British Academy* 71: 429–472.

Wright, C. 2000a. "Cogency and Question-Begging: Some Reflections on McKinsey's Paradox and Putnam's Proof." *Philosophical Issues* 10: 140–163.

Wright, C. 2000b. "Replies." *Philosophical Issues* 10: 201–219.

Wright, C. Forthcoming. "(Anti-)Skeptics Simple and Subtle: G. E. Moore and John McDowell." *Philosophy and Phenomenological Research.*

Wright, C., B. C. Smith, and C. Macdonald. 1998. *Knowing Our Own Minds.* Oxford: Oxford University Press.

Contributors

Jessica Brown is Reader in Philosophy at Bristol University in England. After completing her graduate work at Oxford, she held a Junior Research Fellowship at Wolfson College, Oxford, before moving to Bristol in 1996. Her main research interests are in the philosophy of mind and epistemology, and she has written extensively on reasoning, knowledge of one's own mind, and the conditions for thought. Currently (2001–2003) she is the holder of a two-year research fellowship from the Leverhulme Trust.

Anthony Brueckner is Professor of Philosophy at the University of California, Santa Barbara. He has written articles on transcendental arguments, skepticism, content externalism, the antirealism/realism debate, theories of justification, the metaphysics of death, personal identity, and self-knowledge.

Martin Davies is Professor of Philosophy in the Research School of Social Sciences at the Australian National University and is currently Visiting Professor at the Graduate Center of the City University of New York. He previously taught at Oxford and at Birbeck College, London. He has written on philosophy of mind, epistemology, and philosophical logic, has coedited various collections, and is one of the founders of the journal *Mind and Philosophy*. His books include *Meaning, Quantification, Necessity* (Routledge & Kegan Paul, 1987), and *Knowing What Thought Requires* (forthcoming).

Fred Dretske taught at the University of Wisconsin from 1960 to 1988 and then moved to Stanford University (1989–1998). At present he is Research Scholar at Duke University. His research has been in epistemology and the philosophy of mind, and he has authored several books in these areas: *Seeing and Knowing* (1969), *Knowledge and the Flow* *of Information* (1981), *Explaining Behavior* (1988), *Naturalizing the Mind* (1995), and, most recently, a collection of essays, *Perception, Knowledge, and Belief* (2000).

Gary Ebbs is Associate Professor of Philosophy at the University of Illinois at Urbana-Champaign. He previously taught at Harvard University and the University of Pennsylvania. He is the author of *Rule-Following and Realism* (Harvard University Press, 1997) and of articles in the philosophy of language, philosophy of logic, philosophy of mind, and history of analytic philosophy. A unifying goal of his research is to describe the methodology of rational inquiry from an engaged, practical point of view.

Kevin Falvey is Associate Professor of Philosophy at the University of California, Santa Barbara. His research has been in philosophy of mind, epistemology, and the philosophy of action.

Richard Fumerton is professor of philosophy at the University of Iowa. His publications focus primarily on topics in epistemology, value theory, and metaphysics. Among his writings are *Metaphysical and Epistemological Problems of Perception* (University of Nebraska Press, 1985), *Reason and Morality: A Defense of the Egocentric Perspective* (Cornell University Press, 1990), *Metaepistemology and Skepticism* (Rowman and Littlefield, 1997), and *Realism and the Correspondence Theory of Truth* (Rowman and Littlefield, 2002).

Sanford C. Goldberg is Associate Professor of Philosophy at the University of Kentucky. He has worked on various topics in philosophy of mind, philosophy of language, and epistemology. His current research attempts to motivate various substantive constraints on semantic theory by appeal to the fact that knowledge can be communicated linguistically.

Michael McKinsey is Professor of Philosophy at Wayne State University, where he has taught since 1976. He is the author of many articles in the philosophy of language, the philosophy of mind, and ethics. His work has primarily concerned the semantics of natural language—especially the meaning and reference of proper names, indexical and anaphoric pronouns, and natural-kind terms, as well as the meaning and logical form of cognitive ascriptions. He is particularly interested in the relevance of these semantic topics to traditional metaphysical questions in the philosophy of mind, including the mind-body problem.

Brian P. McLaughlin is Professor of Philosophy at Rutgers University. He has written many articles in a wide range of areas: epistemology, metaphysics, philosophical logic, and philosophy of mind.

Susana Nuccetelli is Assistant Professor of Philosophy at St. Cloud State University in Minnesota. She previously taught at Carleton College, Washington and Lee University, and the City University of New York. Her published articles are principally in philosophy of language, philosophy of mind, and epistemology, but she is also interested in some topics of moral and political philosophy that are broached in her recent book *Latin American Thought: Philosophical Problems and Arguments* (Westview, 2002).

Joseph Owens is Professor of Philosophy at the University of Minnesota, Twin Cities. He has published papers in the philosophy of language, of mind, and of psychology.

Matthias Steup teaches philosophy at St. Cloud State University in Minnesota. He is the author of *An Introduction to Contemporary Epistemology* (Prentice-Hall, 1996) and the editor of *Knowledge, Truth, and Duty: Essays on Epistemic Justification, Responsibility, and Virtue* (Oxford, 2001). His current work focuses on the problem of how experience can be a source of epistemic justification.

Crispin Wright, Fellow of the British Academy, is Wardlaw University Professor at the University of St. Andrews and a Leverhulme Research Professor (1998–2003). He has taught at Columbia, Princeton, and Michigan and is a regular Visiting Professor at New York University. His books include *Wittgenstein on the Foundations of Mathematics* (Harvard University Press, 1980); *Frege's Conception of Numbers as Objects* (Humanities Press, 1983); *Truth and Objectivity* (Harvard University Press, 1992); *Realism, Meaning, and Truth* (2nd edition, Blackwell, 1993); and with Bob Hale, *The Reason's Proper Study* (Oxford University Press, 2001). His most recent book, *Rails to Infinity* (Harvard University Press, 2001), collects together his writings on central themes of Wittgenstein's *Philosophical Investigations*.

Index